1925	1950	1975	2000	

678901234|678901234567890123456789|123456789012345678901234|678901234567890120

UK

Canada

Republic of Ireland

1970 Business ceased — Trinidad & Tobago

1973 Business transferred — Jamaica

Branch closed **1938**   **1946** Business transferred   Joint venture **1995** — India

1968 Branch closed — Uruguay

1937 Business ceased   Office opened in Shanghai **1995** — China

1929 Branch closed   **1952** Business transferred — South Africa

Office opened in Frankfurt **1996** — Germany

...osed — Denmark

1923 Branch closed — Argentina

...osed — Norway

1929 Business transferred — Sweden

1924 Branch closed — Hungary

1930 Branch closed — Egypt

1920 Branch closed   Purchased Prosperity SA in **1993** — Spain

RD LIFE

STANDARD LIFE 1825–2000

The bust of William Thomas Thomson (1813–83), the manager from 1837 to 1874. Without his vision and actuarial skills, Standard Life would not have grown so quickly or so successfully in its first half-century.

The Building of Europe's Largest Mutual Life Company

STANDARD LIFE
1825–2000

MICHAEL MOSS

MAINSTREAM
PUBLISHING

EDINBURGH AND LONDON

Copyright © The Standard Life Assurance Company, 2000

All rights reserved

The moral right of the author has been asserted

First published in Great Britain in 2000 by

MAINSTREAM PUBLISHING COMPANY (EDINBURGH) LTD

7 Albany Street

Edinburgh EH1 3UG

ISBN 1 84018 290 3

A catalogue record for this book is available from the British Library

Standard Life complies with strict European environmental guidelines. The paper used in the production of this book comes from sustainable managed forests

Designed by Janene Reid

Reprographics by Capital Scanning Studios, Edinburgh

Printed and bound in Great Britain by Butler & Tanner Ltd

CONTENTS

LIST OF FEATURES

LIST OF FIGURES

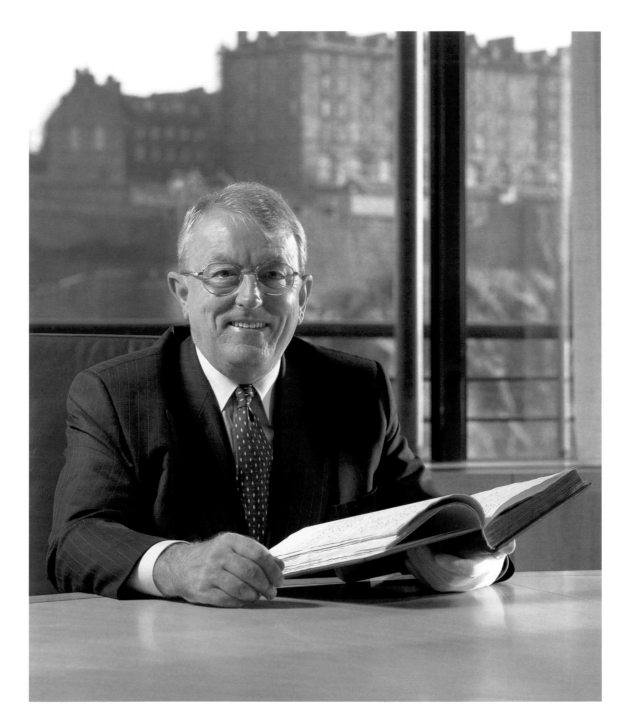

Scott Bell, group managing director in the anniversary year, with the minute book of the Insurance Company of Scotland opened at the page recording the decision on 23 March 1825 to establish the Life Insurance Company of Scotland, later renamed Standard Life.

FOREWORD BY SCOTT BELL

It is a privilege to be group managing director of Standard Life at the time of its 175th anniversary, only the 14th in a succession which includes such famous names as William Thomas Thomson, who made the company such a force in the life insurance industry, and Andrew Davidson, who established its reputation in the pensions market. This book recounts their contributions, and those of many others, to what is a truly remarkable story, starting in Edinburgh and stretching round the globe. We have had policy-holders in almost every country and paid out claims in many different currencies.

Over the years we have grasped every opportunity to invest our capital profitably, from small new enterprises to long-established concerns, whether they be in agriculture, industry or commerce. I am proud and delighted that Standard Life has successfully reached this anniversary in as strong a position financially as it has ever enjoyed. It can now claim to be the largest and one of the most respected mutual companies in Europe. We are proud of our mutual status, adopted in 1925, which enables us to focus solely on the interests of our policy-holders.

I hope you will enjoy reading our history as much as I have enjoyed watching it emerge from our extensive archive which stretches back to the moment we wrote our first policy, in the Old Town of Edinburgh, in 1825.

Standard Life House in Lothian Road, Edinburgh, designed by
The Michael Laird Partnership and completed in 1996.

PREFACE AND ACKNOWLEDGEMENTS

'There is no other kind of business for which a mere decade means so little as for life assurance. Their contracts are for the term of human life. They are themselves mostly centenarians or thereabouts and wish the same for their policy-holders. They are trees of which the girth puts on one more ring a year with the sap of compound interest, and they do not lightly change their address once they have struck root.'

J.M. Keynes's foreword to G.H. Recknell, *King Street Cheapside*, London, 1936.

These words remain as true in 2000 as they did these many years ago despite all the changes in the financial services industry. Standard Life was founded in Edinburgh in 1825 and continued, from 1839 to 1996, at the same address – No. 3 George Street – which now houses its investment company. As Keynes suggested, it has grown and prospered; but the 'sap of compound interest' has never flowed of its own accord. Each generation has worked hard and often taken considerable risks to ensure that investment income more than matched customers' expectations. In the nineteenth century Standard Life's investments supported agricultural improvements, municipal services, shipbuilding companies, New Zealand sheep runs, Argentine cattle ranches, North American railways, small farmers in the United States and Canada, and, later, management buyouts. The company was among the first to invest a large proportion of its funds in equities in the 1920s and remains committed to holding more of its assets in this form than the majority of its competitors. The striking characteristic is how consistently successful Standard Life has been in its investments. Throughout its history, this adventurous strategy has been balanced by prudence in assuring lives and designing new products to allow policy-holders to receive maximum benefit. Inevitably there have been setbacks, sometimes the result of wider economic problems as between 1929 and 1931, and sometimes caused by poor management, as in 1905 when the bonus was passed for the only time in the company's history. British industry is often accused of being unadventurous in exploiting world markets and of being resistant to change. This cannot be said of financial institutions such as Standard Life which, from their foundation, have adapted to new circumstances and challenges and were amongst the first to operate in a global market in the days when travelling to North America or Australasia took several months. Today Standard Life remains a major company in the financial services sector, with a widening range of products and services in the United Kingdom, Canada, Ireland and increasingly in other parts of the world.

I am most grateful to Standard Life for inviting me to write the history of this remarkable enterprise, and to Sir Graeme Davies for releasing me from the University of Glasgow to undertake the project. In writing the book, the work of previous historians was invaluable, particularly that of Sir William Schooling, author of the centenary history, George Norman, author of the monumental overseas history, Professor John Butt and Dr Jim Treble of the University of Strathclyde, who prepared an unpublished volume to mark the 150th anniversary in 1975, and Peter Glover, the retired general manager (sales), who wrote a more recent account. Throughout, Peter generously answered my many questions.

I was helped by many people in the company and retired directors and members of staff too numerous to name individually. I am much indebted to them for the cheerful way in which they offered advice, guidance and support. There were many outside the company who assisted me in my task whom I wish to thank:

Derrick Barclay, Carnegie Birthplace Museum; Vivian Bone; K.V. Bligh, House of Lords Record Office; Professor Tom Brooking of the University of Otago, Dunedin; the late Sir Alec Cairncross; Professor Roy Campbell; Lt-Col J. Clark Kennedy; Chris Close, photographer; Lord Cochrane of Cults; Jocelyne Cunningham; Alastair Cruick-shank of Perth; the family of Andrew Rutherford Davidson; Dr Derek Dow; David Dowie of Leven Golfing Society; David Duguid; Dr Marguerite Dupree of the Wellcome Unit for the History of Medicine, University of Glasgow; staff of the Edinburgh Central Library and particularly Ann Nix, the Edinburgh room; the Earl of Elgin; Jørgen Fink; Rhoda Fothergill of Perth; Sir William Kerr Fraser; Colonel Stephen Furness; John Gourlay; Ian Gow, Curator, National Trust for Scotland; Zara Phillips of the Group Archives at HSBC; Sally Grover, Librarian, Institute of Actuaries; the Earl Haig; Ken Hannigan and Kieran Hoare of the National Archives of Ireland; Vivienne Heffernan of the Research Library, Muckross House, Killarney; Nigel Houldsworth; John Hume; Andrew Jackson and the staff of the Glasgow City Archives; Berit Wulstrup Jensen; Lord Joicey; Patrick Cadell, the Keeper of the Records of Scotland, and the staff of the National Archives of Scotland, particularly Linda Ramsay; Julie Anne Lambert, Supervisor of the John Johnson collection at the Bodleian Library; Hamish Leslie Melville; the president of the Faculty of Actuaries and Dorothy Lewis, Sharon Jamieson and Christine Morgan in the Library; the Librarian and Staff of the Bodleian Library, particularly those on floor L of the book stack; Anne Lightwood; Angus McLaren; David McLoughlin of the National Library of Ireland; the Earl of Mar; Major Andrew Napier; John Norman; Niamh O'Sullivan, Kilmainham Gaol, Dublin; Richard Oliver of Gordonstoun School; Althea and Benedict Parsons; Greg Ross of

Strathallan School; W. Runciman, Carnegie Hero Trust Fund; H.E. Scrope, formerly of Vickers plc; the Lady Sinclair, Knocknalling, Castle Douglas; Martin Sinclair, Chiene and Tait; Bill Smith of Robert Fleming & Co.; Paula Smith of ICI; Joanne Soden, RSA; Robert Steuart Fothringham of Murthly Castle; Stuart Strachan of the Hochin Library, Dunedin, New Zealand; Professor Bruce Strauch; Moira Thorburn of the Mitchell Library; Charles Tod, Wemyss Estate; Alma Topen of the Scottish Brewing Archive; Alison Turton and her staff in the archives at the Royal Bank of Scotland; Isobel Weber of the Research Dept of the Institute of Chartered Accountants in Scotland; the Honourable Mrs Margaret Williams of Udny; and John Wotton of the Association of British Insurers, for arranging access to the records of the Life Offices Association.

I was fortunate to have a group of dedicated supporters without whom the history would never have appeared, at least not on time. The internal reading committee (Scott Bell, Alison Hewat, Tom King and Iain Lumsden) along with Jim Stretton, Sandy Skinner, Morgan Jones, Neil Geddes, Joan Forehand, Peter Stubbs, Nikki Brown and Sandra Ramage met seemingly impossible deadlines and were always ready with help and advice. At an early stage Alan Cameron, archivist of the Bank of Scotland, provided invaluable advice in the design and inauguration of the project. Edwin Green, archivist of HSBC, read all the draft chapters and was a source of inspiration and guidance. Kate Hutcheson, the Standard Life Group archivist, worked hard to organise and then move the archive, to find suitable illustrations and to meet equally punishing deadlines. She was assisted by Eilean Malden whom we sent on what seemed fool's errands only to be dumbfounded when she returned with the relevant information or missing illustrations. In Canada Diana Sheinnan, Bonnie Auger and Suzy Davidkhanian responded to our many queries. Sandra Glen and Louise King of the marketing design department were indefatigable in their help with the design and layout and in commissioning photographs and artwork. Meg Rodriguez, the secretary in the legal department, was a source of good counsel and humour. John and Jackie James at Kingsmeadows House, Peebles, kept me supplied with tea and biscuits on my sojourns amongst the company's records. Our editor, Judy Diamond, was scrupulous in spotting errors and omissions. Lastly, David Simpson, the retired company secretary and investment manager, who was in overall charge of the project, was a tower of strength. He smoothed paths, answered innumerable questions, researched aspects of the history, particularly the company's Perthshire associations dear to his heart, and learned some of the skills of the publishing trade.

MICHAEL MOSS
Borlandhills
2000

Standard Life's motto *Prospice Aspice Respice: Haud Immemor Futuri* means *Look forward, look round, look back* and *Not unmindful of the future*. Standard Life's original coat-of-arms was used on policy documents from 1832 until 1974, when the Lord Lyon King at Arms objected to their similarity to the royal coat-of-arms. The coat-of-arms was redrawn in 1989 and it is this version that is displayed in the foyer of Standard Life House in Lothian Road.

CHAPTER ONE

'WITH CAUTION AND PRUDENCE': 1825–45

'It is imperative on [the directors] as men of Honour, of Principle, of Trust and integrity, to do their utmost for their constituents and act with caution and prudence by satisfying themselves that the party to be insured or the loan required be properly represented and deliberated upon, before it is entertained.'

Lieutenant-Colonel James McBean, a director, October 1830.[1]

The Life Insurance Company of Scotland (later to become the Standard Life Assurance Company) was established on 23 March 1825 in Edinburgh by some of the proprietors of the Insurance Company of Scotland, a fire insurance office which had been set up four years earlier.[2] Political and social allegiances were decisive in the formation of the new company. At the time, Scotland was beginning to struggle free from long years of Tory rule at the hands of the powerful Dundas family, who controlled not only the country's politics but also much of its financial system. Led by the Whigs, the attack on this stranglehold was two-pronged: the political campaign to widen the tiny franchise (just 4,500 voters in the whole country) and the creation of financial houses such as the Commercial Bank of Scotland (established in 1810)[3] and its associate, the Insurance Company of Scotland. Henry Cockburn, a prominent Whig lawyer and a founding director of the Commercial Bank, commented:

No men were more devoid of public spirit and even the proper spirit of their trade than our old Edinburgh bankers . . . All the Whig business of the country would not have kept them going for a week; and the Government dealt out its patronage in the reception and transmission of the public money to its own friends. So they all combined banking with politics . . . A demand for a bank founded on more liberal principles was the natural result of this state of things.[4]

The first governor of the Insurance Company of Scotland, the Duke of Hamilton, and his deputies, the Earl of Roseberry and Lord Blantyre, were all prominent Whigs. These new institutions hoped to win custom from the many enterprises that had sprung up since the 1780s to exploit novel industrial techniques in metalworking, engineering and above all textiles.[5] It was the owners of these businesses that had most to gain from political reform. In Edinburgh it

The High Street in Edinburgh in 1793. It was here at No.200 on
the right-hand side of the street that the Life Insurance Company
of Scotland, later Standard Life, opened for business in 1825.

was impossible for these new finance houses to establish offices in the Tory-controlled New Town so they had to find premises in the cramped confines of the Old Town instead. The Insurance Company of Scotland's first office was in the Royal Mile at 200 High Street, and very quickly it was accepting large industrial risks, and even insuring the steamboat *Rothesay Castle* that plied between Glasgow and Inveraray.[6] By the first annual meeting in 1823, a hundred agents had been appointed throughout Scotland and the north of England.[7] Profits were slim, however, driven down by competition from London fire offices and by a number of serious fires not least in Edinburgh itself during 1824 when much of the south side of the High Street (including the Tron Steeple) was destroyed.[8] These obstacles to progress persuaded the directors to consider opening a life department rather sooner than they had planned. Providing the shareholders agreed unanimously, the deed of the Insurance Company could simply be widened to include life business, imitating other concerns which provided both fire and life cover.[9]

THE INSURANCE MARKET

Rate cutting was the worst feature of competition from other offices, an outcome of intense activity in the Scottish insurance industry at the time. During 1822 the long-established and prestigious Phoenix Assurance Company of London had offered to buy the North British Insurance Company of Edinburgh, which in the 13 years since its foundation had gained control of a fifth of the Scottish market.[10] The North British directors, who also had Whig sympathies, rejected the approach outright and immediately decided to 'establish a Life Office' as a separate department within the company, 'believing Life Insurance was a business now much more generally understood and beginning to be much more acted upon in Scotland' – almost certainly a clear reference to the remarkable success of the Edinburgh-based Scottish Widows Fund since its formation in 1815.[11] The Palladium Life and Fire Assurance Society, established in London in 1824, from the outset had an Edinburgh board chaired by the Whig Sir Michael Shaw Stewart of Ardgowan in Renfrewshire.[12] The Tory response was rapid. They formed the Edinburgh Life Assurance Company in 1823 and in the following year the Tory Lord Provost of Edinburgh, Alexander Henderson, floated the Scottish Union Insurance Company, a fire and life office with a capital of £5 million. This was one of the few successful concerns to be formed north of the border during the 1820s joint stock mania.[13]

THE EARLIEST POLICIES

In the 1820s the market for life assurance was nothing like as well developed as that for fire insurance. Nevertheless, a range of products was already available. The simplest forms of policy were the insurance of a life for the payment of a specific sum of money at death (called 'whole term', later 'whole life') or in the event of death taking place within a specific period or 'term',

DEALING WITH LANDED FAMILIES

At this time landed families were the most important customers for life assurance companies. Agricultural improvement had been fashionable from the late eighteenth century but often could only be paid for by massive borrowings from anyone willing to lend, including legal practices, banks and insurance companies.[1] The majority of estates were 'entailed' and had to pass intact to the next generation.[2] Since the Scottish Entail Improvement or Montgomery Act of 1770, it had been possible for proprietors of entailed estates to obtain loans providing that in the event of their death the interest and repayments did not commit their successors to more than two-thirds of the income from four years' rent.[3] In these circumstances judicious borrowers insured their lives for the value and duration of the loan. Heirs at entail could also borrow against the certain expectation of inheritance; but to do so without insuring their own life or survivorship would have been foolhardy.[4] An heir who was not in immediate line might also wish to insure against the birth of a more direct heir, particularly if borrowings had been made against expectations. During the French wars nearly all financial institutions stopped making such loans, preferring instead to invest patriotically in government securities. Lending to landed families did not resume until the late 1810s, some time after the Battle of Waterloo, usually by means of what were termed 'redeembale annuities'.[5]

These were pioneered by the Pelican as a means of advancing money to the landed gentry whose estates were entailed.[6] An annuity was considered in law to be 'in the widest sense of the term, a yearly sum not payable as interest and chargeable both upon real and personal estate of the grantor or person who created the annuity'.[7] Since they were not considered to be interest they were outside the scope of the usury laws, which from the early eighteenth century prohibited charging rates above 5 per cent unless there was an element of chance. Breach of the law could result in the forfeiture from the lender of a sum equivalent to three times the value of the loan. Under the terms of a redeemable annuity a capital sum was advanced to a landowner, which was repayable after a fixed period and was secured against the proceeds of a whole-life without-profits policy. Such policies were not considered in law to be 'an absolute security for repayment of the principal [as] the policy may be forfeited by suicide and the like'.[8] This element of hazard also placed the loan outside the scope of usury law. 'It was very early decided that an agreement to pay double the sum borrowed or other penalty on the non-payment of the principal debt at a certain day is not usurious because it is in the power of the borrower wholly to discharge himself by repaying the principal according to the bargain.'[9] The landowner agreed in return to pay an annuity to the lender out of the rents of the property. Although the annuity was not considered in law to be an interest charge and the rate was deliberately not recorded in the legal agreement, in fact rates were adjusted at the discretion of the lenders to reflect movements in the cost of borrowing. Changes in rates in either direction were not automatic and applications for reductions were regularly turned down. Under the

Lady Mary Montgomerie and her son, the thirteenth Earl of Eglinton. Lady Mary borrowed heavily from Standard Life to improve her Ayrshire properties and, unusually for her, paid the money back.

The cover of William Thomson's book on the rights of heirs of entail, 1849.

Freeland House, extended in the 1830s by James, Lord Ruthven (1777–1853), with the help of loans from Standard Life. It became Strathallan School in 1920.

annuitant's advantage if death occurred well before the end of the agreed term as interest payments would cease within four years and the capital be forfeited unless it was recovered from the proceeds of a life policy assigned to the insurance company. On the other hand, if an annuitant, who had borrowed against expectations, proved exceptionally long-lived (often the case with the aristocracy) interest payments could be crippling. The courts increasingly came to consider redeemable annuities usurious 'if the total amount of the annual payments is more than sufficient to pay the principal sum and legal interest'.[11]

The whole-life without-profits policies which supported redeemable annuity loans guaranteed a healthy stream of premium income for their duration and made life offices reluctant to allow early repayment.[12] Landed families were ready customers for policies for other purposes. Nearly all their marriages were supported by carefully drafted legal contracts, especially if the wife was wealthier than her husband. Prudent lawyers stipulated that contracts included appropriate assurances, for example against the husband dying before his father or before the birth of a male heir, and the purchase of a deferred annuity to provide for the wife if the husband predeceased her.[13] As a result of a new Scottish Entail Act in 1824, which made possible the payment of pensions to proprietors' spouses through the creation of life-rents over entailed estates for as much as one-third of the rental income, demand for insurance and annuities for women multiplied to reduce such burdens.[14]

terms of the agreement, any default in payment triggered a penal annuity rate and if payments were still not made the lender could seek to recover the debt by distraining the rents. There were risks in such transactions as on many estates, particularly in the Highlands, tenants were in considerable arrears and actual rents far lower than the notional values.

Under the terms of the Montgomery Act of 1770 proprietors of estates in Scotland could, with their agreement, bind their heirs to meet interest and repayments for four years after their death, providing the loans were only used for improvements and all expenditure was recorded with the relevant Sheriff Clerk.[10] This could work to the

which could be for any period but not normally for more than ten years. Term insurance could be improved by an endowment policy which, in addition to guaranteeing the payment of a specified sum if death occurred before the end of the period, also yielded a fixed payment at termination. All these policies could also be taken out on joint or several lives and on 'survivorships' – in other words on one person outliving another.[14]

Many insurers, in return for higher premiums, allowed policy-holders to share in the returns of the company – a 'with-profits policy'. A bonus was declared at the end of a certain period, usually three, five or ten years, when an 'investigation' of the accumulated assets and liabilities was conducted and a profit or loss declared. The first insurance company to conduct such an investigation was the Equitable Life Assurance Society in 1776.[15] Some insurers, such as the Equitable, the Norwich Union and Scottish Widows, were mutual companies organised for the benefit of their 'with-profits' policy-holders, in which case all the profits were available for distribution to them. Other insurers, such as the Sun and North British, were owned by partners or shareholders, who were also entitled to a division of the profits. There were two methods of distributing profits to policy-holders. The oldest was the 'tontine' scheme by which a 'reversionary' addition to the sum invested was declared at each investigation and multiplied by the number of years a policy had been in force. As time went on, the inequitable benefit of the tontine system to long survivors persuaded many companies to issue policies with reversionary bonuses independent of the number of years in force, often referred to as the 'Equitable' principle.[16] In addition life offices sold annuities, which provided an annual income, either payable immediately or from some date in the future. Every type of product could be purchased either by a lump sum or by annual instalments at rates determined by the age, health, occupation and lifestyle of those insured.[17]

Several products catered for the requirements of the landed gentry (see pages 18–19) and could easily be adapted to meet the needs of families engaged in commerce and industry. Consequently, life assurance companies came to occupy an important role in the acquisition of capital to launch, expand and even wind up an enterprise. Trustees for bankruptcies could insure the lives of bankrupts if assets were not readily realisable or as part of a composition whereby creditors agreed to accept a proportion of what they were owed.[18] For example, after Sir Walter Scott's spectacular failure in 1826, he was heavily insured by his creditors.

ESTABLISHING A LIFE DEPARTMENT

The Insurance Company of Scotland formally decided to open a life department to complement their fire business on 9 February 1825, summoning the partners to a general meeting on 23 March.[19] Since there were objections from some of the directors and shareholders to extending the partnership and changing the objectives of the company, the board had no alternative but to agree to establish a separate concern which would share offices and staff. There were several precedents for such an arrangement, among them the Phoenix Fire Office whose partners had formed the Pelican Life Office in 1797;[20] the Norwich Union Fire Insurance Society which had set up a Life Assurance Society in 1808;[21] and the Sun Insurance Office which had established the Sun Life Assurance Society in 1810.[22] The first board meeting of the Life Insurance Company of Scotland was held on 30 March. Since two of the directors of the Insurance Company had been among the objectors to the project, new recruits had to be found. The original Life board comprised Archibald Campbell, George Square, Edinburgh; Alexander Scott, a farmer of Myreside, near Edinburgh; Miles Angus Fletcher, an advocate whose family was renowned for its commitment to political reform; Forest Alexander, an Edinburgh merchant and a director of the Commercial Bank of Scotland; David Clyne, a Solicitor of the Supreme Court; and Alexander Wood, an advocate.[23] They quickly added to their number William Henderson, another merchant in Edinburgh; William Wyld, a merchant in Leith; and William Wallace,[24] professor of mathematics at the University of Edinburgh, 'whose scientific knowledge might be highly beneficial to the Institution'.[25] William Wallace had been persuaded to leave the Edinburgh boards of the County Fire and Provident Life offices, whose life department was presided over by none other

The minute of the board of the Insurance Company of Scotland recording the decision to open a life office, 23 March 1825.

than the leader of the Whigs in Parliament, Earl Grey.[26] There he had learned much about the methods of calculating life assurance risks and the likely return on investments in annuities. Within the year, two of the original directors, Scott and Wood, had to be replaced when they defected to the Norwich Union's newly established Scottish board.[27] Ironically one of the replacements, Lieutenant-Colonel John Munro, was already well insured with the Norwich Union.[28] Robert Alexander, manager of the Insurance Company of Scotland, and his brother William Alexander WS, the law agent, along

The distinguished Scottish judge and diarist Henry, Lord Cockburn (1779–1854), who played an important part in the establishment of the Insurance Company of Scotland. In the background can be seen his home, Bonaly Tower, which later belonged to his kinsman William Thomas Thomson, the manager of Standard Life.

with William Peddie, the secretary, were to fill the same positions with the new Life Company until Whitsun 1831 when the agreement to share premises would be reviewed.[29]

The first tasks of the board of the new company were to issue a prospectus, which appeared in *The Scotsman* on 9 April, and to draw up with the help of Henry Cockburn the contract of co-partnery. The prospectus appealed unashamedly to national sentiment:

> *While we have only four Native Establishments for Life Insurance, the number of Agencies for English Companies exceeds twenty. Of these, nine have been appointed within the last six years; and by the whole together, Premiums to a very great amount are remitted annually to England.*

Given the strength of the competition, the prospects for success were greatly exaggerated: 'it may be doubted if any Insurance Company was ever formed under auspices so favourable, or commenced with more flattering prospects of success'.[30] The contract of co-partnery, which was ready for signing in July, spelled out the parameters of the company's activities, embracing the whole range of life insurance products and every opportunity for investment. It was left to the discretion of the board when to distribute profits, and in what proportion, to 'with-profits'

policy-holders. The authorised capital was £3 million, divided into 60,000 shares of £50 each, of which only 10,000 were ever issued and then only with a call of £1 per share (see page 192). There was to be only one general meeting of the partners or shareholders each year on or near 15 December to receive the annual accounts which were to be balanced a month earlier on 15 November.* The directors, who had wide powers to manage the enterprise, were to meet weekly and their deliberations were to be recorded in a 'Sederunt' or minute book. The company was to continue for 45 years and after the first year dividends could be declared. As with the Insurance Company of Scotland, there were powers to appoint a governor and a deputy governor and to apply, should the need arise, for an Act of Parliament or Royal Charter.[31]

Altogether 116 people subscribed for shares, several of whom were not investors in the Insurance Company of Scotland. Some 51 shareholders lived in Edinburgh but more capital was invested by the 28 shareholders living in and around Perth. Some of the Edinburgh investors also had Perthshire connections. The remainder of the shareholders were mostly scattered up the east coast of Scotland. There was only one shareholder in each of Glasgow and Argyllshire and one south of the border, George Macintyre, a Leeds merchant who subscribed for just two shares. The majority described themselves as

---

* It was the practice of institutions in Scotland to balance their books at about the time of the summer or autumn quarter days (Lammas on 1 August and Martinmas on 12 November) when rents were paid.

lawyers or merchants, titles that often implied extensive family, social and business connections with landed wealth. Under the terms of the contract of co-partnery, the partners were required within a year to take out policies on either their own life or those of others or to purchase annuities.[32]

THE FIRST POLICIES

Before any policies could be issued, rates for the premiums had to be set with advice from Professor Wallace. Rates were calculated on the basis of the life expectancy of the person to be insured, with either additional premiums or outright refusal in the case of certain medical conditions, places of residence or social habits. In computing rates, the most commonly used mortality statistics were based on death rates in Northampton over the period 1735–80 compiled by Dr Richard Price for the Equitable.[33] It was widely recognised by the 1820s that these tables were misleading as they represented the mortality experienced by the whole population rather than the much longer-lived well-to-do, who could afford the luxury of life insurance. As a result premiums on younger lives were much too high, condemned by the mathematician Charles Babbage in 1826 for yielding 'immense' returns to insurance companies.[34] Impervious to the concerns of his professional colleagues, Professor Wallace recommended in July the use of the Scottish Widows tables 'with a participation in profits as having been approved by the experience of that Company to be perfectly safe,

PROSPECTUS OF THE LIFE INSURANCE COMPANY OF SCOTLAND,

FOR THE INSURANCE OF LIVES, PURCHASE AND SALE OF ANNUITIES, GRANTING ENDOWMENTS TO CHILDREN, &c.

THE Projectors of THE INSURANCE COMPANY OF SCOTLAND, established at Edinburgh in May 1821, for Insurance against *Fire*, aware of the advantages resulting from *Life* Insurance, had it from the commencement in contemplation to extend the objects and business of the Company to Insurance on Lives. It was deemed prudent to begin with Insurance against Fire ;---and the success which has attended the *Fire* Insurance Company, joined to the increasing attention that has of late years been directed to *Life* Insurance in Scotland, induced the Partners, at a General Meeting held for the special purpose, on the 23d day of March last, to resolve to form a Company for the objects above mentioned, to be called, " THE LIFE INSURANCE COMPANY OF SCOTLAND."

The advantages of Life Insurance are now so well and so generally known, as to render any enumeration of them superfluous. But in proposing the Establishment of a New Company, it may be necessary to state the probability of its success, and the consequent profits to be derived by the Shareholders.

The Native Establishments for carrying on the business of Life Insurance in Scotland are only *four*. The Scottish Life Assurance Society, formed on the principle of *Mutual Assurance*, having no *Proprietary*, has, after ten years standing, amply rewarded the labours of its Founders. The Edinburgh Life Insurance Company, established in 1823, originating with Gentlemen of the Law, and embracing a Proprietary composed chiefly of that Profession, has been so successful, that its Stock already commands a Premium of from 30 to 40 per cent. ;---the Partners, however, as that Company is established, drawing no Dividend for five years.

The prospectus of the Life Insurance Company of Scotland which appeared in the *Scotsman* newspaper, 9 April 1825.

and as correctly calculated from the Northampton Tables and only differing from the Equitable by taking the interest at 4 per cent instead of 3 per cent'. This was agreed and the following month a blend of the tables of the Equitable itself and the Scottish Widows was adopted for without-profits policies.[35] Later, in August, physicians and surgeons were appointed to referee proposals for policies. The tables, together with printed instructions, were distributed to the

George Gray, a Perth lawyer who played a prominant role in the establishment of Standard Life, with his family, including his daughter Effie (seated, far right), who married John Ruskin. The marriage was annulled and she later married the artist Sir John Millais (standing, right). Gray, one of Standard Life's largest shareholders, contributed more than 10 per cent of all new sums assured in the early years. He died in 1877.

agents of the Insurance Company of Scotland, who were to act for the fledgling business.[36]

Shareholders in Aberdeen and Perth took seriously their duty to recruit policy-holders. The first proposal was reported to the board on 12 September and was made by Alexander Gibbon, an Aberdeen advocate, who held ten shares and wished to insure the life of Mrs Sophia Urquhart or Munroe, widow of Captain Charles Munroe, for £40 without-profits.[37] Learning that Mrs Munroe had been born in India, a decision was delayed while enquiries were made to find out if she was of native descent, since at the time insurance companies, lacking adequate mortality statistics, would only accept European lives. Surprisingly, it turned out that both her parents were from St Helena and the proposal was accepted a week later.[38] The delay prevented Alexander Gibbon from being the first policy-holder. Instead this accolade went to Mrs Janet Wood, aged 60, wife of Dr James Wood of Keithock, near Perth, for a without-profits whole-life policy of £500 arranged by George Gray, a lawyer who held 50 shares and was the Perth agent.[39]

Mrs Munroe was not the only early proposal the directors treated circumspectly. They would not insure Captain John Thornton, late of the 42nd Foot, until they knew what wounds he had received in action,[40] and they wanted to know why Mrs Janet Murray or Dow of Springkerse was described as being of a 'lusty habit'.[41] In mid-October the company received the first request for a loan of £500 covered by a with-profits policy from James Murray, a surgeon in Leith. The board cautiously agreed, rejecting collateral securities in the shape of government stock and insisting on two sureties or guarantors from amongst Murray's friends, who in the event of a default would be responsible for repayment of the interest and capital. This was good business as not only was the interest on such loans 4.5 per cent compared with the 3 per cent available on government stock, but premiums would also be received.[42] The request for Murray to provide guarantors prevented him from becoming the first with-profits policy-holder and instead the first with-profits policy was issued on 5 December to Alexander Horatio Simpson, a Paisley lawyer, as part of a similar loan arrangement. In return for a loan of £1,500 to fund his burgeoning business interests in the town, he insured his life for an equal sum with a single premium of £670.[43] The directors were concerned that this initial large transaction should not send out an inappropriate signal that might trigger a flood of requests, and so that they would have no more money to lend, wisely invested £2,000 in Bank of England stock.[44] Showing little loyalty to his new financiers, Simpson within three years had become the Paisley agent for the Norwich Union.[45]

INSURING THE ARISTOCRACY

All insurance companies had a ceiling on the size of any risk they would accept; but rather than refuse rewarding business, they were accustomed to sharing or reinsuring the risk with their

A certificate for the purchase of Bank Stock from the Bank of England in 1832. This was a secure and readily realisable investment.

A policy of the Life Insurance Company of Scotland on the life of Alexander Shulze, 1826, with the honours of Scotland displayed at the top.

competitors. During the 1820s and 1830s the majority of all very large life policies were issued to the aristocracy and landed gentry, usually as the corollary of equally large 'redeemable annuity loans'. The first request for reinsurance to the infant Life Insurance Company of Scotland was made as early as September 1825 for a policy of £2,000 on the life of the Duke of Argyll by a consortium comprising North British (£2,000), Edinburgh Life Assurance Co. (£2,000), Scottish Union Insurance Co. (£5,000) and Scottish Widows (£3,000) – a total of £14,000. The board was pleased to support a fellow Whig, providing half their risk could be shared with another life office – which, as it turned out, proved impossible.[46] In June 1826 the board took the initiative in negotiating reinsurance on a policy of £3,000 on the life of Archibald Farquharson of Finzean MP from Aberdeenshire.[47] Other reinsurances soon followed within a limit of £1,000 on the lives of the Earls of Errol, Mar and Moray, and Sir David Moncreiffe of Moncreiffe.[48]

Although profitable, dealing with the aristocracy could be hazardous. The Earl of Mar died within two years of taking out his policy, in September 1828, and immediately his bankers, the respected Edinburgh firm of Sir William Forbes & Co., applied for his policies (totalling £7,000) to be redeemed to pay off his debts to them.[49] With rumours circulating that there were suspicious circumstances surrounding the Earl's death, the Life Insurance Company and the two other insurers refused. On investigation it emerged that the Earl had been addicted to laudanum (opium), taking as much as three ounces a day.[50] On the grounds that this information had not been made available at the time the policies were taken out, the claim was contested in March 1830 in the Court of Session in Edinburgh. Sir William Forbes & Co. advanced medical evidence to suggest that the taking of laudanum was not dangerous and the jury supported this view. The insurance companies appealed on the grounds that the judge had misdirected the jury.[51] On reflection the court came to this view but in the interval the reforming Whig government, which came to power in November 1830, had abolished jury trials in such cases without making provision in the Act for the conclusion of outstanding proceedings.

John Francis, seventh Earl of Mar (1770–1825), and his family painted by David Allan. This painting, with Alloa House in the background, originally included his eldest son, John Thomas, who succeeded as eighth Earl in 1825. He lived such a dissolute life that his father had his likeness painted out and replaced by the top-hat to be seen hanging from the branches on the right. Standard Life insured the eighth Earl, who died, as a result of drug addiction, in 1828.

By the time this oversight had been corrected and a retrial ordered for early in 1832, one of the principal witnesses was dead and the other – the eldest son, the new Earl – considered to be insane. Frightened they would lose, Sir William Forbes & Co. accepted the offer from the insurance companies of the return of the premiums less their legal expenses.[52] This was a significant victory as it not only prevented a large loss, but it also established a view that unless such habits were disclosed to insurers, policies would be considered invalid – establishing the principle of *uberrima fides*.

In the early years the directors placed faith in their partners or shareholders as a means of recruiting policy-holders. The directors believed that they had:

much in their power towards promoting the prosperity of the Company. Life Insurance is only beginning to be thought of in this Country and the prejudices against the practice of it are daily wearing off, these prejudices the partners should lose no opportunity of eradicating and proving the superiority of institutions of this nature to the provident societies and widows schemes generated by the prevailing inattention to Life Insurance even among the middling and comparatively enlightened part of the community.[53]

They hoped that through their connections the shareholders would be able to recruit policy-holders from just this section of society.

Although never satisfied with the level of new business that was generated, the board was pleased with early progress, particularly given the onset of a serious trade recession within months of opening. Over four hundred policies with a total risk of £200,000 were taken out in the first five years.[54] Most were with-profits and well below the £1,000 ceiling. Increasingly, policies were linked to loan agreements, making the company a useful source of venture capital for small enterprises. Policy-holders included in 1828 William Houston, a cotton spinner of Blackburn in Lancashire, who borrowed £700 and insured his life for £1,000;[55] William Chambers, the Edinburgh bookseller, who borrowed £200 in 1830 and insured his life for £400; and Peter Somerville, a cabinetmaker in Edinburgh, who borrowed £150 and was insured for £300.[56] The company now had strict rules for such advances. No loans were to be secured against property or expectations and all borrowers had to find two sureties.[57] Moreover, until 1830 the board insisted that the insurance be roughly twice the value of the loan and took a very rigid view of the medical evidence.[58] By July 1828 over £10,000 had been loaned in this way with supporting policies of almost £21,000. All policies stipulated that they became void if the holders left the United Kingdom without informing the company, while sureties had both to make a similar undertaking and to agree to notify any change in their own financial circumstances which would prevent them from paying.[59]

With Scotland's well-established links with

William Chambers (1800–83), the well-known Edinburgh bookseller, who borrowed money from Standard Life to help fund his publishing company, W. & R. Chambers of dictionary fame.

North America, Australasia and India, requests to travel were inevitable from the outset. In November 1826 Mrs Christie from Huntly asked to insure her husband William, who was about to visit his estates in Surinam, Berbice and Demerara. This was agreed with an additional premium of two and a half guineas for the voyage out and for three months' stay and a further eight guineas for longer.[60]

CONFLICT WITH THE INSURANCE COMPANY

The Life Insurance Company was still in its infancy when serious differences arose with its sister company. A life office could afford to lock up its assets in high-yielding personal loans as there was little likelihood (if the business was prudently managed) of a sudden large call. This was very different from a fire office, which needed to have a large proportion of its funds invested in assets that could be quickly realised to meet emergencies such as the enormous fires in the High Street in Edinburgh in 1824.[61] Within three years, David Clyne, the only remaining Insurance Company director on the Life Company's board, questioned the wisdom of seeking more policies merely to expand the loan business.[62] Clyne's position, however, was ambivalent even on the board of the Insurance Company, as he was a large shareholder in the Tory-controlled Royal Bank of Scotland.[63] In any event his view was firmly rejected by the other directors, who, in January 1829, welcomed a committee report which showed that the return on the £13,220 advanced to date was £661 – twice what could have been earned from buying government stock – and in addition premiums of £786 had been paid.[64]

The Insurance Company board was not satisfied but, with mounting losses, was itself embroiled in a fierce internal argument about the future direction of their business. The chief critic of the Insurance Company's management was James Inglis, another Edinburgh lawyer, who replaced David Clyne as the Life Company's representative on the Insurance Company's Board in June. Dissatisfied, he resigned two months later, severing the link between the two boards.[65] At the end of the year David Clyne was again in dispute with his colleagues in the Life Company when it was decided to cut the insurance cover for loans to about the same value.[66] Meanwhile the outlook for the Insurance Company had continued to deteriorate and in February 1830 their directors resolved to let the Life Company's offices unless their wayward offspring was prepared to pay an economic rent. This was merely a prelude to an economy drive on all aspects of the Insurance Company's business supervised directly by the board, which was effectively what James Inglis had been calling for a year before.[67]

Relations deteriorated rapidly following the death in June 1830 of William Peddie, the secretary of the two companies, and reached a crisis in mid-August over what in effect was a trivial incident.[68] After the regular meeting of the Life Company board on 16 August, George Paton from Caithness called at the office requesting a policy which he wanted issued that night as he was returning home early the following day. In accordance with the quorum rules in the contract of co-partnery, three directors met that evening and accepted the risk.[69] On learning of this a month later David Clyne protested that the meeting was 'premature, irregular and illegal'.[70] The board was deeply divided. Lieutenant-Colonel James McBean of Parkside, a man of independent means and a director of the Life Company since 1826, investigated the incident, supporting Clyne's view that responsibility was vested in all the directors when he reported in October:

> The Board of Directors has not only an arduous but a difficult duty to perform, . . . it is imperative on them as men of Honour, of Principle, of Trust and integrity, to do their utmost for their constituents and act with caution and prudence by satisfying themselves that the party to be insured or the loan required be properly represented and deliberated upon, before it is entertained.[71]

The quarrel did not rest there, as within a fortnight the board was considering investing in reversionary interests and, more importantly, redeemable annuities on entailed estates. Clyne was opposed to such innovation and let his concerns be known to the Insurance Company.[72] When in December the Life Company directors tried to discuss the appointment of a new secretary with the Insurance Company, they were rebuffed as the sister company had decided to freeze the post until Whitsun 1831 because of lack of funds.[73] Infuriated, the Life Company board appointed their colleague William Hackney Kerr, an Edinburgh accountant, to examine their own books. His report was a devastating indictment of the management:

> In the books there is no proper division of the various kinds of risks:– that while interest is calculated upon some of the accounts, it is not calculated upon others, and that at no one balance in any one occasion has there ever been an attempt made to determine the values of the risks, so that obviously it was utterly impossible in such circumstances to form an accurate Profit & Loss Account, or even to ascertain whether the Company was a gaining or losing concern.[74]

Worse was to follow when it emerged that some of the bonds for the company's loans had been drawn up by a clerk in the office – not by reference to the law agent but on the authority of the difficult David Clyne, admittedly a qualified lawyer.[75]

GOING IT ALONE

On 27 January 1831 the directors decided to break with the Insurance Company and asked for the resignation of both the manager and the law agent – the two Alexander brothers.[76] Within a week temporary premises had been found on the north-east corner of North Bridge Street[77]* and on 18 February James A. Cheyne, a well-connected Edinburgh accountant and Writer to the Signet who had worked for Scottish Widows, was appointed second manager.[78] Ten days later James Anderson, formerly cashier of the Scottish Union Insurance Company, was appointed secretary and cashier.[79] Although the directors of the Insurance Company had misgivings about the conduct of their manager Robert Alexander, they did not hesitate in accepting his spiteful recommendation to participate in the sequestration or bankruptcy of William Hackney Kerr, who was a guarantor on a debt to the company for £250.[80] At the same time the chairman of the Insurance Company, Colonel H.V. White, persuaded a meeting of shareholders to open a new life department in direct competition with the Life Company.[81] This scheme came to nothing because the Life Company commenced legal action 'in respect of the evil and inconvenience that will result'[82] and early in 1832 the Insurance Company was more preoccupied with the acquisition of the fire business of the Dundee Assurance Company.[83] If it was any comfort to the directors of the Life Company, the troublesome David Clyne was forced to leave their number because of financial difficulties and, after his death a few months later, was declared bankrupt.[84] Two years later, against a background of mounting losses, Robert Alexander was dismissed as manager of the Insurance Company of

Declaration signed by Sir James Boswell, baronet, a policy-holder and borrower, and endorsed by James Cheyne, who was responsible for the change of name to The Standard Life Assurance Company in 1832.

Scotland when it emerged that he had not only tried to defect to a London competitor but had also contributed directly to Kerr's embarrassment by withholding funds.[85]

These bitter disputes had taken their toll on the Life Company's business and the first task of the new manager and secretary was to restore confidence. Custom revived in the early spring

---

* Within a year permanent premises were leased in the New Town at 21 South St Andrew Street.

of 1831. Four Banff businessmen – Andrew McEwen, banker; James Duff, baker; John Aitken, vintner; and William Allan, shoemaker – who took out policies in March, were typical new risks.[86] With the Insurance Company's threat to enter the life business and competition from another new life office (the Scottish Equitable Life Assurance Company founded in Edinburgh in 1831),[87] the board urgently reviewed its agencies, resolving that in the future no one who represented another institution could hold an agency.[88] In the summer James Cheyne visited a number of towns, including London, to assess prospects. New agents were appointed in places as far apart as Lerwick, Dundee and Fort William.[89] This was a prelude to a more radical overhaul in 1832 when, following the lead of other companies, commissions began to be paid to other life offices on reinsurance and to banks and agents who recruited new policy-holders.[90] The company also adopted the Norwich Union's table for annuities and held urgent discussions with the other life offices about the risk posed by the epidemic of cholera that was sweeping the country.[91]

At the same time local boards of directors were appointed in Aberdeen and Perth. Although Aberdeen was believed from the beginning to be fruitful territory for insurance, after the initial interest the company had failed to attract business and it was hoped that a local board and new agents, Adam & Anderson, advocates, would make for improvement. In contrast, the establishment of the Perth board was a recognition of George Gray's success.[92] A visit by the manager and directors to Glasgow, where there were very few policy-holders and still no more shareholders, was largely a failure. Thomas Buchanan, an accountant and a member of the powerful Buchanan family with extensive commercial interests in Glasgow and North America, was appointed agent with offices leased directly by the company. He persuaded two wealthy textile manufacturers, Samuel Higginbotham and William Leckie Ewing, and a lawyer, Alexander Morrison, to take shares and policies but there was not enough interest to form a local board. The existing agents Wyld & Orr were understandably annoyed and refused to resign.[93] Unable to make inroads into the whole of the Scottish market, a decision about representation in London was postponed.[94]

RENAMED STANDARD LIFE

There were disadvantages in making small loans to businesspeople; they were relatively costly to administer and there was the ever-present danger of bankruptcy. Recovering debts that were not directly secured against real property (land and buildings) was time-consuming and could be expensive. There were several such cases in 1831 and 1832, among them that of Mrs Adams, an Edinburgh dressmaker, who had borrowed £250 to help finance her business at 95 Princes Street and that of her husband, Robert Adams, an ironmonger. They had both offered generous terms to their well-to-do clientele who, in the time-honoured tradition, failed to pay.

Sometimes bankruptcy also pulled down the sureties for the debt, making it unlikely that the full amount of a loan would be recovered through the courts.[95] Under partnership law such legal proceedings had to be conducted in the names of all the partners, which could create difficulties if they themselves were either sureties for a debt or also creditors. In December 1831 the board petitioned for an Act of Parliament to allow legal proceedings in Scotland, England and Ireland to be initiated in the name of the company by either the manager or three directors.[96] While the Bill was being drafted, it was decided on 23 April 1832 to change the name of the company to The Standard Life Assurance Company so as to draw a line under the past and to reflect the ideal risk. This was a healthy adult living in the United Kingdom with temperate habits and a secure occupation free of hazards – in other words a standard life.[97] Otherwise the Act passed in June simply repeated the terms of the original contract of co-partnery.[98]

By this time the character of the business had begun to change following the decision to enter the market for redeemable annuities. This was neither for the faint-hearted nor for those with inadequate legal controls. Since the end of the boom in agricultural prices during the French wars, incomes from agricultural rents had fallen sharply; but many of the gentry had refused to cut their expenditure and instead borrowed heavily. It was reported by several commentators at the time that as much as half of all rental income was committed to repayment.[99] Redeem-

able annuities with their high interest rates were considered by most to be the last resort when all other avenues of credit had been exhausted. As a result such borrowers were amongst the most profligate and indigent members of the aristocracy. They were not above pretending that there were no existing mortgages over their properties, their rental income was larger than it really was, or that they had title to estates they had long ceased to own.[100] Some were simply impecuniously improvident such as the ninth Lord Elibank, whose father had inherited the title from an uncle. Others were notorious spendthrifts such as the first Marquess of Breadalbane, the father-in-law of the self-indulgent Richard, second Duke of Buckingham.[101] Only a few, such as Sir James Boswell, sought financial help genuinely to improve their patrimony.[102] With its strong links to the Edinburgh legal profession, Standard Life would have been well aware of the dangers. A newly appointed law committee and legal agent, David Campbell, would bear the heavy responsibility of investigating titles and securing valid bonds over the rents of entailed properties.[103] In Scotland, this was less of a problem than for most counties in England and the whole of Ireland, as all transactions over land were recorded in the Registers of Sasines.

The initial request for a very large loan of this kind came in November 1831 from General Lord Glenlyon for £13,000. This was declined as it was probably more than Standard Life could afford.[104] It was not until the following February that the first loan was made, of £4,000, to General

Duncan Darroch, who wished to develop his Gourock estate on the lower Clyde as a resort for the well-to-do.[105] Immediately new requests came in thick and fast. In processing them, the company set four prudent criteria: loans would only be made on Scottish properties; certified copies of the rentals had to be produced; all loans had to be backed by an insurance policy of an equivalent sum; and in every case two sureties had to continue to be found for both the premiums on the policy, the interest and, in most cases, the loan itself.[106] Other redeemable annuities arranged during 1832 included an advance of £1,000 to Captain Donald Campbell of Barbreck in Argyllshire; £6,000 to Captain Richardson who had property in Perthshire; £1,500 to Lord Elibank secured against his Darnhall estate in Peebles; £5,000 to Sir James Boswell of Auchinleck in Ayrshire; and £4,000 to Lord Ruthven of Freeland in Perthshire.[107] Lord Ruthven soon became Standard Life's largest borrower with an advance of £18,000, largely used to pay for the impulsive development of his mansion and its surrounding gardens.[108]

Insuring the aristocracy was also perilous as many travelled widely and indulged in dangerous sports such as sailing and steam yachting. When Donald Campbell of Dunstaffnage in Argyllshire and Sir W.C. Anstruther took out policies in 1833 and 1834, they were allowed 'to sail about the shores of Great Britain in yachts or pleasure boats' with no extra premium.[109] Any travel outside the United Kingdom had to be notified. John Kinloch of Kilnie, who had just

been loaned £5,000, was charged an extra premium of ten guineas when he went to fight for the Queen in the Spanish Civil War in 1835, and the following year the company went to considerable trouble rearranging the reinsurance on the Duke of Buccleuch so that he could take his steam yacht to the Mediterranean.[110]

The large advances on redeemable annuities in 1832 left Standard Life strapped for cash and the shortfall was made good with an overdraft of £6,000 sanctioned by the Commercial Bank of Scotland, even though Colonel H.V. White (of the Insurance Company) was a director.[111] Undoubtedly Standard Life did not want to be left out of this lucrative market in which the other life offices were already major players. Despite the fact that yields from redeemable annuities were much higher than the interest payments on borrowing from a bank, there was a considerable risk in lending long (however good the security) and borrowing short if for any reason the Commercial Bank was forced to call in its loan to meet its own liquidity problems. In August the company publicly confirmed its new-found commitment to the landed interest by changing political allegiance to the Tories in appointing the Duke of Buccleuch governor and the Marquess of Lothian deputy governor. Both immediately took out big policies.[112]

GOVERNMENT ANNUITIES

In 1833 agents were told that small loans of under £1,000 would no longer be considered and enquiries should be directed elsewhere, presum-

Walter Francis, fifth Duke of Buccleuch (1819–84), a
distinguished figure in Scottish public life, who was governor of
Standard Life from 1832 until 1884.

Reverend Henry Duncan (1774–1846), minister of Ruthwell in Dumfriesshire and founder of the savings bank movement. He purchased an annuity for his wife Mary from Standard Life in 1837.

ably to the banks. This decision was as much a reflection of another new and very profitable source of investment than a consequence of the growing emphasis on larger loans.[113] Since 1808 the government had sold annuities to help fund the National Debt, basing their calculations on the imperfect Northampton Tables. When used to calculate rates for selling policies these produced large profits for the life offices, but when used to calculate annuities, they provided handsome returns for the purchasers and size-able losses for the Treasury. It was possible to buy government annuities on a nominated life without the person concerned ever knowing or benefiting from the transaction. In 1829 the Treasury prepared new tables based on more

representative mortality statistics. It soon became known to actuaries in life offices that the new tables still significantly underestimated the life expectancy of those they insured. All they needed to do was to buy annuities on older lives selected from their policy registers to guarantee a healthy income.[114]

In July 1833, on the advice of Professor Wallace, Standard Life bought £6,000 worth of government annuities on 20 lives of 'persons of advanced years' who held annuities from the company.[115] This was followed by further purchases later in the year valued at £11,000 in the belief that the existing arrangements were likely to be changed. When this did not happen, £9,400 more was invested in 1834.[116] At the same time Standard Life's own annuity business was promoted in the hope of finding more suitable lives. In the summer of 1835 all the annuitants of the Glasgow Society of Teachers,[117] which was winding up, were taken on to the company's books and in 1837 a long list of annuitants was acquired from the Earl of Hopetoun.[118] During March of that year the Reverend Henry Duncan, Minister of Ruthwell in Dumfriesshire and the founder of the savings bank movement, purchased an annuity of £25 payable on his death to his wife Mary.[119] No new government annuities were bought by Standard Life until 1844, when £30,000 was invested on 64 lives.[120]

OVERSEAS TRAVEL

With the rapid development of steam shipping during the 1830s, it was not just the rich who could afford to travel by this new form of transport. Regular transatlantic services began early in the 1840s and soon provided cheap passage for emigrants. The board gave permission in March 1835 to Monsieur Beard to travel home to France in a decked steam vessel without additional payments.[121] In 1836, though, it surcharged Mrs Mary Russell, stewardess on the *Royal Adelaide*, and, in the following year, Robert Stevenson, engineer on the *Queen of Scotland*, and George Thomson, engineer on the *Brilliant*, both of Aberdeen.[122] As it happened, Thomson was killed in an accident on the *Duke of Wellington* while at her moorings.[123] More significant was the calculation of the additional risk in travelling to various countries at a time when little was known about how life expectancy might be affected. Requests to pay visits and for longer-term residence outside the United Kingdom, particularly in North America, increased during the mid-1830s as the pace of emigration quickened. The company was forced to reduce its foreign travel and residence premiums in 1835 to bring them into line with those of other offices.[124] This set the scene for formal discussions with the other Edinburgh life offices in April 1836 to agree such rates along with those on 'damaged' lives – in other words people who suffered from a medical condition.[125]

UNDER NEW MANAGEMENT

In the mid-1830s the directors of Standard Life had once more been reviewing future strategy. James Anderson resigned as secretary in January 1832 less than a year after his appointment. He was replaced by an accountant, Archibald Borthwick, who stayed for two years before deciding to return to his original profession.[126] In July 1834 he was succeeded by William Thomas Thomson, who, at the age of 21, had just completed his training, also as an accountant.[127] His father, William John Thomson, a well-known Edinburgh artist, and his uncle, Anthony Todd Thomson, a leading London medical practitioner and the professor of *materia medica* at University College London, were close friends of

William Thomas Thomson (1813–83), the manager from 1837 to 1874.

Henry Cockburn. They seemingly used their influence with Cockburn and Cockburn's nephew David Davidson, a Leith merchant and a member of a prominent Edinburgh family, to obtain the position for him.

PLANS FOR EXPANSION

William Thomson brought new vigour to the post of secretary, immediately encouraging a reconsideration of the plans for expansion. At the end of September 1834 the board held a special meeting to discuss representation in the larger towns in England and Ireland, in European cities with large Scottish communities such as Danzig and Hamburg, and, remarkably, in Quebec.[128] Although new agents were appointed in some towns in the north of England, little came of this flurry of activity. The suggestion of Quebec, on the other hand, which later was to prove momentous, almost certainly came about as a result of a chance meeting between James Cheyne and John George Irvine, 'a highly respected gentleman from Quebec', who was visiting London. Within a fortnight he had been offered the agency, but the directors had declined to provide an extra seal of approval by forming a local board. The Canadian business did not take off, probably because, over-cautiously, the directors refused to remove the extra premiums for residence there with the exception of Quebec City and Montreal.[129] Nevertheless, the commitment to the Canadian market remained strong.

It was another two years, just after the completion of the first valuation, before a serious attempt was made to extend into the Irish markets with the appointments of agents in Dublin and Cork.[130] Neither choice was without its problems. The Dublin agent, Mark Corin, a lawyer, soon departed after demanding that Standard Life meet all his office expenses,[131] while the Cork agent Edward Robinson, a wine and spirit merchant, proved an unreliable correspondent. Unusually, as a Protestant married to a Catholic, he had his own way of doing business which straddled both communities. In an effort to make him more responsive a local board was appointed composed largely of Protestants.

THE FIRST INVESTIGATION

The first investigation completed in March 1836 was a big project involving not only the calculation of the surplus earned since 1825 but its distribution to shareholders and to all 'with-profits' policy-holders on the tontine principle. The balance sheet revealed that Standard Life had assets of just over £250,000 compared with liabilities of about £240,000, leaving a return of £10,000 – sufficient for a bonus of 1.25 per cent for every year a policy had been in force. With-profits policies totalled almost £230,000 of sums assured and without-profits just over £117,000. The greater part of the assets comprised future premiums, with redeemable annuities contributing roughly £40,000.[132] It was agreed that from now on investigations would take place every five years.[133] Although creditable, the board did not consider the results good enough to justify an assault on the London market, notwithstanding that a new firm calling itself the Standard Life Assurance Reversionary Interest and Annuity Co. was launched there in May 1836. The Lord Chancellor granted Standard Life an injunction against the use of the name but still allowed the new firm to trade as the Standard of England Assurance Co.[134]

BAD LOANS

Other setbacks came thick and fast. There was concern throughout much of the year that the Scottish courts might follow their English counterparts in deciding that the terms of some redeemable annuities placed an unacceptable burden or 'irritancy' on the heir and were therefore grounds for breaking an entail.[135] There was some justification for such criticisms. On the unexpected death of General Duncan Campbell of Lochnell in April 1837, his heir, Captain Donald Campbell of Barbreck, who had borrowed £1,000 from Standard Life against his expectations in 1832, found himself liable to pay an annuity to the company of £275 a year for the rest of his life. Given that he lived for another 20 years this would have resulted in total payment of £5,500. As it turned out, he was unable to meet even the first instalment as his affairs were in total chaos. Eventually Standard Life agreed to advance a further £1,000 'to enable the estate to be brought into order' and appointed William Spens, an accountant, to collect the rents on its behalf.[136]

Potentially more embarrassing was the company's involvement with the luckless and unpleasant Colonel Roderick Macneil of Barra. The Colonel was advanced £6,000 in February 1836 to refinance his kelp-processing alkali works on the island. These had been completed three years earlier in partnership with Harold Littledale of Liverpool, who acted as surety for the loan. Macneil's method of financing this enterprise had been ingenious. He divided the crofts on the estate in half but continued to charge the same rent as for a whole croft. Rather than give in to this extortion five hundred of his crofters left for America and were replaced by newcomers from elsewhere in the Western Isles, whom it was claimed 'the other proprietors were anxious to get rid of'.[137] By the autumn of 1836 Macneil was bankrupt. Reports from the island during the winter were alarming and indicated that most of the population was unemployed and starving. Further emigration seemed the only solution.[138] As by no means the largest creditor, Standard Life had no alternative but to let events take their course. Eventually after several false starts, in a complicated deal involving further funds from the company and an enormous loan from the Commercial Bank of Scotland, Barra was purchased in 1841 by Colonel James Gordon of Cluny, an Aberdeenshire landowner.[139] At the same time as Macneil's failure was reported in 1836, news came that another annuitant, Sir James Boswell of Auchinleck, had defaulted on his payments. Despite the threat of legal action, it took Sir James 18 months to clear his debts.[140] To add insult to

Black houses on the island of Barra in the Outer Hebrides. Embarrassingly, Standard Life loaned money to Macneil of Barra shortly before his bankruptcy in 1836.

injury, H.G. Watson, a director and the auditor of Standard Life, defected in September 1836 to the Glasgow-based Scottish Amicable, which was opening an office in Edinburgh.[141]

The response to these reversals was to raise the insurance ceiling to £3,500 to attract more large lucrative policies[142] while resisting the temptation to move out of redeemable annuities altogether into investment in the fast expanding but no less risky canal, rail and road network.

When it became clear that pleas of 'irritancy' could be avoided if all those involved in the entail agreed the terms, the board lifted the embargo on annuities, which had been imposed after the loan to Macneil of Barra. The first new advance was for £20,000 in October 1836 to Lady Mary Montgomerie. This was secured against her extensive Ayrshire estates in the rich farming land of the south-west. Reinsurance of so large a sum was difficult, involving no fewer than ten life offices.[143] Luckily for Standard Life, Lady Montgomerie and her son and heir, the Earl of Eglinton, who were not noted for their prodigality,[144] honoured their commitment and used at least part of the loan for estate improvements.

With such attractive investment opportunities and security available locally, the directors declared that 'except in cases where the transaction is very desirable they confine their investment to Scotland'.[145] The first loan secured against an English property was made in 1837. This was for £5,000 to improve Etal estate in Northumberland, admittedly owned by a Scottish peer, Viscount Kelburne, the heir of the Earl of Glasgow. This transaction provided useful experience in verifying English titles and in the practice of entails south of the border, both of which differed markedly from Scotland.[146] No further advances on redeemable annuities were made in England until 1842, however, when Robert Ilderton of Springhill in Berwickshire borrowed £3,000 secured against his Northumberland properties. Unfortunately Ilderton was dead within a year when it was rumoured that at the time of his insurance he was 'a person of dissipated habits'. Preferring not to attract adverse publicity, the board (in agreement with the reinsurers North British) decided to honour his policies.[147]

THOMSON TAKES CONTROL

During the autumn of 1837 James Cheyne indicated that he wished to resign as manager to devote time to his many other business interests including banking, the Edinburgh & Glasgow Railway Co., property in Edinburgh and the Kilmaron Castle estate near Cupar, Fife. The directors, reluctant to lose his influential connections which extended to the great London financial houses, offered him the post of actuary with responsibility for overseeing the compilation of tables of rates, the annual balance sheet and the quinquennial valuations. William Thomson, who had fewer outside interests, was promoted to the position of manager and Thomas Robertson was appointed clerk and sub-cashier.[148] Just as he had done when he was first recruited, Thomson at once sought to revive the business, this time by fostering shareholder and customer loyalty. He persuaded the board to follow the example of Scottish Widows by making small loans available to policy-holders on the security of their policies (a privilege later extended to shareholders on the security of their shares). The conditions of redeemable annuities were improved by offering on redemption 'a policy of Assurance to the extent of the whole sum advanced upon the same beneficial footing as to rate of premium as if the policy had been issued at the date when the transaction was originally entered into'.[149] Early in 1838 he aggressively tried to capture the business of Scottish Equitable by advertising the advantage of taking out a policy with Standard Life before the next bonus was declared the following year.[150] Again taking the lead from competitors, policies began to be issued on an ascending scale

George Street, Edinburgh. In the distance on the left is No.3, Standard Life's head office from 1839 to 1996. This was the original building completed in 1839 and designed by the well-known architect David Bryce, who did much work for Standard Life in his later career.

of payments. The scale was designed to meet the needs of those starting out on their careers; an early example was John Hare Duck, an undergraduate at Trinity College Dublin, who took out one of these policies in January 1839.[151]

Thomson was also anxious to expedite the removal of the offices to larger premises. This had been under consideration since the start of 1836. He recruited his friend, the architect David Bryce, to assist in the search for new premises. After two abortive offers, No.3 George Street in the heart of the New Town was bought for £2,400 in December 1837 and Bryce was commissioned to carry out the necessary alterations, which included a pediment with a sculpture of the parable of the ten virgins by John Steele.[152] No sooner had this been installed than Scottish Provident, the occupants of No.1, complained it overhung their property. The ensuing acrimonious dispute was only settled when Standard Life agreed to make minor modifications.[153] The new office was ready for occupation on 8 June 1839.[154]

There were two strands in Thomson's plans for expansion. The first was to develop the existing business and the second was to search for suitable candidates for takeover. George Gray's Perth agency, which had provided so much business, was given special attention with renovations to the offices carried out by Bryce and the printing of copies of the annual report for distribution to local shareholders and policyholders.[155] Likewise, encouragement was given to the Cork agency, which was already securing a steady flow of business. Following a visit to

Ireland to inspect the agencies, the board learned in December 1838 that the Hiberian Assurance Co. was about to sell its life business; but the deal was concluded before Standard Life had time to arrive at a valuation.[156] Bidding for a life office required a scrupulous analysis of the books to make certain there were no poor risks or bad investments.

One of the obstacles to insuring lives in Ireland was the lack of adequate baptismal records, as the agent Edward Robinson explained:

With respect to proof of age generally in this Country, – I fear it never will come up to the clearness we would wish. – The fact is, Baptismal Certificates are next impossible to obtain, owing to the want of regularity of the Churches and Chapels – I suppose you would not find one Parish in ten that could produce the registry books of Baptisms in this Country after a lapse of 20 years. Another difficulty of obtaining proof from family registries in Bibles or Prayer Books arises from the fact of the vast portion of Insurers being Roman Catholics and to think of getting Bibles with them is out of

The frieze in the architrave over the head office building in George Street, showing the parable of the ten virgins carved by (Sir) John Steele. An engraving of the sculpture was used on Standard Life's literature for much of the nineteenth century. When the head office was extended westwards in 1976, a modern version of the sculpture was included on the façade.

Proof of age was essential when accepting a life. Before civil registration was introduced in the mid-1850s, proposers had to submit an extract of the entry in the baptismal register, such as this one for David Nicol in 1827.

The elegant South Mall in Cork where Standard Life had its first office in Ireland.

the question. This last remark however is not applicable to me.[157]

Despite Robinson's claim that the majority of policy-holders were Catholics, many were un-mistakably Protestant. Robinson attributed this to the Protestant composition of the local board: 'I have met with some instances lately where parties would not come to the Office because their proposals were to be brought under the cognisance of Citizens which they would not wish to be acquainted with their affairs.' The credibility of this allegation was lost when he admitted in the same letter that he had been in the habit of paying premiums on some policies himself 'to preserve business to the Office'.[158] Although they were willing to forgive him with a reprimand, the directors in Edinburgh were emphatic that not only was the local board to stay but other boards would be set up elsewhere in his territory (for example at Waterford and Limerick).[159]

CROSSING THE BORDER

Fundamental to the plans for growth was a determined effort to penetrate the English market.

During 1838 deputations of directors visited London and the manufacturing districts of England. Agents were recruited and, over the next two years, offices were opened in Liverpool and Manchester, where local boards were also appointed.[160] On Cheyne's suggestion, it was decided to appoint a London agent but not a board until the results of the second investigation were published. Cheyne proposed that Standard Life should gain information about the metropolitan market by buying stock in such London life offices as Universal, Rock, Crown, Palladium and the General Reversionary and Investment Co.[161] When an attempt in March to subscribe for £7,000 worth of shares in the old-established Westminster Life Office was rebuffed, the plan was abandoned and directors were encouraged to take personal holdings.[162] Instead Peter Ewart, a well-connected Scottish wine and spirit merchant in the City, was recruited in 1840 as London correspondent. His task was to seek out new business and also to report on the life offices, particularly what he could glean about their investment portfolios and any opportunities for acquisitions.[163] These initiatives south of the border were much more successful than before, generating policies ranging from £200 on Thomas Shirt, a gentleman's coachman in Liverpool in 1838,[164] to £5,000 on the notorious Duke of Buckingham, described as 'a well-known life and considered a favourable risk' in 1839,[165] and £5,000 on the hard-hunting George Wyndham, the adopted heir of the last Earl of Egremont of Petworth House, Sussex, in 1840.[166]

When he advised caution in any assault on the London market, Cheyne clearly had in mind a fundamental review of the terms of business at the second investigation. He switched from the out-of-date Northampton mortality tables to the more accurate Carlisle tables drawn up by Joshua Milne, the actuary of Sun Life, in 1815.[167] The valuation work undertaken by William Thomson was on this basis, corroborated where appropriate by the government annuity tables, the experience of the Equitable and the reports of the Registrar General. At the same time, the interest rate was reduced from 4 to 3 per cent. This reflected the current yield on government stock in which many of the London offices had invested heavily. The results, presented to shareholders at an optimistic meeting in March 1841, revealed substantial growth in business, with assets of almost £596,000 and liabilities of £571,000, leaving £25,000 for distribution. This again allowed for a bonus of 1.25 per cent per annum to policy-holders. The funds held by the company now totalled £197,000, of which almost £140,000 had been loaned either on redeemable annuities or on personal bonds and bills. There had been some interesting new recruits amongst the annuitant borrowers including Lord Glenlyon (£7,000), the son of the General and heir of the Duke of Atholl; Thomas Davidson of Muirhouse (£11,000) whose uncle David had sponsored William Thomson for the post of secretary; and the eccentric Sir William Drummond Stewart of Grandtully in Perthshire (£7,000).[168]

Sir William Drummond Stewart (1795–1856) of Grandtully in Perthshire. This painting, by the American artist Charles Martin Hardy, shows him amongst Cree Indians. An intrepid explorer, Sir William applied to Standard Life for permission to make expeditions to remote parts of Russia and North America.

Claiming that Standard Life's earlier policies had 'a greater amount of vested additions than those of any other Scottish Office', Thomson compiled a table illustrating the returns obtained by policy-holders compared to those with Scottish Widows which distributed its bonus on the Equitable principle. Although he admitted that Scottish Widows held back funds to pay a 'prospective bonus' on policies that matured between investigations, his directors saw little merit in such an arrangement which favoured those who died young or had recently taken out policies. Without the addition of a notional 'prospective bonus' to the Scottish Widows' policies, Standard Life's policies gave a better return across the board.[169] There was a certain irony in this outcome since John Mackenzie, Standard Life's auditor, had resigned two years earlier to become manager of Scottish Widows.[170] This was the opening round in a bitter feud with Scottish Widows which continued throughout Thomson's career.

Growing financial strength and better-than-average lives on their register allowed the Standard Life directors to treat the occasional misfortunate death sympathetically. In November 1845 James Whirland, a flesher in Nicolson Street, Edinburgh, who was insured for £200, committed suicide. He had become profoundly depressed when pursued for an obligation on a bond he had signed in his youth to help pay for a church building. When it was reported that his widow and family were destitute and he was clearly insane at the time he took his life, Standard Life honoured the policy.[171]

ENTERING THE OVERSEAS MARKET

The Marquess of Lothian, the deputy governor, died in November 1841, and was replaced by the Earl of Elgin, who had just succeeded to the title and whose life was already insured with the company.[172] This was a significant choice as the Earl was not only committed to life insurance, but was about to embark on a brilliant diplomatic career by becoming Governor of Jamaica the following year.

Requests from policy-holders for permission to travel on business and for pleasure had become much more frequent in the late 1830s. Standard Life remained reluctant to remove additional premiums without agreement from the other Edinburgh life offices but, from 1842, policy-holders were authorised to travel without penalty in decked steamships throughout European waters during peacetime.[173] Voyages beyond this limit still required notification otherwise policies would automatically be void – as James Christie, the owner of the Helmsdale Distillery in Sutherland, had found out to his cost two years earlier. With his business in

James, eighth Earl of Elgin (1811–62), governor-general of Canada and viceroy and governor-general of India. He was deputy governor of Standard Life from 1841 until his death and played an important role in the foundation of Colonial Life.

serious financial difficulties and owing Standard Life £3,000, he panicked and fled to New York, immediately forfeiting his policy and making his situation even more desperate.[174]

Calculating the hazards of residence in ever more remote parts of the world necessarily continued to be problematic, but this did not prevent the company from accepting such business. In May 1838 James Innes was allowed to travel to Canton and the coast of China to work for Jardine Matheson, the great Far Eastern trading house, providing he paid an additional three guineas premium on his £2,000 policy.[175]

He died three years later of fever.[176] The board was much more concerned when, in the autumn of 1841, Sir William Drummond Stewart, with whom they were about to conclude a further annuity loan of £15,000, proposed to travel to the interior of Russia and, more alarmingly, to the largely unexplored far west of the United States.[177] Although they agreed reluctantly, they had good cause to be worried as Sir William had a reputation for living dangerously. On this expedition he was seriously injured and only nursed back to health by an American Indian family in Oregon – a territory the United States was then disputing with Britain. Most requests were less exotic but many like Sir William wished to stay abroad for some time, if not to settle permanently. In June 1837 Archibald Ewart insured his son Peter, a farmer in Van Diemen's Land (Tasmania) for £500;[178] in March 1839 Dr William Wood junior, an employee of the Hudson's Bay Company and the son of Dr William Wood, the company's medical officer and a director, was insured for £600;[179] and in September George Sackville Cotter from Toronto, who was visiting Cork, was insured for £500.[180] Standard Life insured its first resident in continental Europe, Hans Rosenørn of Copenhagen, in 1840.[181]

These travellers and expatriate residents provided Standard Life with an excellent base from which to relaunch their foreign representation. A request in 1843 from David Davidson, William Thomson's sponsor, for permission, as a policyholder, to sail for Montreal to take up the position of manager of the British Bank of North America, prompted a fresh look at the North American market. Annoyed by the surcharge, Davidson protested that the other Scottish life offices had ceased to impose extra premiums for residence in the principal towns of Canada. The board at once wrote to Dr Wood junior to seek his advice. On receiving his favourable report the following year, it was decided to begin trading in earnest in Canada.[182] By this time Thomson had been casting his ruler over other countries where there was a resident British community. During 1843 he sought medical opinion on life in Madeira, where none other than the company's governor was spending the winter. Dr Renton's report was both a masterly understatement and a gross exaggeration:

1st – That there is nothing in the Climate likely to render the life of an English or European subject more precarious than it would be in his own country provided that he take care of himself which a residence in any warm climate renders necessary. The British residents here, and many of them by no means remarkable for their temperance in former times, are a remarkably healthy race of people and have generally died at a good old age.

2nd – With respect to the natives of the Island I should feel disposed to give a much more cautious opinion, in reference to any life assurance transaction – Their mode of life, from the earliest years, is not likely to be

*productive of much firmness of constitu-
tion – While their indolence and guzzling
propensities in after life must tend in a
great degree to shorten the appointed term
of human existence under common sense
rules of management.*[183]

Despite the usefulness of such information in calculating risks, at least to European lives, Thomson's plans to expand overseas were interrupted by fresh opportunities to expand at home.

EXPANSION AT HOME

The whole insurance industry was rocked during 1841 by the exposure of the Independent West Middlesex Fire & Life Insurance Co. which had been established six years before by 'two scoundrels, one of whom had been a journeyman shoemaker and a smuggler, and the other, William Hole, had been a tallow chandler and a bankrupt. These two men contrived to draw from the public no less than £200,000 or £250,000'.[184] The popular author William Thackeray immediately satirised the whole insurance industry in his short novel *The History of Samuel Titmarsh and the Great Hoggarty Diamond*, dubbing the company the West Diddlesex Fire & Life Assurance Company.[185] Such public opprobrium hit home and the directors of several recently formed insurance companies resolved to close their books. William Thomson learned during the summer of 1841 that the City of Glasgow Life Assurance Company was putting its business up for sale. After the failure to buy stock

in the Westminster Life Office, some directors had taken shares in this company when it was established in 1838. This was precisely the kind of opening Standard Life had been looking for, in a part of Scotland where almost no progress had been made despite the best efforts of the board.[186] With no time to lose, Thomson set to work to value the business. An analysis of the 120 policy-holders, insured for a total of £72,000, confirmed a strong base in the west of Scotland manufacturing community but with representation elsewhere in the country. Seventy-six of the lives were classified as good and only ten as very doubtful. The investments were all in small loans, mostly to manufacturers, and well secured.[187] After all his exertions, Thomson was deeply disappointed to be outbid in December by the Aberdeen Assurance Co.[188]

Sensing that similar acquisitions could be made in London, given the lack of confidence in the market, the board bravely decided early in 1842 to open an office at 32 Lombard Street. This had formerly been the City office of the Marylebone Bank which had collapsed the year before.[189] As part of a general overhaul of publicity literature, a separate pamphlet was produced for the London office.[190] In May Peter Ewart was promoted to the new position of resident secretary in London with authority from the autumn to accept business up to £3,000.[191] He almost immediately negotiated a policy and loan of this amount for the Reverend A.C. Tait, who came from Clackmannanshire and had just been appointed to succeed Dr

The Reverend A.C. Tait (1811–82), who borrowed money when he succeeded Thomas Arnold as headmaster of Rugby School in 1842.

Lombard Street, where Standard Life had its first London office in 1842, which it shared with the champagne-importing business of its agent Peter Ewart.

Thomas Arnold as headmaster of Rugby School.[192] He was later to become Archbishop of Canterbury. Ewart also made a great catch by insuring the life of the fabulously wealthy merchant and Lloyd's underwriter John Angerstein.[193] Enhancing the London presence of the company more than matched Thomson's expectation, for by December Ewart was in serious negotiations to acquire the business of an unnamed life office with an annual premium income of £19,000 from some 800 policyholders. When it emerged that the company wished to merge rather than sell out, Standard Life withdrew.[194]

It was to be another 12 months before an approach was made by the York and London Fire & Life Insurance Company, which had sold its fire interests the year before. Anxious not to be disappointed again, the Standard Life directors pressed for a quick deal. At the end of February 1844 the Chairman of the York and London, George Frederick Young, a shipowner and shipbuilder, proposed terms. A settlement was agreed and in April Standard Life received £26,000 in cash in exchange for taking over all York and London's life assurances and deferred annuities. Seven of their directors were appointed to a new Standard Life London board (in effect a committee of the main board), which had powers to accept business without reference to Edinburgh and whose members were full directors of the company. These directors were Lord Ernest Bruce MP, Sir James Eyre MD, Matthew Forster MP, James Gadesden of Ewell Castle in Surrey,

William Haigh, a London merchant, Edward Thomas Whitaker, and George Young himself. So as to sustain such a large presence in London, Standard Life needed a quick means of transferring funds to and from Edinburgh. The terms proposed by the Commercial Bank of Scotland were unacceptably slow and expensive, so the company switched for this purpose to the National Bank of Scotland.[195] The following year Standard Life transferred all its Scottish banking business to the Bank of Scotland, as the Commercial Bank of Scotland was unwilling to raise the ceiling on the overdraft.[196]

The acquisition of the York and London was a fitting prelude to the third investigation which

Lord Ernest Augustus Bruce (1811–91), later third Marquess of Ailesbury and a director of the York and London Life Assurance Society.

A policy on the life of the Reverend Henry P. Hope of the York and London Life Assurance Society which merged with Standard Life in 1844.

showed a massive leap in assets to almost £1.35 million compared with liabilities of just £1.3 million, once more permitting a bonus of 1.25 per cent per annum – now totalling a hefty 60 per cent for a policy taken out in 1825. By now any policy taken out more than ten years before yielded markedly better returns than those with Scottish Widows; for more recent policies, though, Scottish Widows was the better option. Redeemable annuities and loans totalled £240,000, including the largest advances made so far of £41,000 to Colonel John Fullarton Udny of Udny and Dudwick in Aberdeenshire and his son, Major John Augustus Udny; £35,000 to Sir William Maxwell of Monreith in Wigtownshire; and £24,000 to George Duncan Robertson of Struan in Perthshire.[197] The arrangements with the Udnys and Robertson of Struan were part of

Udny Castle in Aberdeenshire, the home of Colonel John Fullarton Udny of Udny, Standard Life's largest borrower in 1845.

pressing debt reconstruction and bore high rates of interest; but in both cases the security was good.[198] Although Lord Kelburne, now the Earl of Glasgow, had redeemed his annuity over his Etal estate in Northumberland, no further advances had been made on English property, much to the annoyance of the English agents and the local boards.[199] The roll call did contain a loan of £2,000 made only that year to Robert Hedges White of Glengariffe Castle, who had massive estates in west Cork – the first Irish loan.[200] The investment portfolio had been enlarged to embrace for the first time heritable securities or mortgages totalling nearly £60,000. Many estates were only partially entailed and any unentailed land could legitimately be mortgaged. The largest borrowers were Duncan Davidson of Muirhouse, Thomas's son (see page 45), with £25,000 on his property near Edinburgh, followed by the Earl of Galloway with £15,500 on his lands in the south-west, no doubt to finance the exorbitantly costly reconstruction of Galloway House, and finally Lord Macdonald of Skye with £5,000. Although there had been a big jump in the number of with-profits policies, partly as a result of the acquisition of the York and London register, without-profits policies had kept pace and still accounted for about a third of all sums assured.[201]

What had not kept pace with the expansion of the business was the number of staff at the new head office in George Street, which was operated by Thomson, along with three clerks, two apprentices and a porter. The staff received six days' holiday a year – New Year's Day, Queen's marriage day, Good Friday, Queen's birthday, Queen's accession day and Christmas – considered 'sufficient to give a fair and reasonable recreation . . ., although they are fewer by four than those kept by the Banks . . .'[202]

COMING OF AGE

By 1845 Standard Life was very different from the enterprise which had originally been conceived by the Insurance Company of Scotland. The attraction of doing business with the landed gentry had drawn the company towards the

Tories and this was reflected in many of their transactions. On the whole, policy-holders came from an older Scotland before the age of steam and factories, from long-established royal burghs and villages, from estates, from craftsmen and women and the professions, particularly the lawyers, who all worked for the gentry. Paradoxically, the Edinburgh-Perth axis, which had laid the foundations of the Whig company, was fundamental to its success under new colours. In these circumstances it is not surprising that Standard Life found it easy to develop a market in Cork and Waterford, which on a smaller scale

St Andrew Square, the commercial heart of Edinburgh in the 1840s.

were remarkably similar to Edinburgh and Perth. The business in England was more diverse but the largest value policies were, as in Scotland, from the aristocracy – such as in 1843 the Duke of Beaufort (£5,000) and Sir Henry Chudleigh Oxenden (£5,000).[203] Only in Ireland did the company with good reason eschew the largely unreliable and untrustworthy members of the so-called Protestant Ascendancy, who owned the majority of the great estates and who were to be the cause of so much trouble later in the century (see page 107). Instead Standard Life preferred business and professional people.

Amongst such customers policies were needed increasingly, either by employers as a deposit to guarantee good behaviour, or by institutions or individuals lending money. This was part of the complex credit structure of the early-nineteenth-century United Kingdom. Despite Lieutenant-Colonel McBean's forthright declaration that it was the duty of the board to act 'with caution and prudence', the directors had been prepared to take big risks by investing in redeemable annuities to achieve good returns. This would not have been possible without a secure and flexible banking system in Edinburgh, which operated within a legal framework where transactions were more transparent than elsewhere in the United Kingdom. For these reasons the directors remained sceptical of English and Irish securities. Where the board was cautious was in accepting lives, in the rates that were charged and in the overall direction of the business. The company may not have grown as quickly as some of its competitors but, as the investigation of 1845 clearly demonstrated, by any statistical measures it was outperforming them both in the quality of its policy register and in returns. With the York and London takeover complete and almost 700 new policies issued during 1845 with sums assured of nearly £450,000, Standard Life had come of age.[204]

CHAPTER TWO

A 'FIRST-CLASS' BUSINESS: 1845–74

'The business may be regarded . . . as one of the great provident institutions of the Country. Large as the sums are they could have been greatly increased had the company extended their investments to personal securities or entertained second-class transactions in connection with which Life Assurances are frequently offered as an inducement but the Directors have not entered on these fields of business and they are therefore entitled to designate their business a first-class one purely and entirely.'

Report of the Investigation Committee, May 1866.[1]

By the mid-1840s there were unmistakable signs of crisis and sudden change in European society. In Britain the population flow from the countryside to the towns was given added impetus by the terrible famine which gripped Ireland and parts of Scotland when successive potato crops failed from 1845 to 1849 and a million people died. More and more people looked for alternative opportunities in other countries, particularly the United States, Canada, Australia and New Zealand. In 1846 the repeal of the Corn Laws, which had offered some measure of protection to British arable farmers, heralded the end of the political influence of the great Tory landowners and marked the beginning of Britain's commitment to free trade. Competing in the world grain market encouraged many landowners to employ new methods, notably the use of artificial fertilisers and later improved machinery, to raise output and productivity. Free trade stimulated the export market for British goods and led to the massive expansion of British shipping. Over the next 30 years manufacturing industry grew swiftly and in many sectors Britain dominated the world markets: the Clyde in shipbuilding, Lancashire in cotton and Dundee in jute. The British colonies initially were dismayed by the abolition of preferential terms for their trades when the Navigation Acts were revoked in 1849. In countries as diverse as Canada and the West Indies there was concern that the future for their economies, based, as they were, largely on natural products, was bleak. Although such fears were exaggerated, the going was tough as farmers, plantation owners and timber merchants adjusted to the unfamiliar trading conditions. In continental Europe a series of revolutions in 1848 brought new constitutions but also an authoritarian political reaction which was to last for at least two decades.

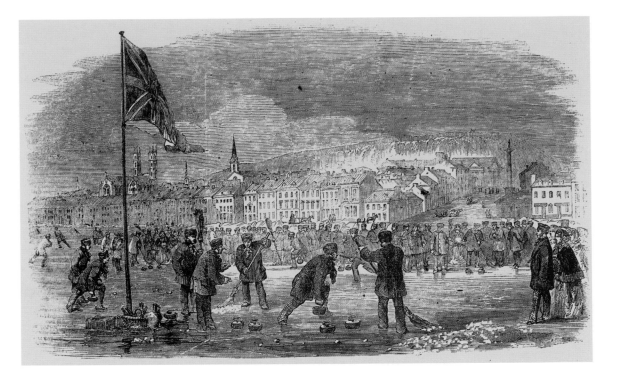

A curling match at Montreal where Standard Life has had its Canadian headquarters since 1845, following an earlier office in Quebec City in 1833. There were strong links between the city's merchant and financial community and Edinburgh.

FORMING COLONIAL LIFE

The directors of Standard Life needed to chart a course for their expanded business through these treacherous waters. With so many unknowns, the temptation was to continue much as before, building on the foundations of what was largely a rural enterprise and trying where possible to break into the urban market. There is much to suggest that this is what they had in mind. As a board they were not enthusiastic about taking overseas risks nor were they keen on the concept of enlarging the portfolio of personal loans.[2] Their manager, William Thomson, took the opposite view. His father had been born in colonial America and he was concerned that not only life cover but finance should be available for those who chose to live and work overseas. From his experience in Standard Life he was conscious that a good number of emigrants came from relatively well-off backgrounds and intended either to buy farms, to set up in business or enter the professions; some already held government appointments. Many of these people needed the security of life assurance to further their careers, and, to this end, Thomson had for some time been collecting mortality statistics and medical reports from other countries. During June 1845 the board discussed the possibility of extending the business to India using tables based on those of other offices doing business there, and the following month considered rates for new agencies in Calcutta and Montreal.[3] On 20 November, however, the board gave its support to a proposal that all overseas business should be handled in future by a new company – the Colonial Standard Life – formed for the purpose and sharing offices and staff with Standard Life.[4]

This initiative was the brainchild of Thomson and two long-serving directors, George Patton, an advocate, and David Smith WS, together with James Kinnear, Smith's partner in his legal practice. Both Smith and Kinnear had extensive connections with Scottish financial institutions and won support for the project from other Edinburgh life offices, which were not as yet represented overseas. Thomson was appointed actuary and Henry Jones Williams secretary of the nascent company, which held its first board meeting on 27 January 1846 under the revised name of the Colonial Life Assurance Company. Half of the directors were drawn from the Standard board; the remainder, like their colleagues, were mostly Edinburgh merchants and lawyers together with an accountant and a banker. The Royal Bank of Scotland – Thomson's own bank – was to act for the company. The chairman was William Stuart Walker of Bowland, a director of the Scottish Equitable Life Assurance Society, and the governor the Earl of Elgin, who had just been appointed Governor General of Canada. Elgin, as deputy governor of Standard Life, championed the new enterprise, helping to recruit influential shareholders in the West Indies and Canada.[5]

Thomson drafted the prospectus for the Colonial Life, which was to have a capital of £500,000 divided into 10,000 shares of £50 each. The partners in Standard Life were entitled to subscribe for one Colonial share for every five shares they held, and the rest of the shares (apart from those issued to the other promoters) were to be made available pro rata, depending on their importance, in the four areas targeted for initial operation – Australia, North America, Ceylon and the West Indies (Australia was later discounted). In keeping with this undertaking, the roll-call of shareholders in Canada included: Peter McGill, president of the Bank of Montreal; David Davidson, manager of the British Bank of North America; and William Walker, president of the Board of Trade of Canada. In the West Indies were: Matthew Davis, Public Treasurer of Granada; William Rennie, manager of the Colonial Bank of Trinidad; and Hon Charles William Warner, Barrister at Law and a leading political figure in Trinidad. In the United States were: Joseph Blunt, Chancellor at Law, Wall Street, New York; and Wats Sherman, banker, New York. There were no shareholders in India or Ceylon but there were several British shareholders with strong links in the East, notably Patrick Alexander Reynolds, Captain of the Honourable East India Company; Frederick Arrow, a shipping agent in London; and George and Thomas Brooking, London merchants.[6] Local boards with the power to accept risks up to the equivalent of £2,000 were to be established in Bombay and Colombo, and in Montreal. Since policies were

MEDICAL OFFICERS

During the nineteenth century the medical profession and the development of medical knowledge went hand in hand with the evolution of actuarial science. Standard Life's first medical officer, Dr William Wood, was a director of the company and helped to draw up the rules for the approval of new risks, which included references as to health, character and habits, an interview by the directors and a medical examination. As its name implied, the company was determined only to accept good or standard lives. On the advice of the medical officer those considered to be sub-standard were either charged an extra premium or rejected.

As business grew Standard Life became more and more dependent on reports from its medical officers in Edinburgh and in other towns and cities where business was transacted. By 1847 in addition to the chief medical officer in Edinburgh and two in London Standard Life employed medical advisers for every local board.

During that year Robert Christison, professor of *materia medica* and therapeutics at the University of Edinburgh, became chief medical officer and undertook to attend the office an hour before each board meeting to go through the list of new applicants to 'single out those proposals, which might require explanation on medical points'.[1] Finding the existing reports did not provide sufficient evidence on which to make a judgement, he and William Thomson issued a new medical referee's report which included questions about the age and cause of death of close relations. Christison demanded that the stethoscope be used to examine the heart and lungs of all applicants and, later, introduced new diagnostic techniques as they became available.[2]

With a background in forensic medicine and as the witness for the Crown at the trial of Burke and Hare in 1829, he was interested in morbidity and began to draw up a quinquennial analysis of Standard Life's underwriting experience.[3] Thomson was no stranger to such medical data as his uncle Anthony Todd Thomson was professor of *materia medica* at University College London and acted as a medical adviser to the Experience Life Assurance Co. Thomson drew on the

Left: Dr William Wood, Standard Life's first medical officer and director, 1838–58.

Centre: Professor Anthony Todd Thomson (1778–1849), who was involved in the founding of University College London. He was the uncle of William Thomson, whom he helped draw up the table of rates for the Experience Life Assurance Company in the 1840s.

Right: Professor Sir Robert Christison (1797–1882), who did much to shape Standard Life's use of medical evidence in assuring lives.

morbidity statistics collected for Standard Life to devise new tables for risks both in the United Kingdom and, more importantly, elsewhere in the world, giving him the confidence to launch Colonial Life in 1845.[4]

Robert Christison became physician to Queen Victoria and was created a baronet. He died in 1882 at the age of 87 and was followed as Standard Life's medical officer after two years by his pupil Professor Thomas (later Sir Thomas) Fraser, one of the most distinguished pharmacologists of his generation.[5] After his death in 1920 he was succeeded by Dr David Halliday Croom, another distinguished Edinburgh physician, who was followed by his son Dr (later Sir) John Halliday Croom.[6] On his retirement in 1978, Dr David Seaton took over and was succeeded by Dr Alec Proudfoot, a poisons expert, in 1989.[7]

With all the advances in medical science since the Second World War, medical advice remains vital to the continued success of Standard Life in the life assurance market.

A Private Friends Report on the life of James Fuller Whiskin, of Highbury, north London, completed by his neighbour, James Gregory, 1861.

to be issued in local currencies, cash balances would have to be held locally, particularly if the rate of exchange was unfavourable. As a result, the local boards had permission to invest funds in government stock, local-authority bonds and heritable securities without reference to the Edinburgh board up to the same limit.[7] The first Colonial Life policy for £1,000 whole-term with-profits was issued on 6 November 1846 on the life of George Smith, a 28-year-old merchant in Ceylon.[8]

In constructing the table of rates for Colonial, Thomson and Dr Henry Marshall, the medical adviser and formerly Deputy Inspector-General of Army Hospitals, divided the risks into four classes based on their own knowledge and the experience of competitors already operating in overseas markets. Class A included Europe; any part of North America north of the 38° latitude but not to the west of the Mississippi River; the Cape Colony in Africa south of the 30° latitude; and Australia and New Zealand south of the same latitude. Class B covered North America to the north of the 35° latitude but not to the west of the Mississippi River, and from November to June to the north of the 30° latitude; Bermuda and South America south of the 20° latitude. Class C was for India, Ceylon, Mauritius and the treaty ports in China, while Class D was reserved for the unhealthy West Indies. Thomson's strategy was to build the business using the contacts he had already made through Standard Life.[9]

The Standard Life board remained cautious. During the course of the 1845 investigation,

Thomson came to the conclusion that the rates Standard Life charged for residence in many countries were excessive, and as a first step he proposed that in future policies should not be 'forfeited in the event of the assured going beyond the limits of Europe until 6 or 12 months after such departure provided always that in the event of death beyond these limits a fine shall be deducted at settlement . . .' This recommendation was not accepted, possibly because the directors were preoccupied with more urgent issues, and in any event any new overseas risks would be offered to Colonial Life.[10]

DIFFICULTIES AT HOME AND IN IRELAND

The life business of the York and London, acquired in 1844, extended to Ireland and the opportunity was taken to strengthen Standard Life's involvement in that market. In June 1844 a local board and new agents were appointed in Dublin.[11] Ten months later, with little new business having been transacted in Dublin at a time when the Cork agency was reporting a flood of proposals, the Standard Life board reviewed the whole of its Irish business.[12] It was decided in the autumn of 1845 to open a head office in Dublin's Sackville Street and to transfer Edward Robinson from Cork to the new post of resident secretary in Ireland.[13] Some months later William White was appointed inspector of Irish agencies.[14] There could have been no less opportune time to expand business in Ireland. By the spring of 1846 there was little food in

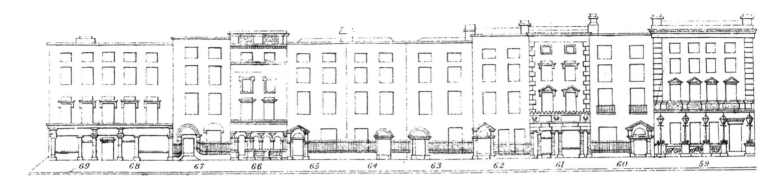

UPPER SACKVILLE STREET

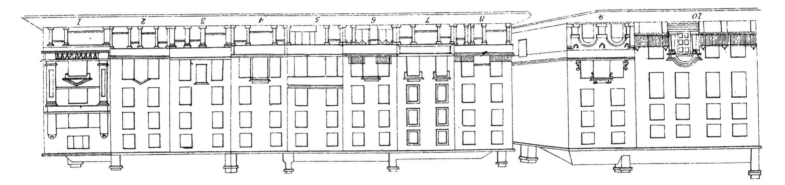

Upper Sackville Street, Dublin, where Standard Life had its Irish office at No.66 from 1845 to 1904. This was one of Dublin's most fashionable streets. The interior of the office was remodelled by David Bryce, the Edinburgh architect, who also added a pediment with the ten virgins.

many parts of the country, particularly in the west, and many tenants were quite unable to pay their rents. For Standard Life matters were made worse by Robinson's deceit and duplicity. Although he had always been something of an unknown quantity (see page 38), the board had been willing to overlook his indiscretions because of his remarkable success in securing good risks on both sides of the religious divide. Matters came to a head in the early months of 1846 when the weekly remittances from Ireland became increasingly irregular. Anthony Trail, a director and an Edinburgh lawyer, was sent to investigate. He discovered that Standard Life's affairs were intertwined with those of Robinson's other interests which included his wine and spirit business and managing his property in Cork. When Robinson promised to make amends and provided reasonable excuses for all the irregularities, he was once again given the benefit of the doubt. It soon emerged that he had no intention of complying with his instructions, however, and in August, following a visit by Thomson himself, he was summarily dismissed for defrauding the company by using funds sent from Edinburgh to redeem policies to support his own failing finances.[15] At once James Stirling, a member of the local board, was appointed managing director in Dublin and Samuel Smylie, one of the clerks, was promoted to be his chief clerk and book-keeper. Simultaneously Benjamin Hall Todd, the chief clerk in London, was dispatched at a moment's notice to Cork to sort out the agency. Thomas Fraser was sent from Edinburgh to take his place.[16]

A BOARDROOM DISPUTE

Unaware of the seriousness of the situation in Ireland, the members of the London board, with one exception all previously York and London directors (see page 51), were outraged at these changes which totally ignored their role as main board directors. When the merger had taken place, they had reluctantly agreed to Peter Ewart being confirmed as resident secretary in London in preference to a member of their own staff. They were determined not to accept a similar reverse without a fight. The chairman, George Frederick Young, protested vehemently that at the very least the London board should be consulted by their fellow directors about such appointments. The Edinburgh directors, who were in the majority, insisted that, as it was their responsibility to manage the enterprise, they alone had control of staff.[17] As the autumn wore on the dispute became increasingly acrimonious. In mid-October the London directors resolved to resign, but the Edinburgh directors still hoped to avoid such an outcome.[18] On 30 November Matthew Forster MP resigned, writing a scathing letter in which he claimed that 'he early perceived that the affairs of the Standard were conducted at Edinburgh on a very questionable and unsatisfactory footing'. His chief concern was that the company was run in practice by Thomson alone with little reference to the board, reminiscent in his mind of the West Middlesex fiasco (see page 49).

Although this was certainly not true, Forster's other criticisms struck home. He was appalled that Standard Life had recently switched its account to the Bank of Scotland so as to obtain a larger overdraft: 'Now the idea of a Life Assurance Coy borrowing money at 4 per cent in these times of its Banker is a thing so startling that if it were to get wind with the public in this country it would be fatal to its credit and the character of those concerned in it.' He attacked the practice of buying back shares on the grounds that it would leave the company under-capitalised and concentrate power in the hands of the directors and managers. George Young forwarded the letter to Thomson with an equally uncompromising covering note. Stung into action, the Edinburgh directors dissolved the board's London committee but left the members as directors of the company.[19] Matters did not rest there and the dispute rumbled on throughout December and into early January 1847.[20] It was to be another year before a new London board was appointed, composed entirely of the members of Colonial Life's London board which had been set up when that company was founded.[21] Like their predecessors, they were also appointed directors of Standard Life.

The crisis occupied much of the time of the Edinburgh directors during 1846; but, as Forster predicted, if so much as a whisper had become public knowledge, Standard Life's reputation would have been seriously damaged. For Thomson it could not have come at a worse time. He was busy launching Colonial Life and conclu-ding the successful negotiations for the acquisition of the Commercial Life Assurance Company which had been founded in Glasgow in 1840. Despite its relatively small size, with total insurances of about £175,000, this was an attractive proposition, providing not only entry to the lucrative west of Scotland market which had for so long evaded Standard Life, but also an established connection in the West Indies. Directly the takeover was agreed, the manager of Commercial Life, William Hunter, was appointed to the new post of resident secretary in Glasgow for both Standard Life and Colonial Life.[22] He was dismissed two years later when Thomson discovered that he had deliberately falsified the certificates on 16 policies reinsured by Commercial Life so as to obtain cover more easily and cheaply. Luckily for Standard Life the sums were small, and only four of the policies were over £3,000.[23] This was a serious setback as Thomson had hoped not only to build Standard Life's presence in the west of Scotland but also to draw on Glasgow's extensive connections with overseas markets to win business for Colonial Life. The only scrap of comfort was a developing connection with the Western Bank of Scotland, which had recently been rescued by a loan from the Bank of England. The Western Bank had a reputation for aggressive lending which, where no alternative was available, was secured against insurance policies taken out by the bank itself.[24] Consequently Donald Smith, the manager of the Western Bank and brother of David Smith, one of the promoters of Colonial Life, was recruited to the Glasgow boards of both companies, which were also strengthened by other appointments.[25] Although Thomson was disappointed at this turn of events, he had been able to capture all Commercial Life's overseas agents and directors for Colonial Life, including an effective local board at St John's, New Brunswick; John Morrison, agent in St Thomas; and Archibald Stevenson, agent in Trinidad.[26] Together with introductions provided by the Earl of Elgin, these established connections provided an excellent base for the entry of Colonial Life into the West Indies and Canada.

THE CANADIAN MARKET

From its conception, the principal target for Colonial Life was clearly Canada, where Standard Life already had a number of policy-holders and powerful friends. Prospects were believed to be good with the completion of the St Lawrence canal system in 1848, providing access for a much longer period of the year to the United States and other foreign markets. Alexander Davidson Parker, the Edinburgh agent of the East of Scotland Assurance Company, was recruited as manager for Canada. Thomson knew his father, John Parker of the Register Office in Edinburgh, well. A policy-holder since 1839, John Parker had close ties with Canada where he had been a partner in the respected merchant house of Parker, Gerrard, Ogilvie & Co. There he had become a good friend of one of his partners, Peter McGill, later described as 'the most popular Scotsman who had lived in Montreal'. McGill

had been a member of the Lower Canadian Provincial Legislative Assembly at the time of the 1837 rebellion and had played a leading role in the union of Upper and Lower Canada three years later. By the time Alexander Davidson Parker left for Canada, McGill was president of the Bank of Montreal and one of the principal politicians in the country. Parker arrived in Montreal late in 1846, armed with introductions to many local shareholders and policy-holders, including McGill and David Davidson, by then manager of the Bank of Montreal, and David

Alexander Davidson Parker, Colonial Life's manager for Canada from 1846 to 1857. He was well connected in both Edinburgh and Montreal.

A Colonial Life Assurance Company policy in the name of Archibald Hamilton Campbell, 1847.

may take two or three years before the company can be well established or at least in a position which will justify any conclusions as to what may be done'. Parker quickly enlisted as local directors McGill, Davidson, Alexander Simpson, cashier of the Bank of Montreal, Christopher Dunkin, advocate and secretary of state of Canada East, and Hew Ramsay of Armour & Ramsay, printers and publishers. He also appointed as solicitor John Rose, later a Minister of Finance, and as medical officer Dr G.W. Campbell. The opening of the Canadian Office on 25 February 1847 in the fashionable Great St James Street was announced in the press with articles in English and French by David Kinnear.[27]

From the outset the intention was to build a network of agencies covering the whole country. William White, Standard Life's inspector of agencies in Ireland, was seconded to Canada in the summer of 1847 to help Parker with this task. To supplement the existing Commercial Life board at St John's, New Brunswick, additional local boards were appointed at Toronto; Quebec; Halifax, Nova Scotia; and St John's, Newfoundland. Parker and White toured the country distributing hundreds of circulars and interviewing prospective agents, local directors and medical officers. In a country where communications were slow, Parker penned a booklet explaining the benefits of life assurance which he forwarded to his agents. By the close of 1847 some 64 policies had been issued in Canada, assuring a sum just short of £50,000. By the time White left for home in March 1849 no fewer

Kinnear, a leading journalist and a relative of James Kinnear, the Edinburgh lawyer. Parker's first impression was that 'even among the better classes of society here Life Assurance is not yet appreciated'. He was warned 'against being too sanguine as to immediate success. They say it

than 26 agents had been appointed.[28] On McGill's advice and with encouragement from Lord Elgin, the board had been enlarged the year before to make room for two French-Canadians, Hon. A.N. Morin (shortly to be elected Speaker of the Legislative Assembly) and Benjamin H. Lemoine, cashier of Le Banque du Peuple in Quebec; but no French-Canadians had been offered agencies. The agent in Quebec was William Bennet and in Trois Rivières James Dickson.[29]

INDIA AND THE FAR EAST

At the same time as the Canadian business was being established, Thomson was attempting an assault on the Indian and Far Eastern markets where many of the agency houses, which now dominated trade, had Scottish connections.* At first he had hoped to recruit a resident manager but, unable to find a suitable candidate, he opted for representation through agency houses. In June 1847 Macvicar Smith & Co. were appointed agents in Calcutta and their associate houses Macvicar Burn & Co. in Bombay and Macvicar & Co. in Shanghai. A month later James and George Smith became agents at Kandy for Ceylon and Binny & Co. for Madras. Progress was painfully slow with no new business and simply the collection of premiums from policy-holders resident in the country. Binny & Co. reported the following year that there was little

chance of competing with the local Madras Equitable and other British companies with local directors, whose only qualification was that they should be policy-holders rather than share-holders as Colonial Life required. In the autumn of 1849 the Macvicar partnerships broke up. The Bombay and Shanghai houses closed and the Calcutta house was renamed Smith, Farie & Co. The new agents in Shanghai and Canton were Rathbones, Worthington & Co., which had links with the powerful Rathbone family in Liverpool. They were immediately successful in securing proposals.[30] Encouraged, the directors of Colonial Life persevered in their efforts to establish a presence in India, dispatching their secretary Henry Jones Williams in December 1851 with instructions to appoint local boards, medical officers and solicitors: 'When the plans in each case are thus far matured a clerk acquainted with the system of book-keeping and having a knowledge of general business shall be sent out from home to work out the plans . . .'[31]

At both Bombay and Calcutta Williams found the business in disarray because of the predatory activities of the Medical and Invalid Life Office, which believed in saturating a market with agents 'who are active in making the institution known'. On the insistence of the agents, he at once advertised in the local press but was concerned that Colonial Life rates were completely uncompetitive. Thomson was not

---

* Agency houses were companies based in India, most often in Calcutta or Bombay, with a diversity of interests and connections in India and the Far East and were usually connected to East India merchant houses in the United Kingdom.

Calcutta photographed from a balloon in the 1860s. Colonial Life appointed their first agents in India here in 1847.

From 1846 Colonial Life regularly published an almanac for their agents containing useful information along with tables of rates.

unsympathetic to reducing the rates and made urgent enquiries at home for more up-to-date mortality statistics including an abortive approach to Medical and Invalid Life itself. Not until new with-profit rates were agreed could Williams with confidence appoint a board and new agents in other towns in the region. He then left for Ceylon to set up a local board in Colombo. He was persuaded to extend his visit to Kandy to consult a Scottish doctor about the mortality experience of Europeans in the sub-continent and the advisability of extending life cover to Burghers (Eurasians) living in the country.

Arriving in Calcutta on 6 December on the way to Madras, he wrote to Thomson expressing thanks for improved rates but emphasising that vigorous efforts needed to be made if Colonial Life was to maintain its toehold in India. He suggested that it should be possible to pay premiums monthly rather than quarterly and that endowment policies, which were not available, would be popular since most policies were used as collateral for borrowing. He re-invigorated the agency in Madras, which was still held by Binny & Co., to such an extent that by August 1853 some 1.23.700 rupees* of new proposals were in hand. Until the Indian Mutiny in 1857 Madras and Colombo produced as much new business as the whole of Canada.[32] Although

Thomson had originally wanted him to continue his tour to China and Australasia, Williams was recalled as it was now planned to extend the North American interests into the United States, which was in the process of negotiating a reciprocal tariff treaty with Canada.

A FORAY INTO THE USA

Following a discussion at the Colonial Life board on 22 June 1853, Thomson left for New York, taking with him Charles Martin, a clerk from the London office, who was to handle the day-to-day affairs of the new agency. Thomson had no difficulty in recruiting a local board but had some trouble in finding a suitable manager. Eventually his brother, George Augustus Thomson, who had been manager and actuary of the Experience Life Assurance Company, was appointed first president and manager. William

FIGURE 2.1
Progress of Colonial Life's business 1847–65

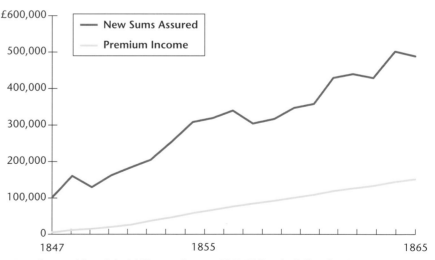

Note: Abstracted from Colonial Life annual reports 1847-65 (Standard Life archives)

---

*   The exchange rate with sterling at the time was about 22 pence (9 new pence). Rupees are counted in lacs (100,000) which is expressed as 1.00.000.

Colonial Life intended to use Atlas holding the world on his shoulders as its motif; but The Atlas Assurance Company protested that it infringed their trademark (top right). William Thomson, the manager, replied it was Hercules despite the fact there was a Hercules fire office. When Colonial Life amalgamated with Standard Life in 1866, Standard Life adopted the emblem (bottom right) on all its overseas literature. All Standard Life's buildings incorporated a statue along with the tympanum of the ten virgins. These can be seen clearly on the Glasgow office (far right) on the corner of Gordon Street and Hope Street, designed by James Thomson in 1890. This building still stands.

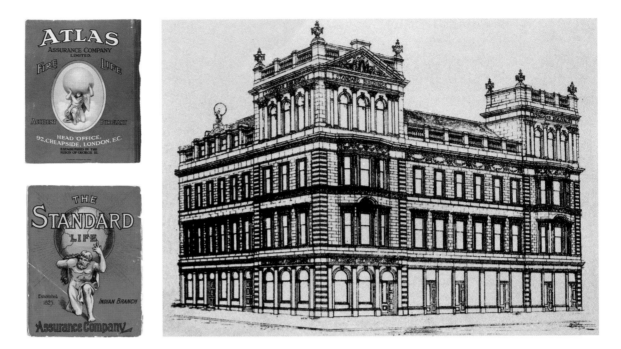

Thomson was persuaded that the $100,000 which the company was required to hold in the country under federal law should be invested in securities rather than mortgages.[33] Thomson returned 'full of wonder at the resources of the Country and the intelligence and activity of the people'.[34] Despite a good start, the American venture did not match his expectations, largely because of the forceful selling techniques of local competitors, and was wound up within four years. Nevertheless, overall, Colonial Life was an outstanding success: new sums assured trebled from just over £100,000 in 1847 to over £300,000 in 1854 and the annual revenue climbed from £5,300 to £58,000 (see Figure 2.1).[35] Reflecting its world-wide ambitions, when new London offices were opened in 1856 in Lombard Street, Colonial Life chose as its motif a statue of Hercules holding the world on his shoulders. Like Standard Life's symbol of the ten virgins, this soon began to be used on promotional literature, reports and policy documents.[36]

FAMINE IN IRELAND

Much as he enjoyed developing Colonial Life, Thomson necessarily had to devote the lion's share of his time to Standard Life. There were several compelling problems which demanded his attention. The most pressing was the continuing deterioration of the situation in Ireland as the famine tightened its grip. With new proposals dwindling to a trickle, it was decided in May 1847 to concentrate representation on Dublin, Belfast and Cork. Local boards were to remain in

Londonderry and Limerick, but all the sub-agencies were to be closed with the exception of Clonmel, Sligo and Waterford.[37] Of greater concern was the possible effect of the epidemics triggered by malnutrition on the lives already assured. A rigorous analysis conducted in the summer by Thomson and one of the directors, Dr William Wood, failed to show any clear connection between the company's mortality experience in Ireland and infection. They reassured the directors that the lives Edward Robinson had accepted were as good as those assured in other parts of the British Isles. The only occupations which appeared to be particularly at risk were doctors and clergymen because the nature of their calling required frequent attendance on the sick and dying. A 5 per cent surcharge was imposed. Although Samuel Smylie, the chief clerk in Dublin, was warned to be especially diligent in the selection of lives, there was no question of Standard Life abandoning the country.[38] Testimony to its commitment was the decision in 1848 to allow Irish policy-holders to borrow on the same terms as those elsewhere in the British Isles and the illumination of the Dublin Office for Queen Victoria's visit in the summer of the following year.[39] By that time there were signs of resurgence in the increasingly prosperous Protestant north. Smylie had established a special relationship there with the Ulster Banking Company which now represented Standard Life in eight local towns.[40]

Following the passing of the Encumbered Estates Act of 1849, which provided a mecha-nism for freeing property from legal restraints preventing either mortgage or sale, the board relaxed the prohibition on lending on Irish property. With large tracts of property coming on to the market through the Encumbered Estates Courts, demand for loans was strong. The first beneficiary was James Stirling, the company's Dublin managing director, who borrowed £14,000 in 1853 to buy an estate to the north of Dublin.[41] He was followed by James O'Reilly, a Dublin property speculator, who obtained a loan of £26,000.[42]

CHANGES IN INVESTMENT POLICY

This decision to lend in Ireland reflected funda-mental changes in the approach to investments elsewhere in the British Isles. By 1845 it had become evident to Standard Life, with over 80

Evictions during the Irish Famine of the late 1840s. These events seriously affected Standard Life's business in the country.

per cent of its funds in redeemable annuities, that changes in legislation meant making further advances was no longer prudent. In fact other insurance companies had long since forsaken them as being too risky and, in any event, the courts were tending to regard the high rates of interest and stringent conditions as inequitable.[43] The need for landed families to borrow money was growing, particularly as more children were surviving into adult life and required settlements to provide for their future.[44] In 1846 the government made available a new source of finance for land drainage secured against mortgages of £2 million in Great Britain and £1 million in Ireland.[45] The law of entail in Scotland, from which nearly all of Standard Life's redeemable annuities had arisen, was reformed by the Rutherford Act of 1848. This did away with the need for costly private Acts of Parliament for disentailing estates. Instead a simplified procedure allowed proprietors, with the Court of Session's consent, to grant bonds over their rents (effectively mortgages) for up to 25 years.[46] Within a year William Thomson had published a book on the working of this new Act.[47]

Standard Life immediately switched to lending almost exclusively on heritable securities (initially only in Scotland) without the need for supporting life assurance, for example lending £22,000 to Lord Kinnaird in 1849, secured by a mortgage over his property at twice the value of the loan.[48] The directors remained unwilling to lend on some properties, however, turning down a modest request for £6,000 from McLeod of McLeod, 'not being desirous of dealing with securities over Highland Properties of such description'.[49] Since drainage loans could only be obtained after work had been carried out, short-term advances had to be negotiated. In the spring of 1850 Standard Life agreed with the Enclosure Commissioners in England, which administered the loans, to make such short-term facilities available south of the border.[50] The following year the Marquess of Londonderry, who had extensive estates in County Durham, paved the way by borrowing £10,000;[51] but few followed, almost certainly because for the next 30 years English agriculture was very profitable and there was no shortage of finance. The final decision to abandon redeemable annuities altogether was not taken until the Usury Acts were repealed in 1854. These removed the prohibition on rates of interest above 5 per cent, but made it necessary to state the rate charged in any bond. If they wished to continue their loans, annuitants were given the option of providing bonds under the Rutherford Act over their property at twice the value of their advances. Both the Earl of Galloway and Sir William Drummond Stewart of Grandtully agreed to these onerous terms.[52]

With 20 years' experience in dealing with landowners, the directors laid down clear procedures before a loan was approved. This involved a careful scrutiny of the title by the company's law agents and the provision of an independently verified rental, along with a statement of all existing outgoings. Such enquiries were thorough and searching, making it almost impossible for would-be borrowers to mislead or deceive. Wherever possible, the board was keen that Standard Life should hold the only mortgages over a family's estates, requiring the repayment of existing loans. This was a condition for advances in 1857 to the Earl of Aberdeen, who had recently been prime minister, and to his son, Lord Haddo.[53] Most borrowers wanted additional funds to improve their patrimony, such as the Duke of Atholl, who was loaned £10,000 for drainage in 1855.[54] On the whole, Standard Life avoided making large advances, turning down out-of-hand most requests for more than £100,000 – for example refusing Sir Robert Clifton of Clifton in Nottinghamshire who wanted £150,000 in 1869.[55] There were special cases, such as the Duke of Richmond, who borrowed £130,000 in 1868,[56] and the fabulously rich industrialist, Henry Houldsworth of Coltness in Ayrshire, whose total borrowings by 1867 were almost £166,000.[57] In many cases these large transactions underpinned complicated family settlements; for example, the wealthy Duke of Hamilton, whose annual rental income in Scotland alone was £112,000, borrowed £160,000 in 1869 to provide under the terms of his father's will for his brother, Lord Charles Hamilton, and his sister, Lady Mary, who was about to be married to Prince Albert of Monaco.[58]

Even such a seemingly good risk had to be approached with caution, however, as the Duke was well known for cutting 'a great figure in fashionable, betting and racing circles'.[59] In one instance, the borrower, the Earl of Strathmore, another racing peer, was in serious financial difficulties. By 1851 he had borrowed £70,000 from the Royal Exchange Assurance and £10,000 from the Royal Bank of Scotland against a rental income of almost £15,000. Given the size of his income and the security of his estate, Standard Life was willing to make further advances.[60] By 1857 he had been loaned £70,000. Alarmed by reports that he was considering leaving the country, the directors refused the importunate Earl any more assistance, only to be told that his horses were 'advertised for sale' and that 'it was with the same view of economy and to escape from temptation that he proposed to go abroad'.[61] He repaid his loan in 1860 when he persuaded Royal Exchange to lift his ceiling to £130,000 secured in part against his Standard Life policies, which totalled £70,000.[62] When he died in 1865 his English creditors tried to claim the proceeds but were blocked in Chancery on the grounds that since Standard Life was a Scottish company, these should be used to defray his Scottish debts. The case was settled out of court with agreement that the proceeds should be divided equally between the two jurisdictions.[63]

Smaller loans could also run into difficulties; but the exposure was less, and following the Rutherford Act the sale of an entailed property was straightforward. In 1862 Duncan Davidson was forced to put his estate at Tulloch on the shores of Loch Broom on the market to clear his debts, including a loan of £12,500 from Standard Life.[64] More public was the failure of the Earl of Buchan in 1865. The twelfth Earl died in 1857

Henry Houldsworth of Coltness (1797–1868), ironmaster, who was Standard Life's largest borrower in the late 1860s.

Thomas George, twelfth Earl of Strathmore (1822–65), who heavily indebted his Glamis estates to finance his passion for racing.

and the entailed estates at Dryburgh passed to his granddaughter for her lifetime while the other estates were inherited by his second son, the new Earl. These properties at Almondell and Strathbrock to the west of Edinburgh had been hopelessly neglected and were in urgent need of improvement. Most of the land had to be sold to meet his father's debts, however, and the new Earl was in danger of losing even his home. Rather than see 'Lord Buchan's house sold over his head', his trustees in 1862 repurchased the Almondell estate with loans from the City of Glasgow Bank and Standard Life on the understanding that if the rich deposits of shale oil, which the Earl owned in the area, did not produce sufficient income to pay off the debt quickly, the estate would be put back on the market.[65] Although the Earl was sequestrated in 1865, Standard Life was willing to stand by him after his discharge from bankruptcy, making a further advance of £4,500 in 1868 to enable him to retain the estate.[66] More bizarre was the disappearance during that year of the Earl of Orkney, who had borrowed £10,000, making it impossible for his Edinburgh lawyers Tods Murray and Jamieson either to meet the interest or sell his Groundwater estate in Orkney. Standard Life immediately took possession of the property and advertised it for sale.[67]

INVESTING IN LAND, PROPERTY AND TRANSPORT

Such problems with advances were exceptional. The majority of borrowers on heritable securities were provident, meeting their interest payments and repaying the capital. Of greater concern to Thomson in the early 1850s when interest rates were low was whether this very secure form of investment would provide sufficient income to sustain future returns on policies and bonus payments. In 1852 he proposed that Standard Life should buy land which would yield rents and might also produce a capital gain, particularly if the property could be developed for housing.[68] Accordingly, the estate of Lundin and Aithernie near Leven in Fife was purchased from Admiral Wemyss for £90,000. Within reach of Edinburgh and on the shores of the Forth, there was potential for holiday development when the East Fife Railway was completed in 1856. Feus were offered for sale in 1857 but none was taken, even after Standard Life had invested £1,150 in a station and station keeper's house. Nevertheless,

Lundin House in Fife which was acquired with its estate by Standard Life in 1852.

Leven golf course in the early twentieth century with Standard Life's housing development in the distance beneath Largo Law.

The trophy presented to Standard Life Golf Club by Spencer C. Thomson in 1891. Winners have included four chief executives – A.E. King, A.R. Reid, D.W.A. Donald and A.S. Bell.

SPORT AND STANDARD LIFE

The Standard Life golf club challenge medal and the Standard Life golf club medal, 1889.

Almost since the company's foundation, sport has played an important part in the social fabric of Standard Life. In the early days the most popular recreation was rifle-shooting, reflecting the pre-occupation of many middle-class men at the time with the volunteer movement. This was gradually replaced by golf and, later, football. When the Lundin estate was sold in 1870, Standard Life presented the Innerleven Golf Club with the amateur champion gold medal (opposite, far left) to be competed for annually in open competition on a course which now includes part of the Lundin estate. This was almost certainly the first open amateur stroke play championship. Standard Life's own golf club was established in 1889 and made its first outing to Musselburgh and its second to Leven. Trophies were soon presented by senior members of the company. These include the McCulloch Cup donated by John McCulloch in 1889; the Ramsay Medal presented by William M. Ramsay, the Canadian manager; and the Calcutta Cup, a gift from Thomas Lang, the representative in India.

It soon became the practice for the head office staff to organise an outing on the Whit-Monday bank holiday. As the company grew in size, golf and football competitions were arranged between offices on that day. News of these and other fixtures were featured regularly in the *Standard Newsletter* which began publication in 1922. Albert King, joint actuary, was one of best sportsmen of this period, a brilliant billiards player and in later life a talented if unorthodox golfer.[1]

Andrew Davidson, who succeeded him as manager, inaugurated an annual football fixture between the London and Edinburgh offices, and presented a cup (below) for the match on his retirement as manager. He regularly attended the competition, filling his cup with champagne for 'victors and vanquished alike'. Brem Dow later presented a challenge cup for an annual golf tournament between the company and Scottish Widows, and Scott Bell a trophy for a competition between staff and pensioners. Sport remains an important part of the social fabric of Standard Life with staff participating in a bewildering variety of activities, sometimes in support of charity.

the board was sufficiently confident to buy the adjoining Balcormo estate for £13,650. So as to stimulate custom, the company built two villas on its own account in 1858 with equal lack of success. When a further four cottages constructed in 1862 still failed to attract holidaymakers, building work ceased.[69] The estate was put on the market in 1870 and sold two years later for £151,250.[70] More successful was Colonial Life's purchase in November 1852 for £15,000 of the Trinity estate immediately to the north-west of Edinburgh. Colonial began building villas and feuing plots the following spring.[71]

Although Standard Life was willing to be involved in building on its own land, the directors remained cautious in making advances for property development, largely because house prices fluctuated markedly, and as a result the security was far less than on conventional mortgages. In 1856 the Kelvinside Estate Company, with property along the line of Great Western Road in Glasgow, requested a loan of £50,000 to help finance the completion of several magnificent new terraces.[72] Despite agreeing to this transaction, the directors steadfastly refused to make any more funds available to the company even though properties in Kelvinside became very fashionable. This reluctance stemmed in part from the risk of large-scale urban property development, which necessarily required more than one source of finance, making it difficult for Standard Life to be guaranteed preference for its loans. It was not until 1869, when demand for loans over agricultural estates had almost dried up, that a further £109,000 was made available to the Kelvinside Estate Company.[73] At the same time an advance of £80,000 was made to Bruno Austin for the development of the Castle Hill estate in Ealing to the west of London as a residential suburb. Austin, who had already borrowed £230,000 from the Union Assurance Society, agreed that all his plans would be submitted to Standard Life for their approval.[74]

Apart from property development, the other investment opportunities open to Standard Life remained making advances to railway and other companies secured over assets. The directors had been reluctant to consider such proposals in

Looking eastwards along Great Western Road in Glasgow with terraces built by the Kelvinside Estate Company and financed by Standard Life. It took almost a century for the Kelvinside Estate Company to repay the £50,000 it borrowed in 1856.

Villa development on the Castle Hill Estate in Ealing to the east of London, proposed by Henry De Bruno Austin and partly funded by Standard Life, 1869.

view of the risk because, like financing building, they were complex. In 1846, however, a loan of £25,000 at 5 per cent was made to the recently incorporated Aberdeen Railway Company, which was building a line to connect the north-east with Edinburgh.[75] This was followed in 1847 by the purchase of debentures in two railway companies, the Glasgow, Paisley & Greenock, and the Edinburgh & Glasgow, regardless of concerns that holding such stakes might not be within the permissive terms of the company's Act of Parliament.[76] Two years later £15,000 worth of debentures were taken in the newly formed Edinburgh, Perth & Dundee Railway Co., which almost immediately plunged into financial difficulties.[77] In November 1849,

£30,000 (later raised to £47,000) was made available innovatively to the Northumberland and Durham District Bank to assist in the financing of the proposed amalgamation of the Hartlepool West Harbour & Dock Company and the Stockton & Hartlepool Railway.[78] The merger did not progress smoothly and the companies were unable to discharge their bank loans as quickly as anticipated. Matters dragged on until 1857 when the Northumberland and Durham District Bank collapsed, still owing Standard Life £15,000.[79] These two experiences confirmed the board's distrust of railway investments and, with the sole exception of the East Fife Railway Company, which borrowed £8,500 in 1858,[80] all requests for loans were turned down and

In 1849 Standard Life unusually provided venture capital to the Northumberland and Durham District Bank to help finance the merger of the Hartlepool West Harbour (above) and the Stockton & Hartlepool Railway.

advances against the security of railway stock were regarded equally unfavourably.[81]

LENDING TO LOCAL AUTHORITIES

Disappointed, Standard Life explored the possibility of lending to local authorities to finance a variety of projects, most of which reflected the new approaches to the provision of social welfare and improvements in amenities, particularly public water supplies and the clearance of bad housing. Such opportunities had existed since the introduction of the New Poor Law in 1834; but no requests for funds had been received or solicited. The attraction of such loans was that they were essentially annuities, repaid over a long period of time (usually 25 years) at relatively high rates of interest. In February 1851, in response to an approach from Middlesex County Council, the board indicated it was willing to provide a loan for a new lunatic asylum, but refused to participate in a competitive tender.[82] Nothing came of this proposal; but the following month £10,000 was advanced to Liverpool Corporation to build a new prison which was to be mortgaged to Standard Life.[83] There were no further requests until March 1854 when it was agreed to buy out the existing bondholders in the Edinburgh Water Company and make additional funds available to a total of £133,000 secured over works at Bonaly and Loganlea.[84] The directors refused to countenance any local-authority loans against rates, turning down both Glasgow Corporation, which wanted £30,000 to lay out a park, in 1857 and Leeds Corporation in 1867, as they did 'not consider such securities clear and satisfactory'.[85] Since they also wanted their loans to have preference over all other debts, they were more willing to entertain proposals from smaller burghs and rural areas. The loan of £4,000 to Peebles Parochial Board in 1859 to build a poorhouse set a pattern,[86] which others quickly followed. This included financing in 1860 the North Leith and Lochgilphead poorhouses,[87] in 1864 a sewerage scheme for St Andrews and police houses and stations in Ross-shire,[88] in 1869 the Darlington Union workhouse,[89] and in 1870 the London Hospital for Women.[90]

Although Standard Life continued to make advances to shareholders and policy-holders against these securities, such business was not encouraged and was never for more than half the value of the shares or policy held. As Thomson intended, Colonial Life from the outset actively offered such facilities up to the total value of the policies. This proved so attractive to civil servants and army officers of all ranks taking up positions abroad that the practice was soon extended to include the United Kingdom. In 1863 Colonial Life loaned £200 to Patrick

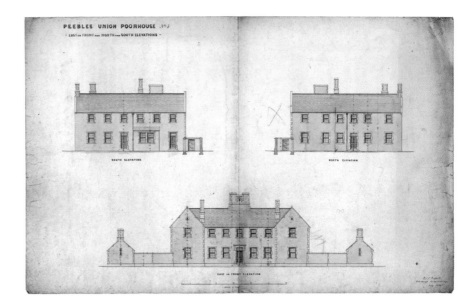

Peebles Union Poorhouse, built with funds provided by Standard Life in 1859.

The London Hospital for Women (1870), with which Standard Life had a long association as a source of capital for new buildings.

Anthony, seventh Earl of Shaftesbury (1801–85), the social reformer, whom Colonial Life helped rescue from financial difficulty in 1864.

foreign local authorities and railways, recognising as impractical insistence on preferential terms for repayment but being no less thorough in investigating the adequacy of any security.

THE STRUGGLE FOR URBAN MARKETS

The decision by Standard Life to lend on the security of bonds without supporting policies had immediate and unforeseen ramifications for securing new risks. No longer could Standard Life rely on a regular stream of large premiums from its borrowers and expect to make handsome returns on reinsurance. As a result, more small policy-holders would have to be recruited from the ranks of the expanding urban middle classes. This was the thinking which lay behind the shift in emphasis in Ireland away from the famine-stricken south towards the more industrialised Ulster. Although a similar strategy was pursued in the rest of Britain, it was not straightforward to implement. Scotland's industrial heartland in the west had so far eluded Standard Life, and the setback following the acquisition of Commercial Life had done nothing to improve this. There were some encouraging signs that the link with the Western Bank of Scotland would help gain industrial clients, however. In 1849 Standard Life insured all the partners in the Glasgow engineering firm of Lyon, Lawson & Co., a condition of their new contract of co-partnery,[94] and the following year insured James Caird, the Greenock shipbuilder, when he became a partner in the family business.[95] Policies were also accepted for several managers

MacNiven, a Dublin pawnbroker, and £1,500 to A.E. Kennedy, who was preparing to take up his appointment as Governor General of Vancouver Island.[91] A year later Colonial Life came to the rescue of the Earl of Shaftesbury, the philanthropist and great social reformer. They participated in a consortium led by the Scottish peer, Lord Kinnaird, a Standard Life client, to allow the Earl to meet his household expenses.[92] Such an overt political advance would have been unthinkable at Standard Life. The only time the company came near to such a transaction was in 1870 when a loan of £7,000 was made to Edward Marjoribanks, who had been more or less disinherited by his father, to enable him to continue as a senior partner in Coutts, the London merchant bankers.[93] Colonial Life was also rather more adventurous in lending to in local textiles mills, such as James Jack of the Milton Mills in the Campsies.[96] This progress was not sustained, except for policies issued to the Western Bank as collateral for its reckless lending. This hastened its collapse with debts of nearly £3 million in 1857.[97] Despite its close affinity with the bank, this disaster did not warrant so much as a mention in the Standard Life minutes, but the consequence was that nothing more was done to foster business in the west for another decade. On the whole, such policies as were written continued the established trend of policy-holders in Scotland being clergymen, lawyers, shopkeepers and craftsmen. Instead, attention was directed towards the industrial north of England where the company had also failed to make much headway in the past.

Thomson had hopes for Liverpool, which had close links with Scotland and where a strong local board was in place. On his return from Canada in 1849, William White was appointed manager and inspector of agencies in England for Standard and Colonial Life based in Liverpool – one of the first inspectors appointed by any British insurance company.[98] He quickly began to expand business in Liverpool and, with Peter Ewart's advice, to root out ineffective agents.[99] He fell foul of Thomson in 1851, however, when he waited ten days before notifying the theft of the office cash box by Edward Robinson's son.[100] White, who had witnessed the effects of the famine in Ireland at first hand, clearly believed Robinson had been badly treated and had become friendly with him, eventually helping him to start a new life in New Zealand.[101] This was too much for Thomson, who recommended White's dismissal. The board disagreed and instead proposed that he should be offered a post at head office. White was delighted to be able to reply that he had been appointed the first inspector of agencies for Scottish Equitable based in their London office.[102] Standard Life could not afford to lose men of such experience; a further

The port of Liverpool in the 1850s. Liverpool was one of the most prosperous cities in the United Kingdom at the time. It had strong Scottish connections, which Standard Life hoped to use in order to gain business.

blow came within two years when Benjamin Hall Todd (the company's first apprentice), who on his return from Cork had become the secretary of the company, was appointed secretary (in effect, manager) of the Crown Life Assurance Company in London.[103]

It was difficult to find good agents in other northern towns. In Manchester between 1850 and 1855 there were no fewer than four changes of agent; while at Leeds the agent J.B. Preston became bankrupt in 1858. The continuity of an agency was not a guarantee of progress, however. At Bradford, where the agent was the brother-in-law of the celebrated woollen manufacturer Sir Titus Salt, progress was painfully slow.[104] There were several obstacles, some of which were outside Standard Life's control. With hindsight it is now known that the middle class in the towns of northern England grew much more slowly than in Scottish cities. Consequently, the directors may have been misled about the potential in English towns by their long familiarity with attracting new lives in Edinburgh and Aberdeen, where demand was inevitably stronger. In addition Standard Life, unlike many of its competitors, was solely a life company and had no association with a fire office. Thomson was well aware that integrated fire and life offices enjoyed an advantage in manufacturing towns, as the first point of contact with insurance for many industrialists was to arrange fire cover for their wares and premises. Since the directors would not contemplate entering the fire market, all that could

be done was to relax the rules which prevented agents from representing other insurance companies, providing they were not in competition with Standard Life.[105] In 1854 the legal practice of Sheil & Small, the company's Dundee agents, was allowed to act for the fire department of the Lancashire Insurance Company.[106] Three years later Thomson approached the Law Fire Insurance Society about the possibility of joint agencies in London and other large towns, but nothing came of the discussions.[107]

REORGANISATION IN ENGLAND

After White's departure emphasis switched to London where, after a delay of two years, William Bentham succeeded him as inspector and resumed the task of overhauling the English agencies. Between 1850 and 1855 a third of the 152 existing agents were dismissed and 177 new agents recruited in every part of the country; of these, 53 were rejected when they failed to produce sufficient new lives. Similar efforts were made by the new company secretary, George Todd, to reinvigorate Scottish agencies, particularly in the north-east where there was still 'a great amount of ignorance and indifference to the advantages of Life Assurance, . . . which tho' no doubt discouraging to the Agents for a time might by more vigorous personal operations on their part be gradually overcome'.[108]

Bentham had not been in his post in London for long when Peter Ewart died unexpectedly in June 1854 of what was described as 'softening of the brain' attributed in part to 'his constant labour, worry and anxiety . . .' He left a young family and the London directors were displeased at Thomson's steadfast refusal to allow his widow a pension, as he believed it would set a precedent for others who died in service or were forced to resign on the grounds of ill-health.[109] They were, however, delighted with their new resident secretary, Henry Jones Williams, previously the first secretary of Colonial Life. This was a masterful appointment as the London boards of the two companies were identically composed and Williams could use his experience to further both businesses. He lost no time in making his presence felt. In January 1855 he proposed a radical reorganisation of the method of doing business south of the border. He advocated the publication in leading newspapers of 'special notices' briefly introducing the company and listing the names of the directors. These would also be mailed directly to about 1,500 selected individuals who at a later date would also receive copies of the annual report. He was also convinced that commissions had to be increased if Standard Life was to have any chance of recruiting the best agents, particularly among the legal profession. He and Bentham were opposed to the current practice of advertising locally, believing that the large-circulation national newspapers such as the *Illustrated London News* and *The Times* had a much greater impact. They also proposed the award of annual prizes for agents who secured the most business. With the exception of prizes, which offended their Presbyterian conscience, the Edinburgh

board endorsed these reforms enthusiastically.[110]

From 1856 England consistently produced more new business than Scotland (see Figure 2.2 on page 86), though the character of assured lives in both countries was remarkably similar, with ranks of shopkeepers, artisans, public officials, teachers, officers in the armed forces, clergymen, doctors, lawyers, clerks and farmers, predominantly from rural towns and villages. The majority were insured for relatively small sums of between £100 and £500 and most insured themselves in the middle years of their lives, between the ages of 30 and 45. Undoubtedly a large number of these policies were taken out to provide collateral for loans or as guarantees as part of the condition of employment in positions of trust. With the exception of policies

THE STANDARD LIFE ASSURANCE COMPANY. Established 1825.
LONDON .. .. .. 82, KING WILLIAM-STREET.
EDINBURGH (Head Office) 3, GEORGE-STREET.
DUBLIN .. .. .. 66, UPPER SACKVILLE-STREET.
GOVERNOR.
His Grace the Duke of BUCCLEUCH and QUEENSBERRY.
DEPUTY-GOVERNOR.
The Right Hon. the Earl of ELGIN and KINCARDINE.
LONDON.
CHAIRMAN OF THE BOARD.
The Right Hon. the Earl of ABERDEEN.
ORDINARY DIRECTORS.
F. Le Breton, Esq., 3, Crosby-sq. | Alexander Gillespie, Esq.,
John Lindsay, Esq., 26, Laurence | Billiter-court.
Pountney-lane. | Alexander Macgregor, Esq.,
Thomas H. Brooking, Esq., 14, | Arlington-street.
New Broad-street. | John Scott, Esq., 4, Hyde-Park-
John Griffith Frith, Esq., Austin- | street.
friars. |
THE BONUS YEAR.
All persons who now effect Assurances will participate in the Division of Profits to be made this year, and will secure an ADDITIONAL YEAR'S CLAIM for Bonus, at all future Divisions, above later Entrants.
THE FUND DIVISIBLE will be derived from the Profits which have accumulated since 1850.
THE COMPANY HAVE DIVIDED PROFITS on four occasions— in 1835, 1840, 1845, and 1850.
A Policy for £1000 opened in 1825 has been increased to £1873.
A Policy for £1000 opened in 1826 has been increased to £1825.
Subsequent Policies have also received large additions according to their standing.
UNCHALLENGEABLE CERTIFICATES.
The STANDARD COMPANY introduced, in 1851, most important changes in the "Conditions of Policies," conferring valuable privileges on Assurers. WILL. THOS. THOMSON, Manager.
H. JONES WILLIAMS, Resident Secretary.
London, 82, King William-street.

An advertisement for Standard Life in the *Illustrated London News*, 24 February 1855. At the time the company restricted its advertising to the quality national press.

for £1,000, which were required as guarantees in certain classes of employment, Standard Life attracted hardly any large risks. Such large policies as were in force had mostly been issued as part of the now discontinued redeemable annuity transactions. Even in the £1,000 category, demand was poor. This profile of policies reflected the company's base in rural Britain where, although incomes and wealth were lower (the landowners apart), they were more evenly distributed.

MERGERS AND ACQUISITIONS

A large number of small policies distributed widely throughout the country was inevitably expensive to administer. It was, nevertheless, the natural outcome of the innovative national advertising strategy. This was quickly imitated by other long-established life companies, which had encountered similar difficulties in making progress in the industrial towns. During the late 1840s and throughout the 1850s many new life offices were established, taking advantage of the joint-stock legislation of 1844;* of these, a good number were inadequately capitalised and lacked a sound actuarial base.[111] Bentham commented on their impact in 1856: 'The excessive competition in this Country [England] has led to enormous commission being offered for new business, in some instances as much as 33 per cent of first premiums with 5 or 7½ [per cent] on renewals, and there is hardly a Town or I may say Village where agents do not jostle over one another.' He believed that the only reason for the survival of 'Companies proven to be of the most worthless description' was the willingness of 'gentlemen of high position' to act for them.[112] Many offices gave up the struggle and were taken over, while a few collapsed. The most acquisitive were the Albert (founded in 1839), the European (1853) and the City of London (1845).[113]

At first Standard Life seemed to be willing to follow the fashion. In May 1849 the life policies and surpluses of the small Edinburgh Friendly Insurance Society, which had been set up in 1720 and had recently sold its fire business to the Sun, were acquired for £7,000.[114] This was followed in December by the acquisition for £6,200 of the Experience Life Assurance Company, so called because its mortality table was based on the experience of 17 life offices.[115] Founded in Edinburgh in 1842 with assistance from Thomson and other members of his family, it had grown slowly with total assurances of a little under £250,000 and assets of just over £25,000.[116] Thomson initially hoped that a merger could be arranged with Colonial Life, but the Experience directors were 'afraid their Policyholders would not be content to have their risks guaranteed by so young an office'.[117] In the

---

* The 1844 Joint Stock Companies Act allowed for the formation of companies with unlimited liability by 5 or more members (shareholders with freely transferable shares), which were to be registered with the newly formed Register of Joint Stock Companies. Limited liability was introduced in the 1855 Companies Act.

event, Colonial took over Experience's offices at 22 St Andrew Square. It is not clear why Thomson was keen to promote a merger of a domestic insurance company with Colonial Life, which, given the joint directors, could only have been done with the full knowledge of Standard Life. The most likely explanation is that it would have provided a vehicle for the provision in the United Kingdom of 'untrammelled assurance' whereby policy-holders were free to travel anywhere in the world without notification. Indeed the contract of co-partnery, which regulated the business, explicitly allowed Colonial Life to insure 'lives of persons residing in Great Britain or Ireland, but in connection with whose lives any special contract shall be entered into with reference to residence abroad'.

Following the 1850 investigation Thomson succeeded in persuading the Standard Life board to introduce unchallengeable 'select policies' with such privileges available to anyone who had held a policy for five years or more.[118] Because he failed to seek clearance for this innovation from the Association of Scottish Life Offices (which operated as a cartel for overseas risks), he was expelled and not readmitted until 1867.[119] Thomson's ambitions for Colonial Life, however, seem to have extended beyond such marketing devices to the creation of an enterprise of equal scale to Standard Life itself. He was involved in 1852 in abortive negotiations with the promoters of the Marine Life and Casualty Mutual Assurance Society for a joint venture to provide cover for the London shipping indus-

try.[120] Instead they chose to establish their own company – the Marine and General Mutual Life Assurance Society.[121] During the same year, Colonial Life acquired the business of the small Dundee-based East of Scotland Life Assurance Company, established in 1842, which had a little less than £100,000 of assurances in force. The manager, E. Erskine Scott, and the board were retained to represent Colonial Life in Dundee.[122] Thomson still hankered after a much bolder merger or acquisition. In 1860 he attempted unsuccessfully to bring about a merger with the London-based Universal Life Assurance Society, which was about the same size as Colonial and had branches in Madras, Calcutta and Bombay. Thomson believed that together the two companies would 'command not only the largest Colonial business but also a most extensive business at home'.[123]

From 1850 until 1857 Standard Life stood aloof from any takeover proposals, preferring, like most of their competitors north of the border, to let their business grow organically. Nevertheless, in 1857, an approach was received through Henry Jones Williams to acquire the medium-sized Minerva Life Assurance Company,[124] which had been established in London in 1836 and which in recent years had found it hard to cope with the competition. With some 8,000 shares valued at £5 each, this was a much larger proposition than any of the previous acquisitions.[125] Standard Life was interested but lacked the legal powers to take over an existing enterprise. This was corrected in a new Act of

A prospectus for the Albert Insurance Company, which failed spectacularly in 1869. Standard Life acquired all its interests in India.

A policy of the Experience Life Assurance Company taken out by William Thomas Thomson in 1844 on the life of his brother George Augustus Thomson, the Experience's first manager and later Standard Life's representative in New York.

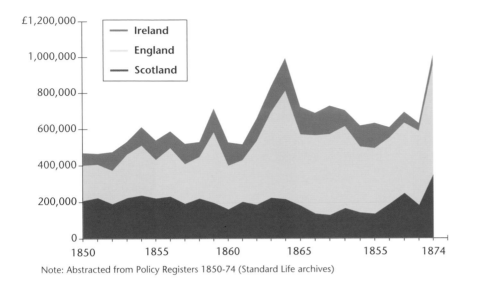

£1,200,000

1,000,000

800,000

600,000

400,000

200,000

0

— Ireland
— England
— Scotland

1850   1855   1860   1865   1855   1874

Note: Abstracted from Policy Registers 1850-74 (Standard Life archives)

FIGURE 2.2
New sums assured by country
1850–74

Parliament in 1859, which also allowed the company to conduct business in any part of the world.[126]

By this time negotiations with Minerva had been suspended and the directors had once again turned their attention to expanding their existing activities. They had dipped their toe into Europe in 1856 when they agreed to accept 125 German lives insured with an 'unsound' Hamburg office;[127] but the main thrust was concentrated on London where Williams and the London board were convinced there was considerable potential. Bentham devoted much of his time in the spring of 1857 to gathering information about insurance agencies in the City and reported that he could 'find no Office having more than one or two Agents and these appear born for their occupation, not made, and it is only by accident these are to be met with'.

He proposed a blitz approach, seeking 'to interest all persons with whom we come in contact, resident in London; and to make Agents or Correspondents of all men at all likely to serve our purpose in the hope that eventually we may procure a dozen good Agents out of a hundred appointments'. He was also keen to recruit solicitors but was convinced they would not be interested unless Standard Life abandoned the practice of refusing commissions on policies taken out as collateral for loans from whatever source, a concession already granted in Scotland. Finally he recommended the appointment of an assistant inspector to help with all this additional work. Once again the board was supportive, but it proved impossible to find a suitable candidate for the new post.[128] It was not until an assistant was engaged following further representations from Bentham in 1862 that these reforms were reflected in a sustained advance in premium income south of the border (see Figure 2.2).[129]

ATTACKING SCOTTISH WIDOWS

During that year Thomson launched his final onslaught against the Scottish Widows in a well-advertised pamphlet in which he condemned their prospectus and the whole concept of mutuality. This produced a stinging rejoinder in May 1863 from Samuel Raleigh, the actuary of the Scottish Widows, in *Mutual and Proprietary Life Assurance Compared* in which he countered Thomson's allegations. All the Edinburgh life offices were quickly caught up in an acrimonious and unedifying war of words with claims and counter claims from both sides. Raleigh was forced back on the defensive and had to vigorously fight off calls for his resignation from with-profits policy-holders who had been persuaded by Thomson that there was something inherently unsound about a mutual company. Underlying the dispute was intense competition with Standard Life threatening to overtake Scottish Widows' long-cherished position as the leading life office in Scotland (see Figure 2.3).[130] Thomson, who was undoubtedly the most able actuary of his generation, got the better of the argument and thereafter ceased to make any further criticism of Scottish Widows' management or results.

TROUBLE IN IRELAND AGAIN

In 1858 Samuel Smylie, resident secretary in Dublin, had sought permission 'to extend the company's operations in Ireland . . . from a firm conviction that social progress has made great strides in that Country within the last few years resulting in an entire modification of the habits of the people, Ideas of Business and general improvement; and that Ireland now presents a fair and safe field for extended operations in most mercantile as well as agricultural pursuits'. While this may well have been an exaggeration, he could point to a modest rise in new business over the past five years (see Figure 2.2 above left) in convincing the directors to instal Hillgrove Robinson as inspector of Irish agencies to 'extend the Agencies of the Company . . . to all

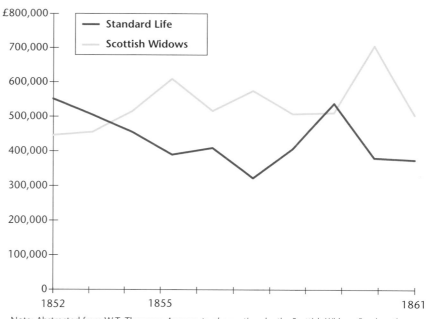

Note: Abstracted from W.T. Thomson *Answers to observations by the Scottish Widows Fund on the comparative merits of Life Assurance Companies and Mutual Assurance Societies*, Edinburgh, 1863 (The Library, the Faculty of Actuaries, Edinburgh)

towns of easy access where the services of a first-class agent and Medical man can be obtained'.[131] He had already been allowed to appoint seven new agents a year earlier.[132] Robinson died suddenly 12 months later and was succeeded by two temporary inspectors shared with Colonial Life, who together re-established Standard Life's representation in the south and deepened it in the north with new agents in places as far apart as Magherafelt and Skibbereen.[133] As in the past, the directors were soon disappointed by their experience in Ireland when it emerged during their annual visit to the Dublin office in 1859 that Samuel Smylie, who had eight children, had allowed his personal finances 'to get into a state

FIGURE 2.3
New sums assured Scottish Widows and Standard Life 1852–61

of confusion'. Although there were irregularities in the way in which the company's books were kept, no funds were missing and it was considered of 'the greatest importance' to retain his services. Because of his close links with Thomas Ringland, the general manager of the Ulster Bank, Smylie was let off with a serious reprimand and Standard Life advanced him £600 to help clear his debts.

With new business in Ireland rising, the directors appeared to be justified in the belief that the warning would make him 'a better officer of the company than ever'.[134] Towards the close of 1861 the architect David Bryce was commissioned to design a new Dublin office on the same site in Upper Sackville Street. This was completed in 1863 along with a pediment of the parable of the ten virgins again sculpted by John Steele (see page 43).[135] Almost immediately it opened, Smylie was discovered to have systematically defrauded the office and was dismissed in July. He was, however, given help to go to Canada with his wife and children, of whom there were now nine. William Bentham was hurriedly transferred from London to repair the damage, particularly the relationship with the Ulster Bank.[136] With the same zeal he had displayed in England, he had visited all the agents in Ireland by the end of December and was able to report a record year in January 1864.[137]

COLONIAL LIFE BUSINESS

With the establishment of Colonial Life, the focus of Standard Life was entirely domestic; but inevitably some policy-holders settled overseas – not always of their own volition, as in the case of George Rose, who in 1853 'sailed for Australia as a convict'.[138] On the whole, Standard Life followed Colonial Life's lead in setting rates for foreign residence and in assessing unusual risks such as working in the gold diggings in either California or Australia.[139] More problematic was deciding rates for war risk in the increasing number of crises in far-flung parts of the world in which Britain became involved during the middle years of the century, such as the Maori wars in 1863 and the Abyssinian war of 1867.[140] Although rates were generous, the board still required notification of participation in armed conflict even if the policy-holder had come to no harm. When Dr D.J. Lewis, a surgeon in the Confederate Army, died at Florida in the winter of 1862, Standard Life paid out his policy less an extra premium of 10 per cent to cover the risk and a fine of £10 because he only had an ordinary licence to reside.[141] Colonial enforced a similar code, annulling the policies of miscreants. When John Gibson, who had recently been insured through the Shanghai agents, was severely wounded in 1863 'while heading a party of Mandarin Soldiers against some Rebels near Tientsin', his policy was forfeited. He complained that he had been 'ordered' to enlist and as a special gesture his premium was returned.[142] Likewise, when it was discovered that Colonel Grenfell had not only run the Northern blockade but also served the Confederacy in Bragg's Army and 'exposed himself much in action', he was asked to surrender his policy.[143] For both companies such colourful risks were unusual; most policy-holders wished either to travel on business or pleasure or to take up foreign appointments or to settle permanently, which the unchallengeable policy gave them the freedom to do.

Since 1854 Colonial Life's new business had stalled with new sums insured consistently at between £300,000 and £350,000 a year (see Figure 2.1 on page 67). This pattern disguised shifts in the structure of the business, however. The failure to penetrate the United States given the heavy casualties of the Civil War was probably a good thing; whereas the decline in Canadian business in 1855 was discouraging and made worse by a disagreement between Thomson and the Canadian manager, Alexander Davidson Parker, about his personal expenses.[144] Alexander Brand, an Aberdeen chartered accountant, was sent out in 1856 to wind up the New York office and to investigate prospects in Canada, particularly the advisability of constructing new offices. As a result of his visit the status of the Toronto branch was enhanced with its own local board; but irregularities were discovered in the management and in November Parker and his clerk Henry White were asked to resign from May 1857. The local directors, chaired by Peter McGill, were furious and only agreed to stay reluctantly.[145] Parker, for his part, was soon snapped up as local manager by Scottish Provincial, which was about to open in Canada.[146] James Gilchrist Dickson, an Edinburgh stockbroker, was dis-

General William Braxton Bragg of the Confederacy. Colonel Grenfell, one of Colonial Life's policy-holders, served under his command. Since he had failed to get permission to do so, his policy was rescinded. Grenfell was a colourful character who spent his life in daring military exploits. He fought pirates off the coast of Morocco, served with Garibaldi in South America and rode in the charge of the Light Brigade. Shortly before joining Bragg's army, his uniform had been pierced 11 times by bullets in a furious charge with General Morgan's troopers. It was reports of this action which so disturbed the directors of Standard Life. Grenfell vanished in 1868 after escaping from the notorious American Dry Tortugas prison in a make-shift boat.

patched by Thomson to take over, with this revealing advice: 'I find little business comes through the directors in any of our branches so you must not be disappointed if you find yours bring you less than you anticipate. If they do the business carefully that is the main point . . .'[147] Dickson was to be assisted by William Miller Ramsay, a 25-year-old clerk in the London office, who was seconded as inspector of agencies. Together they set about enlarging Colonial Life's representation through the appointment of new agents at various places including Galt, Napance and Collingwood and the creation of local boards at Hamilton, Kingston, London, Quebec, and later Ottawa, all chaired by prominent people. Within a year they could report sufficient improvements to warrant the Edinburgh board raising their insurance limit to £6,000. By 1859 the company had policies totalling some £544,000 in force in Canada.[148] Dickson's health broke down the following year and he was forced to retire. He was succeeded by William Ramsay who, since his return from Canada, had been working as inspector of agencies in Scotland. His elder brother Gordon, also trained at Colonial, had recently been appointed manager of Canada Life at Toronto.[149]

William Miller Ramsay, Standard Life's manager in Canada from 1860 to 1901.

Like Dickson, Ramsay was to be helped to establish himself with the assistance of the newly recruited inspector of agencies for England, the remarkable 32-year-old John O'Hagan. Nothing is known about O'Hagan's early career except that he greatly impressed Thomson. He spent six months in Canada, visiting all 78 agencies and also investigating the company's investments in the United States. His report to the board in Edinburgh in December 1860 held out the prospect of further development, provided the bridge with the French-Canadian community was strengthened through the selection of a bilingual inspector. Inevitably the local board would have to find a suitable candidate, who would be confirmed by head office. This was the first time Thomson had allowed any official to be recruited locally. He had little alternative but to accept the nomination of Richard Bull of Hamilton as first permanent inspector of agencies in Canada.[150] The outbreak of the American Civil War in 1861 disrupted the economy and disturbed the uneasy political balance between the two Canadian provinces, leading to the postponement of plans for expansion. There was serious danger of invasion by the Northern States as a reprisal for what was perceived to be British support for the Confederacy. This threat was a powerful stimulus to negotiations in 1864, which led to the creation of the Dominion of Canada with a federal government three years later – but not before there had been some so-called 'Fenian' raids from the south. Ramsay himself volun-

JOHN O'HAGAN'S SALES TOUR

John O'Hagan (1827–94), the inspector of agencies at Colonial Life, undertook this remarkable sales tour outlined on the map below between the autumn of 1862 and the winter of 1865. Travelling in the interior of Australia was difficult, with the ever present danger of attack by bushmen. He had often to swim swollen rivers and creeks and camp under the stars. Wherever he went he described the economic conditions and the way of life for the directors in Edinburgh. If he believed there to be a market for life assurance, he appointed agents and, in some instances, recruited new local boards as in Melbourne and Sydney. His efforts in Australia and New Zealand came to nothing because of the strength of local competition; but those in India and Ceylon contributed directly to the growth of business in those countries. Such an extended tour at the time was most unusual. (Inspectors in other financial institutions could expect to be away from their desks for six months on trips to India and the Far East.) O'Hagan later became manager of Standard Life's London West End branch, from which he retired in 1892 at the age of 65. He died two years later.

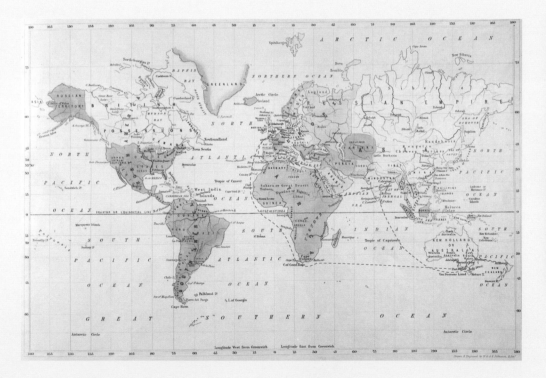

Sydney, which was visited by John O'Hagan on his extended sales tour in 1863.

teered in 1861 at the beginning of the crisis and was called out in 1866, belatedly asking permission and sending Thomson a piece of a Fenian flag as a keepsake.[151] The difficult situation in North America forced Colonial Life to look for growth in other parts of the world.

Although the West Indies economy was buoyant during the Civil War, the market was not large enough and Colonial's eyes turned eastwards towards India. Even before the Indian Mutiny in 1857, Colonial Life had encountered resistance in many places, notably Calcutta where the whole of the local board resigned in 1856 when new agents were appointed.[152] In the wake of the Mutiny, Frederick Arrow, a member of the London board, was sent out to prod agents into life or appoint new ones. Little came of this visit, largely because of the lack of demand and the continuing strong competition from the Medical and Invalid Life Office. In 1861 this office was taken over by the Albert, notorious for offering very low rates and large commissions.[153]

Against this background Thomson instructed O'Hagan to undertake an astonishing sales tour to the Antipodes, India and Ceylon.[154] He left

London in the autumn of 1862 and did not return until late in 1865, providing Thomson with detailed reports on every place he visited. His journey took him first to Sydney, then to Melbourne and on to Adelaide, with frequent stops in between. He then visited Tasmania and New Zealand. Although he was taken aback by the intemperance in Australia, he believed the outlook was good and recruited agents wherever he went.[155] In India he advocated perceptively that Colonial needed urgently to open a branch in Calcutta with a network of sub-agents – 'I . . . think that Bengal, the North West Provinces and the Punjab will in future be much too important and extensive a field to be left in the hands of mere agents, none of whom will ever give sufficient attention to it, or work it as it should be worked.'[156] Although he had intended to return via the Straits Settlements and China, he was recalled home. In any case Thomson had been gathering intelligence about conditions in the Far East from other sources, notably G.N. Young, who wrote of Hong Kong in 1863: 'Before trees were planted, the drainage executed and the vast improvements that have taken place there of late years, no doubt Hong Kong obtained for itself an unenviable notoriety, but now it is used as a sanatorium for the Invalids from Shanghai.'[157] Nevertheless, no agency was established and even the Shanghai agency lapsed. It was not revived until the arrival in 1866 of James Tod, who had been trained at the Colonial Life head office and was now working for the agency house of Williams & Tod.

THOMSON'S MANOEUVRES

By the time O'Hagan returned, Colonial Life was in the process of merging with Standard Life and had absorbed Minerva and the Victoria and Legal and Commercial Life Assurance Company in a complex sequence of manoeuvres. The bargaining with Minerva, which had been broken off in 1857, resumed in the spring of 1864 and was concluded finally in January of the following year.[158] In exchange for a payment of a little over £100,000, Standard Life acquired total risks of some £2 million along with assets of over £485,000. A sizeable proportion was invested in railway stocks and debentures, consistently avoided by Standard Life. Although the managers left, the clerks were offered either a year's salary or positions with Standard Life, which six accepted. The Cannon Street office was sold; but the office in the West End in Pall Mall was retained as a branch with some of the Minerva directors forming a new local board with O'Hagan as resident secretary. This significant deal was entirely to the credit of the London secretary Henry Jones Williams, who had probably done more than anyone to build Standard Life's business in the previous decade. He was paid a bonus and given the new title of general secretary for England, which merely reflected his actual duties rather than any additional responsibilities.[159]

By now Thomson, even though he was only in his early fifties, was beginning to think about the succession and was determined to frustrate any ambitions Williams may have had. There is

A policy taken out by Frank McGechy, land agent in the County of Armagh, on the life of Roger Leigh of Arundel in the County of Sussex with the Victoria Legal & Commercial Life Assurance Co., July 1863.

little doubt that, despite his reputation as perhaps the most influential and innovative actuary and manager of a life office in the United Kingdom, Thomson was autocratic and not always easy to work with. In 1861 George Todd, who had succeeded his brother as secretary, left

to become manager of Scottish Equitable[160] and four years later in January 1865 his successor, A.H. Turnbull, departed to manage the City of Glasgow Life Assurance Co.[161] By this time, and on his own admission, Thomson was anxious to advance the interests of his son, Spencer C. Thomson, who had just graduated from Cambridge and joined the company as a clerk in the head office. On Turnbull's departure he persuaded the board to promote his son, who was only 23, to the new post of actuarial assistant.[162] It is not clear at this juncture what he had in mind. Although later in the year he was to claim that he had always intended for Standard Life and Colonial Life to come together, his previous negotiations suggest that this was certainly not the case and what he seems to have been doing, difficult as it is to believe, was trying to improve his son's chances of becoming manager of Standard Life should he, himself, leave to lead an enlarged Colonial Life.

Unknown to the board of either company, he had been discussing during the closing months of 1864 the possible amalgamation of Colonial Life with the London-based Victoria and Legal and Commercial Life Assurance Company. The Victoria Life Assurance and Loan Company had been established in 1838 and had merged in 1857 with the Legal and Commercial Life Assurance Company, which itself in 1853 had acquired the business of the London and Provincial Joint Stock Life Assurance Co. By 1864 Victoria and Legal had assets of some £422,000 and risks of about £1.6 million, mostly on

English lives. Thomson intended to launch Colonial Life in the domestic market in direct competition to Standard Life using Victoria's established network of agents, which had the added attraction of also representing the associated fire office – Legal and Commercial Fire Assurance Company.[163] When the Standard Life directors learned of the almost completed merger in February 1865, they were understandably furious. Thomson deftly suggested that the crisis could be diffused by 'a junction between the Offices', which would retain for Standard Life 'the advantage of the Colonial connection, while it would enable the Colonial to establish and consolidate its position'. Recognising the advisability of such an outcome, James Hay, the chairman of Colonial Life and also a director of Standard Life, wholeheartedly supported Thomson's sudden change of tack and it was Colonial Life which proposed the three-way merger in March. An agreement had been reached by the end of April whereby Colonial Life would dissolve in March 1866 and in return shareholders, for every four shares, would receive one share in Standard Life valued at £60. Standard Life assumed responsibility for the 5,385 policies with a total risk of a little over £3 million and took over assets of £500,000. The with-profits policy-holders were given a special bonus of 1.5 per cent per annum for the years 1864 and 1865 and allowed to share in the bonus to be declared in 1870. As a consequence Standard Life also agreed to acquire Victoria Life as from 31 December 1864 on the same terms as had been

agreed with Colonial Life – the repayment of the capital of 8,166 shares of £5 each with a premium of £7. Apart from the manager, who retired, all the Victoria staff were offered positions with Standard Life or a year's salary in lieu. The assets valued at £422,354, which were transferred to Standard Life, included, like those of Minerva, about £100,000 worth of railway stock. As a result of these mergers the company's accumulated fund rose from £2.6 million in 1864 to almost £3.9 million in 1867 and the number of accepted policies from 1,428 to 1,820.[164]

MANAGING THE ENLARGED BUSINESS

Thomson may have been despondent at this turn of events, but at least he ensured that Colonial Life would continue to enjoy a measure of independence in conducting overseas business within Standard Life. In any event, he had no time to be depressed, with four businesses to bring together and an investigation to complete within a year. The mergers brought to a head the need to make a decision about the future of the tontine bonus system, which, as a result of the company's rigorous insistence on accepting only first-class and therefore longer-lived risks, had become impossible to sustain at the early level of 1.25 per cent a year. In 1850 the rate was cut to 1.1 per cent and in 1855 to 0.75 per cent. The principal reason given for the large reduction in 1855 was to create a bigger reserve fund 'as the great aim of the Institution is to be as nearly as possible a Mutual Assurance Association without

The last Colonial Almanac, published in 1868

all the drawbacks to which Mutual Assurance is liable'.* Henry Jones Williams, who was engaged in overhauling the London office, suggested as part of the programme of reform that the tontine system should be abandoned in favour of the equal scheme as employed by Colonial Life, which he believed would improve competitiveness. Although Thomson tended to agree, the directors decided they had no alternative but to persevere with the existing arrangements.[165]

The request was made again at the time of the 1860 investigation and again rejected, even though the rate of 0.67 per cent a year was only achieved by slashing the allocation to shareholders. On this occasion the investigation committee was willing to admit that: 'This diminution of rate arises from the peculiar mode of division followed by the company.' Thomson, however, was now less inclined to support a change, as he could show that the decline in bonuses had not dented demand for new policies. The investigation committee claimed that 'the Standard can now claim the highest position among British Assurance Institutions, as having transacted a larger amount of Business during the last 15 years than any other office', without offering 'the inducement of personal loans' or 'assuring deteriorated lives on enhanced terms'.[166] With the absorption of Minerva, Victoria and Colonial, all of which employed the equal scheme, further resistance

was impossible and, following the 1865 investigation, when the bonus rate came down to 0.58 per cent, an equal scheme was introduced to run in parallel with the tontine: 'That mode of division is attractive to some persons who make assurance an Investment as well as provision looking forward to prolonged life, but to others it presents less attraction . . . To lives after middle age it holds out few inducements comparatively and at the Younger Ages although the benefits in the case of lengthened Survivance are very great the rates of premium are considered high . . .'[167] Within ten years the tontine scheme was closed to new entrants and all Standard Life's new policies were issued on the equal basis.[168]

The strain of all this activity began to tell on the 53-year-old Thomson in the spring of 1866 and, to support him, his son was appointed joint actuary.[169] By the autumn his health had completely broken down and he was away from the office for several spells, leaving his son in charge. Finally in December the directors decided that he should take three months off to recover from his breakdown.[170] During these critical months there was a great deal of work to be done apart from completing the investigation and dealing with the complexities of the Strathmore case (see page 72).

From the outset the directors recognised that it would no longer be possible for the whole board to conduct the entire business, approving

* The advantage of mutual status was that dividends did not have to be paid to shareholders. The disadvantage was that they often lacked an adequate capital base from which to develop their business.

every new life and receiving reports from all the branches. In March 1866 it was agreed that the full board would meet weekly as before on Mondays at one o'clock to discuss 'all subjects connected with investments' and what were known as 'red-ink subjects'. The board would then divide: one half to discuss 'Colonial and Foreign business' and the other half 'Standard or Home proposals'.[171] This reflected the new office structure, which had been divided for convenience into a Home department with Thomas Robertson as secretary and a colonial and foreign department under the Colonial Life secretary D. Clunie Gregor.[172] Two years later these arrangements were modified as the Thomsons were unable to keep control of transactions after the board had split and from October 1868 all new lives, whether domestic or foreign, were to be reviewed by a committee of three directors which met immediately after the weekly board.[173] The flaw in these arrangements was that nothing was done to relieve possible tension with the London board and management, which had led to the crisis 20 years earlier. Although the London directors, like those in Dublin, had considerable discretion over accepting risks, they had no influence over investments, unlike their counterparts in other countries, and, perhaps more importantly, given their status as full members of the main board, over the general direction of the company. This was unfortunate as they were effectively the powerhouse of the enterprise, generating the bulk of new business and with direct access to the expanding London financial market. With the preferment of the young Spencer Thomson, friction with London and even Dublin was inevitable; but the main board in Edinburgh totally failed to appreciate the likely consequences.

INDUSTRIAL LOANS

The railway investments of Minerva and Victoria were now a pressing concern, given Standard Life's continuing opposition to such holdings. By this time such an attitude was irrational, as even very conservative insurance companies, such as the Royal Exchange Assurance, had been investing in railway stock for more than 20 years and the Government Actuary had endorsed such strategies by insurance companies in his evidence to the Select Committee on Assurance Associations in 1853.[174] Equity investment did require good market intelligence, however, and this was more readily available in London than Edinburgh. At first the directors persisted in their refusal to countenance any dealings with railways, turning down a loan to the well-respected London, Brighton & South Coast Railway in March 1866.[175] By the end of the year they had relented and agreed to advance £30,000 to the Highland Railway as part of the funding for the line from Dingwall to Stromeferry; this was secured not on the assets but on the personal security of the directors, most of whom were local landowners, among them the Earl of Seafield and the fabulously wealthy China merchant, Alexander Matheson.[176] The embargo on lending on railway stock remained in force; a

PUNCH'S FANCY PORTRAITS.—No. 87.

SIR JOHN BENNET LAWES, BART.

THE AGRICULTURAL LAWES, THE NEW WHEEL-BARROW-NET.
MOTTO, "LAUS ET HONOR."

Sir John Bennet Lawes (1814–92), a pioneer in the use of artificial fertilisers, who borrowed money from Standard Life to finance his new factory in Deptford in 1867.

further loan of £20,000 to Henry Houldsworth on the security of his shares in the Lancashire & Yorkshire Railway in December 1867 was explicitly an exception to the rule.[177] Within a month the directors were forced to change their minds only because demand for loans on heritable securities in both Scotland and England had simply dried up as a result of a commercial crisis in London. Affirming that 'the most eligible Investment is that which the board has hitherto relied on all along to the greatest extent, viz. Investments on Heritable Securities in

Scotland and to a lesser extent England and Ireland', the directors in January 1868 bought through James Capel, the London stockbrokers, £50,000 worth of debentures of four railway companies.[178] Taking debentures rather than stock guaranteed income and gave preference in the event of failure. Having made this decision and despite a recovery in the market for heritable securities, other railway investments followed including further loans to the Highland Railway and the purchase of stock in the East Indian, Great India Peninsular and Tasmania Railways.[179] The London directors' attempt to influence this change in investment policy was at first rebuffed.[180] Realising the importance of having regular contact with Capel's, Spencer Thomson intervened and asked the London board for advice about Indian railway investments. Delighted at this display of confidence the London board 'took it up *con amore* & sat three hours on it'.[181] No further consultations took place for some time, however.

Even before the reaffirmation of the central position of Scottish heritable securities, the directors had made large loans south of the border. In 1867 they advanced £72,000 to John Bennet Lawes on the security of his Rothamsted estate in Hertfordshire, where he had been conducting pioneering agricultural research for over 30 years. This was almost certainly Standard Life's first industrial loan, albeit made unwittingly, as Lawes needed the money to develop his very successful artificial manure business with a factory in Deptford in south-east London.[182] Like other insurance companies, Standard Life was circumspect in dealing directly with commercial companies, rejecting a request for £40,000 from the Vulcan Foundry in Manchester in 1865[183] and for £15,000 from the Killyheagh Spinning Company in Belfast in 1870,[184] but the next year advancing an equivalent sum to the New Zealand Scotch Trust on the personal security of the directors chaired by Lord Gifford.[185] In 1872 the board took the bold step of lending £66,000 to Merry & Cunninghame Ltd, which had been recently formed to acquire the Glengarnock iron-works in Ayrshire from a partnership of the same name.[186] This was followed in 1874 by an advance of £40,000 to the Inns of Court Hotel and £80,000 to the newly established Railway Clearing House towards the finance of its offices.[187]

Nevertheless, the bulk of new investments remained in Scotland, with substantial loans to long-term borrowers such as the sixth Earl of Glasgow, whose headlong enthusiasm for the Catholic revival in the Scottish Episcopal Church had led him to the brink of ruin,[188] and to the Earl of Galloway whose improvidence, particularly the expenditure on the gardens and massive estate wall at Galloway House, was relentlessly destroy-ing his patrimony.[189] Apart from the Dukes of Hamilton and Richmond (see page 71), there was one other large recruit, Sir William Gordon Gordon Cumming of Gordonstoun, who bor-

Gordonstoun House, the family seat of the Gordon Cumming family, which was mortgaged to Standard Life in the 1870s. It is now the well-known Gordonstoun public school.

rowed £110,762 to pay off gambling debts, which his grandfather had incurred before 1830.[190] There were two big English loans at this time, £87,000 to Lady Langdale, the widow of the Master of the Rolls, in 1869[191] and £110,000 in 1870 to Lancaster Lucas against his Kent estates.[192] Once the directors had been satisfied that Gladstone's Irish Land Act of 1870, which offered some measure of protection to tenants, would not damage their security, they entertained loans of £90,000 in 1871 to Sir Charles Compton William Domville, who owned Templeogue and Santry House at Howth near Dublin,[193] and of £65,000 the following year to Lord Dunalley of Kilboy, Nenagh, County Tipperary, on condition he provided a personal bond and accepted Standard Life's choice of agent.[194] Remarkably, in 1875, loans on heritable securities in the United Kingdom totalled in excess of £3.5 million and represented almost 72 per cent of the portfolio.[195] This policy of lending principally on landed estates was perfectly satisfactory as long as the prosperity of agriculture in the United Kingdom sustained the value of agricultural properties.

RESTRUCTURING THE COMPANY

Perhaps the most pressing issue which needed to be resolved for the long term in 1866 was the overall structure of the enlarged company in the domestic market. The two inspectors in London, George Edwards and Stephen Hudson, under Williams' direction continued the careful scrutiny of agents in England and Wales, dismissing no fewer that 188 between 1865 and 1870.[196]

The decision in September 1868 to reorganise the West End branch and dismiss the local board, who left with ill grace, was a prelude to the abolition the following month of all the local boards in England with the exception of London.[197] Whatever misgivings William Thomson may have had about the effectiveness of local boards, it is difficult to envisage how the two inspectors based in London could promote Standard's interest satisfactorily throughout the length of England unless something was put in their place.

Strengthening local commitment became essential in 1869 after the spectacular collapse with massive debts of the two most aggressive insurance companies, the Albert Life Assurance Society and the European Assurance Society;[198] but at this crucial juncture Williams' commitment was beginning to wane. After Spencer Thomson was promoted to assistant manager in 1871 because his father's health was continuing to deteriorate,[199] the London board demanded better treatment for their manager, only to be rebuked with a stinging reminder that the 'duties of general secretary for England are entirely ministerial and in no way independent of the Head Authority in Edinburgh'.[200] Disaffected as he was, Williams took some action in 1872 by securing the appointment of Stephen Hudson to the new post of local secretary in Manchester and a year later of M.B. Hick, the long-serving and very successful agent in Wakefield and Dewsbury, to the same position there.[201] Nevertheless, this was a half-hearted response lacking

Wakefield in Yorkshire, where Standard Life had one of its most successful English agencies in the 1860s.

the vigour of the root-and-branch reforms he had pushed through with Bentham's help a decade earlier.

In Ireland Bentham, whose efforts to maintain Standard Life's position had scarcely been rewarded, did little except keep things ticking over. He was hardly encouraged by Thomson's scathing critique of Irish business after a visit in 1868: 'Much of the business was of an undesirable kind . . . Material facts were suppressed about the assurers; there were too many early claims and the tendency of life companies to dispute claims had engendered a want of confidence in the public, whose demand for insurance was falling off.'[202]

In Scotland new sums assured fell from £221,598 in 1863–64 to £126,365 in 1867–68. Thomson, alarmed, instructed John O'Hagan to inspect all 200 agencies in the summer of 1868. Although he was able to recruit new agents in a few places, such as Ayr, Invergordon, Kirkintilloch and Stirling, he 'found it impossible to obtain additional Agents in towns where the company was already represented, as all the parties disposed to undertake the agencies were engaged for other offices . . .' On the whole he was impressed with the quality of agents and all he could recommend was that they were kept 'up to the mark, by correspondence and inspection'. With over 40 life offices competing for business, he was pessimistic about future prospects.[203]

William Thomson was more confident and determined on yet another assault on the west of Scotland market. In 1867 he recruited the talented young accountant Alexander Sloan to be resident secretary in Glasgow where the local board was reprieved.[204] Sloan's first annual report was depressing reading, with only £19,000 of new risks during the year, which he attributed to 'the failure of the European and Albert Companies; disasters which have certainly a more intimidating effect on the class of people amongst whom our district Agents labour than they have on the more shrewd and calculating Mercantile community'. At the end of his penetrating report, he suggested that to introduce business Standard Life should enlist private agents from among 'City Travellers (Grocers, Drapers etc.), Heads of Department in large Warehouses, Foremen in large Public Works, Clerks etc. to whose income an addition of £10 to £15 a year . . . would be a matter of considerable importance'.[205] There was no response to this imaginative proposal and within three years Sloan had lost interest.[206] Even when Spencer Thomson pointed out to the board in 1870 that

other companies regularly inspected their agents in Scotland,[207] no action was taken until 1873 when a Scottish inspector was appointed to strengthen the Glasgow office.[208] William Thomson did, however, respond to pressure from agents to improve the terms of endowment policies, which were becoming increasingly popular, by persuading the board in 1870 to introduce with-profits endowment policies.[209]

OVERSEAS

Abroad, with the exception of India, there was a similar lack of resolve in addressing local weaknesses and strengthening competition. At the head office in Edinburgh, despite the transfer of D. Clunie Gregor, the secretary of Colonial Life, to the post of colonial and foreign secretary, the overseeing of operations abroad in practice remained in Thomson's hands, even more firmly after the abolition of the separate Colonial committee in 1868. Moreover, the versatile John O'Hagan was fully occupied as resident secretary in the West End branch in London and no longer available to undertake lengthy inspection tours. As a result Thomson and the board lacked the first-hand information about local conditions they had received so regularly in the early days.

Success in India was due entirely to the fortuitous appointment in 1869 of George Lucas Kemp as secretary to the Calcutta board. Previously the India manager for the Albert, he had hurried home on learning of his company's difficulties and volunteered his services to

Colonial. Within a few months of his return he had travelled nearly 3,800 miles by train, by dâk gharry, by palki and on horseback, securing where possible all the Albert's agents for Standard Life and appointing new ones at towns such as Allahabad, Benares, Cawnpore, Delhi, Lahore, Lucknow and Umballa. Taking advantage of the gap in the market in the aftermath of the Albert catastrophe, Kemp rapidly built up the business, helped by forging a close link with the Delhi and London Bank Limited, which adopted Standard Life policies as its collateral for loans. Partly to meet the needs of the bank, the company began to insure Eurasian lives and to offer automatic increases in cover up to 10 per cent of the value of a policy. Native lives, however, were 'rigorously excluded'.[210] Within a year Kemp had accepted 16 lacs of rupees of business,* much of them direct and free of commission.[211] Kemp's success was acknowledged late in 1871 when he was promoted to permanent secretary with an assistant, Thomas Lang, sent out from Edinburgh.[212] By 1873 the Calcutta branch had far outstripped all the other overseas branches, most of which languished in the doldrums. Competition from local life offices was severe in Australia and New Zealand and, despite complaints that rates were too high and commissions too low, the directors refused to make any adjustments. Nor were they prepared to replace the lackadaisical Sydney agent, who was better at complaining than seeking business.[213] In Shanghai, meanwhile, James Tod and his successor Edward Holdsworth failed to make any impact.[214]

Most worrying was the downturn in the Canadian business due in large measure to the belligerent marketing and sales techniques of American and, later, Canadian companies. They nearly all offered a non-forfeiture option on their policies, whereby if payments lapsed a policy up to the value of the premiums received was issued. Also, instead of paying bonuses, they used their profits to reduce premiums. Their sales force was organised into districts with agents, paid on commission, who used canvassers to attract new lives by visiting every office and store in a neighbourhood in a concerted campaign. American firms made lightning raids to set up new districts, offering very attractive terms to potential agents. In 1870 Standard Life lost its Canadian inspector, Richard Bull, to the American Travellers Insurance Company in one such sortie. William Ramsay persuaded Thomson to allow him to experiment with the appointment of two canvassers, A.H. Fox (soon replaced by Alfred Shortt) in Montreal and John Fulton in Toronto. After three years, following a visit by Fulton to Edinburgh, it was decided to abandon the scheme and revert to inspection.[215] From the results of a tour of agencies during 1873 at a time when competition from newly formed Canadian life offices was at its height, Ramsay concluded that canvassing was the only

---

* The sterling exchange rate was still about 22 pennies (9 new pence).

Standard Life's Calcutta Office in the 1860s. This photograph
comes from the collection of George L. Kemp, secretary to the
Calcutta board.

way to proceed, but he confessed he had no stomach for such high-pressured selling.[216] The reaction from Edinburgh was to order the abandonment of both canvassers and inspectors and revert to agents. Although Ramsay was able to reverse this decision, the argument did nothing to improve morale.[217] Many of these problems in the foreign branches could easily have been avoided if, as in the past, visits had been made by officers from the United Kingdom to report first hand to the board.

THOMSON'S LEGACY

After the mergers in 1866 the whole management structure of the company should have been reorganised to match its far greater size, with much more emphasis both in the United Kingdom and overseas on inspection as the main means of communication between branches. This failure can be attributed largely to Thomson's breakdown, as he was the linchpin which held the entire enterprise together. After he returned to work in the spring of 1867 he lacked the drive and enthusiasm of his earlier days and his preferment of his son alienated his senior managers, who understandably hoped to succeed him. So as to process the greater volume of business, the offices in Edinburgh and London necessarily grew bigger but still lacked any integration. By 1872 there were 27 men including Thomson in the Home department and 16 in the foreign and colonial department in Edinburgh, while there were 18 staff in London. Thomson was paid £3,000, twice as much as

Williams in London, and more than three times as much as Bentham and Ramsay.[218]

In order to accommodate the larger staff, Nos. 5 and 7 George Street were acquired in 1851 and in 1863 No. 1 was bought from Scottish Provident for £7,000.[219] Although David Bryce was commissioned to design a new building to cover the whole site, the directors opted just to refurbish the existing offices.[220]

In some ways the board could be forgiven for allowing the company to coast when all the evidence suggested that Standard Life was outperforming the industry. Confidence in the life market, which had been badly buffeted by the collapse of the Albert and the European, was further damaged when, during their liquidation in the full glare of publicity, it emerged that the business of the two companies had been conducted fraudulently. There was clamour for legislation to prevent such abuses in the future. William Thomson, who had been elected chairman of the Association of Scottish Life Offices, saw it as his duty to speak for the whole industry throughout the United Kingdom in the protracted and time-consuming negotiations with the Board of Trade, which led to the passing of the Life Assurance Companies Act in 1870.[221] This required all new companies to hold £20,000 in public funds, to adopt a standard form of accounts, to publish regular valuations, to make annual returns to the Board of Trade and, in offices where other types of insurance was conducted, to account separately for their life funds. Thomson's hand was evident in every section of the Act, particularly in the structure of the form of accounts.[222] These new regulations did not present any problems to well-conducted insurers such as Standard Life or Scottish Widows; but the damage had been done and all offices reported a decline in new business. A comparison between the major life companies published in 1873 by the *Post Magazine*, which reported on the industry, showed that over the previous decade Standard Life had secured more new business than any other office. Although it had not grown as quickly as either Scottish Widows or Scottish Provident,[223] Standard Life could justifiably claim to be 'one of the great provident institutions of the Country'.[224] Gratified by this momentous achievement, William Thomson retired as manager at the age of 61 in November 1874 and was immediately appointed consulting actuary at a salary of £2,500, 'more as a retiring allowance in consideration of his long and valuable services'.[225] Shortly afterwards, Thomson joined the board of the Royal Bank of Scotland where, ironically, he played an important part in expanding their London business.

There can be no doubt that since he joined Standard Life in 1834, Thomson had been the driving force behind its development. As a young man he had become the doyen of the actuarial profession. He had been instrumental in the formation in 1848 of the Institute of Actuaries (whose first meeting was held in the London offices of Standard Life) and of the Faculty of Actuaries in Scotland in 1856.[226] He had compiled widely used actuarial tables, written extensively on insurance and conducted actuarial investigations for the widows' funds of a number of bodies, including Church of Scotland Ministers, the Writers to the Signet and the Royal College of Surgeons in Edinburgh.[227] He could claim to have trained more managers and actuaries of United Kingdom life offices than any of his contemporaries. His inflexible commitment to only accepting 'first-class' lives and to the probity of his officers had guaranteed success to Standard Life, and his interest in mortality in other parts of the world had provided the vital ingredient in the launch of Colonial Life. He was a stalwart advocate of the advantages of a proprietary company over that of a mutual. He had helped shape the Companies Act of 1855 and the more recent insurance legislation.[228] Like many great men, he had fallen into the trap of nominating his son as his successor long before he retired and consequently stifled management initiative in his final years. Thomson left a market-leading enterprise, which depended for its success on a profoundly conservative strategy: only accepting the best lives, still dominated by policy-holders in country towns and villages and with a very restricted approach to investment.

CHAPTER THREE

SITTING ON THE SAFETY VALVE: 1874–1904

'We have no sympathy with the big man when he wears himself out in trying to look bigger, or with the captain of the fast steamer who piles on the coals and sits on the safety valve when there is no good reason for forcing the pace . . . Such expenditure cannot be justified in the case of Standard and it is not in the interest of the policy-holders, who should be the first consideration. We do not know why or how but it seems to us beyond question that the business is being unduly forced . . .'

The Financial Times comments on Standard Life's results in 1893.[1]

For any business connected with the land, such as Standard Life and other life offices, the final decades of Victorian Britain provided an unprecedented challenge. After 1875 the prosperity of British agriculture began to wane in the face of foreign competition. Although the British market had been open to overseas imports of grain since the repeal of the Corn Laws in 1846, foreign growers had lacked access to an efficient cheap transport system. Technical advances in the design and construction of ships and locomotives during the 1870s combined with the building of new port facilities and many miles of railroads, particularly in North and South America, served to drive down freight rates. As a result prices of grain and wool and then those of meat tumbled and many British farmers were faced with ruin, particularly those on marginal and heavy lands. Matters were made worse by appalling wet and cold weather between 1878 and 1882. Rents went unpaid and rent reductions were inevitable. Land values collapsed by as much as half and showed no sign of recovering by the end of the century. Increasingly it proved impossible to find new tenants for vacated farms or purchasers for estates. The bad weather brought potato blight back with a vengeance in the Highlands of Scotland and the west of Ireland. Although a repeat of the famine of the 1840s was avoided, there was widespread agitation in both places against landowners. With much of its life business in rural communities and a large proportion of its capital tied up in mortgages over landed estates, Standard Life was very exposed to this reversal in agricultural fortunes.

WORSENING SITUATION IN IRELAND

It was not until the rent riots in Ireland and the formation of the Irish Land League in the

Valentine Augustus, fourth Earl of Kenmare (1825–1905), to whom Standard Life lent £100,000 from 1875 to build the magnificent Kenmare House overlooking the lake at Killarney. The house was destroyed by fire in 1913.

KILLARNEY HOUSE. 1702. W.L.

autumn of 1879, however, that the directors appreciated the seriousness of the company's position.[2] Until then, following the time-honoured policy of investing in heritable securities, confirmed as recently as 1868 (see page 98), Standard Life continued to make large advances to the landed gentry. By far the greatest proportion of these new loans were made to Irish landowners, particularly to the Lord Chamber-lain of Ireland, the Earl of Kenmare, and his son Viscount Castlerosse, who were Catholics and owned large estates in Kerry and Cork and were engaged in building Kenmare House at Killarney for the colossal sum of £100,000.[3] These new mortgages were accepted despite the fact that some existing borrowers were already showing signs of strain. The Marquess of Queensberry, a long-time borrower, had difficulty in repaying his loan of £7,200 when it fell due in 1874,[4] and two years later Sir Charles Domville was declared bankrupt. Standard Life, owed £93,000, took possession of his Sangtry estate outside Dublin.[5] Even as late as August 1879 Spencer Thomson reported after an audit of the Dublin office that there was nothing to worry about:

I found all people in Ireland a good deal concerned with the prospect of continued hard times on account of the Agricultural depression already existing, and the anticipation of another bad harvest, a prospect which is already leading to a fall in the rents from Land, and to some difficulty in collecting those which are due. The directors have already had before them one or two cases of delay of a few months in payment of the Interest on Irish Loans, but I am assured that these will eventually be recovered . . . without difficulty, the considerable margin in all the company's transactions being a safeguard against loss from any diminution in the value of the security.[6]

Within a few months the riots had dispelled this confidence and William Bentham, the resident secretary in Dublin, was instructed to review the security of all the company's mortgages in the country.[7]

Convinced that the disturbances were 'of a temporary character', the board remained willing to commit further funds, lending £48,000 in January to the Earl of Gosford against his estates in Armagh and Cavan.[8] On learning later in the month that Standard Life had over £1 million tied up in Irish mortgages – some 20 per cent of the whole investment portfolio – the London-based directors cautioned their Edinburgh colleagues that 'it would be unwise to make any further loans at present'.[9] The board concurred unless the borrower 'exhibited a very full margin of security' and at the same time improved security by requiring existing borrowers to take out policies.[10] This decision came not a moment too soon, as many landowners found it impossible to collect the 'gale' (instalment) on the rents due in May and allowed it to 'hang over' until the end of the year. When it proved impossible even to collect this hanging gale, the Earl of Kenmare, recognising that Standard Life could take possession of the whole of his estate, petitioned for a postponement of all payments until 1882. In common with other Scottish life offices, the board, not wishing to draw attention to the extent of their Irish mortgages at a time when events in that country were under intense public scrutiny throughout the United Kingdom, agreed and at the same time began to monitor arrears on such loans monthly.[11] When Bentham was reported in the newspapers to have attended a 'great' meeting of landowners, he was cautioned by Spencer Thomson that it was 'highly injudicious to do anything to bring us before the world in such a conversation'.[12]

Although the focus of agitation in Ireland had switched by 1882 to Home Rule, there had been no improvement in the plight of landowners.

Muckross Abbey at Killarney, which Standard Life acquired in 1898 after the owners, the Herberts, became bankrupt. It is now the focal point of the Killarney National Park.

The Earl of Kenmare, who now owed Standard Life £146,000, was effectively bankrupt. In the circumstances the directors concluded they had no alternative but to advance a further £40,000 on very strict conditions which included breaking the entail and the appointment of trustees to manage the Earl's property, the sale of the Limerick estates for not less than £100,000 to reduce the debt to £87,000 within two years, and maintenance of premiums on a policy of £153,000 assigned to Standard Life.[13] Since no buyers could be found for the Limerick estates, Standard Life was forced to manage the Earl's

affairs directly for the remainder of the century. This was both time-consuming and frustrating.[14] In 1892 the board dismissed the Earl's agent and appointed their own receiver, who at once sold all the horses and cattle on the estate.[15] By careful management, the debt was reduced to £111,000 by 1902.[16]

In the case of Henry Arthur Herbert, the owner of the nearby Muckross estate also in Killarney, who was unable to repay his loan of £36,000, the board took more direct action by buying Muckross Abbey and all the property in 1898.[17] The farms were sold to the tenants and after three false starts the abbey was bought by Arthur Guinness, Lord Ardilaun, in 1899.[18]

The financial world, rife with rumours about the company's exposure in Ireland, repeatedly called for more precise information, particularly in 1890 when almost £77,500 was written off the value of property. The directors steadfastly refused, reassuring customers quite truthfully that investment in Ireland yielded higher returns than mortgages elsewhere in the United Kingdom. This explanation did not convince commentators in the press, who regularly warned of the peril of substantial losses.[19]

AGRICULTURAL CRISIS AT HOME

Although Irish loans gave the directors greatest cause for concern, there were similar problems closer to home. During 1886 Standard Life called in their loan of £55,000 to the Earl of Glasgow, precipitating the sale of his estates and his four grand homes on which he had lavished money.[20] The following year Skibo Castle, which had recently been rebuilt, and its surrounding estate in Sutherland were repossessed from Ewan Charles Sutherland, a West Indian merchant, whose speculation in Highland Railway stock had contributed to his failure.[21] It was ten years before the sale of Skibo to Andrew Carnegie, the Scottish-born American magnate, was concluded for £85,000.[22] From then on, where there was any doubt about an advance against a heritable security, it was revoked when due for renewal. The Earl of Denbigh was asked to repay £57,000 in 1888 because it was feared that the 'diminution of rents since 1881' would make it impossible for him to maintain interest payments. As a result his Leicestershire and Warwickshire estates were put on the market without attracting buyers and he was obliged to give additional security.[23] In several cases, with the bulk of their rents committed to interest payments, impoverished borrowers were dependent for their living expenses on whatever Standard Life would let them have.[24] Some landowners, alarmed by this tough attitude, found other means of finance and repaid their advances. One such was the Earl of Galloway who switched his borrowing to the less exacting Scottish Provident.[25]

Skibo Castle in Sutherland, which was repossessed by Standard Life in 1887 and managed by the company for ten years. It was eventually sold to the American steel magnate, Andrew Carnegie, who greatly enlarged it.

An illustration from one of the books forming part of the *Bibliotheca Lindesiana* in John Rylands Library, University of Manchester. James Ludovic, 26th Earl of Crawford (1847–1913), borrowed from Standard Life to finance his passion for collecting books, naming his library after his subsidiary title of Lord Lindsay. The Earl sold his library to assist with his loan repayments to Standard Life.

reported: 'I know the family Establishment expenses are kept as low as possible, and that especially during the "pinch" of the last few years, household and other expenditure has been reduced to meet the deficiency in income to a very great extent. His Lordship does not bet or gamble in any way and if any of his tastes may be said to be expensive they are in connection with literature and science and these have been and are regulated according to his means.'[26] This was an understatement. The Earl borrowed heavily to fund his passion and was obliged to sell his magnificent *Bibliotheca Lindesiana* to the new John Rylands Library in Manchester for £155,000 in 1901.

With evidence that prospects in Ireland were improving, the embargo on lending there was lifted in 1895.[27] By this time the board's policy was to invest in other sectors. Nevertheless, two of the loans to the aristocracy in the 1890s were very large – £200,000 in 1895 to Sir John Sinclair of Ulbster, who owned valuable property in the City of London as well as his Caithness estates,[28] and £180,000 in 1898 to the Earl and Countess of Warwick.[29]

RESTRUCTURING THE INVESTMENT PORTFOLIO

When the directors began to consider restructuring the investment portfolio in the 1870s, they remained wary of railway and harbour stock and loans for housing and industrial development, but welcomed applications from local authorities. In 1877 some £120,000 was advanced to the

The deepening agricultural crisis did not prevent the directors from considering further applications from Scottish and English landowners, but they were much more circumspect than in the past. They usually required evidence of prudent living and some other source of income than just rents, for example mineral rights. When the Earl of Crawford applied successfully for a loan of £50,000 in 1888, his lawyer

Manchester Corporation Property Co. for slum clearance and £163,000 to the Barony Parochial Board in Glasgow to pay for Barnhill Poorhouse, the largest in Scotland.[30] There were exceptions. Although a request for £20,000 made in 1878 from W.H. and H.V. Haig, the owners of the Cameron Bridge Distillery, was turned down as being 'beyond the scope of the company's usual investments',[31] some £10,000 had been made available in 1875 to the South of Ireland Distillery and £30,000 to Charles Palmer, the well-known Tyne shipbuilder and engineer, to help finance the ill-fated Tyne Plate Glass Works.[32] During that year the directors refused to buy ground in St Paul's churchyard in London as they were 'disinclined to invest the company's funds in the purchase of property',[33] but in 1877 lent the

Mercantile Heritage Company £30,000 to buy property in Princes Street, Edinburgh.[34] The market for property in Scotland collapsed shortly afterwards and early in 1882 the Mercantile Heritage Company claimed that it was unable to dispose of their Princes Street investment even at less than 20 per cent of the price it had paid for it.[35] Because of such difficulties, interest rates on heritable securities had been reduced by the Association of Scottish Life Offices to 3.5 per cent a year earlier.[36] As a consequence the board looked seriously for new investment opportunities.

The weakness in the property market in Scotland was partly due to the collapse in the autumn of 1878 of the City of Glasgow Bank, which had fuelled speculation by fraudulent lending. The bank had close links with the

Matakanui sheep station, near Dunedin, New Zealand, shortly after the discovery of gold in the late 1880s. The gold workings are in the foreground. Standard Life loaned £40,000 over the property in 1887.

Antipodes through investment in the New Zealand and Australian Land Company, also based in Glasgow.[37] Badly affected by the removal of the bank's support, this company had to be reconstructed and, public-spiritedly, Standard Life offered in April 1881 to take £20,000 of debenture stock from the liquidators. Despite its subsequent withdrawal, this proposal marked a significant turning point in Standard Life's investment policy.[38]

Within a month £8,000 had been advanced to Archdeacon Wilson on the security of property in New Zealand – the first advance against a heritable security outside the United Kingdom.[39]

Formal approval for this change in direction was given in January 1883 when £120,000 was loaned against New Zealand and Australian mortgages.[40] Other loans followed, mostly to sheep-farmers, with sureties provided by partners in Borders textile mills, who had switched to buying cheaper wool from those two countries. The advantage to Standard Life of these loans was that rates of interest in the colonies were much higher than those prevailing at home. By 1885 there was such demand for mortgages from New Zealand that local agents were appointed to value property and draw up deeds,[41] and in 1887 the board formally adopted

The Roman Catholic Bishop Fabre of Montreal to whom Standard Life made large advances for new church buildings, including schools.

St James Street, Montreal, where Standard Life had its office at no. 157 and helped to finance the building at the corner with Victoria Square (top left) in 1895.

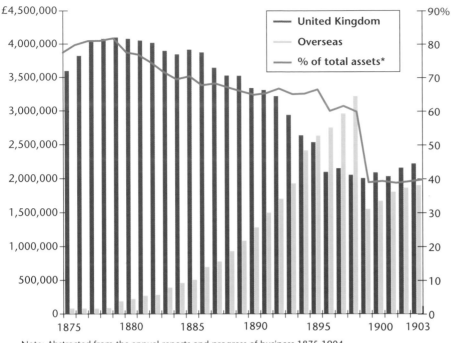

FIGURE 3.1
Mortgages 1875–1903

Note: Abstracted from the annual reports and progress of business 1875-1904

*Total assets include British Government securities, Indian and Colonial government securities, foreign government securities, Indian and Colonial municipal bonds, railway shares and other debentures and debenture stock, bank deposits, house property, stocks of Scottish chartered banks, rents and loans

rules for such investments in the Antipodes. These included a charge on the stock as well as the land, the need for the borrower to have property and a secure source of income in the United Kingdom, and the provision of guarantees by 'a bank or mercantile firm of undoubted standing in this country'. On the whole, preference was to be given to borrowers 'resident in this country and in a responsible position in business'.[42] Standard Life was not alone in pursuing this business; Scottish Widows opened an office in Sydney in 1886 to negotiate mortgages.[43]

Although £50,000 was tentatively contributed to a consortium advancing £200,000 to the Canada North West Land Co. in 1883,[44] Standard Life did not invite proposals for loans from other parts of the world until the financial crises in New Zealand and Australia in the mid-1890s brought the land boom there to an end. Thereafter they diversified swiftly, in 1895 lending $90,000 (£18,000) on land at the corner of St James Street and Victoria Square in Montreal and $300,000 (£60,000) to the Roman Catholic Archbishop of Montreal secured over church property.[45] This marked the start of a long-term relationship with the Catholic Church in North America with several large loans to fund new buildings both to the Church itself and also to religious orders. Funds also began to be made available to cocoa plantations in Trinidad.[46] By the turn of the century Standard Life had become very adventurous, making $200,000 (£40,000) available in 1900 to Señor Alvera in Santa Fé,[47] 700,000 Austrian florins (£58,000) in 1901 to HRH Archduke Joseph, heir to Emperor Franz Joseph, on the security of his Tapolesany estates,[48] and £103,000 in 1903 to the New Club in Johannesburg.[49] This further diversification was prompted largely by the continuing dullness in the market for land in New Zealand and Australia and concerns over the title to property purchased from Maoris, which led to an embargo on all loans in 1902.[50] Overseas mortgages overtook those in the United Kingdom in 1895 and peaked at just over £3.2 million (see Figure 3.1).

Thereafter they declined as the investment strategy changed.

INVESTING IN SECURITIES

Following the cut in interest rates on heritable securities in Scotland in 1881, Spencer Thomson persuaded the board to use Henry Jones Williams, the general secretary for England, to revive the contact with James Capel, the London stockbrokers, and to look out for other investment opportunities in the London market.[51] This led to a change in policy to lending to industry and on city-centre properties. In 1881 some £30,000 was made available to the Appleby Iron Co. and the Mid-Lincolnshire Hematite Iron Co. together to finance expansion.[52] Three years later Standard Life joined forces with the Scottish Union and National Insurance Co. to advance £150,000 to the Barrow Shipbuilding Co., which at that time belonged to the Duke of Devonshire.[53] The most extraordinary industrial loan was 160,000 Danish rigsbank dollars or krone (roughly £16,500) made in 1900 to the Copenhagen shipbuilders and engineers, Burmeister & Wain, representing 50 per cent of the cost of their new works.[54] As significant was the decision to finance property development. During 1882 £75,000 was invested in Members' Mansions in Victoria Street, Westminster, and £60,000 in the Drapers' Building in the City of London.[55] Other property transactions followed not just in London but in Glasgow and the north of England. In 1898, despite the fact that publicans

Robert Fleming (1845–1933), who pioneered investment trusts in Dundee and then founded the London merchant bank which bears his name. He advised Standard Life on their American investments.

were considered a very poor life risk, Standard Life acquired the Crown public house in Rupert Street in London because it was considered to be a good investment opportunity.[56] These two avenues for new investments were a prelude to a more determined assault on the equity market in the mid-1890s.

For more than a decade Scottish investors had been buying speculative stock in American railways and other utilities, which, although high risk, provided healthy dividends.[57] Several investment trusts had been set up to channel savings into such lucrative outlets including those administered by Ivory & Sime in Edinburgh and Robert Fleming in Dundee and later

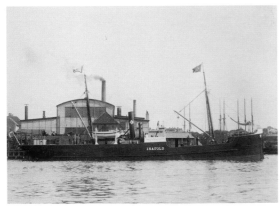

The new engine works at the Burmeister & Wain shipyard in Copenhagen paid for by Standard Life. It was here that the company's well-known marine diesel engine was developed.

The lathe shop in the engine works at Barrow shipyard in Cumbria which was financed in part by Standard Life in 1881.

in London. In July 1891 Standard Life secured permission from its shareholders to reform its investment regulations to allow for the purchase of debentures and preference shares in commercial companies in 'the United Kingdom, India, or any British Colony or Dependency' (shortly afterwards extended to include the United States and other foreign territories).[58] Directly this was known, the board began to receive a steady stream of investment proposals from stockbrokers such as Bell Cowan in Edinburgh, Penny & McGeorge in Glasgow and the newly formed Rowe & Pitman in London,* accountants such as Martin Currie in Edinburgh, and lawyers – all of whom had stock to place. Although the board continued to use Capel's, they turned elsewhere for some advice, notably to Bell Cowan and to Robert Fleming himself, who was retained to help the directors review the existing portfolio of American railway investments in 1897.[59]

Drawing on the accumulated expertise of the London and Scottish financial markets, the spread of investments was remarkable, ranging through a variety of state bonds to railway company stock, including the Niagara Falls Park and River Railway Co.,[60] the Great Northern Railway of Minnesota,[61] the Atchison Topeka and Santa Fé Railway[62] and the Canadian

Atlantic Railway.[63] There were investments in bonds in other parts of the world including Africa, Burma, India and later mainland Europe. The advantage of these foreign stocks was that the rate of return, at between 6 and 7 per cent, was considerably higher than prevailing rates in the domestic market. They were also cheap to administer, with none of the legal costs and hazards of advances against landed property. In a few instances equity investments were accom-

A locomotive on Canada's Grand Trunk Railway to which Standard Life made a substantial loan in 1904.

---

* Fred Pitman, one of the two founding partners of Rowe & Pitman, was the younger brother of Archibald Pitman, a partner in the Edinburgh legal firm of J.& F. Anderson, who had joined the Standard Life board in 1887. Fred Pitman soon began to handle business for both for J.&F. Anderson and Tods Murray & Jamieson, another Edinburgh legal firm with which he also had a close family relationship. The Pitman association with Standard Life continued until Ian Pitman WS retired from the board in 1977. (Andrew Lycett, *From Diamond Sculls to Golden Handcuffs*, London, 1998).

panied by loans on advantageous terms, such as $200,000 advanced to the railway promoter Señor Alvera in Santa Fé in 1901[64] and $800,000 advanced to the Grand Trunk Railway in Canada in 1904.[65] Although the directors exercised their prerogative to reject some recommendations, they were largely reliant on the advice of the growing band of professional investment brokers with specialist knowledge of different markets. For this reason the board, which devoted the bulk of its time to the management of the portfolio, took good care to draw on as wide a range of expertise as possible. By 1903, £4,164,051 was invested in government and local-authority stocks and in equity, a

little more than in mortgages (see Appendix 6 on page 386). Although personal loans on the security of policies continued to be made, they were not actively promoted because they were too small to be cost-effective. One well-known borrower was the Polish-born novelist Joseph Conrad, who took out a loan of £250 in 1901.[66] Overall the painful task of restructuring the investment portfolio had a profound effect on Standard Life's ability to recruit new policy-holders.

GETTING THE BEST OUT OF AGENTS

The agricultural crisis had equally far-reaching ramifications for Standard Life's market for its policies as it had for its investments. The decline in commodity prices and the accompanying fall in rents hit rural incomes and jobs, forcing more people to leave the countryside for the rapidly expanding industrial towns where the company had always been poorly represented. This weakness had long been recognised and many efforts, mostly abortive, had been made to attract urban business. Spencer Thomson, following his father's lead and the inclination of the directors, believed that there was no room for American sales techniques in the United Kingdom market. In 1874 he had firmly rejected a proposed experiment with their use in Ireland, made by William Bentham and endorsed by Henry Jones Williams in London: 'If the American system were introduced into this country . . . our whole system would require to be changed, but I object very much to its introduction . . . although a

Spencer Campbell Thomson's farewell dinner menu (1904) with his portrait and views of his Highland home on the island of Eilean Shona in Loch Moidart. He succeeded his father as manager in 1874 and retired 30 years later.

SPENCER C. THOMSON ESQ:

THE STANDARD LIFE ASSURANCE COMPANY

EDINBURGH 13TH MAY 1904

larger amount of business may be got by pressure on the American plan we do not care to do it.'[67] This angry response failed to recognise that Standard Life's competitors, such as Scottish Amicable, had already started using such methods to attract new business in what was an increasingly crowded market.

Thomson was adamant that the time-honoured system of agencies was the best and cheapest method of recruiting good lives. He was, however, prepared to admit that agents, rather than waiting for business to come to them, had to be encouraged to 'canvas' by regular inspection.[68] After Bentham submitted a detailed report on the lacklustre performance of the Irish agencies early in 1876, Thomson insisted that the remedy lay in Bentham paying more frequent visits to each agent and in the regular removal of agents who failed to produce results.[69] He explained somewhat patronisingly: 'I myself and my assistant manager are only too glad when we can have a few days to perform this duty and any idea of it derogating from our position has never occurred to us.'[70] This was the prelude to a programme of retrenchment. In Scotland, where some local directors had survived the purge south of the border in 1868, all the remaining boards, with the exception of Glasgow, were wound up.[71] An initiative to drum up business in Barrhead to the south of Glasgow through a network of sub-agents was abandoned as a failure with no attempt to investigate the cause.[72] Likewise in England two years later, it was decided to close the Manchester office,

opened in 1872, as the expense could not be justified, to dismiss Stephen Hudson, the local secretary as well as inspector for the north of England, and to appoint a local firm of East India merchants as agents. Since new agents were to be 'men of influence' and the 'inferior class' were to be avoided, not all the existing sub-agents of the Manchester office were offered agencies.[73] This attitude, redolent of a market-town mentality, was ill-suited to the cut and thrust of the new conurbations. The only concession the board was willing to make to American practice was the introduction in 1875 of 'secured payments policies' limited to 11 or 22 payments under which 'a proportionate part of the sum assured is secured, payable at death, in the event of the Premiums being discontinued'.[74]

CONCERN ABOUT EXPENSES

Spencer Thomson's opposition to American methods was almost certainly influenced by the high cost of maintaining offices and employing managers in each district, along with hiring large numbers of canvassers. The returns to the Board of Trade under the 1870 Act, which were published for the first time in 1873, included management expenses. These contained such things as the cost of employing staff and maintaining offices, commissions paid to agents and advertising expenses. When expressed as a percentage of premium income, these were measurably lower than those of North American competitors and were seized on by the financial press as evidence of the robust performance of

British companies.[75] Such a comparison was misleading, as American policies were designed differently from those in Britain and rarely included any bonuses.[76] Moreover, by focusing attention on expenses without using other measures of performance, such as rates of return on investment, commentators encouraged conservative management. Throughout the 1870s the Standard Life directors were preoccupied with the expense ratio to the exclusion of long-term strategic goals. This concern was reinforced by regular criticism of Standard Life in the press, orchestrated by disaffected tontine policy-holders, who were convinced they were being short-changed. Their leader was an Inverness accountant, Andrew Dougall, whose trenchant criticisms were widely circulated and extensively reported. In effect he accused William Thomson of misleading customers: 'I have a strong feeling that I have been deluded.' His attack reached a crescendo after the declaration of the bonus in 1881:

> In 1866 the late manager persuaded me that if I continued a Policy-holder under the Tontine system, the profits added to my Policy would grow in a rapidly increasing ratio. I perceive now that such a result was not only improbable, but absolutely impossible, because the more numerous the new policies became, as they were bound to do year by year, a constantly increasing share of the profits must go to them, and a constantly decreasing share must go to the old policies, by

> which the whole profits were earned, and which were entitled to the whole of the profits made by them.[77]

As a proprietary company, Standard Life was also exposed to criticism for paying too high a proportion of profits to shareholders.[78] In an effort to redress the balance the dividend was cut in 1882, undermining the share price, drawing stinging rebukes from shareholders and further adverse press comment.[79] Coming at the time of one of the most serious recessions in the nineteenth century, these protracted assaults damaged Standard Life's reputation. New premium income and the total income stagnated while at the same time claims mounted, reflecting the age profile of the policy-holders (see Appendices 1 and 2 on page 376 and 378). Successive annual reports put a brave face on the figures. In 1881 the directors declared triumphantly: 'The result is that our Business for the past five years exceeds that of any previous quinquennium.'[80] They were well aware, however, that such comparisons were erroneous as they excluded returns for Minerva, Colonial and Victoria. In grim mood, the Committee on Annual Expenses, assisted by the new home secretary, John H.W. Rolland, an accountant, had already conducted a vigorous review of head-office expenditure. The committee compared Standard Life's practices with other Edinburgh offices where mergers had occurred recently and therefore where expenses were likely to be higher, notably North British and Mercantile, and Scottish Union and National Insurance.[81]

Although the policy of retrenchment and restraint brought temporary relief, it did nothing to address the fundamental problem of recruiting more customers. Responding to a sharp decline in new premium income, the board in the spring of 1878 conducted a wide-ranging review of the 'sources of supply of the company's home business, and the best means of multiplying and invigorating them . . .' From their knowledge of the market, Henry Jones Williams, the general secretary for England, and his inspectors recommended the appointment of 'the smaller class of agents . . . men who send in £500 to £2,000 in the course of the year, but never more'. The directors refused to listen and instead harked back to the cherished 'influential man', who 'from his character and position is able to influence others to the largest extent'. Such a reaction overlooked the past difficulties of finding such men in towns and cities who were not already acting for other life offices, and the introduction of American selling techniques by competitors, which depended crucially on large numbers of small agents or canvassers. There was, however, grudging admission that the failure of the Manchester experiment may have been due more to Stephen Hudson's failure to generate new business rather than to the concept of district agencies, which had been successfully introduced by Scottish Widows. Williams was instructed to identify possible new districts and make efforts to revive representation in Liverpool. Although the system was to be welded

together by the inspectors 'spending some time with any Agent of promise, and urging him to go out with him among his friends', Hudson was not to be replaced as an inspector and his duties in the north-east of England were to be carried out from Scotland.[82]

This work was assigned to a new inspector appointed as a result of an inquiry into the collapse of new business in Glasgow from almost £47,000 in 1875 to less than £10,000 for the first ten months of 1878. Recognising that closure of the branch would be a public admission of failure, Spencer Thomson accepted the opinion of Alexander Sloan, the Glasgow secretary, that Standard Life's commissions were uncompetitive.[83] Revised west of Scotland rates of commission, which improved returns to agents during the first ten years of a policy, were issued and were to be heavily promoted by the new inspector, George Thomson, previously an agent, who also worked two months of the year as librarian of the Church of Scotland.[84] When these rates proved successful in attracting new agents, they were extended to the rest of Scotland and subsequently to the whole of the United Kingdom.[85]

HOME BUSINESS

The first fruits of the reappraisal of home business were the appointment in July 1879 for two years in the first instance of two more local secretaries – Ebenezer Prosser in Bristol and W.H. Taylor, manager of the Staffordshire Fire Office, in Manchester – at annual salaries of £200.[86] Within

a year they were joined by R.B. Duncan, formerly an official with the Raipurtan Railway in India, as district agent in Newcastle.[87] Their initial achievement in three very different cities persuaded the Edinburgh directors to hold a conference with their London colleagues in London in April 1881 to take a fresh look at the company's representation in England. Spencer Thomson, Henry Jones Williams, and William Bentham were in attendance. It was decided to extend the powers of the existing districts by giving them responsibility for canvassing by all the sub-agents within their area and to create two new districts in Liverpool and Birmingham.[88] At the same time Arthur Hines was recruited from the Life Association of Scotland to be local secretary in Liverpool,[89] W. Nichol opened the Birmingham branch in 1883 and two years later the firm of J. & L. Watson started the Leeds branch.[90] The board agreed in 1883 to construct new office blocks in cities with district status 'provided the investment could be remunerative' through renting most of the premises.[91] Williams was also permitted to appoint a superintendent of district branches and additional inspectors to help canvas business.[92]

In Ireland a district was established at Belfast.[93] Alexander Sloan was replaced as local secretary in Glasgow, which was also to be run as a district, by R.E. Forbes, who had been working for the Life Association of Scotland in London.[94] Inch by inch Williams and Bentham were bringing the directors around to their point of view. Although Spencer Thomson in his 1882 annual report publicly endorsed the establishment of districts – 'The extreme competition for life assurance business has rendered this plan of extension necessary'[95] – in private he made it clear that the new arrangements would be judged on their merits. Already George Thomson had been told to work for five months of the year rather than ten, when it was judged that the costs of his inspections 'were greater than the results'.[96] Such insecurity bred distrust when new premium income failed to match expectations. In 1885 Spencer Thomson blamed another poor year on the system of inspection and to the chagrin of the chief inspector in England, George Edwards, attempted to tell him his job.[97]

The real cause of the poor performance was the failure of the board to adopt the new selling techniques and to appreciate that much new life business was now derived from brokers, whose chief purpose was to recommend companies providing the best value for money. Brokers could draw on a number of publications, which ranked insurance companies by various measures derived from the Board of Trade returns. Joseph Allen in *Where shall I get most for my Money* in 1883 put Standard Life 47th out of 81 life offices and reserved the top places for the mutuals.[98] In 1886 William Bourne's widely used *Expenses Ratios of Life Offices* placed Standard Life a long way behind the more progressive Prudential, Scottish Widows and Scottish Amicable.[99] The Prudential with its enormous muscle was diversifying away from its original base as an 'industrial collecting society', providing funeral benefits for the less-well-off, into ordinary life business.[100] In March 1885 the *Insurance Spectator of London* commented on the Prudential results: 'In all the records of life insurance no such announcement has ever been made . . . [the industrial branch] long since passed into the range of the marvellous and now ordinary business begins to assume abnormal proportions.'[101] Although Standard Life sounded a note of caution, suggesting that the Prudential's method of weekly payment was expensive and the number of lapsed policies high, most commentators shared the enthusiasm of the *Insurance Spectator*.[102] Bruised by this experience, the Standard Life board made it a rule in future not to comment on either the performance or products of other life offices – 'we are to stand on our own merits and not on some real or fanciful superiority'.[103] Comparisons with their competitors in the domestic market simply reinforced the board's commitment to reducing expenses at a time when, on the investment side, they were grappling with the serious consequences of the agricultural crisis. Instead the directors looked overseas to enlarge their portfolio of risks. They

KEEPING IN TOUCH WITH THE BRANCHES

In the late nineteenth and early twentieth centuries the most formidable obstacle in managing a large business which was represented in many countries and markets remained communications. The development of the international telegraph in the 1880s had made it much easier to monitor progress. Leonard Dickson, the manager from 1905 to 1919, insisted that results should be wired to Edinburgh to be reported at the weekly meetings of the board, making it possible for the agency manager to keep expenses under constant review.

Most contact, however, continued to be by letter. Although Standard Life had purchased its first typewriters in July 1893, these were used largely for reports and circulars. Dickson preferred to write most of his letters by hand, particularly those which concerned future policy. During the crisis years following the passing of the bonus in 1905, he complained that he was often kept late at 3 George Street dealing with correspondence.

Correspondence with managers was in English, but in many markets knowledge of other languages was essential, particularly in Europe but also in India and Latin America. The board refused to confirm the appointment of David Scott Moncrieff to the Egyptian branch until he had proved himself willing and able to learn French.

Letters to overseas branches, especially to India and the Far East, took several weeks to arrive, by which time the situation might have changed markedly. In such circumstances there was no substitute for regular visits to branches by the manager, the agency manager and the investment manager. These trips were expensive, time consuming and, although not as arduous as in the past, still exhausting, involving as they did thousands of miles of travel by boat and train. When he visited North America in 1909, for example, Dickson was away for two months and made a heroic journey by train across the northern USA to Seattle, returning across Canada by way of Vancouver. By this time he was able to be contacted by telegraph in case of emergency.

Above: Printing the Standard Life diary at the works of George Stewart, 1899. A century later, they still printed the company's diaries.

Left: The Standard Life code book for coding and deciphering cable messages, 1934

Above: The Canadian Pacific liner SS *Empress of Britain*, which provided regular sailings to Canada, 1931

Left: Standard Life's first typewritten letter, July 1893

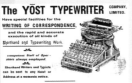

The YŌST TYPEWRITER COMPANY, LIMITED.
Have special facilities for the
WRITING OF CORRESPONDENCE,
and the rapid and accurate execution of all kinds of Shorthand and Typewriting Work.

competent Staff of Operators always employed.

Shorthand Writers and Typists can be sent to any Hotel or Address at a moment's notice.

127 HOPE STREET, GLASGOW.
Telegrams—"Yost." Telephone No. 4979.
ABERDEEN: 137 UNION STREET. EDINBURGH: 17, N. ST. ANDREW STREET.

were in good company. The Royal, the Liverpool and London and Globe, and the North British and Mercantile pursued similar strategies of expansion into foreign markets.[104]

BUILDING BUSINESS IN CANADA

Like his father, Spencer Thomson enjoyed Standard Life's participation in foreign markets; but, unlike the older Thomson, he was prepared to allow managers in different parts of the world greater autonomy. Throughout his career he made regular overseas tours, usually in the company of one of the directors, to observe local conditions at first hand. In the mid-1870s there was no doubt that there was much to be learned from Canadian experience in grappling with the onslaught of American competition. Shortly after William Ramsay, the Canadian manager, intervened to prevent the board from abandoning his experiment with new selling techniques (see page 105), Alfred Shortt, one of his canvassers, visited Edinburgh. Echoing the views of Williams and Bentham, he told Spencer Thomson that the only way to proceed was to adopt American practice by replacing all local agents, who were 'men engaged in other pursuits', with full-time district agents who, 'receiving all commission on old and new business, would find it worth while to work up the business with vigour'.[105] Unconvinced of the merits of district agencies at home, Thomson did nothing until April 1877 when Sir Alexander Galt, the railway magnate and chairman of the Canadian board (in effect a local board), warned

that unless there were radical changes Standard Life would find it difficult to continue to compete in the Canadian market.[106] Direct canvassing was adopted and over the next two years district agents were appointed at Toronto, Pembroke, Bradford and London (Ontario) and in Manitoba and Nova Scotia.[107]

At the same time Galt insisted that new business could only be secured if the existing Canadian tables were overhauled 'to be more in accordance with those of other Companies of good standing'. What he wanted was a reduction in premiums across the board, which he argued could be offset by the higher rates of interest available in Canada (normally 2 per cent above United Kingdom rates).[108] This of course required Standard Life to increase its dollar balances and

Sir Alexander Galt (1817–93), the Canadian railway magnate and sometime Canadian Minister of Finance, who was chairman of Standard Life's local board in Canada. He was the son of John Galt (1779–1839), the Scottish novelist.

THE SELECTION
OF A
LIFE OFFICE.

THE STANDARD
Life Assurance Company.

HEAD OFFICE: EDINBURGH.

HEAD OFFICE FOR CANADA, MONTREAL.

Promotional literature from
Standard Life Canada with a
picture of Edinburgh's Princes
Street on the cover.

investments in North America. Having just lost £26,000 advanced against mortgages in New York as a result of a fraud, the directors needed reassurance that their Canadian investments of some £118,000 were safe. On learning that 'all the investments were of a first-class character' and that the Canadian mortgages were stored securely in a fire-proof safe, they consented.[109] In any case it was hard to argue with someone as distinguished as Galt who had an impeccable Scottish pedigree – his father was the famous novelist, John Galt. By mid-May 1877 Spencer Thomson, on instructions from the Edinburgh directors, had drafted new tables.[110] This was an important victory for Ramsay and his colleagues, leading to further adjustments in the 1880s and to improvements in the terms of policies. He was quick to take advantage of these concessions to recruit and retain a high calibre of staff, whose progress he monitored regularly. Failure was met either with dismissal or a reduction in salary, whereas success was well rewarded. His admiring staff nicknamed him the 'Auld Chieftain'.[111]

Against a background of severe depression in the Canadian economy in the late 1870s which encouraged a mood of economic nationalism, it took some time for the reforms to work through. Insurance legislation in 1877 blatantly discriminated in favour of Canadian life offices, persuading some American and British companies to cease issuing new policies, notably New York Life and the Life Association of Scotland.[112] Although concerned about the prospects of

challenging an expanding Canadian life insurance industry, Standard Life with its long association remained committed to the country. Spencer Thomson did not visit Canada for the first time until 1882, when he sanctioned expenditure on a grand new Canadian head office in St James Street, Montreal.[113] From his experience, he was persuaded to extend home rates to the whole country two years later and, with the completion of the Canadian Pacific Railway, to place Newfoundland and British Columbia under Montreal. The Canadian board was given permission in 1884 to begin writing polices in Montreal from 1887, rather than having them all sanctioned by the Edinburgh head office.[114] By 1885 business had recovered with new sums assured of almost $1.2 million, accounting for some 20 per cent of all Standard Life's sales. This total rose to $1.5 million in 1890 and exceeded, for the first time, $1.7 million in 1894–95. There were serious setbacks in 1887 and 1890, but the overall trend was upwards.[115]

By the 1870s Standard Life was the principal British insurance company in Canada, with net premium income of almost $150,000, over $30,000 more than its nearest rival. By 1890 net premium income had almost tripled and only just failed to equal the combined income of its two main United Kingdom competitors, British Empire Mutual Life and London & Lancashire Insurance. In 1892 Standard Life could claim 42 per cent of all Canadian life assurances accepted by British companies; but as this represented only 3.5 per cent of the market, there was still considerable room for expansion.[116] Under Ramsay, who was now at the end of his career, Standard Life failed to make further inroads, however. This was largely because the Canadian manager, schooled by William Thomson, refused all but the best risks. When Standard Life's results for the 1895 quinquennium were disappointing, Ramsay emphasised that 'security' was paramount.[117] He retired in 1901 and was succeeded by David Mackay McGoun (see page 135), who most recently had been in charge of opening Standard Life's South African branch. Notwithstanding his determined efforts to promote the company in British Columbia and

Manitoba, he was at first no more successful than his predecessor.[118]

TENSIONS IN THE INDIAN MARKET

Just as in Canada, rates for India, Standard Life's largest overseas market, were in urgent need of revision by the mid-1870s because of 'the improvement which has taken place in certain conditions . . . of recent years'. Refusing prudently even to contemplate following the lead of some competitors in insuring Indian lives at home rates, the directors made some concessions for younger lives in new rates published in 1876. At the same time they tackled the growing problem of the depreciation of the rupee due to

A group of Scottish officers with their sepoys in attendance photographed in India. Such men were Standard Life's principal customers in the country.

From left to right: Thomas Lang, George Oliver and George Kemp with two unknown friends on the terrace of the Calcutta office, 1872.

the sharp fall in the price of silver on which it was based. Policy-holders in India had enjoyed the right of paying premiums in rupees and having the proceeds paid in sterling at the official fixed exchange rate of two shillings to the rupee, while the actual market rate was no more than one shilling and sixpence and falling. These privileges, which were expensive for the company, were cancelled in August 1876 when for new policy-holders the market exchange rate was substituted for the official rate. Only the beneficiaries of policy-holders who died in Europe would continue to be paid at the official rate.[119] This still left Standard Life with a considerable liability if the price of silver continued to slide. No sooner had this decision been taken than the company's Bombay agents, the London Asiatic and American Company, went into liquidation. George Kemp, the manager in Calcutta, hurried to Bombay to assess the situation, with letters of introduction to no fewer than 16 businessmen and lawyers. After interviewing them, he recommended that his assistant Thomas Lang should be manager in this fast-expanding western city – 'He thoroughly understands the administration of a Life Office in India, and also the manner in which Agencies are formed and worked to best advantage.' The board agreed and a new branch office was opened in Bombay.[120] In 1877 Kemp proposed that Standard Life take over the small India Life Office with 444 policy-holders insured for a total of £172,000, which had close ties with several Indian banks, especially the Bank of Upper India – a reliable source of good European risks.[121]

Spencer Thomson took the opportunity of putting the finishing touches to this acquisition by visiting India and Ceylon. While there he arranged for the Calcutta office to move into the premises of the Delhi and London Bank in Council House Street. On his return home he recommended that all business should be channelled through Calcutta or Bombay and the two local boards strengthened by the appointment of men with strong connections with the mercantile and banking communities. As a result the Madras agency of Binny & Co. was placed under the Bombay office, the local board discontinued, and all sub-agents in the Madras Presidency made answerable to Lang.[122] The Ceylon agency of Alston, Scott & Co. followed suit in 1882 when the local board was also abolished.[123] From 1881 it was decided to begin accepting native lives, but as neither Indian board was keen to accept such risks, little new business was forthcoming.[124]

Despite the changes in the currency clauses of

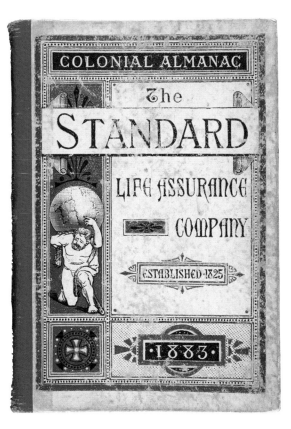

After Standard Life took over Colonial Life, the almanac continued to be published for overseas agents.

policies, Standard Life continued to dominate the Indian market, outperforming the four other offices which actively sought custom in the country, the Commercial Union, Oriental & General Marine, Positive Government Security Life and Universal Life.[125] The Calcutta branch averaged new business of Rs 12-13 lacs a year and Bombay Rs 9-11 lacs, secured by issuing circulars 'four or five times a year to all the best class of Europeans throughout the country and by judicious advertising in the local newspapers and leading periodicals'.[126]

Tensions soon began to appear between the two Indian offices. Kemp, who had effectively laid the foundations of Standard Life's representation in India, believed he should have precedence over Lang, his more junior colleague, and was irritated when the main board in Edinburgh refused him the title of general secretary for India.[127] Nevertheless, they still had to work together. After it was decided to close the dual currency scheme to new policy-holders in 1883 since the price of silver showed no signs of recovery, they pressed in March 1884 for a reduction in rates which were higher than those of competitors. Small modifications were made

in anticipation of a major review of the company's mortality experience in the subcontinent.[128] Conducted in 1887, this resulted in completely new tables which cut premiums for younger lives by as much as 10 per cent and for older lives by about 5 per cent. The impact was immediate. Within a year new policies in Bombay climbed from Rs 12 lacs to Rs 19 lacs sums assured and in Calcutta from Rs 9.7 lacs (admittedly a poor year) to Rs 18 lacs.[129] Impressed by Lang's achievement in Bombay, Spencer Thomson tempted him home in 1887 with the offer of the new post of superintendent of district branches and inspectors based in London.[130]

The bungalow of Thomas Lang, when he was Standard Life's representative in Bombay.

A Standard Life advertisement in *The Times of India*, 1878.

Before he returned he completed a year-long tour of the Far East, following an inspection by Kemp in 1884. His extended visit took in Colombo, Singapore, Penang, Shanghai and ended with five weeks in Japan, which he found remarkably 'like Scotland with the advantage of being free from smoke'.[131] One consequence of these visits was a reduction in the extra premiums for local lives and the extension of home rates to Shanghai, Chefoo, Tientsin and Nanchang, where mortality was low.[132] Lang was succeeded by George Oliver, a former Glasgow inspector who, for a decade, had been the company's third European officer in India.[133]

Kemp, who was on home leave, was furious at his protégé's promotion. Lang had already beaten him in getting approval in 1884 for a purpose-built office in Bombay's Hornby Row and he believed, incorrectly, that Lang would now succeed Henry Jones Williams, the general secretary for England, whose health was failing fast. In a fit of pique Kemp resigned and immediately transferred his allegiance to the Universal as inspector of agencies in India. He toured the country seeking to persuade Standard Life's agents to defect, with some success in the North-Western Provinces and the Punjab, most notably the Alliance Bank of Simla.[134] In the event William Bentham, the company's secretary in Dublin, got Williams' job.[135] Lang agreed to return to India as general secretary for the East with responsibility for India, the Straits Settlements, China and Japan, a post denied to Kemp.[136] George Oliver took over as superinten-dent of district branches and inspectors in the sub-continent.

On his arrival Lang recruited R.H. Seaton of the Alliance bank of Simla as chief agent for the North Western Provinces to keep him informed of Kemp's activities.[137] These did not last long. After 18 months Kemp moved to Sun Life of India, which largely insured native lives, and in the early 1890s joined the Alliance Bank of Simla where he once again acted for Standard Life.[138] Although London & Lancashire Insurance and North British and Mercantile began actively prosecuting business in India in the early 1890s, Standard Life at first held its ground, continuing to gain new custom through established connec-tions with banks both in London and in the Far East.[139] Since Lang discouraged the acceptance of native lives, the company's market remained confined to Europeans, whereas other life offices were filling their registers with good local risks. Nevertheless, returns from India reached a record level in 1893–94, despite Lang's attention being diverted by planning the new prestigious office in Calcutta and by the problems caused by a further deterioration in the exchange rate. Amidst mounting public concern at home about exposure to the collapse of the rupee, the board in Edinburgh decided there was now no alternative but to realise rupee investments to meet current liabilities and, when appropriate, to convert funds into sterling despite the inevitable losses. These would have to be written off at the next valuation in 1895.[140] Altogether Standard Life had invested over Rs 10 million, which was

Edward T.J. Blount, who began his career with the company in Shanghai in 1900 and later became a legendary agency manager.

valued in the balance sheet at just over £1 million (about 15 per cent of the portfolio) using the official exchange rate of two shillings, whereas the real rate had fallen to almost one shilling and two pennies. The company only needed to hold an estimated Rs 3 million to meet its liabilities in India.[141]

By this time Lang was a sick man and he died in England in 1896. He was succeeded in Calcutta by George Stewart, who was left to wrestle with growing competition from both British and American companies. Attracted by more favourable rates and similar comparisons of performance as those available in the United Kingdom, 'a good number of our Assured holding policies for considerable amounts have either surrendered their policies or taken up Paid-up ones in lieu thereof and effected Assurances on their lives with other Offices'.[142] At the same time, the government of India and commercial concerns were opening to Indians positions previously reserved for Europeans. This reduced Standard Life's traditional custom, which was further eroded following the outbreak of the Boer War in 1898 when several regiments were moved to South Africa. In these circumstances there was no alternative but to begin insuring native lives. This was helped by the issue of revised tables in 1902. Of the risks accepted by the Bombay office in 1903 some 40 per cent were native lives, with 16 per cent in Calcutta. Even this change of direction could not halt a decline in business which was more a reflection of outmoded sales techniques than uncompetitive products. Stewart

and his successor in Bombay, F.A. Prevost, continued to rely on direct selling through circulars, appropriate for contacting the relatively small number of Europeans in India, rather than fostering the network of agencies, more suited to recruiting Indian lives. Moreover, in selecting agents, they preferred men with a 'public-school stamp',[143] whereas even the public-school-educated Spencer Thomson was beginning to think 'a more middle-class type of man with his own way to make in the world' might do better.[144]

EXPANDING WORLDWIDE

The indifferent performance of its two principal overseas branches prompted the directors to extend into other countries. For all their pre-occupation with expenses, they cast their net very wide. Almost any country with a European population was considered, however remote. The objective, with a certain air of desperation, was to secure good risks to fill the vacuum left by the failure to break into the urban market at home. Kemp and Lang had already explored the potential in the Far East, but expansion was postponed until after the war between Japan and China in 1894–95. A branch in Shanghai was opened in 1900 with Edward T.J. Blount from the London office as its first secretary.[145] He quickly made an impression, addressing the problem of writing policies in the silver-based currencies of the area and extending the coverage of local lives by recruiting two Chinese canvassers.[146] Austra-lasia was discounted because of local opposition from mutual companies, but Central and South

America were considered to provide good opportunities and could be serviced from the existing base in the West Indies.

Following a visit there by Thomson in 1888, the company's organisation in the region was centralised under Thomas Atkins at Barbados, and agencies and local boards were appointed in Mexico City and in Montevideo.[147] When Atkins died suddenly in 1891, David McGoun took over and energetically pursued an expansion programme. He travelled to most Latin American countries to recruit agents, canvassers and, in some cases, local boards, in Haiti, Cuba, Puerto Rica, Venezuela, Argentina, Brazil and Chile.[148] All these initiatives were failures. At Montevideo the choice as agent of a rich, well-connected American, Señor B. Lorenzo Hill, seemed fortuitous. In an already crowded market he quickly developed a large business; but this soon tailed off and in December 1900 Thomson warned him: 'Unless we can find Inspectors who are capable of securing proposals I fear we shall have to consider the propriety of closing the office altogether.'[149] Hill managed to convince him that what was needed was extra investment, particularly splendid offices to be known as the Standard Palace in Montevideo's most fashionable thoroughfare.[150]

Although the board had considered opening a branch in South Africa in 1887 to take advantage of the goldrush boom, there was no sustained development for a decade when, with spectacularly bad timing, McGoun was sent out to establish a branch with offices at Port Elizabeth.

Standard Life's palatial office in Montevideo under construction in 1904.

The Boer War, which began in 1898, delayed progress and soon after peace was declared the office moved to Johannesburg. As in other parts of the world competition was strong and Standard Life found it hard to recruit suitable agents.[151]

Nearer to home, Spencer Thomson investigated the potential of mainland Europe in 1890, appointing general superintendents for Belgium and Luxembourg based in Brussels, and for Denmark, Norway, Sweden and Finland based in Copenhagen.[152] In Scandinavia Billy Thalbitzer,

An advertisement in Hungarian from 1910 for the Budapest office, which had opened ten years earlier.

the agent, was industrious in establishing agencies and providing a constant stream of advice about investment opportunities.[153] By 1897 he had extended Standard Life's representation as far as Helsingfors in Finland.[154] Although the board were willing to begin lending against mortgages, initially in Denmark in 1898, they had misgivings about the conduct of the agency.[155] Thomson had cautioned Thalbitzer about the need for 'keeping daily in view the question of expenditure'; but this advice was ignored.[156] George Oliver reported after a visit to Copenhagen in 1898 that the branch was 'being conducted in an extravagant and unbusinesslike manner' and that there was little control over the cost of the new office building which was nearing completion.[157] Warned that the office would close if matters did not improve, Thalbitzer was given another chance.[158] There was some immediate improvement, but by 1901 expenditure had again run out of control.[159] Thalbitzer was dismissed the following year and the Scandinavian branch closed with the offices to be controlled directly in the future from Edinburgh.[160] Otto Kaae was transferred from the Budapest office to repair the damage.[161]

After a visit by members of the board to Budapest in 1897, Latzko & Popper had been appointed agents in Hungary.[162] When after two years they had failed to generate sufficient business, they were replaced by Charles Szilagyi who organised the country into eight districts administered from a new Standard Life office in Budapest. Employing an army of more than 300 canvassers, he consistently secured more than £300,000 worth of new risks each year from 1901 until 1904.[163] These results, however, which represented over 13 per cent of all the company's new business, were bought with heavy costs. Within a year of his appointment Thomson had made it clear to Szilagyi that he was operating at a loss, probably because he employed 'dishonest or incompetent' agents.[164] By 1903, with a frightening expense ratio of 51 per cent and escalating lapses, Thomson wrote in alarm: 'We have told you on several occasions that we thought you were moving too fast in the direction of appointing new and untried men, who in most cases brought a large cost upon the company.'[165] The Amsterdam branch, opened at the same time as Budapest, was equally disappointing. Although the experience of doing business in Europe did deter the board from forming a branch in Switzerland and contributed to the closure of the Hamburg agency in 1901,[166] offices were opened in that year in Cairo (largely to cater for Europeans in Egypt) and in Spain during 1904.[167]

NEW PRODUCTS AND HIGHER EXPENSES

The problems Thomson encountered in controlling Standard Life's branches in almost every part of the world raised serious doubts about the wisdom of this helter-skelter race for overseas expansion. Although this diversification was intended to compensate for poor performance at home, it compounded the difficulties by driving up the expenses, which increased from £102,000 in 1886 to £137,000 in 1896, while net premium income only rose from £632,000 to £766,000. In comparison, Scottish Widows' expenses only rose from £77,000 to £96,000, while net premium income climbed from £739,000 to £970,000.[168] Both offices, however, were condemned by the newly formed Insurance Policy-holders Mutual Protection League for their extravagant expenses.[169] In response to such criticism, the Standard Life directors regularly attributed their high expense ratios to the initial start-up costs of their overseas branches. When the *Post Magazine* had the temerity to suggest that the price of entering some markets might be too high, the directors countered that the cost of the foreign business was met entirely by the extra premiums paid by overseas policy-holders.[170] This was hard to believe, particularly as home rates were increasingly applicable in certain markets for European risks, and the cost of employing staff, office rents and inspecting and auditing foreign branches was a general charge against the company. Moreover, as time went on and competition increased from British and American companies following similar strategies, more and more local risks had to be accepted and Standard Life lacked sufficient actuarial knowledge to offer competitive rates. More often than not, adjustments in rates were a reaction to market pressures rather than being based on a sound statistical reappraisal. As with any programme of expansion, it was difficult, once expenditure had been committed, to withdraw from a market and write off the losses, as this would only attract

Standard Life's Cairo office at Midan Soleiman Pasha, opened in 1904.

further press criticism. Probably the most damaging outcome of these foreign adventures was that it diverted the board's attention away from the home market, which was left largely in Thomson's hands.

DIFFICULTIES AT HOME

Conscious that Standard Life was not 'getting the business we ought from several of the large English towns' in the mid-1880s, the terms of policies had been improved to match those of competitors.[171] This work was carried out by the newly appointed assistant actuary, Neil B. Gunn. He had been recruited from Scottish Provident, which was regularly reported as having better products than Standard Life.[172] The first concession in 1885 was to entitle with-profits policy-holders to an intermediate bonus after having

The Leeds Office in 1910. All large insurance companies built prestigious city-centre offices prominently displaying their names to attract custom.

medical examination scheme was introduced for existing policy-holders.[176] This proved so popular that it was extended to all types of policy at the turn of the century and included both India and Argentina.[177]

Williams retired in June 1888, Lang returned to India and Bentham moved to London. At the same time, George Edwards was replaced as inspector of English agencies by his assistant, Andrew A. Wood.[178] With his experience of handling the crisis in Ireland, Bentham set about investigating the underlying cause of the Standard Life's weakness in English cities. He concluded that there was 'no sudden fall, no cause at work which can be seen or which has not been working for years . . .'[179] This clearly came as news to the Edinburgh-based directors, confirming the long-held view of the London directors that they did not understand the predominantly rural composition of their customer base south of the border. In any event, the organisation of the English business was completely overhauled and placed directly under Bentham.[180] Andrew Wood was promoted to general superintendent of branches and agencies for England with instructions 'to receive the monthly reports from the branches, to analyse them with a view of ascertaining that each local manager is properly working his districts . . .' In addition to annual 'surprise' inspection visits, he was also to make regular calls at branches to encourage the staff and learn of any problems.[181] At the same time the districts were given greater autonomy with more control over the agents in their area, a

paid one or more premiums. This had always been a feature of Scottish Widows' policies – much criticised in the early years by Standard Life (see page 46).[173] This was followed almost immediately by bringing bonus rates on the increasingly popular with-profits endowment policies into line with other with-profits products.[174] Such reforms, which were hardly innovative, did little to improve returns until Henry Jones Williams and Thomas Lang, while temporarily superintendent and inspector of branches for England, urged the board to raise commissions by 10 per cent in 1887.[175] In 1889 policies were granted unchallengeable status (entitling the holder to travel or settle anywhere in the world) after two years instead of five, and a year later a limited non-budget for local advertising and power to hand over cheques for matured policies. Nevertheless, there were caveats: district secretaries retained the right to communicate officially with the manager without reference to London, and the northern districts were to continue to be inspected from Scotland.[182] Wood immediately set about his task, visiting the branches and recommending the appointment of more canvassers and travelling agents to work with local secretaries.[183] At the same time, the Glasgow board was abolished and the whole of the west of Scotland, including Dumfries and Galloway, was placed under the Glasgow branch.[184]

The dust had hardly settled after these changes before Bentham and John O'Hagan, the secretary of the West End branch in London, decided in 1892 to take advantage of the pension scheme introduced for all staff from the age of 65.[185] John H.W. Rolland, the company secretary, became general secretary for England based in London, and Neil Gunn, who had succeeded Clunie Gregor as colonial secretary in 1890 became sole secretary.[186] He left within three years to become manager of Scottish Amicable and was replaced by George Oliver, who had succeeded O'Hagan at the West End branch in 1892.[187] The appointment of these men strengthened Spencer Thomson's control over the home market. Although he corresponded with Rolland almost daily, their relationship, even when Thomson was expressing his worst fears for the future of the company, was formal to a fault. Occasionally Thomson responded to Rolland's suggestions but

on the whole he threatened and bullied.[188] When Rolland told him that Standard Life's rates for without-profits policies were still high, he agreed to a reduction early in 1895 in the clear expectation that business would improve. When it did not, retribution was swift.[189] Already Thomson had used his increased authority to cajole the district secretaries in England. In 1894 he had made it clear to the Newcastle manager, R.B. Duncan, that if he continued to devote so much time to the local Sanitary Association instead of canvassing, either his salary would be cut or he would be dismissed.[190] A year later Charles Stewart was summarily dismissed because of the 'want of success of the Manchester Branch' and the Bristol inspector was warned that he could expect a similar fate unless there was a considerable improvement in results.[191] Likewise in 1896 when the Glasgow agent, D.A. Hunter, returned to work after a long illness, he was left in no doubt of the 'absolute necessity of more vigorous work and better results so as to make up for lost time'.[192] These ill-tempered actions were a response to Thomson's growing conviction that 'the English business is going to the devil'[193] and of the dire consequences for Standard Life if it was unable 'to supply the places of those going off by death'.[194] One solution to this problem was another amalgamation and in 1896 there were once more abortive negotiations with Universal Life (see page 85).[195] In a mood of growing anxiety, Thomson refused to believe Rolland that the principal cause of the company's serious difficulties was uncompetitive products and terms for agents. Yet this was the opinion of an increasingly critical and sophisticated insurance press.[196]

PUBLIC CRITICISM

Expense ratios continued to concern commentators and they began to publish comparative tables showing the relative rates of return of similar products from different companies. An Edinburgh actuary in the handbook *Life Insurance Up-to-Date*, published in 1890, ranked the leading life offices as the Equitable, Metropolitan, Prudential (Ordinary Branch), Scottish

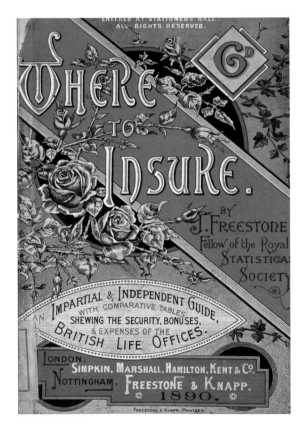

A typical insurance pamphlet of the late nineteenth century purporting to offer impartial advice as to which company to select, published in 1890.

Amicable, Scottish Provident and Scottish Widows. Standard Life did not merit a place.[197] Three years later C. Spensley in *A Thousand Tips about Life Assurance Offices* placed Scottish Amicable well in front of the competition.[198] Charles Cox in *How and Where to Insure* (1903) contrasted the yields for normal life expectancy of with-profits policies taken out at the ages of 30 and 40 with £10 annual premiums. At the age of 30 Scottish Amicable produced £696, Scottish Provincial £701, North British & Mercantile £634 and Standard Life just £608. At the age of 40 Standard Life performed no better.[199] Such statistics, used by brokers to recommend life products, were disturbing. Part of the explanation for the low yields on Standard Life's policies was undoubtedly the weak performance of its investment portfolio, caused especially by the difficulties in Ireland and the rupee exchange; but equally significant were the high costs and poor returns from overseas expansion and the failure to retain or recruit new custom at home. Net profits at Standard Life only rose from £265,000 in 1886 to about £351,000 in 1899 with funds advancing from £6 million to £9 million, whereas Scottish Widows' net profits soared from £358,500 to £555,550 with funds almost doubling from £9 million to £17 million.[200]

Until Standard Life could improve its revenue, agents at least in the home market were fighting an uphill struggle. Even if they could secure new lives, there was the ever present danger that policy-holders would be enticed to switch to other offices which seemed to offer more attractive terms. Judging from the returns, this appears to be what was increasingly happening after the turn of the century. Nevertheless, Thomson continued to blame the agents for the company's shortcomings. In June 1897 he wrote to Rolland: 'I am sorry to see such a large falling off in the English business. Something must be done,'[201] and two years later he urged: 'Birmingham and Bristol must be tackled at once – and Manchester has something wrong with it too. One hears of little offices like the City of Glasgow and even Scottish Life doing much more than we do.'[202] The number of lapsed policies reached record levels in 1900. Although he realised correctly that 'a large proportion of our English business is of an unstable character and not the permanent family class which is most desirable', Thomson still persisted in finding fault with the district secretaries and agents.[203] Dismayed by the collapse of the English market, which had been the cornerstone of the policy register, he decided to bring it under his own control by abolishing the London board but he had no clear marketing strategy to put in its place.[204] Where other life offices had started to arrange annual conferences of their local secretaries and principal agents to report progress and learn about conditions in the market, all Thomson could do was to criticise. The London directors, who all still had seats on the main board, were furious and did their best to frustrate the proposal: 'The Management of the English business from Edinburgh, besides being inconsistent with its very nature of English business and

a departure from the practice of 59 years, would necessarily be productive of great inconvenience and delay in carrying on of business and would also prejudicially affect the obtaining of fresh English business . . .'[205] Their main concern was that Thomson and the Edinburgh directors simply did not understand the changing nature of the English market, which had a much greater demand for endowment policies to pay for house purchase or to provide for retirement from work than in Scotland. By the time this dispute came to a head in 1903, all the directors had compelling reasons to be concerned with Thomson's management of the company.

WEAKNESS EXPOSED

The quinquennial investigations since 1875 were based on the English Life Table (No.1) which had been calculated by the Registrar General from the mortality experience for the whole of England and corresponded closely with the company's own experience. By 1890, however, actuaries considered these tables to be inaccurate. The Institute of Actuaries had already published its own tables, which the *Post Magazine*, in commenting on the results of the investigation of that year, recommended in preference to the English Tables.[206] Such objections were the prelude to a major review of mortality experience by the Institute and the Faculty of Actuaries, using data for the previous 30 years from life offices and the Registrar General. This was a massive undertaking, in which Standard Life took part, and it was not until after the 1901 investigation was complete that the new ordinary males (O^m) and the ordinary annuities (O^a) tables were complete.[207] The findings in both tables were that men and women, who took out life policies, were living longer. Although this was welcome news for life assurance business, it was bad news for annuities, requiring companies with a large commitment to make bigger provisions at their investigations particularly if the lower interest rate of 3 per cent was used. Standard Life had always had a large exposure to annuity business, with annual outgoings in 1901 of over £90,000, compared with just £21,000 at Scottish Widows and £22,000 at Scottish Provident.[208]

It did not require an elaborate analysis to guess what effect the adoption of these tables would have on the Standard Life balance sheet at a time when the growth in net income was failing to keep pace with rising expenses. The reserves had already been seriously depleted by writing off £77,500 against property losses in Ireland in 1890 and £425,438 in losses on the rupee exchange – altogether more than 6 per cent of the company's assets. In both cases the directors had put a brave face on these decisions. They explained with great circumspection in 1891 'now that these unfortunate investments (made, it must be remembered, when Irish securities were looked upon with favour, and indeed sought after) have been dealt with in detail in the light of existing circumstances, and with the benefit of information obtained from persons skilled in the value of Irish property, the

Committee and the board feel but little anxiety for the future'.[209] In 1895 the full extent of the rupee exchange loss, which was described as 'only a book entry', was disguised.[210] Having rejected the possibility of passing the bonus so as to strengthen Standard Life's position, the directors used 'hidden' reserves (in other words, not separately identified in the balance sheet) to maintain it. To his credit Thomson cautioned against this course of action as it was at 'the expense of using up Reserves, which had better have been retained'. One casualty of this decision was the postponement of the building of a new Edinburgh head office on the George Street site to designs by Peddie & Brown. Neil Gunn, who attended the public meeting at which the results of the investigation were declared, wrote from Scottish Amicable to congratulate Thomson on having 'done the right thing by burying the Rupee question out of sight. You may and probably will lose a portion of your business – but loss of business does not necessarily mean loss of profit . . .'.[211] In his constant search for new lives in many different markets, this was a lesson Thomson never learned. Although improvements in both the rupee and in Ireland allowed the bonus to be maintained in 1900 and the construction of the new head office to go ahead, there was almost no fat left in the balance sheet.[212] Moreover, the results of all these investigations continued to be greeted with a litany of complaint from the tontine policy-holders, who remained convinced they were still being badly treated.[213]

No.3 George Street, Edinburgh, the site of Standard Life's
head office from 1839 to 1996. This building was constructed
in 1900 to designs by the well-known Edinburgh architects
Peddie & Brown.

THE MANAGER GOES

By early 1903 the directors were convinced that Standard Life was in difficulty, overstretched and unable to compete effectively with its Scottish rivals. Surrenders were escalating and net premium income still lagged behind that of Scottish Widows.[214] At the end of May Spencer Thomson gave notice that he would retire at Whitsun 1904 after 30 years as manager but short of his 65th birthday, ostensibly to leave his successor time to conduct the 1905 investigation on the basis of the new O^m and O^a tables.[215] He was almost certainly encouraged to go, as with uncanny speed the directors nominated one of their own number, Leonard W. Dickson, a chartered accountant who had joined the board in 1900, as his successor.[216] Against a background of runaway expenses which had climbed from £165,000 to over £190,000 in three years, they began to review the company's operations both at home and overseas. Within weeks George Oliver was sent to India to carry out a thorough investigation of the underlying causes of the decline in business.[217] The Dublin premises were sold to the Northern Bank, Belfast, and part of the Bombay office to William Watson & Co.[218] The contract for the new premises in Montevideo was suspended.[219] Although the board understood the reasons for the concern of the London directors about the future conduct of the English business, the London board (still in effect a committee of the main board) was nevertheless abolished. It was replaced by a local board of four directors who no longer held seats on the main board.[220]

In the closing months of his career Spencer Thomson can have had no doubt that he had failed in his stewardship of his father's legacy.[221] He was not solely responsible, however. The directors had encouraged the overseas expansion. Although unconcerned with the detail of the salesforce, they had insisted that Standard Life continue to appoint the better class of man as agents and focused attention on the expenses ratio to the exclusion of other yardsticks of competitiveness. Overall, the greatest obstacle to progress since Spencer Thomson's appointment had been the long crisis in agricultural Britain, which could not have been predicted. This had eroded the company's traditionally strong representation in rural Scotland, England and Ireland and forced attention on urban centres where there had been constant difficulty in gaining a foothold. In the circumstances, the decision to extend foreign activities was logical. The failure of both the manager and the board was to control the expanded business effectively and to recognise that the market for their products was changing, particularly outside Scotland where saving for saving's sake remained a virtue. Their achievement was in decisively changing the investment strategy away from domestic mortgages towards overseas securities which gave better returns.

CHAPTER FOUR

'TO IMPROVE OUR BASIS OF VALUATION': 1904–19

'The two things which I desire more than any others are to bring down expenses and to improve our basis of valuation. The second really depends upon the first.'

Leonard Dickson, the manager, to John H.W. Rolland, general secretary for England, 6 April 1905.[1]

The opening years of the twentieth century were an inauspicious time to attempt to rebuild any business. After a boom in the late 1890s, the world economy was in serious recession and interest rates were low. In many sectors companies ran for shelter by joining defensive amalgamations or, hopelessly overstretched, were taken over or simply succumbed. This was the era of the birth of Britain's first large-scale enterprises and the insurance industry was not exempt. Several long-established, well-respected and sizeable companies were swallowed up, such as the Hand-in-Hand by Commercial Union in 1905, Provident Life by Alliance and the Westminster & General Life by Guardian in 1906. The creation of massive integrated fire, accident and life companies was undoubtedly encouraged by the Employers' Liability Act of 1906. Because it applied for the first time to all types of employment, it led many corporate customers to seek cover for all their risks from one company. Reflecting on events of the previous four years, the Actuary of the Royal

Exchange Assurance commented perceptively in 1911 that life business would be dominated in the future by 'influential "composite" companies transacting all classes of business' and by 'a few large mutual offices, who, by maintaining a high rate of bonus in the future, will be enabled to support a separate existence'.[2]

In a nutshell this was the dilemma which confronted Leonard Dickson when he entered the manager's office in May 1904: how, in the face of such pressures, could Standard Life – with its record of poor bonuses and high expenses – survive. As a proprietary company with a tiny number of shareholders, there was nothing to prevent a predator launching a hostile bid on attractive terms, which it would be difficult to defeat. The only scrap of comfort Dickson had was that Standard Life, despite its mixed performance, was too big to be acquired by all but the largest companies. If Standard Life was to remain independent, he knew instinctively that he had to develop clear strategies and make the day-to-day direction of the business more effective and

Leonard Walter Dickson
(1867–1919), the manager from
1904 to 1919, with his son,
Thomas, at Monybuie, his
Kirkcudbrightshire home, during
the First World War.

clear cut. Immediately he developed a rapport with John H.W. Rolland, the general secretary for England, whom he regarded as essential in re-establishing the company's base south of the border. His predecessor, Spencer Thomson, had treated Rolland badly, repeatedly interfering directly with the branches under his control in the south of England. Dickson reassured him by insisting that it was essential for the directors to meet regularly with the members of the new London local board to gain first-hand knowledge of the English market.[3] With more than 50 per cent of new premiums coming from outside the United Kingdom, Dickson appreciated that rebalancing the business would take time. It was essential that the management and control of the foreign operations should be improved as quickly as possible. Within weeks he had also written to all the Standard Life agents at home and overseas to ask for their continued loyalty, and by the end of the year he had visited the Scandinavian and Hungarian branches to assess their performance.[4]

FIRE-FIGHTING ABROAD

Dickson's most pressing problem in May, however, was to respond to George Oliver's gloomy report on the Indian business, which had been commissioned a year before (see page 144). He wrote to the two secretaries in India, George Stewart and F.A. Prevost (see page 134), making it clear that the board no longer considered the old gentlemanly way of doing business appropriate: 'It is quite necessary in these days of keen competition to adopt a more commercial and pushing style of transactions and seeking business than in the past.' All agents were to be visited every year and alternative rates of commission were introduced as an inducement. 'Special native agents' were to be appointed in Bombay and Calcutta but were to confine their activities as far as possible to 'natives possessing a knowledge of English, such as Government Servants, Barristers, Pleaders, Judges in the Mofussil [country districts], Clerks in European firms, Banks, etc.' who were thought to be a better risk.[5] Disappointed with the slow progress in implementing these reforms, Dickson wrote again in November 1904 expressing the hope that there would be an improvement in the coming bonus year.[6] When matters still showed no sign of getting any better, Prevost, who was home on leave, was quizzed by the Edinburgh board in June 1905. On learning that, if the business was to grow, there was now no alternative but to cultivate native business more generally, the directors endorsed plans for appointing new Indian agents in Lahore, Bangalore, Shimoga and Madurai.[7] The effect was rapid, with a marked upturn in business which now represented some 10 per cent of all Standard Life's new risks.[8] Any optimism was soon quenched by news of George Stewart's death of typhoid on Christmas Day at the age of just 39.[9]

Hungary presented a much more intractable problem. After an audit revealed a total loss since the branch opened in 1898 of 2 million Kreuzers

Edward Blount, the agency manager, with Charles Szilagyi, the company's representative in Budapest, and Thomas Darling, who also worked in Hungary and later in South Africa, photographed after the war.

(some £80,000), Dickson's reaction was to close it as the cost was 'more than the company could afford'. Before taking such drastic action, the board insisted on a visit by a deputation of directors.[10] They were persuaded by the manager, Charles Szilagyi, that expenditure would be cut, despite his past history of ignoring similar undertakings. They even mildly rebuked Dickson by telling him: 'We are not satisfied that we can judge a young branch at any period of its existence by simply striking a balance between surplus of actual receipts over expenses on the one hand, and the actuarial sum required for reserve on the other.' As a result the branch was given a reprieve for a further two years.[11] As Dickson predicted, Szilagyi had no intention of reducing costs and instead chose to seek more new risks at whatever the expense. Although new business climbed by £40,000, it was only secured at a high price and the ratio of expenses

to new premium income actually rose from 144 to 150 per cent.[12] It was to be another 20 years before Standard Life finally left Austria-Hungary. Dickson met similar opposition to his attempt to withdraw from Scandinavia. Although most of the agencies in Denmark, Finland, Norway and Sweden were closed, the offices in Copenhagen, Stockholm and Christiana remained open but were refused permission to employ expensive canvassers.[13] He did get his way in closing down the hopelessly unprofitable Amsterdam branch in 1905.[14]

By contrast, the newer offices in Barcelona, Cairo and Johannesburg were encouraged, at least in the short term, as prospects appeared to be good. In the first seven months of operation in Spain during 1904 Ernest Noble, the agent who had previously worked for Sun Life, secured 74 policies valued at just under £38,000. Noble with his partner, Señor M. Calzado, also acted as agents for the non-life business of the London and Lancashire Insurance Company.[15] Their success encouraged Standard Life to open offices in Cadiz in 1906.[16]

Elsewhere in the world, although there were causes for concern, such as the recession in North America and the continuing flouting of the company's rules by Lorenzo Hill, the agent in Montevideo (see page 135), the returns were sufficiently healthy not to warrant immediate investigation. The only new development Dickson vetoed was the formation of a branch in Japan after Standard Life's application to the government for registration failed. Dickson noted accurately, 'Japan for the Japanese will more and more be the cry.'[17]

CHALLENGE AT HOME

Undoubtedly Dickson's chief preoccupation, like the Thomsons' before him, was how to break into the English urban market. He was conscious that disengagement from the overseas market would have been suicidal if there was little indication of any recovery at home. Between 1900 and 1905 the value of policies in force in the domestic market as a proportion of those in force abroad fell by nearly 3 per cent.[18] With Rolland's advice, Dickson's first effort early in 1905 was to circulate all military centres and garrison towns in the United Kingdom. Standard Life was already well known to those leaving for overseas postings, both for the competitiveness of its policies and the attractive terms of its loans.[19] In April he decided to abandon expensive advertisements in national newspapers in favour of local campaigns.[20] This was a prelude to a thorough review of expenses, which had continued to nudge upwards everywhere, exceeding 21 per cent of premium income in 1904 compared with about 10 per cent at Scottish Widows. By this time Dickson had come to the conclusion that the home establishment was over-staffed and required to be completely overhauled, beginning with inspectors who were failing to recruit sufficient business – 'The men themselves must see that it is out of the question for the Company to go on paying them for such wretched results.'[21] At a time when the demand

for life cover was depressed, prospects for recovery were not good, but Standard Life was still slipping behind its rivals in the home market. In Newcastle upon Tyne R. Cook Watson, who had replaced the lackadaisical R.B. Duncan in 1903 (see page 139), was only able to make an initial impact before being overwhelmed by the competition in 1906.[22] As the author in a personal capacity of *Life Assurance Premiums charged by various companies for the guidance of brokers*, Cook Watson was well aware that Standard Life's products were without exception poor value.[23]

PASSING THE BONUS

Nevertheless, as a result of growth in overseas markets, albeit at considerable expense, total new business did reach new peaks of £2.5 million of sums insured and over £125,000 of premium income in 1904–5.[24] Even more encouraging was a sharp decline in surrenders. With this better news Dickson and the company's actuary, George Cameron, turned their attention to the difficult task of the 15th quinquennial investigation. Apart from the almost predictable impact of the use of the new O^m and O^a tables on the results (see page 142), the investigation also had to take into account a decline since 1896 in the value of all stock-exchange investments, which represented some 40 per cent of total assets. It soon became clear that there would be no alternative but to pass the bonus so as to improve the strength of the balance sheet. In part this was to satisfy the

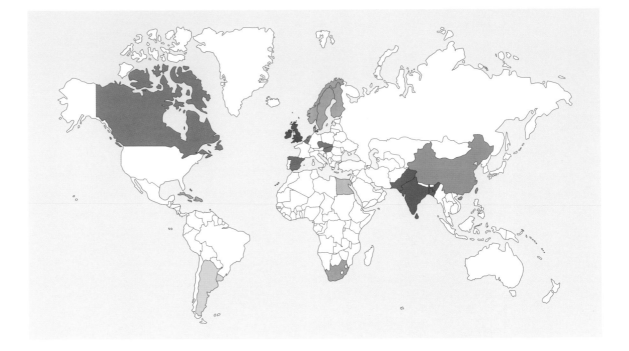

■ United Kingdom 31%

■ Scandinavia 4%

■ Hungary 13%

■ Belgium 2%

■ Spain 2%

■ Canada 18%

■ India 10%

■ West Indies 4%

■ South Africa 5%

■ South America 7%

■ China 2%

■ Egypt 2%

FIGURE 4.1
Distribution of new sums
assured 1905

Note: Taken from Standard Life's
archive material

exacting criteria of the insurance legislation in some of the countries in which Standard Life did business. It was decided to write £188,000, about 5 per cent, off the value of investments, and because of Standard Life's large annuity commitments to make a provision of £483,000 as a consequence of adopting the new tables.[25]

There was no doubt there would be repercussions. Dickson was concerned that his predecessor Spencer Thomson, who was largely responsible for the crisis, might challenge the basis of the valuation and whip up resentment amongst the shareholders – with fatal consequences for the future of Standard Life. For this reason he went out of his way to consult Thomson at every step, even leading him to believe he had suggested

passing the bonus and persuading him to draft the 'report by the board to the annual meeting and also the chairman's speech'.[26] By accepting some of the blame, Thomson suffered the humiliation of having his pension cut permanently by the board from £2,500 to £2,000 a year.[27] The dividend to shareholders was declared at the existing rate of 10 per cent but with no added bonus, even though there was a danger that with-profits policy-holders, who had been denied a division of the profits, might mount a legal challenge.[28] The other consequence, which could be predicted from the advice offered by insurance brokers to would-be policy-holders,[29] was that the balance of new business would move sharply away from with-profits towards without-profits policies until a bonus was declared. This was almost certainly what Dickson hoped, as such a shift would only serve to reinforce the balance sheet further by yielding good returns while at the same time reducing the proportion of policy-holders entitled to share in the profits. He actively promoted the growth of without-profits business in the design of new products. Much of the life assurance industry failed to grasp the significance of this relationship. Even in the 1980s and 1990s, many demutualisations were a direct result of companies writing more with-profits business than they had capital to support.

With the hatches well battened down, the outcome of the 15th investigation was presented to a meeting of shareholders on 10 May 1906. The report was masterly, playing to strengths and providing a full explanation as to why the use of the up-to-date O^m and O^a tables had resulted in the passing of the bonus. To sweeten the pill and as a token of good faith, with-profits policy-holders were offered an intermediate bonus of 1 per cent for every year after 1905 on claims maturing before the next investigation.[30] Only the most senior of Standard Life's officials were warned in advance of the meeting; the rest of the staff and agents learned the news afterwards individually from Dickson. In his letters he emphasised that, despite 'the intense disappointment', Standard Life was 'stronger and more able to face the world than it has ever been.'[31] The press reception was mixed. The leading daily papers were hostile. *The Times* condemned the high expense ratio and called for early cuts in the overseas operations. The insurance and financial press was less harsh. The *Insurance Observer*, referring to the use of the new tables, commented encouragingly: 'These striking and valuable reforms, which will enable Standard Life to hold its own against the most powerful competition in all countries where business is carried on, could not be carried out without some immediate sacrifice . . .' The *Post Magazine* reflected later that 'passing bonus sometimes wins praise for a company which perhaps somewhat belatedly has decided to strengthen its reserves at the expense of its immediate popularity'.[32]

Any hopes which the board might have had that the skilful presentation of the results would forestall a hostile response were soon dashed when a committee of with-profits policy-holders was formed in London to commence legal proceedings. There was no doubt that this was a serious challenge. The committee was chaired by Sir Christopher Furness, one of the most able and determined business leaders of his generation. He was both a borrower and a policy-holder. The secretary was Maurice Jenks, a respected London lawyer. The committee retained Sir Robert Finlay, a future Lord Chancellor, to represent them and advertised the intended action in national newspapers in the United Kingdom and India, calling for the support of other policy-holders.[33] As there was no precedent for such a case, press interest was intense, whipped up particularly by the mercurial financial commentator Horatio Bottomley in his newly founded paper *John Bull*, which was later to run a vindictive campaign against the Prudential.[34] *John Bull* and other papers printed letters from with-profits policy-holders complaining that since they had paid more than without-profits policy-holders they were entitled to compensation.[35] Standard Life warned its staff around the world, however provoked they were, 'on no account to enter into newspaper correspondence'.[36] The board quickly retained Charles Scott Dickson, a Member of Parliament and Dean of the Faculty of Advocates, and James Clyde, later Lord President of the Court of Session, to act for them.[37]

Sir Christopher Furness (1852–1912), chairman of the committee of policy-holders, who threatened legal proceedings against Standard Life after the passing of the bonus in 1905.

With the battle lines drawn, Leonard Dickson urgently sought to prevent such a high-profile and damaging engagement. He instructed Rolland to build a working relationship with Furness in the hope that he 'may "smash up" the agitation'.[38] This tactic was largely successful as, unlike some members of the committee, Furness accepted that 'the welfare of the company should be the first consideration'.[39] The committee's main objection was not to the passing of the bonus but to the payment of dividends to the shareholders during the period covered by the quinquennium. This hinged on the delicate point as to whether the directors had any inkling that the bonus would be passed before the investigation had taken place. Although it seems unlikely that an accountant of Dickson's ability could not have easily guessed the likely outcome, he strenuously denied any such knowledge. He was, however, prepared to consider the committee's suggestions for reform.[40] The proposal that the policy-holders should be represented on the board was turned down out-of-hand, while the concept of terminating dividend payments in anticipation of future profits and fixing the proportion of profits divided between shareholders and policy-holders at 9:1 was accepted and approved. At the same time it was agreed to hold interim investigations to give fair warning of a similar crisis in the future.[41] After protracted negotiations following the issue of a writ in the High Court in London, the committee were satisfied with this response and withdrew their action in October 1907.[42]

The case, however, was not closed, as one of the committee's members, Otto Barlein, a Manchester merchant, issued his own writ in November, claiming he was entitled to a 'reasonable share of the company's profits earned during the said quinquennium'.[43] There was no possibility of negotiations, as to admit there was any justification in such an assertion would have had serious repercussions not just for the management of Standard Life but the whole life industry at a time when other companies were being forced to pass or cut their bonuses. The case, the first of its kind, was tried in Manchester in May 1909. Defended by two of the most respected commercial counsels, Rufus Isaacs (later Marquess of Reading) and Robert Younger (later Lord Blanesburgh), Standard Life won the case.[44] An immediate consequence of these legal proceedings and another contemplated action in Denmark[45] was the need to limit the liability of the shareholders in the event of large damages being awarded against the company. A new Act of Parliament in 1910 incorporated The Standard Life Assurance Company as a limited company, allowing shares for the first time to be quoted on the stockmarket.[46] Dealing with the lawyers and drafting the legislation distracted the attention of Dickson and his directors for almost three years, when they should have been devoting their energies to addressing the company's deep-seated problems. For Dickson the only good that came of all this activity was that it spelled out clearly to his directors the precariousness of Standard Life's position and made them

reluctant to challenge his judgement in the future.

DRIVE FOR EFFICIENCY

The passing of the bonus did not seriously affect the volume of new business, which declined to a little below £2 million of sums assured in 1907–8 and hovered around that level until 1914. New premium income, on the other hand, declined more sharply from about £106,000 in 1905 to £86,500 in 1910 as cheaper without-profits policies became more popular both at home and overseas.[47] Of perhaps more concern to Dickson was the rapid escalation of surrenders at Standard Life, which soared from £68,000 in 1905 to £110,294 in 1906 and remained at above this level until 1908. Although other Scottish life offices experienced rises, Standard Life's record was the worst, a reflection of the adverse publicity surrounding the lawsuits.[48] Dickson was not greatly troubled by either the only-to-be-expected loss of custom or the lack of growth in new business except for the impact it might have on the expenses ratio. As he readily admitted to Samuel Robinson, the Dublin secretary, in 1907, 'What we need are substantial bonus results, and I have not the least desire to see inflation for the sake of inflation . . . I can assure you that nothing is more present to me than the crying need for economy in all directions. The difficulty is that we have a huge permanent staff all over the world and if our premium income goes down through the want of new business, the salaries of the staff remain practically constant and up goes the ratio of expenses'.[49]

As a first measure all salaries were frozen in April 1906 and increases were only allowed for 'exceptionally deserving cases' and then had to be paid for out of economies made elsewhere.[50] Recognising that the company was in serious danger of losing its best staff to competitors, Dickson introduced a system of annual confidential staff reports – 'I certainly wish to know whether one man is quick and interested in his work and another the reverse.'[51] Tied by the legal actions and the need personally to keep control of the Edinburgh head office, Dickson in February 1908 recalled Edward T.J. Blount, the secretary in Shanghai, to the new post of general superintendent of foreign agencies (extended two years later to include the United Kingdom with the abbreviated title of agency manager). His responsibilities included all Standard Life's overseas operations with the exception of Canada, which Dickson kept in his own hands.[52] This was an inspired appointment. Blount was a natural auditor, who used his excellent actuarial skills with great effect in scrutinising the performance of the branches in the context of the business as a whole. His lengthy, searching reports explored every nook and cranny of a branch's activities and were full of suggestions of ways of improving performance.

With such a useful lieutenant, who could be relied on to implement and develop policy, Dickson was free to concentrate on strategy and on restoring Standard Life's tarnished public image. He summoned all the branch secretaries in the United Kingdom and Europe to a conference in Edinburgh to discuss the future direction of the company.[53] His first concern was to calculate, with Blount's help, a formula for measuring the cost-effectiveness of any branch or agency irrespective of its location. This was an important decision as it prevented local secretaries from advancing special mitigating circumstances for excessive expenditure, as had happened in Hungary in 1905 when Dickson had been overruled by his board. The first yardstick was that total expenses of any branch or agency (with the exception of the permanent staff and office rents paid for by the head office) should not exceed 70 per cent of its new premiums and 4 per cent of renewals.[54] This was later revised for some branches to 80 per cent and 8 per cent to cover all expenses including the staff and rents. Any branch or agency which exceeded these guidelines could expect the most rigorous investigation and a stern refusal to sanction any further expenditure, however modest, until returns improved.[55]

COMPETITIVE REVIEW

Dickson realised that this crude measure alone was not enough to gauge the health of any branch and he insisted that secretaries and agents should make every effort to recruit only new customers who could be expected to hold their policies until maturity. He was well aware that this almost certainly implied a change in sales strategy away from whole-life policies which actuaries believed everyone ought to purchase, towards endowment policies linked to loans or the purchase of annuities to provide pensions, which customers increasingly wanted.[56] In adopting this course Standard Life was following the market, with endowment policies accounting for more than 60 per cent of all new policies in the United Kingdom by 1910.[57] The experience in other countries was similar.

Dickson wished to provide a range of competitive products to capture a good slice of this business. A new well-priced United Kingdom without-profits endowment scheme, modelled on those available in America, was introduced in 1906. Terms of surrender were liberal and cleverly designed to increase at least in the short term the proportion of without-profits policies. There were three options guaranteed at maturity: a lump sum to pay off a mortgage or a loan; the purchase of an annuity for the remainder of the life; or a cash payment and the ability to remain insured under a with-profits policy for a fixed sum without further premiums. It proved so popular that it was extended to other countries in 1907, when another new endowment policy to help pay for children's education by means of annuities was launched. This was followed in 1911 by improved terms for the revival of lapsed policies and a new system of deferred assurance for children, known as the Early Thrift Scheme, which matured at the age of 21.[58] Delighted with its appeal, further more attractive products were launched and at the same time the terms of personal loans were improved. Although Standard Life had in the past been reluctant to pursue such

Advertisement for a minimum premium policy, revised in 1909 as part of Dickson's review of Standard Life's products.

business, Dickson recognised that the market was changing, with more and more people wishing to borrow against the security of an endowment policy to buy and furnish their homes. Not only were such borrowers provident, they could also be guaranteed to hold policies until maturity.[59]

David Lloyd George, the Liberal Chancellor of the Exchequer, imposed higher rates of tax on 'unearned' income in 1907, and in his famous 'People's Budget' in 1909 introduced super-tax for those earning more than £5,000 a year and raised both income tax and death duties to pay for old-age pensions. Although life insurance premiums had been fully tax-allowable and payments on maturity free of duty since 1853,[60] this concession had not been exploited by life insurance companies in their marketing because few people were affected and levels of tax were relatively low. These increases made life policies a very inviting investment with a return of about 10 per cent for those with large salaries or dependent on 'unearned' income.[61] With this market in view, Standard Life revised its basic endowment rates to bring them into line with those of other major

Brochure advertising the new without-profits endowment policy with three options, 1906.

companies and launched new without-profits policies designed specifically to protect a family's capital from the damaging effects of death duties.[62] As was hoped, these new products proved popular amongst the better-off. Unlike those of its major competitors, the average value of Standard Life's new policies increased, suggesting they were being purchased by well-to-do taxpayers, and the volume of surrenders fell significantly if only temporarily. As a result of the success of all the new products the percentage of without-profits policies, already higher at Standard Life than at the other principal Scottish life offices because of the poor bonus performance, climbed from 30 per cent in 1905 to almost 40 per cent in 1910, remained above 35 per cent until the outbreak of war and returned to 40 per cent by 1919.[63] This ratio, however, was a long way behind Norwich Union and Legal & General, the two offices with among the best bonus records at the time, which had a 50:50 split.[64]

WITHDRAWAL FROM EUROPE

Convinced that the branches throughout the world were now being given products to achieve their expenses targets, Dickson with Blount's assistance reviewed all the company's overseas activities. By this time insurance companies were required under the provisions of the Assurance Companies Act of 1909 to disclose in returns to the Board of Trade foreign investments at current prices and the prevailing rate of exchange. The background to this legislation was an inquiry into the industry in the United States which had revealed a quite extraordinary degree of mismanagement and absence of control of extensive foreign operations, confirming much of the criticism levelled at American companies by the British insurance press. Despite plenty of evidence that rates of return were uniformly higher and that even Standard Life's expense ratio was modest in comparison to American companies, these devastating findings were seized on by the Insurance Policy-holders Mutual Protection League (an organisation set up in the 1880s to provide policy-holders with independent advice) as proof that things were no better in the United Kingdom industry. Standard Life was singled out by the League for having only won its case in Manchester by 'introducing obscure and puzzling clauses into their contracts'.[65] More damaging were accusations by E. Piercy Henderson, a self-appointed insurance ombudsman and a long-standing thorn in Standard Life's side, that the company had been guilty of 'fraudulently' misleading prospective policy-holders.[66] In particular he represented General Sir Horace Smith Dorrien, whom he had convinced of having been mis-sold a policy in India of Rs 60,000 (£5,000) in 1902.[67] Although he subsequently withdrew the charge, the damage had been done in a series of pamphlets which even Standard Life had to admit 'whatever fallacies and misrepresentations they contain . . . are to say the least plausible'.[68] Reluctant to become embroiled in any more litigation, Dickson believed that the best way to deal with these allegations and meet the new statutory obligations was by tightening the controls he had already begun to put in place. Blount's brief already included a thorough review of assets, particularly premises over which Standard Life held mortgages.

Not surprisingly, Dickson asked Blount to begin his inspections with Hungary and Scandinavia which continued to exert the greatest pressure on expenses for little return. Even the tough-minded Blount was impressed by Charles Szilagyi, whom 'he considered one of the ablest and cleverest men in insurance I have met'. He had no doubt, however, that these very qualities made it 'absolutely essential that he should be convinced of the necessity of con-ducting our business in accordance with our principles and methods'.[69] Despite all Szilagyi's assurances, there was little improvement and in January 1910 he was warned that the branch was in danger of being closed.[70] Faced with this ultimatum he made efforts to reduce expendi-ture and improve working practices; but before a decision about the future could be made, Austria-Hungary became embroiled in the Balkan War in 1912 which precipitated a massive financial crisis leading to serious inflation.[71] Under these circumstances it was not practical for Standard Life to leave, particularly as there was a large Scottish commitment to the country, notably in the development of the Romanian oilfields. It was decided that in future, business should be confined to towns as the mortality experience in rural areas was poor.[72] To help Szilagyi in what were difficult circumstances,

Kivonat a dijkönyvecskéből

ALAPITTATOTT 1825. ÉVBEN.

THE

STANDARD

LIFE ASSURANCE COMPANY.

A Standard életbiztositó társaság Edinburgh-ban 1825-ben lett alapitva és régóta úgy Angliában mint Indiában, Anglia gyarmataiban és néhány európai continentális államban egyike a vezető biztositó inté-zeteknek.

Évi bevétel és vagyon.

A társaság évi bevétele meghaladja a harminczöt millió háromszázezer koronát és a társaság vagyona most már kétszáznyolczvan millió koronára rúg, a mely az országgyűlési törvényekben engedélyezett értékekben van befektetve.

The Hungarian prospectus, 1906.

Thomas Darling, one of Dickson's close con-fidants, was sent out from Edinburgh to assist him for six months and to review all the existing commitments.[73] His efforts were overtaken by the declaration of war in 1914 after which com-munication became difficult and had to be conducted through neutral countries. Szilagyi continued to write new policies, collect pre-miums, and look after the investments of some £50,000.[74]

In February 1917, by which time Dickson had

was suppressed in August, enormous damage had been inflicted on the branch's finances. Thomas Darling returned to assess what remained and recommended closure.[76] After the government imposed an enforced loan on the branch of 50,000 kronen early in 1921,* Standard Life reached agreement with the Royal Hungarian Minister of Finance for the transfer of the business and exemption from all liabilities. This agreement did not extend to policy-holders, who as a result of the dismemberment of the Austro-Hungarian Empire had become citizens of other countries.[77] It took another four years of lengthy negotiation to find a local purchaser for these risks, and in the meantime Standard Life had to service its customers by purchasing very unstable Czech kroner and Romanian lei. The Budapest office was not finally sold until 1929.[78]

In Scandinavia, although the outlook appeared to be better in Sweden than in either Denmark or Norway, Blount recommended in 1908 that no action be taken until after the declaration of the bonus in 1910. Within a year Otto Kaae, the manager in Denmark, had been sacked for defrauding the company of over £1,300.[79] Sidney Melville from Edinburgh was placed in temporary charge and remained for two years. The firm of C.A. & K. Leth were appointed agents, the Copenhagen board disbanded and the offices were sold in 1911.[80] The decision in 1916 by the Swedish government to

Copenhagen, where Standard Life did business from 1890 until 1911.

resolved to kill off Standard Life's European involvements, it was decided to sell the branch to the government 'at a fair ante-bellum valuation' as soon after the end of hostilities as possible.[75] The coup by the communists in March 1919 resulted in the nationalisation of Standard Life's business. By the time the coup

---

* Because of the excessive post-war inflation in enemy countries, it is difficult to provide an accurate sterling equivalent, but it was probably in the order of £500.

require insurance companies to invest in state bonds to cover all liabilities accelerated the closure of the Scandinavian operations. The Stockholm agency was shut in that year and no new risks from Sweden were accepted.[81] In 1922 the Norwegian business was sold to the Norske Forenede Forsikrings Selskab and the Danish business to Livs-og Genforsikringsselskabet 'Dana' Aktieselskab of Copenhagen.[82] The Belgian branch, which was badly disrupted by the First World War, met a similar fate. No more business was accepted after 1918 and the branch was placed on a care-and-maintenance basis until 1930 when the agent was dismissed for irregularities.[83]

The venture in Spain, which had started in 1904 (see page 148), at first fared better with a steady increase in premium income which reached 422,000 pesetas (£12,700) in 1909 with relatively low expenses.[84] However, doing business in Spain was problematic because of the fluctuating value of the peseta, which had depreciated rapidly since the end of the Spanish-American War of 1898. Initially the board had insisted that no investments be held in the currency except for Ptas 200,000 in government stock required by law. In 1909 the Spanish liabilities were valued in the company's books at Ptas 33.3 to the pound, whereas the real exchange rate had dropped to Ptas 27. This was the rupee dilemma in reverse (see page 133). The only solution was to begin investing in pesetas – a silver-based currency, which Dickson, mindful of the experience in India, was reluctant to do.

New legislation in 1908, however, required all insurance companies to create actuarially sound reserves – half to be invested in government stock and half in approved securities (not necessarily Spanish). Standard Life complied, but Dickson resolved not to expand the branch any further. The revolution in Portugal in October 1910 added to the uncertainty and increased the board's determination to leave Spain.[85] The branch, nevertheless, remained open until the death of the agent, Ernest Noble, in 1920 when it was closed.[86] The risks were finally sold to Equitativa, a Spanish company, in 1929.[87]

CANADA – WESTWARD EXPANSION

As Dickson was not prepared to run the risk of the sudden contraction of the company, the withdrawal from Europe, which had provided such a large proportion of new premiums in the immediate past, had necessarily to be compensated for by growth in other markets. During 1908 just such an increase had come from Canada, sustaining Standard Life's new business at the same level as the year before.[88] Recognising the central importance of Canada and the United States in the long term, not just as a source of new risks but also as a major place for investment, Dickson in 1909 made a personal visit which lasted from May to July and took him across the continent to the Pacific coast. In his assessment of the company's insurance business, he was not convinced David McGoun, who had been appointed manager by Spencer Thomson, was the right man for the job. He

Canadian pioneers heading westward. After 1911 Standard Life expanded into the western provinces.

described him as 'defending the past arrangements' rather than 'entering cordially into any proposals for alteration', despite the fact that Standard Life's share of a rapidly growing market had dropped since he took over.[89] Well before his arrival he had found McGoun difficult, always standing on his dignity and with a tendency to write ill-considered letters to clients.[90] He had summoned him to Edinburgh in March to be warned that his quick-tempered behaviour would not be tolerated.[91] Dickson had more faith in the very able William Hew Clark Kennedy, the secretary, whom he had known since childhood and who, following a visit to Edinburgh in 1906, had become a personal friend. When Norwich Union tried to poach him to open a Canadian

branch in 1908, Dickson did all he could to keep him.[92] Two years later he became secretary in South Africa, but the altitude did not suit him. In 1911 he returned to Canada as assistant manager with a specific brief to develop new business, particularly in the western provinces of Manitoba, Saskatchewan and Alberta, which were expanding rapidly on the back of the wheat boom.[93] William Mackenzie, who had been recruited in 1901 from an American life company to be chief inspector for the north-west, was promoted to the new post of chief agent with an office in Winnipeg and instructions to appoint inspectors for the larger towns, such as Regina, Calgary and Edmonton. 'Somewhat rough and ready both in appearance and manner', he seemed ideally matched to the job.[94]

Made well aware that in Canada a policy was regarded 'as much as a fund of credit, which can be drawn upon at any moment, as a provision for old age or against death', Dickson asked the actuaries to examine ways in which loan, surrender and paid-up values could be improved. American and Canadian competitors guaranteed their policies with these figures which, for those not fully paid up, were uniformly higher than Standard Life's – in some cases as much as double. Consequently, when guarantees became required by law in 1910, Standard Life were able to offer more competitive terms and in 1912 new tables for Canada were introduced. One of the reasons Dickson was so concerned about this issue and expansion into the western provinces was that the board was actively considering investing heavily in high-yielding farm mortgages, which at the same time would provide an excellent opportunity for selling new policies (see page 171).[95]

These initiatives stimulated new business in Canada during the boom years of 1913 and 1914. On the outbreak of war Clark Kennedy joined his regiment and became one of Canada's most distinguished and decorated soldiers, winning the Victoria Cross, DSO and bar, the Croix de Guerre and being appointed a CMG.[96] Without him, McGoun's weaknesses were exposed. In 1917 he replied to an enquiry from a Toronto lawyer on behalf of a client: 'If the University from which you got your degree to

William Hew Clark Kennedy VC (1879–1961), who was trained by Standard Life in Edinburgh along with his brother Archibald. He served in the Boer War and was wounded. On his return he was sent to Canada and, on the outbreak of the First World War, joined the Canadian Infantry Brigade. He became Canada's most decorated soldier, winning a VC, DSO (and bar) and the Croix de Guerre with Palm. After the war he became Standard Life's manager in Canada and retired in 1945.

practise your profession is not capable of inculcating respectful language in which to couch your enquiries, I would recommend you to send your children to the West Indies where the descendants of slaves would teach them some things you appear to be deficient in.'[97] Unwilling to apologise, McGoun was given early retirement in 1918. As soon after the war as possible Clark Kennedy took over as manager in Canada. During the war new custom had fallen away from $1.95 million sums assured in 1914 to a low of $625,000 in 1917.[98] This was due largely to the better terms offered by American companies, which until 1917 benefited from United States' neutrality.

INDIA AND THE FAR EAST

In 1905 the Indian market was discouraging. The passing of the bonus and the persistent hostile activities of E. Piercy Henderson (see page 156) and a policy-holder, Major Scharlieb, damaged new business and caused a sharp increase in surrenders. However irksome the attacks, Dickson steadfastly refused to countenance any official response in the press.[99] Following Stewart's death, Walker E. Hill was appointed secretary in Calcutta. A public-school adventurer, who enjoyed going on safari in Africa, he lacked the temperament to see off the growing competition from newly established Indian life offices.[100] F.A. Prevost at Bombay, with his passion for horseriding and keeping dogs, was equally unsuited to the changing business environment.[101] Frustrated by his attitude, one of his most able staff, Ian Alston, left to become the manager of the National Indian Life Assurance Company (founded in 1906), which he rapidly made a formidable adversary in securing native risks in the Mofussil and country districts.[102] He was not to be alone in being driven out of

The Bombay staff outside the Standard Life office in 1912, with the manager, F.A. Prevost, in the white suit.

Standard Life by the inadequacy of local management. Continuing to rely on circulars, some addressed directly to old boys of their respective public schools, Hill and Prevost failed to live up to Dickson's exhortation in 1906 'to strain every nerve to keep the business of the company from falling off'.[103] Part of their difficulty was undoubtedly Standard Life's uncompetitive commissions and rates for both European and native lives.

Steuart Edye Macnaghten, who was appointed joint actuary in 1911 and succeeded George Cameron the following year, recognised this problem at once. He came directly from working as assistant to the distinguished actuary George Lidstone at the Equitable Life Assurance Society (actuary of Scottish Widows from 1913) where together they had been responsible in a very short time for totally revising that office's working practices.[104] Dickson hoped he would quickly make his presence felt at Standard Life. One of his first tasks was to draft new rates for India; but in 1913 neither Hill nor Frederick Loch Trevor, who had just been transferred from Shanghai to succeed Prevost at Bombay, considered them sufficiently competitive.[105] Before further revisions could be made, war was declared. Business dwindled; but expenses fell as members of staff left to join their regiments.

By 1915 Dickson and Macnaghten had come to the conclusion that the company's activities in the Far East were in need of drastic pruning. Immediately the Singapore and Straits Settlements branch was replaced by an agency and the local board dissolved because the representative, who had been sent there complete with motorbike to get round the rubber plantations, had proved 'a complete failure'.[106] The following year the Bombay board and branch were abolished. Hill was recalled to Edinburgh and Trevor moved to Calcutta with responsibility for the whole of India and eventually for a short time the whole of the Far East, when the Shanghai branch closed in 1922.[107] At the same time Macnaghten introduced new schemes for Europeans at considerably reduced rates and new tables for native lives. They were to be recruited with greater determination through the establishment of a complete agency system modelled on those of Indian companies. Trevor was more than suited to this task, but unfortunately Henry M. Cook, who, with experience in India and Shanghai, was expected to play a prominent role in the planned expansion, was found to be unstable and unreliable.[108] After a series of violent arguments he left in 1918 to join the Indian branch of the Scottish Union and National Insurance Co.,

which quickly made inroads into Standard Life's business, capturing both customers and agents.[109]

NEW OVERSEAS MARKETS

Dickson had two choices in 1906: either to withdraw entirely from less established markets in Latin America, the West Indies, South Africa and Egypt or develop them. Since there was evidence that because of the premium income generated from these new markets Standard Life was growing faster at least in terms of total funds than the two leading Scottish life offices (Scottish Provident and Scottish Widows), Dickson opted for expansion (see Figure 5.2 on page 191).* Blount was sent to Montevideo in 1911 charged with the sensitive task of pensioning off Lorenzo Hill, now aged 80, while at the same time 'retaining, if possible, his influence and good will towards the Company'. Dickson had tired of his continual refusal to obey instructions, particularly his total failure to provide any information about the likely impact of proposed insurance legislation. The offer of a generous pension, a directorship and a lavish farewell dinner was too tempting for the flamboyant Hill. He was succeeded by his assistant, Aubrey Bertrand Drayton, who had been 'the mainstay of the business for several years'. Drayton was confident that, given the fact that Standard Life was essentially the only foreign life office in Uruguay, he could secure £200,000 worth of new

---

* Between 1901 and 1906 Standard Life's total funds grew by 16.5 per cent whereas Scottish Provident's grew by 14 per cent and Scottish Widows' by nearly 15 per cent.

business a year by extending representation to smaller towns and the 'estancieros who are the richest people'.[110]

No sooner had he taken up his position than the government of the new socialist president Señor Battel Ordonios tried to establish a state monopoly in insurance. This failed but no more insurance companies were allowed to open offices in the country and a State Insurance Bank, providing only without-profits cover, was set up. Seizing the opportunity to sell with-profits policies, Drayton comfortably exceeded his target by 1913 when he contributed about 10 per cent of all Standard Life's new business. Custom fell away during the First World War which seriously dislocated South American trade leading to considerable unrest. Standard Life, however, refused to discuss the sale of the branch to the State Insurance Bank.[111]

Although not such a large market as Uruguay for Standard Life, the West Indies was a similar success story with total premium income achieving a peak of almost £26,000 in 1921.[112] Likewise the Egyptian branch, which had been hampered by a personality clash between the manager and his assistant, prospered after 1909 when David Scott Moncrieff took over.[113] In 1912 he secured £42,000 worth of new sums assured, mostly connected with mortgages, and sustained this level throughout the war.[114]

The South African branch, which had grown swiftly at the beginning of the century, recording about 5 per cent of all new business in 1905, was scarred by internal strife after W.E. Kitson left in

Lorenzo Hill, the flamboyant agent in Montevideo.

1906 to become secretary of the London (West End) office. His successor, Stanley Mugford, was described by Dickson as 'a man of energy, ability and integrity; but he suffers from the complaint which we call "Swollen-Headed" to an objectionable degree'.[115] He left after three years to become agent for Norwich Union in Buenos Aires, where within twelve months he had captured three times as much business as Standard Life.[116] His departure did little to improve the strained relations between the staff and members of the local board, which were damaging the business at a time when competition from other offices, particularly South African Mutual Life Assurance

An aerial photograph of a battle during the brief but successful South African campaign against German South West Africa during 1915, in which Standard Life's assistant manager in the country served.

Society, was growing swiftly. In these circumstances it proved almost impossible to recruit and retain reliable staff to maintain even a shadow of an agency system. Clark Kennedy's altitude sickness while secretary in Johannesburg made matters worse.

Blount was sent out to investigate in 1913. He replaced the chairman and confirmed the appointment as secretary of Edward Scipio Kimber, a member of a distinguished London legal family.[117] Business recovered momentarily; but within a year Kimber was ill and his assistant R. Douglas Wilson had been called up to take part in the brief southern African campaign against the Germans.[118] In their absence the branch was managed for a year by Miss Jean Hancock, the

first woman to occupy such a senior position. The difficulties persisted and in 1919, following the formation of the Union of South Africa and the introduction of new insurance legislation, Dickson decided to replace Kimber, whom he considered an incompetent manager.[119] On learning the news, Kimber defected to South African Mutual Life. His place was taken by Dickson's protégé, Thomas Darling, who, delayed in Budapest, did not arrive until 1921.[120]

HOME BUSINESS: THE FIRST PENSION SCHEME

At home, following the passing of the bonus and the damaging publicity surrounding the legal action, figures for new business made depressing reading. The experience at Manchester was typical. The branch at first seemed to weather the storm with business rising to nearly £82,000 in 1907; but the Barlein case completely undermined local confidence and returns fell. Dickson noted wryly: 'The irony is that when things were in their former parlous state no one said anything. Now when the Company is in a thoroughly sound state the trouble has to be faced.'[121] Standard Life's main problem was that it was very difficult to gain new business without paying agents and brokers big commissions; whereas Scottish Widows, Scottish Amicable, Scottish Mutual and Scottish Provident with 'such good articles to sell' could get away with much lower rates.[122] Dickson's fear was that if business was obtained at whatever the price during the crisis years, 'we shall never be able to draw back when we reach smoother water'.[123] Throughout his career he was totally opposed to the activities of brokers, whom he condemned as caring 'for nothing except their commission'. His strategy was 'systematically to develop an agency organisation'. His attempts to do so were hampered at first by the need for Rolland, the general secretary for England, to devote nearly all his time and energy to the legal proceedings. Shortly afterwards Rolland's health broke down, leading eventually to his early retirement in 1912. With the market for life insurance in Britain stagnating, Dickson took action in 1910 by extending Blount's brief to include all agencies, and demoting T.H.B. Black, who had proved ineffective as general superintendent of home agencies, to be his assistant.[124]

Blount's first visits revealed a collapse in the coverage of agencies and, perhaps more seriously, a complete lack of *esprit de corps* amongst the inspectors. As in the foreign branches, the better inspectors and agents had left to work for other companies. A good many agents, who remained nominally on the roll, had simply given up trying to represent Standard Life and were content just to take their 4 per cent commission on renewals. Circulars and leaflets were left unopened. Moreover, those agents who remained active regarded themselves as the point of contact with the policy-holders and refused to pass on addresses to Standard Life.[125] Reforms were quickly made. Card indexes of the current names and addresses of policy-holders were started in all branches and agency agreements were revised, stipulating that if no new business was received in five years the agency would lapse and commissions on renewals cease to be paid.[126] Neither Dickson nor Blount had any illusions that rebuilding Standard Life's base in the United Kingdom would be an easy task.

There were, however, some rays of light in the otherwise depressing landscape. At Manchester one of the inspectors, A.C. Cutter, negotiated with his brother-in-law, the secretary of the chemical company Brunner Mond (later part of Imperial Chemical Industries), for Standard Life to establish a group pension scheme in 1910. Although Standard Life had been associated with group life insurance schemes in the past, notably for their London bankers the London County and Westminster Bank, this was the first formal pension scheme, supported with contributions from the employer, and was almost certainly one of the first in the world.* Following the success of the Brunner Mond scheme, the Manchester office made approaches to a number of other large local business houses.[127]

The timing of this innovation could not have been better. Retirement from active work for many people was a novel concept, which had been encouraged by the introduction of old-age pensions in 1909. More recent welfare legislation to provide sickness and unemployment benefits and tax concessions for children had radically

---

* The Equitable Life Assurance Company of America is normally credited with issuing the first group life policy in the United States in 1912.

The staff of Brunner Mond's chemical works, who were covered
by Standard Life's first group pension scheme in 1910.

changed attitudes to saving. The old rhetoric of 'saving for a rainy day', characteristic of all thrift organisations and of family insurance, lost much of its credibility and began to be replaced by the notion of 'saving for a purpose' – to protect capital from taxation, to buy a house or a pension.[128] Lloyd George, the Liberal Chancellor of the Exchequer largely responsible for this legislation, recognised from the outset the need to encourage people to supplement what were minimal state benefits. Making it clear that thrift was the handmaid of the new social order, he readily accepted invitations to lend his name to publications extolling the benefits of life insurance.[129] Although Standard Life secured further pensions business, such as the takeover in 1911 of the Widows' Fund of the Glasgow Faculty of Procurators,[130] there was no specific marketing strategy before the First World War, largely because most schemes were negotiated through brokers, who demanded exorbitant commissions. Some brokers, such as the big firm of Sedgwick Collins & Co., refused to deal with Standard Life on the grounds that the commission was too low.[131] With brokers controlling an increasingly large proportion of new business, Standard Life was surely mistaken in persisting to oppose their legitimate role in the insurance market.

Dickson's main concern was to create an effective organisation in the United Kingdom to capitalise on the restoration of the bonus following the 1910 investigation. On receiving Blount's disturbing reports from his first inspections, Dickson decided to bring all the districts under

his control. Investigation dinners were held for the first time to present the results to the staff and agents. Annual targets were set linked directly to staff bonuses.[132] On Rolland's retirement from the London City branch in 1912, the West End branch was placed under the control of his successor C.E. Fox, who was instructed to approach London legal firms armed with the improved rates.[133] Fox failed to make an impact and the only branch in the south of England which prospered was the West End. Everywhere else business continued its downward path and expenses continued to rise inexorably. Most disappointing were Fox's returns for the London City branch itself, which fell sharply up to the outbreak of war.[134]

Standard Life was not alone amongst life offices in experiencing such problems, but its

David Lloyd George (1863–1945) with his granddaughter. As Chancellor of the Exchequer, he introduced National Insurance in his 1911 budget but made it clear that this was not an alternative to life assurance.

The West End branch, originally Colonial Life's London office.

Charles Whigham, who was responsible for arranging the sale of United States securities owned by British subjects during the war. He had been a director of Standard Life between 1904 and 1908.

performance once again lagged behind that of Scottish Widows and was only on a par with Scottish Provident. Although Scottish Widows' surrenders for the first time were consistently higher than those of Standard Life, it recorded a growth of almost 22 per cent in assets between 1906 and 1914 whereas Standard Life achieved only 15.5 per cent.[135]

To allow the London staff to concentrate on sales, from 1913 all Standard Life's policies were registered in Edinburgh and the London local board was abolished;[136] but there was still no improvement. Such expansion as there was came entirely from abroad. By the end of the following year no less than 65 per cent of Standard Life's new premium income came from outside the country. So as to disguise the weakness in the home market, the split between home and overseas business ceased to be disclosed at the time of the investigations. Further action to remedy the problem was delayed by the outbreak of war in 1914.

INVESTMENT – HIGH-RISK STRATEGY

Since 1904 Standard Life had continued to invest heavily in North American railway bonds, advised by the Edinburgh stockbrokers Bell, Cowan and the London merchant banker Robert Fleming. When he became manager Dickson also brought Charles Whigham,* an accountant who represented the American bankers J.P. Morgan & Co in Scotland, onto the board.[137] Two years later James Ivory of the Edinburgh investment managers Ivory & Sime also became a director.[138] Both Whigham and Ivory specialised in risky high-yielding recovery stocks. Whigham also immediately introduced Standard Life to the lucrative market for underwriting new issues of government and industrial stock, beginning with participation in a syndicate for a £30 million loan to the Japanese government in

---

* Charles Whigham's brother, Walter K. Whigham, was Robert Fleming's partner. Charles himself ceased to be a director of Standard Life in 1908 when he left to become office manager for Morgan Grenfell, the London merchant bank. He continued to be a close confidant of Dickson, however, and regularly undertook commissions for Standard Life in North America.

1905.[139] Ivory's expertise, like Fleming's, was increasingly in North America, where he developed close links with the New York firm of G.M. Forman & Co. and the Chicago financiers Peabody, Houghteling & Co., itself connected to Morgan's.[140] On their advice Ivory persuaded the Standard Life board in 1908 to be the first British office to follow the example of American insurance companies by investing in Canadian and United States farm mortgages in the rapidly expanding west.[141] This, at the time, was good business, providing excellent returns secured against rapidly appreciating assets. Within a year $625,000 (£120,000) had been committed to mortgages in Georgia, Florida, Arkansas and Alabama and $360,000 (£70,000) to Manitoba, Saskatchewan and Alberta. On his American tour in 1909 Dickson visited farms at Moosejaw, Saskatchewan, over which Standard Life held mortgages, and was impressed by their quality.[142] He was happy to endorse further loans, provided a system of inspection was put in place. T. Dick Peat, an investment clerk, was immediately despatched across the Atlantic to visit farms and view crops. Dickson himself planned to return in 1911 for discussions with Forman's, booking his passage on the maiden voyage of the *Titanic*, but the meeting was providentially cancelled.[143] Instead Peat sailed later in the year, travelling over 30,000 miles and pledging more funds.[144] On his return Peat was promoted to the new position of investment superintendent and in 1919 became investment secretary with control of the department.

By the close of 1912 just under 45 per cent of Standard Life's assets (£6 million) were committed to North America (23 per cent to Canada and 22 per cent in the United States). The only shadow across this portfolio was the currently low value in the aftermath of the Spanish-American War of 1898 of railway securities with a book value of almost £3 million. Although they provided healthy returns, they could only be realised at a substantial loss.[145] With so many of its assets in North America, Standard Life was exposed to any depreciation in the value of the US dollar against sterling, but with both currencies linked to the price of gold the risk was thought to be minimal. Standard Life's commitment to North America was much larger than any of its principal Scottish competitors. In

A farmstead in Oregon – typical of the American farms mortgaged to Standard Life and other insurance companies during the agricultural boom before the First World War. The inability of farmers to repay these loans during the depression of the 1920s caused considerable problems for the insurance industry.

The burnt-out Post Office in Dublin's O'Connell Street where the proclamation of independence was read during the Easter Rising in 1916. These events led Standard Life to foreclose on many of its outstanding commitments in the country.

1908 Scottish Widows held only £2.8 million in North American securities out of a total capital of £19 million, while Scottish Provident held £2.7 million out a total capital of £14 million.[146]

Outside North America, Standard Life was required under the terms of legislation introduced in nearly all the countries in which the company did business to hold a proportion of its assets locally, usually in government or other approved securities. The long-standing embargo on further Australasian mortgages (see page 116) remained in force. They were replaced by mortgages over *estancias* and other property in the Argentine, which totalled over £1.3 million by 1913, yielding almost 7 per cent – 2 per cent above United Kingdom rates. The only other British insurer with equivalent representation was the Law Union and Rock Insurance Co. After the onset of a serious economic downturn in South America in the second half of 1913, the Standard Life directors became nervous about the security of these investments, which represented more than 10 per cent of the company's assets. Although G.M. Forman himself reported reassuringly on the quality of Standard Life's loans, Peat was sent out to see for himself and confirmed this conclusion: 'The Standard has a good name for dealing justly with its borrowers, and does not need to look for mortgage business.'[147]

Apart from these initiatives, the board had some unfinished investment business to clear up left over from the previous regime. There was still over £1 million locked up in United Kingdom mortgages where the borrowers had either defaulted or were known to be in difficulty. After the passing of the bonus in 1906 the board took tough action against these recalcitrants, since any losses would necessarily have to be written off at the next investigation. Legal action was taken against the Earl of Gosford with estates in County Armagh who owed £48,000, and other Irish landlords were told to pay up or expect similar treatment.[148] A new receiver was appointed to clear finally the debts of the Earl of Kenmare and his son Viscount Castlerosse. These still exceeded £150,000.[149] Recovery was delayed by the supposedly accidental destruction by fire in 1913 of Killarney House, which had been built with £100,000 of Standard Life's money. By the Easter Rising in 1916 Irish loans had been reduced from £600,000 to £300,000[150] and within four years by dint of further draconian measures had been cut to £156,000.[151] Uncertain about the stability of the country, Standard Life foreclosed on Viscount Castlerosse, now the fifth Earl of Kenmare, in 1921 bringing to an end one of its worst investment decisions.[152] With civil war raging in the newly formed Irish Free State in January 1923, the board took comfort from the news that Irish loans on both sides of the border were just £39,000.[153] Given the difficulties in Ireland in the past 40 years, this was a remarkable achievement.

In Scotland Sir John Sinclair of Ulbster was made to repay £87,000 of his £187,000 loan;[154] Sir Kenneth Mackenzie of Gairloch, a long-standing borrower, was forced to sell a large part of his estate;[155] and the Kelvinside Estate Company in Glasgow, which owed £150,000, was pressed to sell land and property. Because of the continuing depression in the Glasgow property market, this did not happen until after the First World War.[156] Amidst a glare of publicity, the well-known naval contractors Thames Ironworks & Shipbuilding Company, to which Standard Life had made loans, was reported to be in serious financial difficulties in 1913. Before foreclosing, the company took the novel step of conferring with Scottish Widows and Edinburgh Life, both of which had also made funds available to the company. This was to become a common procedure when dealing with large corporate exposures where there was public interest.[157]

The share certificate for Standard Life's investment in the Thames Iron Works Shipbuilding & Engineering Company Ltd, 1899.

Sir Thomas Beecham (1879–1961), the conductor, who borrowed £100,000 from Standard Life in 1913 to help buy the Covent Garden Estate in London.

Not all the debts recovered were invested abroad. Loans continued to be made in the United Kingdom. In 1909 the commitment to the London Hospital for Women was maintained with an advance of £2,500 towards the cost of a new building and £10,000 was loaned to William Burrell (the great art collector) to pay for a new steamer.[158] Four years later £100,000 was made available to Thomas Beecham (later the well-known conductor) towards the purchase with his father of the Covent Garden estate for £2 million, believed to have been the largest property transaction in the United Kingdom up to that time.[159]

Dickson was also keen finally to settle the problem of the rupee investments which in 1912 still totalled over £500,000, mostly held in municipal and public utility stocks. Although the official exchange rate had been pegged by the government of India at one shilling and five pennies, its market value had continued to slide, reaching 10 pennies by 1912. With no prospect of any appreciation in the value of silver, on which the rupee was based, Dickson advised the board in 1913 to liquidate its Indian investments and convert them into gold-backed securities. In the current market conditions these traded at a premium on the rupee.[160] The board decided to take no action until a government enquiry into Indian finance and currency had reported.[161] On this occasion the directors' reaction was correct; during the First World War the rupee appreciated by about 8 pennies due to a rise in the price of silver and the revision of the official exchange rate in 1920.[162] As a result Standard Life not only retained its Indian stock but also in 1920 invested in Indian government war loans and speculated profitably by purchasing rupees in the expectation that the currency would appreciate.[163]

FIRST WORLD WAR

In January 1914 Dickson was elected chairman of the Association of Scottish Life Offices and was immediately plunged into discussions with the Treasury about the taxation of profits from foreign investments of life insurance companies.[164] This was a complex subject involving agreeing the basis on which profits were to be calculated with other life offices and raised the issue of double taxation both in the country where the dividend was earned and at home. Dickson had to spend a good deal of time in London meeting his opposite number in the English Life Offices Association, Geoffrey Marks, manager of the National Mutual Life Assurance

Society, and the Chancellor of the Exchequer, David Lloyd George, and his Treasury officials.[165] Dickson and Marks got on well. They were about the same age and shared similar opinions on the management of life offices, agreeing for instance on the importance of the relationship between with- and without-profits business. They had a common interest in the special constabulary and the welfare of servicemen and their families.[166] Moreover, through his friendship with Marks, Dickson encountered the economist J.M. Keynes, who advocated that insurance companies should change the balance of their investments away from fixed-interest securities towards higher-risk equities, which demanded an almost daily review of the portfolio.[167] Keynes was later successfully to put his theories to the test as a director of both the National Mutual and the Provincial Insurance Company.[168] Such a bold investment strategy would undoubtedly have appealed to Dickson.

In late June 1914, exhausted, Dickson contracted a severe attack of shingles, which laid him low for several months. To add to his worries, his son went down with appendicitis but made a good recovery from what at the time was a dangerous operation.[169] Dickson could not have become ill at a worse time. Following the murder on 28 June of Archduke Franz Ferdinand, heir to the Austrian throne, the international money markets were thrown into confusion. By the end of July the London bill market, which kept the wheels of Britain's finance houses lubricated, was on the verge of collapse. When

Austria-Hungary declared war on Serbia on 28 July 1914, panic overwhelmed all the financial institutions. There were fears that people would rashly convert their savings in whatever form into gold. Although the banks reported more activity than usual, there was no hysteria.[170] At life offices requests for the surrender of policies continued to be high, fuelled by the uncertainty. This presented them all with a serious problem as the turmoil in the financial markets had caused the value of their investments both at home and abroad to fall by at least 5 per cent within a week. In some instances the falls had been catastrophic, notably in ordinary stock in Canadian, Indian and United States railways. Apart from gold and gold-backed bonds, there appeared to be no obvious safe haven for investors. During the financial crisis in the week before Britain declared war on 4 August, the stock exchanges in Britain and America were closed amidst fears that a number of stockbrokers would be hammered, because all remittances from abroad had ceased and the clearing banks had called in their advances to billbrokers.[171] Although dealing in shares was resumed in mid-November 1914, the British exchanges did not formally reopen until 4 January 1915 and then only under stringent Treasury control with the value of all securities protected by a minimum price until July 1916. Even with this safety-net, prices remained depressed until the closing stages of the war.[172]

Matters for Standard Life, with its huge overseas business, were complicated at the outbreak

Volunteers joining the colours in Edinburgh at the outbreak of war in 1914.

An advertisement for Edinburgh Aeroplane Week with an offer from Standard Life for an assurance scheme to invest in war loan, 1916.

Edinburgh Aeroplane Week
Buy War Bonds
· £2,500 will provide an Aeroplane
If 5 persons combine and purchase a £500 Bond each, they provide an Aeroplane between them;
BUT
They can achieve the same result by a present payment of
Only £45 each to
The Standard Life Assurance
COMPANY
and an undertaking to make 9 further annual payments of a like sum. The Company will purchase the Bonds at once, handing them over when the 10 annual payments of £45 are completed. Each person will at the end of the 10 years draw £525 in cash for an outlay of £450.
Bonds for £100 and upwards on the same scale.
NO MEDICAL EXAMINATION REQUIRED
For further particulars write to or call on
The Standard Life Assurance Co.
3 GEORGE STREET, EDINBURGH

of hostilities by the rapid appreciation of sterling against most other currencies. This was a technical consequence of the repatriation of Britain's large overseas balances. Most serious was the depreciation in the value of the United States dollar, which lost almost 20 per cent of its value against sterling in the week before the declaration of war. Although the Bank of England took immediate action to stabilise the exchanges, the dollar did not return to parity until the end of the year.[173] Unwell as he was, Dickson hurriedly joined in negotiations with the Board of Trade to allow all insurance companies to value their securities at 1913 prices and rates of exchange until the end of the hostilities and to make short-term borrowings without Treasury approval from the banks to cover any immediate liabilities.

Without such protection most life offices would have been forced to suspend payments.[174]

From the outbreak of war Dickson, who had reached the rank of lieutenant-colonel in the volunteers, had no doubt that the conflict would be both long and costly. He persuaded all the Scottish life offices, unlike the London insurance companies, to allow their staff to join Kitchener's volunteer army. All those from Standard Life continued to receive their salary if it was less than £200 a year or that sum if it was more.[175] Dickson went to great lengths to keep in contact with both members of staff and their sons on active service, entertaining them on leave, visiting them in hospital and writing to them at the front. He took great pride in the military success of W.H. Clark Kennedy and Thomas

Darling and shared in the grief of the families of those who had been killed.

Dogged by the after-effects of his shingles which made reading difficult well into 1915, Dickson as chairman of the Association of Scottish Life Offices found himself locked in discussions with the government on behalf of the whole industry. Together with Geoffrey Marks of the Life Offices Association, he agreed uniform extra rates for war service, negotiated the offset of management expenses of insurance companies against tax, raised the continuing question of the double taxation of foreign earnings and, perhaps most importantly, was consulted about the financing of the war itself. When Dickson threatened to encourage insurance offices to set up overseas subsidiaries if the question of double taxation was not settled, the Treasury provided some relief in the 1916 Finance Act.[176] After taxes were raised in almost every country to 'confiscation levels' the following year, the Association to Protest Against the Duplication of Income Tax within the Empire was formed to lobby for further rebates. Although not a member of the committee, Dickson remained in close touch with the association as all the Scottish life offices had much to lose.[177]

With new issues suspended for the duration of hostilities and all financial markets strictly controlled, insurance companies had no alternative but to invest their balances patriotically in war loans. Within a year of the start of hostilities Standard Life had invested over £1 million. If held to maturity, the yield was good and there were no grounds for complaint.

Of much greater concern to the insurance industry was the Treasury's plan to mobilise British investments in North America for the war effort. In June 1915 the Bank of England began to buy dollar securities from United Kingdom companies which were realised to help meet the cost of war matériel.[178] Standard Life co-operated with the sale in August of all its American securities (mostly gold-backed bonds) which could be realised profitably.[179] This was made easier by the strengthening in value of the dollar and by the fact that the person responsible for the United Kingdom end of the negotiations was Charles Whigham, a former director of Standard Life and now a partner in Morgan Grenfell, the merchant bankers.[180] In the autumn a government committee, chaired by Sir John Bradbury, joint permanent secretary at the Treasury, worked out the details of a formal scheme (later termed scheme A) to be introduced in December whereby securities would be purchased for their prevailing price and at the current rate of exchange.[181] Dickson was in almost daily contact with Bradbury, other senior officials in the Treasury and Bank of England and Ministers, who included his friend the Marquess of Reading. Between the end of August and mid-December he spent almost a month in London in an effort to improve the terms of the scheme for the industry. The problem for holders of American securities was that many stocks had still not returned to their pre-war prices and that with the value of the dollar now rising above parity the last thing they wanted was to have all their assets in sterling, especially if they had American liabilities. At a meeting with the Chancellor of the Exchequer on 11 December, Dickson made this point forcibly and pressed for investors to be allowed if they chose to lend stock to the government as security for dollar borrowings. This was agreed, with the Treasury reserving the right to sell in the event of an emergency. Immediately lists of American stock to be purchased in the first phase of the scheme were circulated to the financial institutions.[182] Exhausted, Dickson pressed his colleagues in the other Scottish life offices to allow him to hand over the chairmanship of the Association at the end of 1915 when his term expired. With his wealth of experience they were reluctant to let him go[183] and, despite his misgivings, he agreed to stay on.[184] Negotiations with the Treasury continued. When the financial institutions failed to comply wholeheartedly with scheme A because they wanted to continue to hold dollar investments directly, the government, under protest from Dickson, insisted on the repatriation of all listed American securities and imposed a surcharge of 5 pence in the pound on the taxation of the dividends of all 'listed' securities remaining in private hands. With the government still seriously short of foreign exchange, a further scheme (B) was planned to cover securities held in other countries. Under this scheme, introduced in August 1916, the investments were to be held on deposit by the Bank of England for five years and then returned. Under both schemes the owners were to be paid the normal dividends along with a premium of 0.5 per cent. As Dickson predicted, scheme B proved much more acceptable to the insurance industry as it protected investments, which had been made not only because interest rates were more attractive than at home, but also to cover overseas liabilities. Consequently scheme A was wound up and all remaining United States' securities were dealt with under scheme B.[185]

More worrying for Standard Life and many Scottish investment trusts was the Treasury's attitude to farm mortgages. In the past as they fell in they had either been renewed or sums realised had been invested in new mortgages. The Treasury was unrelenting, insisting that all dollars had to be deposited with J.P. Morgan & Co. in New York to help pay for the war effort and paid for at the prevailing rate of exchange with British government paper.[186] Although with the improvement in the dollar-sterling rate after 1914 Standard Life did not lose capital in these transactions, the rate of interest on war loans was significantly lower. Largely as a result of the sale of its foreign securities, Standard Life by the end of the war had £6.5 million, almost half its assets, in government stock (see Appendix 6 on page 386).

The lengthy experience of negotiating with the Treasury suggested to some leaders of the insurance industry that a single committee to represent their interests should be established.

Dickson stalwartly refused to countenance any such suggestion, preferring that the Association of Scottish Life Offices remain independent but federated to the Life Offices Association in London. He well appreciated that together he and Geoffrey Marks of the Life Offices Association made an effective pair of lobbyists whereas any amalgamation would leave these complex negotiations in the hands of a single individual.[187] After the United States entered the war in 1917 they were involved in campaigning successfully for the resumption of investment in North America to reduce losses across the exchange as the dollar remained at a discount on sterling. They also discussed how enemy debts were to be dealt with at the end of hostilities. This was of direct concern to Standard Life with its branch in Hungary.[188] In January 1918, after four hectic years, Dickson stood down as chairman with the thanks of the whole life industry.[189]

The cost of the war was financed as much through taxation as by borrowing. Even before the outbreak of war income tax had been raised by Lloyd George in his 1914 budget and the super-tax threshold lowered to £3,000. This should have made life insurance policies attractive to an even larger number of people, but the war intervened and the number and value of new policies fell. For those earning more than £3,000 a year, tax was increased sharply over the next two years.[190] Although it was widely recognised that life policies were an efficient means of tax avoidance for the better-off, there is no evidence that they took advantage of this privilege to avoid heavy wartime taxation.[191] In fact Standard Life's receipts in the home market continued to fall as customers invested in war loans. In the Finance Acts of 1915 and 1916, steps were taken to limit relief on premiums. This was reduced as an emergency measure to half the standard rate of tax and to a qualifying premium of 7 per cent of the total sum assured.[192] Dickson fought hard to prevent these provisions being made retrospective, briefing his friend Sir George Younger MP to support this principle in the House of Commons debate.[193]

At a time of high inflation and interest rates, these big reductions, which were not cancelled after the war, made life policies much less attractive and contributed directly to a decline in new business and an increase in surrenders, particularly of whole-life policies. Indeed it was not until the summer of 1917 after a further increase in income tax that life assurance again became popular. The total new premiums for the whole industry almost doubled from £2.1 million in 1916 to £4.1 million in 1918.[194] Neither Standard Life nor their principal Scottish competitors shared in this recovery (see Figure 5.2 on page 191). This was almost certainly a reflection of the reluctance of Scottish companies to accept poor risks and a limit of £2,000 on any war risks agreed by the Association of Scottish Life Offices.[195] As a result Scottish companies were hardly affected by the devastating influenza epidemic of 1918–19 when other companies reported heavy claims.

LEONARD DICKSON'S HEROISM

At 2.30 on the afternoon of Tuesday, 8 July 1919, Leonard Walter Dickson (1867–1919) (below, right), the manager of Standard Life, was returning along George Street in Edinburgh from a Victory Loan rally accompanied by Steuart Macnaghten, the company's actuary. A horse and cab belonging to George Hall, cab proprietor, and under the charge of Peter Cunningham, bolted. Cunningham was thrown to the ground and at the corner of Frederick Street Dickson grabbed the reins and was dragged by the ex-army horse for twenty yards. He received cuts to his face and head and was knocked unconscious. He was carried to the British Linen Bank and then taken by police ambulance to the Edinburgh Royal Infirmary. He died there a fortnight later. Subsequently his widow was presented with this medal and citation from the Hero Fund Trust, established in that year by Andrew Carnegie (below), the Scottish-born American steel magnate and philanthropist, to whom Standard Life had sold the Skibo estate in 1896.

LEONARD W. DICKSON, Chartered Accountant, 45 Manor Place, EDINBURGH, died on 21st July 1919, from injuries sustained in an attempt to stop a runaway horse in George Street. EDINBURGH, on 8th July 1919.

DICKSON – A VISIONARY MANAGER

Although Dickson's duties at the Association had occupied a disproportionate amount of his time and energy, he kept his finger firmly on the pulse of Standard Life. Indeed during the winter of 1916–17, with Blount and Macnaghten ill, he was working almost single-handedly. Despite this crisis he refused an offer of help from Spencer Thomson.[196] His main concern remained the domestic market, which became even more depressed after the outbreak of war. This general slump did not prevent Dickson from taking tough action to improve business. In 1915, for example, he pensioned off the Newcastle secretary, Cook Watson, and the Liverpool secretary, J.D. Ainslie, because of their failure to generate new business.[197] Subsequently the Liverpool branch was amalgamated with Manchester as part of a programme to rationalise and re-invigorate representation at home.[198] Although there were excellent results at the 1915 investigation, the bonus was suspended until after the end of hostilities, with Treasury agreement.[199] By 1918 there were some signs of recovery with new sums assured up by £200,000.

For some time Dickson had regarded Legal & General (which Spencer Thomson had dismissed as 'third rate')[200] as the leading life office and trendsetter. When it was announced in 1919 that Legal & General was to diversify into the growing market for general insurance,[201] Dickson, taking its lead, concluded that this was the only way forward for Standard Life as well. There were many attractions in such a strategy, not least that by selling a wider range of insurance there was a real possibility of reducing the expenses to something approaching a competitive level. With a large proportion of its assets in readily realisable government stock there could not have been a more opportune time to diversify into shorter-term risks such as accident and fire. Early in 1919 Dickson obtained an Order in Council (subsequently confirmed by Act of Parliament) for Standard Life to undertake 'business of every kind of insurance against any loss, damage, injury, liability, misfortune, contingency, or event . . .' and, if appropriate, to change its name.[202]

The insurance press was agog with interest about what was intended. What Dickson probably had in mind was a merger with either a general insurance office or another life office with a wider range of products (particularly accident insurance) than Standard Life. He almost certainly intended to make a purchase as he arranged a line of credit for the very large sum of £4.5 million (representing about a third of total assets) from the Bank of Scotland, ostensibly to meet liabilities while war bonds were realised.[203] He did not explain what these liabilities were. A number of offices were known to be on the market, such as Edinburgh Life, the University Life Assurance Society, and the Liverpool and London and Globe. It may be that he intended to merge with Legal & General itself, which had a similar mix of life business. This would have been a powerful alliance. Sadly for Standard Life, no one was ever to learn Dickson's intentions as, on 8 July 1919, returning from a Victory Loan rally in Edinburgh, he was seriously injured while attempting to stop a runaway horse outside the head office in George Street. He died a fortnight later a few days short of his fifty-second birthday.[204]

His death was a cruel blow. His contribution had been immense. Without his energy, determination and foresight, Standard Life would probably have foundered. With an accountant's eye to costs, he was not always popular, but he had dragged Standard Life into the twentieth century, reshaping the management and introducing products which met the needs and expectations of the customers. As he would have been the first to admit, he had only partially succeeded in implementing his strategy. He had been hampered by the introduction in every country of legislation which favoured local competitors and by the ill-health of his managers. The strength of the competition and the damaging effects of adverse publicity, both at home and abroad, had undermined his determination to reduce the expenses ratio, which had never fallen significantly. (In 1919 expenses were still almost 19 per cent of premium income compared with less than 10 per cent at Scottish Widows.)[205] Any attempt to withdraw more rapidly from foreign markets would only have served to highlight Standard Life's continuing weakness at home. Against this background Dickson had found it very difficult to reward able staff and retain good managers and agents, who resigned to join more successful competitors, leaving the dead wood behind.

Dickson's strategy for survival had undoubtedly been blown off course, first at home by the Liberal government's welfare legislation and then in every market by the outbreak of the First World War. As a result the insurance industry and other savings organisations found themselves in much more regular contact with government. By chance Dickson became chairman of the Association of Scottish Life Offices on the brink of the war. Recognising that financial and fiscal policies could easily paralyse the industry, he gave priority to the long, difficult negotiations with the Treasury and the Bank of England. There is no doubt that his views were influential in modifying the proposal for the realisation of foreign investments and in reducing exposure to double taxation. Despite his failures, he had navigated Standard Life through perilous waters. The future was by no means assured, but the bonus had been restored and the company was poised for expansion either in the life market or in insurance more generally. Had he lived, Dickson, even though he was not an actuary, would have been recognised as one of the leading figures in insurance of his generation.

CHAPTER FIVE

'A LONG-TERM POLICY': 1919–51

'I am proud of the fact that the Standard is perhaps singular among the insurance companies in this country in that it has had a long-term policy.'

Andrew R. Davidson, the manager, June 1946.[1]

In the summer of 1919 there was an expectation that the clock could simply be turned back to the prosperous years immediately before the war. Europe had not experienced such a major protracted conflict since the beginning of the nineteenth century and no one could recall the serious social and economic problems that followed in the aftermath of the allied victory at Waterloo in 1815. Unaware of the lessons of the past, many predicted unprecedented prosperity in a 'land fit for heroes'. The directors of Standard Life were more cautious, recognising that the enormous cost of the war had greatly reduced the country's financial strength. Stunned by Leonard Dickson's death and anxious to maintain continuity at such a critical time, they quickly appointed Steuart Edye Macnaghten, the actuary of the company, as his successor. Macnaghten, who had come from the Equitable in 1911, had worked closely with Dickson, as well as acting as his honorary secretary at the Association of Scottish Life Offices during 1917.[2] They had similar backgrounds. Macnaghten

came from a distinguished Ulster family of lawyers, soldiers and civil servants in India, tracing their ancestry back to Sir Alexander Macnaghten, who died with James IV at Flodden. Illness had prevented him from following his father, who had been killed in action in 1878, into the hussars, but he remained fascinated by the army and adopted a rather formal manner in his relations with colleagues. There was a family connection with Standard Life as his great uncle Sir Steuart Macnaghten, the chairman of the Southampton Dock Company, was a member of the London board from 1880 to 1895.[3] Although Macnaghten shared much of Dickson's outlook, he believed passionately that life assurance and general insurance did not mix. Consequently, the possibility of a merger with one or more other companies was abandoned in favour of developing Standard Life's own business.

Albert E. King succeeded Macnaghten as secretary and assistant actuary. He had worked with Macnaghten for a year at the Equitable where the two men had become good friends. Said to be

Steuart Edye Macnaghten
(1873–1952), manager from
1919 to 1938.

one of the most brilliant actuaries of his generation, King had a particular interest in annuities from his student days. After Macnaghten left the Equitable in 1911, King became assistant to the manager, George Lidstone, 'who was not slow to appreciate [his] keenness and ability'. When Lidstone was appointed actuary of Scottish Widows in 1913, King worked closely with his successor, William Palin Elderton, who was also a close friend and mentor to Macnaghten. King had been taught by Elderton and together they shared an interest in advanced mathematical statistics. In 1915 Macnaghten had persuaded King to join Standard Life to assist him with the extra work caused by Dickson's frequent absences

in London. In 1920 Macnaghten proposed King as a Fellow of the Faculty, and he became an untiring supporter of it. Macnaghten rarely took any action without first consulting King, who lived near him in Edinburgh.[4]

Their strategy was simple and consistent: to make Standard Life as much like the Equitable as possible and to shift the balance of the business back towards with-profits policies. The Equitable was a mutual company founded in 1762, which uniquely throughout its long history had never paid commission nor appointed agents. Instead, policies were sold direct by inspectors, who could earn generous bonuses if they matched or exceeded their annual quotas. Writing to Elderton, Macnaghten confessed, 'I am afraid we won't be able anyhow at present to attain the high respectability of not employing any agents or paying commission! This I know would be an ideal state of things from my point of view.'[5] He planned to move cautiously in this direction by continuing to improve Standard Life's financial health and by converting, as soon as was practical, to mutual status,[6] which he was convinced would attract custom. In his view, the advantage of mutuality was that, like the Equitable, Standard Life would become the property of the with-profits policy-holders, who would then be entitled to share all the profits rather than divide them with the shareholders. Macnaghten's immediate priority following the decision to abandon Europe, however, was to recover domestic business lost during the war and to try to succeed, where Dickson had failed, in bringing down the expenses ratio. Although at heart he believed that with-profits whole-life policies were best, he appreciated that in the current market conditions other types of assurance were likely to be more attractive.

INTRODUCING COMPETITIVE PRODUCTS

The range of products was overhauled in 1919 with new plans for women at the same rate as for men,* a revised public-school policy (to pay for school fees) and, in response to a further increase in taxation in the Budget, a new death duties policy (later renamed Family Provision) which was designed to take advantage of the difference between the issue and conversion price of Victory Bonds.[7] None of these products was innovative, but they were more flexible than those offered by others. At the same time annuity rates were made more competitive, an outcome of King's analysis of Standard Life's experience.

The Acme scheme, which was already operating in Canada as the 'Perfect policy', was introduced in 1921. This was an improved version of the 'three options policy' with payments limited to 20 annual instalments during which time no bonuses would accrue. At the end of the contract the sum insured was to be increased by one half and there were a number of other additional benefits, such as provision for disability and a guaranteed surrender value. The scheme was not

CENTENARY YEAR 1925

The "ACME" Policy OF THE STANDARD LIFE ASSURANCE Co.

REPRESENTS *the highest point in the development of* LIFE ASSURANCE.

The Standard Life Assurance Co.
(Established · 1825)
Head Office: 3, GEORGE STREET, EDINBURGH.

The brochure for the Acme policy introduced in 1921.

without its critics; Sir William Schooling, a leading insurance commentator, condemned it as offering a poorer return than a with-profits policy.[8] Like the products introduced before the war, all these new policies were intended to discourage early surrender and on the whole appealed to the better-off in stable employment. It was hoped that retention would be fostered by the introduction at the 1920 valuation of a

---

* Until this time premiums for women of child-bearing age had been much more expensive than for men because of the high mortality rate during pregnancy. Some life offices had refused to assure such women because the risk was too great.

The interior of Standard Life's new London office at 46 Queen Victoria Street in the 1920s.

The title page from Edith Beesley's booklet which accompanied her monthly training meetings. She was the first woman to occupy a senior position with the company.

reversionary bonus on a sliding scale – akin to the old tontine scheme – which favoured those who had held policies for more than five years and greatly benefited those who had held them for at least ten years. At the same time, on advice from the branches, Macnaghten persuaded the board to change from quinquennial to triennial valuations which, since bonuses would be added more frequently, was expected to stimulate new with-profits business.[9]

The women's policies were intended to underpin a drive to attract more business from women. In 1920 Edith Beesley, one of the first women to become a senior official in an insurance company, was recruited to open a women's department in the London West End branch. She threw herself into the task with enthusiasm and quickly attracted publicity by flying from Wadden Aerodrome to Paris and back in a day to interview a prospective customer. She began to appoint women agents and inspectors and inaugurated monthly meetings for them 'to take the form of a sort of conference, someone being chosen to read a paper or give an address'.[10] This long-overdue initiative was an instant success. Her efforts in the West End were accompanied by an overhaul of the City branch, which had under-performed for a decade. A.B. Drayton was recalled from Montevideo to take over as manager. The old cramped premises in King William Street were sold and while new offices were being refurbished at 46 Queen Victoria Street the branch moved to 110 Cannon Street. Drayton immediately made an impact, restoring

the branch to its pre-eminent position.[11] This was only just in time as, with the onset of recession, the branches in Scotland and the north of England were faltering. To encourage greater awareness amongst the staff and stimulate sales, an in-house newsletter began to be published in 1922.[12] Convinced that the company was now equipped with competitive products, Macnaghten used the newsletter as a vehicle for the introduction of a quota scheme for the production of new business for all branches based on the previous year's performance and linked at first to an annual competition.[13]

LOOKING ABROAD FOR SUCCESS

At first these initiatives at home were unsuccessful (see Figure 5.1a overleaf and Appendix 2 on page 378), partly because of the economic situation which depressed the whole market, but also because Standard Life still lacked credibility after the difficulties of the previous 20 years. More disappointing than the lack of growth in new sums assured at home was the fall in new premium income as customers elected to take out the cheaper without-profits policies. Worse still, after all the efforts to encourage loyalty, was the rise in surrenders, which in 1924 totalled a record £210,000 – over 10 per cent of all new business – as policy-holders switched their investments to high-yielding fixed-interest securities.[14] Consequently, like Dickson, Macnaghten was forced to look overseas for new business. Canada remained the most important foreign market, which after a strong post-war recovery under Clark Kennedy's

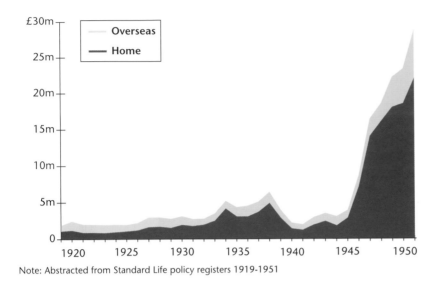

£30m —

Note: Abstracted from Standard Life policy registers 1919-1951

FIGURE 5.1a
Distribution of new home and
overseas business 1919–51

inspired leadership now accounted for over 30 per cent of all new sums assured (see Figure 5.1b overleaf). One drawback of placing too much emphasis on Canada, however, was the large number of lapsed policies and surrenders and the continuing high level of expenses. Macnaghten went to Canada in 1921 to review these issues but failed to reach any conclusions.[15] Progress was disrupted by the total destruction by fire of the offices in St James Street, Montreal, on the morning of 7 February 1922. Luckily the records of the branch, stored in the safes, survived and it was possible to resume business almost at once in temporary offices in the McGill buildings. Although Ernest Lindsay Armstrong was sent out from the London office to maintain contact with the sales force, the attention of Clark Kennedy

and his staff was of necessity diverted by the need to rebuild the St James Street office.[16]

The performance of the South African branch, which by this time should have been realising its potential, was disappointing, aggravated by the effects of the rebellion in the Transvaal during 1922. Thomas Darling, who had taken over the branch the year before, disagreed fundamentally with Macnaghten's strategy of direct selling and believed that the branch should be handed over in its entirety to agents.[17] Dissatisfied, he resigned in 1924 to join the Southern Life Association of Capetown, and was followed a year later by his deputy.[18]

Uruguay and the Argentine, too, remained depressed. In 1920 A.B. Drayton, who had done so much to expand the branch, was replaced by Arthur Leslie Cook, the brother of H.M. Cook, who had caused so much trouble in India (see page 164). In 1923 Blount went out to consider the future of the branch. He closed the Argentine sub-office in Buenos Aires to new business, but reprieved the branch in Montevideo, chiefly because the recently appointed 'Camp inspector', the colourful Don Ramón Paradell, was securing good custom in the Uruguayan countryside.[19]*

With little prospect of immediate improvement in most overseas markets Macnaghten looked to India, which he visited in 1922. Unlike Dickson, he was impressed with the potential of the market, but, as he himself admitted, this may have been more to do with family sentiment

* The whole country outside Montevideo was known as the Camp and was divided into eighteen departments.

than sound business sense. In Calcutta he found a portrait of his grandfather Sir Francis Macnaghten, chief justice of Bengal, and in a cemetery he came across the grave of his great uncle, Sir William Macnaghten, who was assassinated at Kabul in 1841. Nevertheless his confidence was not without justification. The Indian branch had performed well after the war, with new business climbing from £238,154 in 1919 to £316,000 in 1920 and retreating the following year to just under £250,000 with almost negligible surrenders (see Figure 5.1b overleaf). Standard Life enjoyed a monopoly of business from civil servants and service personnel and could rely on agencies with Grindlays and Cox & Co and the newly formed Imperial Bank of India. Macnaghten suggested that the company should catch the nationalist mood by appointing 'an Indian of good standing to the board'; but this did not happen until 1931.[20]

The harbour in Montevideo in the first part of the twentieth century. Standard Life continued to be represented in Uruguay until 1968.

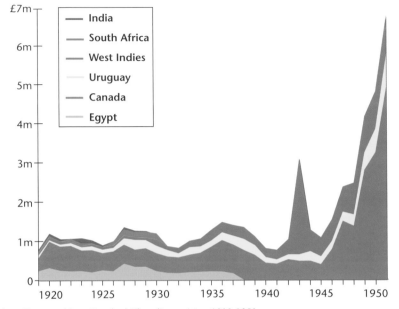

£7m

— India
— South Africa
— West Indies
— Uruguay
— Canada
— Egypt

Note: Abstracted from Standard Life policy registers 1919-1951

FIGURE 5.1b
Distribution of new overseas
business 1919–51

RESTORING CONFIDENCE

Publicly the board put a brave face on Standard Life's indifferent performance in the immediate post-war years, which remained weaker than that of either Scottish Widows or Scottish Provident (see Figure 5.2 opposite). The downturn in 1921 was blamed on the loss of continental business, which had actually contributed little or nothing since 1914. Shareholders and policyholders were encouraged to use every opportunity to promote Standard Life's products.[21] Macnaghten hoped finally to restore confidence in the company by adopting a 'bedrock basis' of 2.5 per cent for the 1923 valuation, which still allowed for a bonus of 1.75 per cent and for almost £140,000 to be carried forward. He was

able to do this because the company's inner reserves had increased from £230,000 in 1920 to almost £1 million by 1923 as a result of the profitable sale of property and investments and a healthy surplus in 1920 on the revenue account.[22]

There were substantial tax advantages in adopting a figure of 2.5 per cent because the Inland Revenue was prepared to accept it as realistic and consequently allow all the provisions needed to meet future liabilities against tax. Other offices quickly followed suit. This method of valuation not only strengthened the balance sheet but also held out the possibility of large bonuses in the future as reserves accumulated. A comparison with other offices showed Standard Life was reserving 27.8 per cent of premium income for future expenses and profits for with-profits policy-holders, more than nearly every competitor and even 3 per cent more than the Equitable.[23] In announcing the result Macnaghten told the 'Field Force' that they were now armed to the teeth against any opposition.[24] The *Stock Exchange Gazette* was unequivocal in its praise: 'The valuation now adopted is, we believe, on a stronger basis – i.e., one requiring larger reserves, and providing a bigger margin for future profits – than has ever been adopted by any Life Office.'[25] At the investigation dinner on 26 February 1924 in the presence of Spencer Thomson, who had been rehabilitated by Macnaghten, a delighted Edward Blount put his feelings into song:

In the realm of Life Assurance
Flies the Scottish Standard high
And for pluck and strong endurance
It all rivals can defy
Though in public estimation
We were once beneath a cloud
Our most recent Valuation
Is a thing of which we're proud.[26]

MUTUALISATION AT THE CENTENARY

No sooner was the investigation completed than Macnaghten began to plan Standard Life's centenary celebrations for March 1925. Two senior managers were put to work to research the history, which was to be written by Sir William Schooling, who had so recently criticised the Acme policy.[27] The motive for inviting him was to ensure a good press for the centrepiece of the anniversary – the mutualisation of the company which Macnaghten believed essential if Standard Life was to remain competitive. William Thomson, who had never had a good word to say about mutual companies, believing them subject to 'excited meetings' of policy-holders,[28] would have been aghast. Although Macnaghten had suggested the idea to the board in December 1921 in a paper addressing the question of increasing once again the policy-holders' share of the profits,[29] nothing was done until April 1924 when a committee was appointed to consider the matter.[30] Macnaghten, whose main concern was to raise the bonus to policy-holders by cutting out the shareholders' entitlement to a division of the profits, canvassed the members

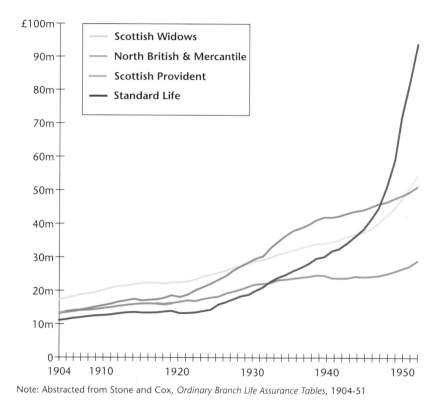

Note: Abstracted from Stone and Cox, *Ordinary Branch Life Assurance Tables*, 1904-51

heavily.[31] The committee hardly debated the advantages or disadvantages and never referred to the need to protect the company from a predator, which was to become one of the main motives for later mutualisations.[32] They quickly endorsed the proposal to issue in 'exchange for each £10 share (£3.50 fully paid) £17 of fully paid 5 per cent stock' at a cost of some £850,000 for all 50,000 shares.[33] There followed a month of intense activity during which opinion from counsel and actuaries was obtained, and stock exchanges consulted.[34] W.P. Phelps, the distinguished actuary and benefactor of the Institute,

FIGURE 5.2
Assets of major Scottish life offices 1904–51

The company, which was established in 1825 as a partnership, had an issued capital of 10,000 shares with a nominal value of £50 but with just £1 paid. This was the only call ever made on proprietors. There was, of course, an outstanding call originally of £49, although this was reduced later as surplus was credited to the shareholders' account. Until Standard Life was converted into a limited company in 1910, the shareholders remained personally liable for its debts. At that time the shares were split into five and a formal Stock Exchange listing was obtained. The nominal value was correspondingly reduced to £10 a share. It was these 50,000 shares that were in existence at the time of mutualisation in 1925.

DIVIDEND

Starting in 1827, an annual dividend was paid at the rate of 5 per cent up to 1855. As the capital was progressively increased at each investigation by capitalising some surplus, the amount paid in dividends rose over this period from £700 in 1835 to £5,000 by 1855. The rate was increased to 7.5 per cent over the next four years and thereafter to 10 per cent.

From 1865 onwards a policy was adopted over each quinquennium of distributing some of the surplus to shareholders by way of cash bonuses. This surplus was determined after each investigation and was fixed for the ensuing five years. Normally between 20 and 40 per cent of the surplus was earmarked for shareholders although by the time of mutualisation, under competitive pressure, this had fallen to 10 per cent. The distribution to shareholders in 1860 at 10 per cent of the paid-up capital was £10,000, rising to £35,000 in the 1870s. The difficulties that the company encountered in the last years of the nineteenth century caused a reduction to £25,000 in 1882 and then to £20,000 in 1896. In 1905, following the passing of the bonus to policy-holders, the dividend to shareholders was limited to 10 per cent on their paid-up capital, some £12,000.

SHARE PRICE

The shares were issued at £1 and, although there was no formal quote until 1911, the company's records indicate prices over the years at which shares changed hands – sometimes these were transfers for value between shareholders and on other occasions the company bought the shares in. In the early years the price fell to 13/6 (a loss of 32.5 per cent) but rose to £4 by 1840, to £12.50 by 1850, to £20 by 1855 and finally to £77 by 1877. This was the highest price ever attained by the shares until mutualisation 48 years later. There was a fairly steady decline to £45 in 1905 with a further slump to £30 following the passing of the bonus and the dividend cut. The shares fell as low as £16 in 1915. At mutualisation in 1925 the shares were valued at £85 per original share and replaced by 5 per cent perpetual stock.

RETURNS TO SHAREHOLDERS

An original investment of £1 in 1825 had turned into £85 a hundred years later. This represented a compound annual rate of return of 4.5 per cent per annum. In addition, there were of course the dividends, whether expressed as interest on the capital or interest on the capital plus a share of the surplus. Over the years, the income was between 3 and 5 per cent of the prevailing share price. The average appears to have been around 4 per cent so that the total return over the whole hundred years was perhaps 8.5 per cent per annum. This was much better than returns from fixed-interest investments over the century of perhaps 3 per cent.

in a remarkably brief report based on information supplied by Standard Life, rather than based on an inspection of the books themselves, had no doubt that the scheme 'will be to the interest of Policy-holders and Annuitants'.[35] The other consulting actuary waited until he had seen what Phelps had to say before submitting his own letter of support. The scheme was made public on 10 July. Some financial journalists, particularly those on the *Financial Times*, and a few stockbrokers hinted that the shareholders were being short-changed: 'We cannot see why holders of Standards should give up their heritage, a real live investment, for a dead one on such terms. Shareholders should demand the opinion of a disinterested actuary.'[36] Such advice was ignored and mutualisation was approved by a large majority of shareholders three weeks later. It took several months to draft the necessary legislation, which was sanctioned by the shareholders in February 1925.[37] By the time of the centenary dinner on 12 June, held at the head office in George Street, the Bill had passed all its main stages in Parliament. With the foundations of his strategy now in place, Macnaghten declared enthusiastically that 'there is no other Life Assurance Company in the world in a stronger position than that which the Standard now occupies, and this cannot but make the task of our Field Force easier and lead to good results in the way of new business figures'.[38] Although the company almost stumbled into mutualisation, there is no doubt of the importance of this decision for its long-term development.

The Standard Life Assurance Co.,
3 GEORGE STREET,
EDINBURGH,   *June* 1925.

DEAR SIR,

I beg to inform you that on the ...... inst. the Royal Assent was given to the Standard Life Assurance Company's Act, 1925, which reincorporates the Company and provides for its control and management as a Mutual Company.

Under the terms of the Act the Share Capital has been cancelled, and in lieu thereof Five per cent. Perpetual Stock has been created, £17 of Stock being issued for each £10 Share (£3, 10s. paid). Interest on the Stock is payable half-yearly on the 15th May and 15th November, and I have pleasure in enclosing herewith Warrant for the half-year's interest due on 15th May 1925, less the payment made on account on that date.

The Certificates in respect of the cancelled Shares should be sent to this Office, in order that the Certificates for the new Stock may be issued in exchange.

I am,

Yours faithfully,

STEUART MACNAGHTEN,
Manager.

PUTTING THE EMPHASIS ON INVESTMENT

Along with other insurance companies, Standard Life had strengthened its investment management in the wake of the collapse in 1922 of City Equitable when stock certificates were discovered to have gone missing.[39] The investment committee began to meet monthly and keep better minutes. With mutualisation complete, Macnaghten turned his attention to improving the performance of investments. He persuaded the board to switch from the long-standing commitment to mortgages to ordinary shares.[40] The

A letter to shareholders informing them that Standard Life had converted to a mutual company and requesting that they send in their cancelled share certificates to be replaced with certificates for the new 5 per cent perpetual stock (opposite).

A paperweight produced to mark the company's centenary in 1925.

inspiration for this innovation came from Albert King and Andrew Rutherford Davidson, an assistant actuary, who had joined the company in 1914 from the Edinburgh office of the English and Scottish Law Life Assurance Association. Both King and Davidson had an interest in investment performance, and the latter's two closest friends in the industry were G. Hugh Recknell, who was to succeed Geoffrey Marks as manager of the National Mutual, and Jim Davie, who was to become investment secretary of Scottish Provident.[41] All four were attracted by J.M. Keynes' belief that a life office 'ought to have only one investment and it should be changed every day', which he was putting into effect as chairman of National Mutual.[42] Standard Life's strategy was to increase the proportion of its assets in marketable securities (government stocks, debentures, preference shares and ordinary stock) from about 65 per cent to over 85 per cent, principally by raising the total investments in ordinary stock from less than 1 per cent of marketable securities to about 20 per cent within five years (see Appendix 6 on page 386). At first only shares in investment trusts were purchased.[43] These were popular at the time and had themselves only recently switched the bulk of their capital into equities.[44] Although Standard Life was no stranger to ordinary stock, having underwritten several new issues since the war, there was a reluctance to confine investments to a single company and a preference for the greater spread of risk and high yields available from investment trusts. To put the new policy into effect, however, the investment department needed to improve the quality of its market information by monitoring the financial press more closely and by arranging to receive a wider range of stockbrokers' circulars. In April 1926 the board approved a list of 55 stockbrokers, including some of the best known London firms such as Laing & Cruikshank, Messel & Co., Kitcat & Aitken and Helbert Wagg & Co.[45] Very quickly the investment department under T. Dick Peat was producing impressive digests of stockbrokers' advice and detailed statistics. Armed with this information the investment committee moved away from investment trusts and began cautiously buying shares on its own account, at first only in telephone and telegraph utilities in North America and in banks, insurance companies and electrical concerns in Britain.[46] With the exception of the oil and financial sectors, there was little attempt to enlarge the scope of the holdings until after the Second World War. After a careful analysis of both returns and performance, the committee gave the investment manager a mandate to buy and sell shares up to a certain value in selected firms and sectors. When the mandate was exhausted further purchases or sales had to be approved.[47] Monitoring the developing portfolio of ordinary shares occupied the greater part of the time of the investment committee. Increasingly they found themselves to be the largest shareholders in some of the country's best-known companies, along with the few other insurance companies which had adopted similar strategies, such as the National Mutual, Prudential, Equity & Law and Scottish Provident.[48] Consequently, as the recession deepened in the late 1920s, Standard Life began to be consulted about rationalisation schemes such as the amalgamation of the steelmakers Bolckow Vaughan and Dorman Long in 1929[49] and the total reconstruction of William Beardmore & Co., the Glasgow manufacturers of armaments.[50] Although concerned about the effect of such events on the share price, the committee did not reply directly, relying on stockbrokers to make their views known. In turn stockbrokers became more proficient in their dealings with their corporate clients. London brokers, especially, reported on visits to companies and sought advice from merchant banks. By 1950 Cazenove were handling about 25 per cent of Standard Life's transactions, followed in order of importance by Bell Cowan in Edinburgh, and then by other London firms, notably Greenwells, Rowe & Pitman and de Zoete & Gorton.[51]

The clear indication that the world economy was sliding rapidly into recession by the late 1920s did not cause the committee to question the strategy. On the contrary, in the summer of 1928 the board agreed to investigate the potential of American common stock (ordinary shares). Macnaghten visited New York in June and returned full of misplaced enthusiasm: 'I was . . . assured by responsible authorities that basic conditions in America today were sound and that for those who were not interested in speculation but needed real investments there

would be ample opportunities.'[52] After a heated debate he persuaded the board to invest £1 million in American common stock on the grounds that 'America has the greatest stock of gold, is the greatest creditor nation and it is in its interest to keep the value of the dollar'.[53] The investment committee, influenced by a sceptical James Ivory, proceeded with caution as prices were high, and only one purchase was made before the Wall Street crash on 29 October 1929.[54] Even when stocks were cheap in the wake of the catastrophe, the committee remained nervous. Although the board renewed the mandate to invest £1 million in 1931,[55] no purchases were made until after the presidential election of

Crowds on the steps of the Subtreasury building in Wall Street on 29 October 1929 awaiting news of the collapse of the stockmarket.

November 1933, which returned Franklin D. Roosevelt. Since his 'New Deal' created uncertainty in financial markets, the investment committee did not rush into purchases and by the outbreak of war in 1939 Standard Life had less than 4 per cent of its assets invested in the United States.[56]

RESPONDING TO THE SLUMP

The Wall Street crash sent shockwaves through international financial markets, precipitating the worldwide slump with accompanying mass unemployment in many basic industries. Standard Life's response to the decline in security values on the London stock exchange from the third quarter of 1929 until 1934 was as measured as it was professional. The relative values of each class of marketable securities was calculated by Albert King so as to allow the investment committee to form a view (Figure 5.3). Concerned but not panicked, the committee adjusted the portfolio away from ordinary and preference stock towards (in equal proportion) British government stock; Commonwealth and foreign government, provincial and municipal securities (overseas securities); and debentures (see Appendix 6 on page 386). In managing these fixed-interest securities, the investment department had discretion to alter the mix of short- and long-dated stock depending on prevailing money rates.[57] Nevertheless, throughout these years Standard Life continued to buy ordinary stock in the financial and oil sectors, while reducing exposure in telephones and telegraphs.

During the spring of 1932 the Treasury and the Bank of England planned in great secrecy to convert the interest rates on the massive short-dated war loan from 5 to 3.5 per cent, heralding the advent of 'cheap money' designed to help lift the economy out of the slump.[58] All large institutional shareholders, including Standard Life, were consulted in advance and requested not to switch to other investments immediately so as to prevent a fall in price. Well aware that this policy was in their long-term interest, the institutions agreed and the conversion was carried through smoothly at the end of June. The operation was so well managed that the price of government securities, along with other fixed-interest stock, rather than falling, rose as investors' confidence returned.[59] With the ordinary shareholdings still

FIGURE 5.3
Ordinary stock investments
1922–51

Year	Ledger value	Market value	Total investment in marketable securities (%)
1922	106,252	136,610	1
1926	1,079,911	1,173,398	8
1927	1,724,663	1,889,615	11.5
1929	2,688,310	3,113,981	18
1931	3,939,840	3,138,709	20
1934	4,569,464	4,274,608	15
1936	6,130,568	7,091,532	21.5
1938	7,020,280	6,605,680	23
1939	7,086,650	5,739,375	23
1940	6,906,724	4,960,798	21
1944	7,435,386	8,066,204	17.5
1950	17,099,899	18,051,456	22
1951	19,538,005	21,710,097	21

Note: Abstracted from Standard Life archives

showing a large loss and with yields on equities of less than 4 per cent, Standard Life increased its holdings of government securities between 1932 and 1934 from just under £5 million to over £6.5 million. Taking advantage of the rising market, investments in debentures and overseas securities were also made. Directly ordinary share values began to recover their losses in the spring of 1935, the directors resumed their strategy of holding about 20 per cent of marketable securities in ordinary shares and now placed greater emphasis on industrial sectors.[60]

Although the proportion of assets in mortgages and loans fell from over 30 per cent before the First World War to 13 per cent in 1930, the company had still been willing to consider advances against good security despite the problems with the outstanding farm mortgages in the United States (see page 178). The boom was over by 1920 and many farmers faced ruin. Nearly all the mortgages still in force required to be refinanced and where farms were repossessed they were usually found to be neglected as families had struggled to keep up repayments.[61] Luckily for Standard Life the quality of its risks was better than most, thanks to the advice of James Ivory, and most of the mortgages were in states and provinces where there had been less speculation. Unable to sell the remaining loans or to recover all of them through the courts, substantial sums had to be written off in 1920 and again in 1925.[62] Loans to the Earl of Kenmare and Lord Napier and Ettrick were

foreclosed in the early 1920s,[63] but Standard Life was still prepared to advance £18,000 to the elderly Earl of Chesterfield in 1924 – the last in a tradition of lending to the aristocracy which extended back almost to the beginning of the company.[64] More typical in the 1920s were mortgages for commercial development, such as £70,000 for cinema construction in Leeds in 1922[65] and £30,000 three years later to Montagu Burton, the Yorkshire clothier who coined the slogan 'the Full Monty'.[66] During 1929 the board agreed to contribute £140,000 to a consortium led by the Royal Exchange Assurance which was

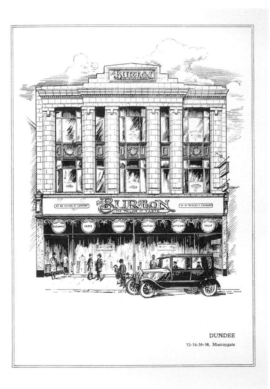

Burton's store at Murraygate, Dundee, 1925. Standard Life loaned Montagu Burton £30,000 to build new shops during that year.

The White Star liners *Britannic* and *Georgic* at Harland & Wolff's Queens Island yard in Belfast in 1931. Two years before, Standard Life had joined a consortium to allow these ships to be completed.

lending £900,000 under the Trade Facilities Acts to the Oceanic Steam Navigation Co. to allow the motor ships *Britannic* and *Georgic* to be completed by the Belfast shipbuilders Harland & Wolff.[67] This transaction gave Standard Life a ringside seat in the reconstruction of the Royal Mail Group* of companies, cementing relations with leading City financial institutions and the Bank of England. Although under the terms of the Trade Facilities Acts the Treasury was supposed to honour loans if the borrower defaulted, this did not happen, and Standard Life was left

*   The collapse of the Royal Mail Group of shipping companies, which included such household names as White Star, Union Castle, and Elder Dempster, in 1931 was the largest corporate exposure during the inter-war slump and resulted in the imprisonment of the chairman, Lord Kylsant. The reconstruction involved all the clearing banks and was masterminded by the accountant Sir William McLintock and General Sir Arthur Maxwell of banking house Glyn Mills (see page 202) with advice from Montagu Norman, the Governor of the Bank of England. (These events are described in Edwin Green and Michael Moss, *A Business of National Importance – the Royal Mail Shipping Group, 1902–37*, London, 1982.)

with a block of shares in the Oceanic Steam Navigation Realisation Company. Having by chance become ensnared in this complex affair, the directors refused to participate in any other reconstruction schemes.

HOUSE PURCHASE BUSINESS

The investment manager, T. Dick Peat, died suddenly in 1933 and was succeeded by Alexander Robert Reid, who distrusted equity investments.[68] It took little encouragement from Andrew Davidson, now the agency manager, to persuade him immediately to review Standard Life's attitude to mortgages. With the rapid growth in private housing in the south of England, Davidson wanted to be able to offer mortgages as well as the supporting life policies so as to meet competition from the building societies which recommended English offices for their insurance needs.[69] As a vehicle for this purpose Standard Life purchased in April 1934 for £250,000 the Heritable Securities and Mortgage Investment Association, which had been established in Edinburgh in 1862.[70] The Heritable, as it was known, was a modest-sized company with assets of a little under £400,000, mostly invested in small property developments and commercial premises in Edinburgh and Glasgow.[71] The plan was for the Heritable to use its expertise in negotiating mortgages to lend £2.5 million initially set aside by Standard Life. A house-purchase brochure was hurriedly produced and a Heritable branch opened in London where demand was reportedly strong.[72] A.B.

A.B. Drayton, the secretary of the London City branch, photographed in his office in 1920.

Drayton of the London office was right to dismiss the whole initiative as 'half-hearted'.[73] There were few takers as terms were uncompetitive. Instead, the Heritable continued its previous investment policy until the outbreak of war, by which time only £250,000 had been drawn from Standard Life.

THE FIRST PENSION SCHEMES

Surprisingly, it was the investment department that provided the introduction to the management of pension schemes, which were to become the core business after the Second World War. During 1920 Standard Life agreed to underwrite the issue of £1.5 million of 7 per cent notes by Vickers, the armaments company.[74] Fortuitously, the company was being encouraged by its

PENSION SCHEMES AND THE INLAND REVENUE

There were two alternative ways of setting up a scheme: either to establish an in-house scheme with independent trustees and actuarial advice, or to use an insurance company. Perversely, the Inland Revenue treated each approach differently. Under the terms of the 1918 Income Tax Act, pension contributions paid to insurance companies qualified for the same rebates as life insurance premiums (half the standard rate of tax up to a qualifying premium of 7 per cent of the total sum assured), providing the scheme was approved by the Revenue. The 1921 Finance Act, amidst widespread protest from the insurance industry, allowed employees who were members of a *bona fide* in-house scheme to claim their contributions as expenses – in other words, they obtained relief at the full rate of tax. Unlike insurance company schemes, however, the proceeds were taxable at a quarter of the standard rate.

These differences caused considerable confusion in the emerging pensions market. Unless a scheme fulfilled very narrow criteria specified by the Act, approval had to be sought in every case. This could be time consuming and frustrating as the Revenue, at least at first, discouraged provision for widows and disliked provision for 'back' or previous service with the same employer. Their motive was to outlaw schemes and policies for the better-off designed not so much to provide for old age but to avoid tax.[1] The Association of Scottish Life Offices and the Life Offices Association were in constant dialogue over this issue with the government throughout the inter-war years, which resulted in legal protection for funds in 1927 and new regulations in the 1930 and 1947 Finance Acts.[2]

Whichever way they were constituted, schemes could either be set up so that the employees contributed or not. Most commentators preferred contributory schemes as they provided members with greater security. There were three types of scheme: 'money purchase' where a fixed proportion of the salary was paid in each year; 'average salary'; and 'service' or 'final' salary, where the employer had to contribute sufficient funds to compensate for pay increases. Average and final-salary schemes required complex annual actuarial calculations 'based on *unknown* rates of salary progression, on *unknown* future benefits, or *unknown* future contributions, on *unknown* rates of withdrawal, and the *unknown* profit thereon;'[3] whereas money-purchase schemes only depended on 'the accurate estimate of the future rates of mortality, interest and, possibly, withdrawal'.[4] In all three types arranged through an insurance company, contributions were used to purchase deferred annuities or, less commonly, endowment policies.

Advertisements from the 1960s and 1970s.

A hand-finishing shop at Vickers' Sheffield works. Standard Life
insured the company's group pension scheme in 1920.

bankers to form an independent pension scheme. Financial institutions and auditors were increasingly anxious that pension funds should be held outside the balance sheet in case of either takeover or failure. At Standard Life itself until the mid-1930s, the establishment fund, which provided pensions, was charged against the assets. Ian Fletcher, the assistant secretary at Standard Life's London office, tendered successfully for the Vickers scheme and then worked out the details with the chairman, Douglas Vickers. Fletcher left shortly afterwards to

Field-Marshal Douglas Earl Haig (1861–1928) on the right with General Sir Herbert Lawrence (1861–1943), his chief-of-staff, and, on the left, Field-Marshal Herbert Viscount Plumer, perhaps the ablest commander of the war. The Haig family had been associated with Standard Life from the company's foundation in 1825, and Earl Haig joined the board in 1922 to cement the relationship with the London bankers Glyn's, of which Lawrence was managing partner.

become life manager for the London insurance brokers Crawley, Dickson & Bowring (later known as C.T. Bowring & Co.) and was succeeded by P.C. Reynolds.[75] Within a year Standard Life had issued 800 deferred-annuity policies under the Vickers scheme and by 1930 the total had risen to 1,800 policies.[76]

Importantly, the contract brought Standard Life in touch with Vickers' bankers Glyn Mills, widely recognised as one of the leading finance houses. Glyn Mills already had close connections with the insurance industry with its partners on the boards of Sun Life, North British & Mercantile and Legal & General, the last named of which was to become the largest provider of pension schemes.[77] Nevertheless, Glyn's were willing to recommend Standard Life to their clients. The relationship was strengthened in 1922 when Field-Marshal the Earl Haig joined the Standard Life board; one of Glyn's managing partners, General Sir Herbert Lawrence, who was also on the Vickers board from 1921, had been his chief of general staff at the end of the war. Contact with Glyn's brought other benefits as the bank under the direction of General Sir Arthur Maxwell, another managing partner whose background, unusually for a banker, had been in the Post Office, was a pioneer of office automation for handling clients' accounts.[78] Such a change in working practices was essential for dealing cost-effectively with the large number of policies issued under group schemes.

Although the London office received several more enquiries about group schemes, nothing was done to foster the business immediately because it could only be secured through brokers – and Macnaghten disliked the large commissions they charged. However, he was keen to use the connection with Glyn's to sell voluntary group life assurance schemes building on Standard Life's existing expertise. In 1927 a special offer was negotiated for the staffs of the leading clearing banks – Barclays, Bank of Liverpool, Lloyds, Midland, National Provincial, Royal Bank of Scotland, Union Bank of Scotland, and the Westminster. Over the next two years similar offers were made to other banks and to oil companies. Group pension enquiries were not turned away and in 1927 a scheme was arranged for Gestetners, the manufacturers of duplicating machinery.[79] The following year the London office, having failed to make much progress in selling group life assurance because of the strength of competition, decided to 'have a go' at pensions, writing to firms which 'had recently published satisfactory annual reports'. The response was 'immediate and striking – but there the real problem started'. Standard Life had no experience of marketing pensions since all the schemes which had been quoted for had been at the request of employers, such as Vickers. The London staff took the novel step of visiting companies to get to know the senior management and discuss the details – a practice which was to become a hallmark of Standard Life's approach to selling pensions. Although a great deal was learnt about 'the employer's point of view – how he was concerned with the problem of providing for his older men, how he viewed the question of cost, how so often each employer had his own pet notions, which must not be ignored', little business was forthcoming.[80] The most significant lesson to come from these visits was that large employers were reluctant to provide deferred annuity or endowment assurance for all their staff because 'younger members, having learned their trade, are inclined to leave after a few years'.[81] The only success of any note was with the great brewery firm of Barclay Perkins.[82]

REORGANISATION AND DEVELOPMENT

In the meantime A.B. Drayton had been fighting hard to change Macnaghten's attitude to brokers:

> *The Broker. For better or for worse he has established himself in the industry on a huge and still growing scale. The City proper is the great centre of his activities. There his offices exist, but his tentacles extend also far beyond, not merely into the surrounding countryside, but throughout England and even into Scotland itself. The stern fact faces us that a large business without him is nowadays impossible.*[83]

Drayton found a convert in Davidson, who, although he had no quarrel with the long-term strategy of turning Standard Life into a no-commission office, increasingly had doubts about the means to the end. No friend of

Special offer brochure to staff employees of Metropolitan-Vickers Electric Co. Ltd, 1925.

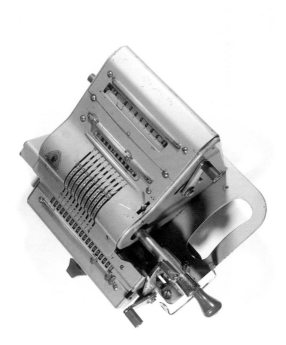

A Brunsviga multiplying machine of the kind used in the office from the beginning of the twentieth century until the introduction of computers in the 1960s.

brokers, he was persuaded they were a necessary evil. In an effort to recruit and retain better staff in March 1925, the quota scheme for new business was linked directly to staff bonuses, which could be as much as 25 per cent.[84] This was followed by some modest reorganisation of the branches in the United Kingdom and the recently independent Republic of Ireland where, with the end of the civil war, the company planned to renew its commitment using bank agents as in the past. A year later products were improved and a new training course for fieldmen was inaugurated.[85] These measures, together with the decision to introduce compound reversionary bonuses and annual valuations from

November 1927,[86] lifted new sums assured at home and overseas to about £3 million and there were indications that at last Standard Life was keeping pace with Scottish Widows and Scottish Provident if not with North British & Mercantile (see Figure 5.2 on page 191). At the same time, however, in line with Macnaghten's plans and reflecting the wider experience of the industry, the proportion of with-profits policies was increasing from around 60 per cent towards over 70 per cent by 1930.[87] Davidson was aware of the danger of placing too much emphasis on with-profits business – 'The effect of this . . . would have been to increase substantially the cost of each bonus declaration and therefore to strain the resources of the Company or to involve a reduction in the rate of bonus.'[88] Moreover, Standard Life may have been catching up in the volume of new business; but its expenses ratio was still 20 per cent compared with 12 per cent at Scottish Widows. North British, which under the leadership of Sir Arthur Worley was rapidly overhauling Scottish Widows to become the largest life assurance office in Scotland, had a ratio of 17 per cent.[89] As Davidson later reflected, Standard Life 'had the heavy expenses of a large company and the premium income of a comparatively small company'.[90]

Macnaghten and Davidson, learning from Glyn's, believed that recent developments in mechanised book-keeping systems provided an obvious means of keeping expenses in check as business grew. Brunsviga multiplying machines had been used at head office since the beginning of the century, an addressograph was purchased in 1920 and a multigraph machine for printing circulars and forms in 1925. After careful consideration, a Powers Samas tabulating machine was installed in 1927 under Macnaghten's personal supervision to cope with the additional work of the annual valuation and the issuing of bonus certificates, which were to be generated automatically.[91] Over the next decade the use of the machine was extended to include the calculation of annuity payments and associated tax, the compilation of new business statistics from the weekly returns from the branches, the tracking of lapses and revivals, payment of invoices, and stock control. Although not the first insurance company to invest in this new technology, Standard Life quickly came to be regarded as a pioneer in the mechanisation of life assurance records.[92]

During 1929 Eric M. Beilby, a partner in the Edinburgh accountancy firm of Howden & Molleson, became chairman of Standard Life. He had been recruited to the board in 1916 by Leonard Dickson with whom he had trained. He was also the managing director of the brewers William McEwan & Co. and was responsible for bringing about the merger with William Younger in 1931 to form Scottish Brewers, which eventually became Scottish & Newcastle.[93] All too aware of the consequences of Davidson's forecasts, he urged his colleagues to consider how the company should be developed. Considering that in current competitive market conditions it was impractical to expand without-profits business,

they decided to enter the domestic market for staff pension schemes on the grounds that there was room in the market for a domestic mutual life office.[94] There were other compelling reasons, too, spelled out by Davidson:

- *the relatively low cost of securing 'substantial and permanent additions to the premium income';*
- *that pension schemes, if designed correctly, would not involve high compound reversionary bonus payments;*
- *that scheme members would provide a ready market for other products offered at a discount.*[95]

To make pension schemes more attractive the single premium plan was pioneered by Standard Life which was 'so arranged that the employer does not make substantial contributions in respect of the younger (and continually changing) employees, but devotes his payments to the cases of those employees who are remaining in the service and are likely ultimately to become pensioners'.[96] Davidson hoped that in the long run it would be possible to sell pensions direct rather than through brokers, a view not shared by Drayton and his assistant P.C. Reynolds from their experience of speaking to potential customers.[97]

Standard Life had already joined the group assurances agreement to regulate commission rates, established the year before by the Life Offices Association with the other providers on the committee – Atlas, British Dominions, Phoenix, Wesleyan & General and North British & Mercantile.[98] It was not long before the members wished to include group pension schemes. A sub-committee chaired by W.A. Workman, general manager of Legal & General, and with representatives of North British & Mercantile, the Prudential and Standard Life, worked out the details of an amendment, which was signed in June 1931 by 29 of the 54 members of the group assurance agreement.[99] This was never more than a loose association and members undertook to compete on product and service, only paying flat-rate commissions to brokers. These agreements were remarkably enduring and survived until 1986 when they were finally ruled as uncompetitive by the Office of Fair Trading (see page 309). As a result they played a significant role in shaping the pension industry.

Beilby realised that the pension strategy could only work if the internal organisation of the company was overhauled. In December 1929 the board committee structure was reconstituted. A general purposes committee was formed to monitor new business throughout the company. Canada ceased to be under the direct control of the manager to make it easier to tackle the long-standing high expenses ratio. The brief of the investment committee was also widened. In keeping with the mood of the times, after several recent scandals where directors were unaware of the activities of their managers, Beilby's objective was to improve corporate governance there-

by ensuring that the board's wishes were implemented. For the first time the whole board was to approve investment policy annually – 'the proportion of funds to be held in (1) long- and short-dated securities, (2) foreign currencies, (3) debentures and mortgages, preference stocks and ordinary stocks and shares, (4) different countries and different classes', along with how much was to be invested in one concern and which brokers should be retained.[100] From the outset Beilby expected the general purposes committee to conduct its affairs in the same businesslike manner as the investment committee which as a member he had helped improve.

By this time Edward Blount, the agency manager, was tired and unwell. His understudy and successor in 1931 was Andrew Davidson with Alec Reid as his assistant. Davidson, 'a hanging judge of pomposity or pretentiousness and his judgements were not pronounced *sotto voce*',[101] had the disarming habit of calling men and women alike 'love' and 'darling' in both praise and fury.[102] Such eccentricity was misleading. In everything he did, Davidson was professional to his fingertips. Directly he became agency manager he toured the country energetically, visiting branches, inspiring the staff and insisting on fuller reports and more detailed supporting statistics. Returns were entered into the Powers Samas machine to calculate expense and other ratios on which were based the annual review of each branch and every member of the sales force. The resulting annual digests, which were considered and commented on by the general purposes committee, were impressive evidence of the new management approach in action.[103]

DEVELOPING GROUP PENSION SCHEMES

The main concern of the general purposes committee was to supervise the assault on the pensions market. At first Reynolds continued to handle enquiries in London and E.J.W. Cossar, an inspector, those in Edinburgh. There was much still to learn about negotiating with brokers and customers, obtaining approval from the Inland Revenue, and producing the individually tailored booklets. During 1931, their first full year together, in the depth of the slump, they completed nine single-premium schemes, which, through accompanying group insurance, also accounted for over 1 per cent of all new sums assured. Encouraged by this achievement a pension schemes department was formed under James Bremner (Brem) Dow and, later, A. Ernest Bromfield, with two young inspectors R.H. Mackay in London, aged 28, assisted at head office by K.W. Marshall, aged 22.[104] During the next two years Standard Life provided schemes for two major London insurance brokers involved in the pension business, Cuthbert Heath & Co. and C.T. Bowring & Co. where Ian Fletcher was still life manager.[105] They were followed in 1936 by another significant player, Hogg Robinson & Capel Cure.[106] These three brokers contributed directly to a boom in pension business targeted at those sectors least affected by the recession, such as brewing, food processing and retailing. By 1938, admittedly a record year, 45 new pension schemes were arranged and altogether group schemes contributed almost 30 per cent of all new ordinary sums assured.[107] The largest single scheme, for Metropolitan Vickers, by then a subsidiary of the American International General Electric Company, was established in 1934. The range of customers was impressive and many were household names, such as Kia-ora in 1932, Fortnum & Mason in 1933, Paton & Baldwins, J. Sainsbury and Taylor Woodrow in 1934, Kraft Cheese in 1935 and Littlewoods in 1937. Although most were designed for the better-paid staff, Standard Life was happy to provide schemes for all employees of large companies, as with Terry's of York in 1931, or for the hardly well-off employees of Sunningdale Golf Club and the servants of Balliol College, Oxford.[108]

The National Savings Committee, which had been established during the war, was concerned that the growth of pension schemes would damage in-house savings plans which were often set up with the help of insurance companies. Fearing retaliation from the Treasury, a handful of the larger life offices, including Standard Life, continued to help organise such plans, which included life assurance cover.[109]

BUILDING NEW BUSINESS

Although the growth in ordinary business after 1934 can be attributed in large measure to the expansion in group business as scheme members

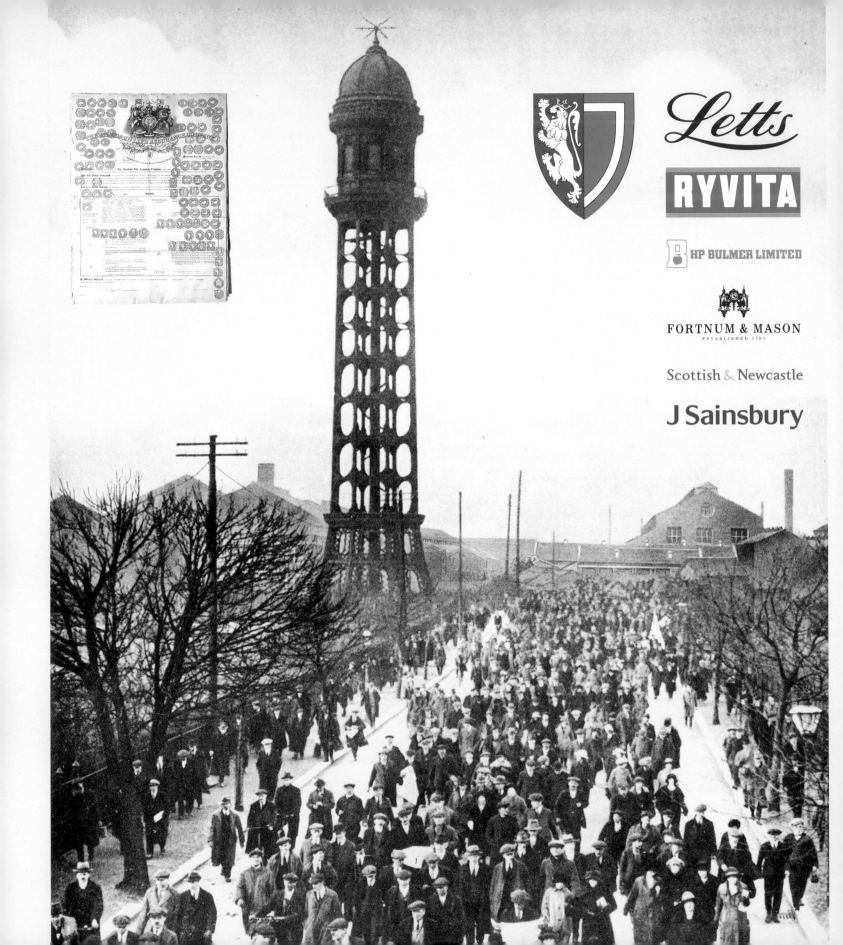

Letts

RYVITA

HP BULMER LIMITED

FORTNUM & MASON
ESTABLISHED 1707

Scottish & Newcastle

J Sainsbury

took advantage of special offers for their own personal assurance, Davidson made heroic efforts to build an effective branch network in the larger towns and cities, staffed by reliable, well-trained inspectors. His views were supported by James C. Campbell, chairman of a Glasgow group of department stores, who succeeded Beilby as chairman of Standard Life in 1932. Speaking at the triennial valuation conference in 1932 Campbell chose salesmanship as his theme: 'You are selling a long-term contract which, if it is a Standard Policy, cannot perish. I am selling articles which I sincerely hope will perish (but not too quickly). The underlying principles, however, are surely the same.'[110] With his guidance, promotional campaigns were targeted at well-defined constituencies (such as teachers, bankers and chemists) with the aim of 'cementing relationships with connections that a few years ago would not look at us'.[111] In 1935 all the company's promotional literature was redesigned, incorporating photographs and written in language which could be easily understood.[112]

With the advent of cheap money in 1932, life assurance gave savers the best rates of return and the market strengthened with total sums assured climbing by over 17 per cent between 1934 and 1939.[113] The Republic of Ireland branch reported sparkling results with total new sums assured trebling from £80,000 in 1931 to over £250,000 in 1938, partly because Scottish Widows and Scottish Equitable withdrew from the market.[114] Unlike the United Kingdom, demand in Ireland

was dominated by traditional with-profits and endowment policies.[115] To Davidson's delight Standard Life outperformed the industry with a growth in new sums assured of more than 20 per cent; importantly, the balance of the business had been moved firmly back in to the domestic market (see Appendices 2 and 3 on pages 378 and 382).

FURTHER CONTRACTION OVERSEAS

Convinced by 1925 that prospects for home business were improving, Macnaghten and Blount undertook a more considered review of the long-term viability of all the overseas branches, taking into account political circumstances, the economic outlook, and the available staff. They visited South Africa for three months at the end of the year to plan 'a scheme of agency organisation for the whole country' with D. Spence Fraser, Darling's successor, as secretary.[116] Fraser was a talented actuary, who had

Standard Life's revamped sales literature, 1935.

Opposite page:
Workers leaving Vickers-Metropolitan works in Manchester in the 1930s. The company's group scheme, established in 1934, was Standard Life's largest. At the top left is the deed establishing the pension scheme for Taylor Woodrow, the contractors, and on the right the badges and logos of other customers, including Balliol College, Oxford, and Bulmer's Cider. Standard Life concentrated on the food and drink industry and the service sector, which prospered during the inter-war years.

served as assistant actuary to Scottish Widows before becoming actuarial adviser to the South African government in 1919.[117] Eric Bell was recruited as agency manager for South Africa shortly after Macnaghten and Blount arrived home and business began to improve (see Figure 5.1b on page 190). Fraser returned to government service during 1926 and was succeeded by Bell, who in turn left in 1929. As in the past, frequent changes in staff against a background of strong local competition hindered development and it was decided to close the branch to new business. For the next 23 years Samuel Thomson & Young, a firm of chartered accountants, acted as chief agents, looking after the interests of policy-holders and collecting premiums. Following changes in legislation, all the remaining business was sold to the South African Life Assurance Company in 1952, exactly one hundred years after Standard Life had opened its first agency at Capetown.[118]

In 1930 the Egyptian branch was also closed for similar reasons. After the end of the British protectorate in 1922, business declined. Outbreaks of violence directed against foreign residents caused many customers to leave the country and locals turned to the growing number of domestic insurers. By 1928 the political situation had worsened and the secretary, David Scott Moncrieff, had been sent home to recover his health. He advised Macnaghten to wind up the branch and transfer such business as remained. Scott Moncrieff returned in 1930 to recruit British lives; but died a few

months later. He was not replaced.[119]

At first India appeared to live up to Macnaghten's expectations and in 1927, the year Frederick Loch Trevor retired as manager (see page 164), new sums assured reached a record £422,000 (see figure 5.1b on page 190). Much of this achievement can be attributed to a determined campaign to secure more native lives using local inspectors. The new manager, T.J. Christie, reported reasonable returns in the following two years in the face of mounting competition from many new Indian companies. These had been formed in a wave of nationalism culminating in Gandhi's eleven-point programme of 1930.[120] By the following year, when new sums assured were less than they had been in 1919, Davidson was persuaded to keep the branch alive until the worst of the recession was over and the political situation was resolved. A strong recovery in the second half of 1933 was encouraging with reports that, apart from North British & Mercantile, Standard Life's rates were more competitive for both European and native lives than any other British office, including the Prudential.[121] Ill health prevented Christie from capitalising on this success and he was forced to retire.

John Hamilton, the able secretary at Dublin, was sent out in a final attempt to revitalise the branch. He immediately set about appointing more Indian inspectors, most of whom had no experience of life assurance and needed intensive training before they produced results. He soon discovered on tours of the country that this

G.A.S. Norman with his staff in the Bombay office in 1937, shortly before the branch was closed to new business.

would be an uphill task. From before the war there had been no procedure for selecting agents and virtually no personal contact with them. Standard Life had lagged far behind other companies, such as North British & Mercantile, in appointing 'inspectors (or Organisers, as they are commonly called in India) whose sole object is to look after the agents and help them secure business'. Hamilton had no doubt that reorganisation would be costly and might not necessarily yield results largely because Standard Life's rates of commission were uncompetitive.[122]

Macnaghten was still hopeful that his early confidence would be fulfilled. During 1937 *The Standard Quarterly*, which had thus been renamed three years earlier, carried a lengthy review of the branch from its foundation by Colonial Life in 1846. George Norman, who was later to write the overseas history of Standard Life and was then serving in India, predicted that the 'ordinary Indian citizen . . . will turn to a company like our own, seeing that after all there is no such thing as nationalism and discrimination in Life Assurance within the British

Empire'.[123] His confidence was misplaced. Business fell during 1937; but Hamilton anticipated that with the newly elected Provincial governments in power prospects would improve. New insurance legislation to tighten control of local companies, many of which had a questionable actuarial base, was passed in 1938. Since it also placed onerous conditions on foreign companies, Hamilton suggested the agency manager should fly out to India to discuss the future.[124] Pessimistic about the possibility of the Indian branch ever earning its keep, Davidson supported the board's decision to close it to new business in July 1938 and went out to make the necessary arrangements. His fortnight-long visit (which included at his own request a visit to a yogi in a muddy cave) left a lasting impression of the high regard in which Standard Life was held by its customers.[125] The Bombay office closed in 1939, while the Calcutta office remained open under Norman's charge until 1946 when the remaining business was transferred to Gresham Life.[126]

Apart from Ireland, by 1939 Standard Life had only three overseas branches left open for new business – Canada, Uruguay and the West Indies – which together still contributed almost 30 per cent of new sums assured (see Appendix 2 on page 378). Although Canada remained the most important, business had never really recovered since the fire at the St James Street office in 1922, despite the efforts of Lindsay Armstrong to overhaul the agency network and to recruit new inspectors. Just as in India, this proved difficult.

According to Clark Kennedy, Standard Life lacked competitive products and paid poor commissions. Davidson was less convinced, pointing at the high expense ratio and the very large volume of surrenders. Comparing Canada unfavourably with India where there were self-evidently problems beyond the company's control, he launched a withering attack on the management early in 1932: 'So far as I have been able to ascertain from the correspondence etc. the Canadian Branch has largely been allowed to manage itself, and while this, no doubt, has been a considered policy, the facts and figures . . . speak for themselves as to whether its results have been satisfactory.'[127] With the support of the board, he insisted that, in future, reports should be fuller and that Clark Kennedy and Armstrong concentrate on improving sales figures. The abrasive William Mackenzie, now aged 68, who had been responsible for the westward expansion in Canada and 'for some years had been of no use as a producer of business', was dismissed and the Calgary branch shut down.[128] New canvassers were taken on, but returns still continued to deteriorate as the economy slumped.

Convinced that there was 'not sufficient premium income to justify our organisation in Canada', Davidson went out to see for himself in the summer of 1933. He appointed Armstrong agency manager with a brief to reorganise the field staff into six newly constituted branches with managers and agents appointed on terms agreed by the main board in Edinburgh. Several more staff were retired and many agents removed. Inspired by Davidson's enthusiasm, Armstrong rapidly made an impact. Clark Kennedy, who had responded positively to criticism, gave him the credit for the sharp upturn in 1935, helped by the economic recovery.[129] Although ceasing to accept reinsurance business held down the figure for new sums assured in the three years before the war, progress continued to be made with, in Davidson's words, 'an improvement in the state of affairs which was ruling in Canada some years ago'.[130]

A marked improvement in the performance of the Uruguayan branch after Blount's reprieve in 1923 had persuaded the board two years later to appoint an accountant, Horace Clifton, a Spanish speaker, from the London City branch. Continuing healthy returns reflected the failure of the State Insurance Bank to extend its monopoly by further legislation and indicated the preference for the more attractive with-profits terms offered by Standard Life. Following the appointment of the forceful J.G. Wright as town inspector in May 1927, the sale of new policies boomed.[131] Even after he was dismissed in 1931, the decline in new business was more a result of the depression than the loss of the connections he had made.[132] Nevertheless, Macnaghten's attitude to the branch remained ambivalent. He refused to allow the manager, Arthur Cook, to tender for group business at the very moment he was negotiating with 'some of the largest institutions in the country'. He also refused to remove the ceiling of $50,000 (about

£10,000) on any new policy.[133] During the early 1930s the Uruguayan economy was overwhelmed by the collapse in the value of the currency and by a devastating plague of locusts.[134] The State Insurance Bank deliberately tried to undermine Standard Life's position during 1933 with a hard-hitting advertising campaign and by having the Camp inspector, Paradell, tailed 'with a view to approaching personally every person known to be assured with us, or interested in our policies'. Cook refused to be intimidated by such strong-arm tactics and, despite the continuing uncertainty, business improved, especially among the country's German community.[135] Although he was well aware that 'in this country there was no natural demand for life insurance', he was always prepared to experiment with new products.[136] He volunteered in the early 1930s to test the market for group insurance, against Macnaghten's better judgement, and sold his first scheme to the Commercial Travellers Association in 1935.[137] On the eve of war the branch broke new records, yielding some 7 per cent of all new sums assured by the company.[138]

There had never been any doubt about maintaining a presence in the West Indies. The branch was reorganised in 1924, when the head office was moved from Barbados to Trinidad, where the economy was prospering with the exploitation of oil and asphalt. A new local board was established, rates revised and canvassers appointed. The anticipated growth in business did not materialise and in 1929 the

Alfred John Mascall, manager from 1939 to 1942.

performance in the West Indies was due to the commitment of the agents in all the islands, particularly J.V. Murray in Jamaica, and Michael Hamel-Smith and later Major J.D. Lenegan in Trinidad. Murray left to become manager at the Vancouver branch in 1935 and shortly before the outbreak of war several other staff sailed for home to join their regiments, leaving Eric Cook with a young and inexperienced staff.[139]

MACNAGHTEN'S LEGACY

Steuart Macnaghten retired in July 1938 after almost twenty years as manager. As Davidson later acknowledged, unlike nearly all his contemporaries, he had a clear strategy for the future development of Standard Life from the day he was appointed. His lasting contributions were mutualisation and the adventurous move into equity investments. He had represented the industry in Scotland in detailed but abortive negotiations with the government in 1930–31 about the possibility of the reform of insurance legislation. From 1931 until 1933 he served on the Cohen Committee on Industrial Assurance, which, during the Second World War, was to inform discussion about the creation of the welfare state.[140] Since his appointment Standard Life's assets had overtaken those of Scottish Provident and were at last gaining ground on Scottish Widows'; but the company had been left behind by North British & Mercantile, whose life department now dominated the industry in Scotland (see Figure 5.2 on page 191). The underlying strength of Standard Life was formidable, with

secretary, F.D. Gray, resigned. He had not been in the habit of making full reports to the agency manager and there was no alternative but for A.J. Mascall, the assistant secretary of the company who had previously worked in Barbados, to go out to appraise the situation. On his recommendation Edward Alexander (known as Eric) Cook, who had recently been invalided home from Bombay, was asked to take over. After a faltering start, the branch prospered under his leadership, reporting record returns throughout the 1930s. The first staff scheme was negotiated in 1932 for the 600 civil servants employed by the government of Trinidad. Standard Life's outstanding hidden reserves (the difference between the book and market value of securities) of some £4.9 million – 13.5 per cent of the assets. Overseas he had continued Dickson's policy of withdrawing from unprofitable markets in mainland Europe, Egypt, South Africa and even, at the very end of his career, India. In every market in which the company still operated, business was prospering and at last the expenses ratio had been reduced to 15 per cent, lower than that of North British & Mercantile and Scottish Provident, and was within reach of Scottish Widows'.[141] It is difficult to know how much of the credit for this achievement belonged to Macnaghten. The directors clearly thought it was mainly down to him and offered him a seat on the board. Where he had excelled, as they later recognised, was 'to gather into Standard Life and to train a large cadre of able young men to provide for the management and development of the various sides of what he realised was to be a rapidly growing organisation'.[142]

Although Davidson had unquestionably contributed more explicitly to the development of the company than anyone else apart from Macnaghten since the end of the First World War, the secretary and joint actuary, Albert E. King, who was then almost 51, became manager. King's expertise was as a theoretical actuary with an interest in mortality, who had worked discreetly

Albert Edward King, one of the ablest actuaries of his generation and manager from 1938 to 1939. Ill-health prevented him from ever entering the manager's office.

STANDARD PERSONALITIES—V.

A. E. K.

If he's made up his mind
You will very soon find
That his reasons are many and solid;
Don't attempt to expound,
Unless sure of your ground,
You'll be caught in the flick of an eyelid.

to refine Standard Life's products and rates. He was also interested in rates of return and had contributed to the decision to invest in equities. Unusually for a senior official in the company at the time, he had joined the board of the Scottish American Investment Company, which also had offices in Edinburgh's George Street, and where R.O. Pitman, a long-serving director of Standard Life, was already on the board. King could be trusted to keep in check Davidson's ambition of making Standard Life one of the major players in the United Kingdom pension market to the exclusion of the traditional with-profits business.[143] King's health broke down and he was forced to enter a TB asylum in Aberdeenshire. Despite his serious illness he kept in touch with the business and the profession. A year later, nine days after the declaration of war, when it was clear he would never recover, he was succeeded by A.J. Mascall who, until he was promoted to be secretary in 1938, had been junior to Davidson. Moreover, he was beyond retiring age. Davidson, who had no doubt that he had been passed over, was made deputy manager and actuary.[144] Eventually, when Mascall retired in 1942, he entered the manager's office. Alec Reid, the investment secretary, then became secretary, and Brem Dow joint actuary. Despite these manoeuvres, it was Davidson who devised the strategy to meet the uncertainties of wartime trading.[145]

THE SECOND WORLD WAR

War made a much more direct impact on Standard Life in 1939 than it had in 1914. Many staff were members of the reserves and, within weeks, 32 of them, mostly fieldmen, had left to join their units.[146] It was immediately decided that, with such staff shortages, it would be possible to conduct only quinquennial investigations until the war was over. Arrangements were also made for a duplicate set of the company's books to be kept in Aberdeen in case the head office was bombed. Although inconvenient, the evacuation of both London offices to Kingswood in Surrey and to premises in the East End was a prudent precaution as the Queen Victoria Street premises were totally burnt out during the Blitz in 1941.[147] Minet May & Co., who had been Standard Life's London lawyers for over a century, provided temporary accommodation in their City office.[148] Recognising that replacing staff would be impossible, Davidson laid down three principles for the duration of hostilities:

1. To obtain as much suitable life business as possible with our present organisation
2. To retain the active collaboration of our agency organisation
3. To reduce the expenses of the head office and branches so far as may be practicable . . .[149]

Anticipating a decline in business, he began collecting statistics from other offices so as to monitor Standard Life's experience. Within two years ordinary new sums assured in the home market had collapsed to £1.2 million, less than 40 per cent of the 1939 total, but this compared favourably with other companies. As in the previous conflict, Scottish life offices were cautious about accepting war risks and refused entirely to cover new civilian lives against the uncertain hazards of air-raids and invasion. Standard Life took the view that it was its duty to look after the interests of existing members.[150] Although demand for pension schemes increased as expenditure could be set against excess profits tax, Davidson believed 'prosperity due to the war does not necessarily form a sound basis upon which to make a permanent arrangement' and refused to push sales until victory was in view. As far as possible contact was to be maintained with existing pension schemes by regular visits to their offices.[151] For much of the war sales focused on children's policies, which would not mature until long after the return of peace.[152] As the war intensified more and more staff, both male and female, were called up. By the close of 1942 only a quarter of the staff remained and the Bristol and Newcastle branches were shut, along with several sub-branches, while employees well over retiring age kept others open. In the circumstances Standard Life did well to raise the volume of ordinary new sums assured at home above the low level of 1941 and maintain it at about £1.6 million for the rest of the war with little corresponding increase in surrenders.[153]

During the conflict there were considerable variations in the returns of the three overseas branches. Since Canada was fully engaged in the hostilities throughout the war, business was depressed. In 1944 the branch actively began to

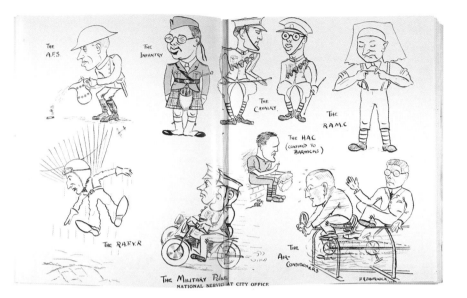

A cartoon of reservists at the London office, who were called up on the outbreak of war in 1939.

The London office, which was gutted during the Blitz in 1941.

Ernest Lindsay Armstrong, the Canadian manager from 1944 to 1957.

promote group schemes, signing up 31 during the year, with ten more awaiting confirmation.[154] Shortly after the defeat of Germany, Davidson visited Canada, taking with him Ernest Bromfield, now the assistant secretary, who was to stay for several months to help establish a pensions department and develop a strategy to sell group life assurance products. The main purpose of the visit was to bid farewell to William Clark Kennedy, who was over retirement age. Two years earlier he had been appointed to the local board in recognition of his long and distinguished service. Lindsay Armstrong, who had served as assistant manager since then, was confirmed as manager, George T. Westwater appointed actuary

and J.A. Anderson group pension supervisor. At the same time, in an effort to retain good sales staff, it was decided to establish a direct sales force, by paying all branch managers and selected agents salaries and bonuses based on quotas but no longer commissions as in the United Kingdom. Canvassers were to be replaced by full-time inspectors.[155] Alec Reid visited Canada in 1946 to review progress and approve the purchase of new offices at 1245 Sherbrooke Street, Montreal, where there was room for expansion. Westwater, who had been sent out from London, later recalled the excitement created by these reforms and the drive for group sales.[156]

Uruguay, a neutral country, recovered strongly from 1943 due largely to Ramón Paradell, who was able to sell policies to some of the country's largest landowners to cover newly introduced death duties.[157] With a growing mood of sympathy for Britain's plight after the battle of the River Plate in 1940, the political environment changed for the better. Following diplomatic representations, proposed insurance legislation, originally intended to drive out foreign companies, was modified and then abandoned. When Standard Life's medical officer Dr Rafael Schiaffino was appointed Minister of Industries in 1945, the outlook seemed excellent.[158]

During the latter part of the war, the best results were secured by the West Indies branch, which in 1944 produced over £500,000 of new sums assured and overtook Canada. This was a fitting end to Eric Cook's career. He retired in

A painting by John C. Little of Standard Life's new Canadian
head office at 1245 Sherbrooke Street, Montreal.

May and was succeeded by John Hamilton, who had been responsible for winding up the Indian branch.[159] This success overseas lifted Standard Life's total assets above those of Scottish Widows for the first time (see Figure 5.2 on page 191).

From the Munich crisis in 1938, which took Britain to the brink of war with Nazi Germany, Standard Life's largest problem was the management of the investment portfolio. The decline in the stockmarket began to erode the inner reserves and the board reduced the proportion of marketable assets in ordinary shares from more than 23 per cent to about 17.5 per cent by switching into debentures (see Figure 5.3 on page 196).[160] From the declaration of war the stockmarket was controlled in much the same way as it had been during the First World War, with all new issues strictly monitored by the capital issues committee. At first prices were depressed but began to recover towards the end of 1941. By this time the Treasury, adopting the formula which Dickson had negotiated in 1917, had again begun to requisition foreign securities to be used as collateral for loans to help pay for the war effort.[161] Since less than 10 per cent of its assets were now held in North America, Standard Life was scarcely involved in these transactions. More significantly, in the summer of 1940, the Bank of England reached agreement with the insurance companies that all new money should be invested in government stock.[162] Companies were allowed some freedom over the reinvestment of existing funds and in February 1941 the Standard Life board decided to place in war loan

only half the proceeds from 'requisitioned securities, maturing investments and loans, and securities sold shortly before maturity'.[163] The board authorised the resumption of purchases of ordinary stock early the following year[164] and in May resolved, as soon as possible after hostilities had ended, to return the proportion of investments held in such securities to the pre-war level.[165] When the war was over the company held £26 million, about half its disclosed assets, in government paper and had at the same time increased its holdings of ordinary shares (see Appendix 6 on page 386).

TAXATION AND THE WELFARE STATE

The Second World War, much more than the First, was paid for by taxation. Between 1939 and 1945 the standard rate of income tax increased from five shillings and sixpence to ten shillings and by the end of the war most people in work were taxed. From the outset relief for life assurance premiums was limited to the lower rate paid on the first portion of taxable income and new 'tax saving' policies were outlawed in the national interest.[166] These changes, coupled with a well-organised and promoted wartime national savings campaign, in which the insurance companies played an active part,[167] depressed demand for life assurance. Moreover, improvements in welfare benefits during the war encouraged many to believe they no longer needed private cover. The whole benefits system was reviewed by an inter-departmental committee set up in 1941 and chaired by Sir William Beveridge, until recently the director of the London School of Economics.[168] Concerned that the committee would recommend a comprehensive system of state pensions, the Association of Scottish Life Offices and the Life Offices Association in their evidence defended the flexibility of voluntary provision, reporting that there were in force 2,939 schemes administered by insurance companies covering almost half a million employees. Drawing on their experience, they warned that: 'If the cost of the scheme is kept sufficiently low to make practical the imposition of the cost upon all industries in all conditions of prosperity and adversity, then the pensions will be comparatively small and much less than some industries will be willing to provide voluntarily.'[169] Dismissing this advice, the Beveridge Report when it was published in 1942 recommended comprehensive and higher pensions paid for out of increased national insurance contributions and the nationalisation of the industrial assurance companies.[170] The report was enthusiastically received and the financial markets responded by marking down the price of all insurance company shares. The post-war Labour government's National Insurance Act in 1946 fuelled the uncertainty by introducing state pensions for everyone and greatly increasing employers' contributions.[171] Despite this improvement, many recognised that the state pensions would be minimal, as the life offices had predicted, and chose to take advantage of the tax relief on life assurance premiums and pension contributions as the most favourable method of saving at a time

of mounting inflation. Employers, who were still subject to high rates of excess-profits tax, were easily convinced of the merits of establishing or extending pension schemes at what was in effect almost no cost to themselves.[172]

In these conditions Davidson's strategy of holding Standard Life's sales organisation together throughout the war with a skeletal staff while at the same time putting in place carefully thought-out plans for the coming peace paid off handsomely. An immediate priority was to find new premises in central London and in 1943 offices were leased in Abchurch Yard. Like Dickson before him, he had kept in touch with members of staff on active service in the hope that they would return to their posts as soon as they were demobbed. The transition to peacetime trading was better than he could have expected: 'All those who achieved positions of responsibility in the forces have accepted their change of status with good humour and patience in the expectation that Standard will not be behind other companies in bringing salaries more into line with the cost of living.' Unlike some of its competitors Standard Life was fortunate to have an experienced, if elderly, sales team in the field within months of the end of hostilities to make the most of the burgeoning demand. These included the appointment of four staff scheme superintendents for London and Birmingham. In contrast, during 1947 staff shortages forced the Prudential temporarily to suspend its group pension business and Legal & General 'to restrict their service to policy-holders and to brokers'.[173]

EXPANDING THE PENSION BUSINESS AFTER THE WAR

Macnaghten, whose opposition to pension schemes hardened after Beveridge reported, retired from the board in 1945, making it easier for Davidson to base expansion firmly on such business – 'doing for the working man, efficiently and cheaply, what the industrial companies have done at the cost of considerable manpower and great expense'.[174] The investment committee, worried that it might prove difficult to place additional funds at 'satisfactory rates of interest', sounded a note of caution in the summer of 1946.[175] Davidson's response was characteristically robust, emphasising that since the First World War 'there has not been (and I

hope will not be in the future) anything haphazard about our development; the whole matter has been continually under observation and is continually in control'. He discounted the threat posed by the new welfare provisions and argued persuasively that expansion promised 'a bright and successful future'. At the same time, worried about the future direction of interest rates, he insisted that the basis for valuation should be reduced from 2.5 per cent to an even more demanding 2 per cent, which the company could afford because of the strength of its reserves.[176]

Over the next six years the volume of group business grew rapidly to reach a colossal £12.5 million in sums assured (Figure 5.4) and £8 million in premium income, three quarters of the total (see Appendix 3 on page 382). In negotiating new contracts Davidson insisted that the pension scheme superintendents continue to make direct contact with the customer rather than relying solely on the brokers, not just to agree terms but also to allow ordinary inspectors to get to know the members.[177] This policy, coupled with Standard Life's refusal to haggle over the level of commission, resulted in some large schemes handled by the bigger London brokers being forfeited to Eagle Star, Legal & General or the Prudential. These three principal competitors for pension business were prepared to pay 'as much as a third more in commission'.[178] Such losses were compensated for by cultivating local connections through the branches with potential customers themselves and their brokers, bankers, accoun-

FIGURE 5.4
United Kingdom group pension business 1930–51

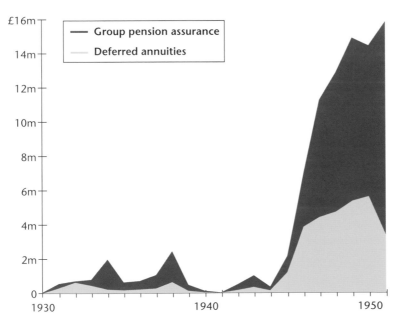

Note: The values of deferred annuities written before 1935 are given at pension age

tants and lawyers. The only disadvantage of this approach was that it produced a large number of relatively small schemes with 50 to 100 members, which were time-consuming and expensive to service. From 1945 until 1953, however, Standard Life refused to quote for very small schemes with fewer than 25 members on the grounds that they were not profitable. Instead they offered such clients separate endowment policies for all staff.[179] With salary levels rising towards the end of the 1940s, many firms realised that their better-paid employees had inadequate pension cover and they were sold special 'top hat' endowment policies to make good the deficiency. In part these schemes were designed to mitigate the effects of the punitive rates of taxation on higher incomes.[180]

As had been the case from the beginning of Standard Life's involvement in the pension market, schemes were used as a fruitful source of ordinary business. Having made contact with members, inspectors were encouraged to draw their attention to the special rates for additional life cover. They were also told to be on the look-out for potential new agents amongst senior staff, who would be able to introduce friends and relations, particularly those who were buying houses or who had withdrawn pension contributions and wished to reinvest the money.[181] A characteristic of the pension business was the high rate of withdrawals as members left schemes to work elsewhere. Standard Life's annual surrenders climbed from less than £400,000 in 1945 to over £1.5 million by 1951.[182]

DISTRIBUTION AT HOME AND ABROAD

Between 1946 and 1950 some 3,600 new agents were appointed in direct conflict with the objective of becoming a no-commission office. This was a feature of the insurance industry as a whole at the time. Recognising the significance of home ownership in England, renewed efforts were made immediately after the war to market loans for house purchase through the Heritable, backed by endowment policies.[183] Within three years such arrangements accounted for almost 20 per cent of a record £9 million new ordinary sums assured in the domestic market.[184] Sales in the Republic of Ireland continued to be unaffected by such changes and the market there was still dominated by traditional with-profits products, largely sold by bank and legal agents.[185]

The performance of the three remaining overseas branches was equally impressive with a similar growth in ordinary business and group pensions. At first the going in Canada was tough because rates offered by the Dominion Government Annuities Branch were difficult to match. These were raised during 1948 at the same time as Standard Life cut its with-profits terms.[186] The resulting growth in new business during 1949 broke all branch records and more than justified the expansion of the direct sales force since the war. Although 350 group schemes had been negotiated since 1945, it was still proving impossible to win custom from large concerns, partly because attitudes to British assurers were coloured by the Labour government's threatened nationalisation of industrial assurance companies and partly because of competition from local providers, particularly Manufacturer's Life.[187] The breakthrough came in 1951 when four large schemes covering about 500 lives each, including Empire Brass, the Ottawa Transportation Commission and Sheraton Hotels, were agreed. To encourage such custom a new type of pension plan was introduced which allowed employers to meet some of the premium costs out of the profits on investments. Lindsay Armstrong, the manager for Canada, had no doubt that, despite the competition, Standard Life was now well placed to win even more business; but this could only be achieved by doubling the sales force to cover more of the country.[188] An unforeseen consequence of setting quotas for the branches at the end of the war was that the Canadian board began to think of the assets, which supported policies written in the country, as somehow separate from those of the whole company, referring to them as 'our Canadian assets'. In an effort to improve relations, the chairman, some directors and the manager began to make annual visits to the country. More often than not these were akin to royal progresses and lacked a serious business focus.[189]

Likewise, the branch in Uruguay reported record returns due largely to the continuing efforts of Ramón Paradell and a newly recruited inspector, Alex Hughes, whose family were old-established English merchants in Montevideo. The only impediment to further development (later to prove decisive) was mounting inflation and strict exchange control.[190] Davidson visited the country in 1948 and authorised the development of group life assurance to supplement the state pension scheme, more generous commissions and the appointment of sub-agents to reduce Paradell's monopoly of rural areas.[191] Cook, who retired at the end of the year, was not convinced that sub-agents would yield much custom as the rates of commission were too low.[192] Davidson insisted that his successor, Leonard King, should at least explore their potential with the help of Dr Carlos Zumaran Arocena, a lawyer, who had recently become an agent. King was also sceptical at first, suggesting that Paradell 'will be the foundation on which the total production of the branch will depend'.[193] When Paradell declared that he had no intention of 'exhausting himself' in Standard Life's service, King began to have doubts. These were confirmed by a 'piratical expedition' in 1950 by Arocena into the countryside, which revealed that in many towns there had been little or no attempt to recruit new custom. Analysis of Paradell's returns showed that his clients were confined to eight of the 18 departments of the Camp and were made up entirely of large policy-holders. Much the same was true of Montevideo itself, with a population of 900,000, where Standard Life was in the hands of four agents, who mostly confined their attention to the better-off. The greatest obstacle to broadening representation was finding reliable agents who could be trusted to establish a network of dependable sub-agents while at the same time not upsetting the sensitivities of the existing agents and their influential clientele. King was, however, optimistic about future prospects.[194]

Davidson visited the West Indies early in 1946 to introduce the same method of direct selling as had been put in place in Canada.[195] Under John Hamilton, the branch continued to prosper, with new sums assured doubling from £500,000 to £1 million between 1945 and 1951.[196] This growth was largely an outcome of mortgage lending both for house purchase and property development, which by 1952 totalled just over £1 million.[197] Although competition from Canadian companies was strong, it was not difficult for inspectors to show that Standard Life's higher rates provided much better yields.[198]

RETURN TO EQUITIES

The anxiety expressed by the investment committee in 1946 – that it would be difficult to place a greatly increased flow of funds 'at satisfactory rates of interest' – was real. The Labour government had at least nominally strengthened the wartime control of the new issues market and was committed to cheap money, making Reid's preference for mortgage investment appear to be the only viable option.[199] Loans to the Heritable rose from £250,000 to £4 million by 1950 and total mortgage investment increased from 3.5 per cent of total assets to 9 per cent by 1951. Although house mortgages helped to generate premium income, yields were less than the 3 per cent which could be earned through the stockmarket and there was no pos-

sibility of capital gain. Reid also urged investment in 2.5 per cent irredeemable annuities issued by the Chancellor of the Exchequer, Hugh Dalton, on the grounds that this represented the future trend in rates. Francis S. Jamieson, who was appointed investment secretary in 1945 after his release as a prisoner of war, took a contrary view in common with his counterparts in other life offices.[200] An Oxford classicist, he had joined the company in 1931 and worked closely with Davidson in the agency department. In the belief that cheap money could not be sustained for long, he won the support of Davidson and the board for the rapid switch of funds into debentures and equities and, when no suitable securities were available, as in 1948, the holding of funds in short-dated government stocks.[201] In practice the capital issues committee was unable to do much to restrict the market, particularly after the economy began to recover rapidly in 1948.[202] Consequently it was possible for Standard Life to resume underwriting new issues sooner than expected, which in itself provided a source of new investment. By 1947 the proportion of stock-exchange securities held in ordinary shares had been restored to 21 per cent (see Appendix 6 on page 386). Over the next two years the appreciation was an impressive 10 per cent per annum. A small decline in 1949, as the market reacted to the recession in the United States, was followed by an even stronger recovery in 1950 and 1951.[203]

Companies such as Standard Life, with large liabilities in dollar areas, were concerned after the war about the future rate of exchange, which had been fixed at just over four dollars to the pound in 1939. By the early months of 1948 it was generally accepted that devaluation of sterling was both necessary and inevitable and most companies had taken the precaution of ensuring that foreign earnings were held in dollar investments to meet overseas liabilities. Standard Life was no exception and between 1948 and 1949 stock-exchange investments in the United Kingdom were reduced by 10 per cent by investing mostly in Canada, which since it was outside the sterling area would be unaffected by devaluation of the pound, and to a much lesser extent the West Indies.[204] An investment department was set up in Montreal under the secretary R. Thomson, reinforcing the belief that the Canadian assets were a local responsibility rather than 'owned',[205] as was the case, through the investment committee in Edinburgh. This decision was fully justified when sterling was devalued by 30 per cent in the autumn of 1949.

Throughout the period from 1919 until 1951, the whole of Standard Life's increasingly complex investment portfolio was handled by a tiny department. Apart from the investment manager, in 1925 there were three clerks and one typist and by 1950 this had only grown to eight clerks and three typists.[206] As well as buying and selling securities, the department kept in close contact with an ever increasing number of stock-brokers, monitored the performance of investments, collected market intelligence from the press and prepared detailed statements for the investment committee. Jamieson's shrewd assessment of the market in 1946 more than vindicated Davidson's commitment to expansion. By 1949 the price of debentures and preference shares had risen so much that Standard Life temporarily withdrew from the market, correctly predicting a downturn.[207]

THE LARGEST MUTUAL IN EUROPE

By 1951 Standard Life had outstripped all its Scottish competitors, leaving North British & Mercantile and Scottish Widows far behind, and had even overtaken Commercial Union and the Co-operative Insurance Society. Although still smaller than the giants of the industry (Legal & General, the Prudential and the Pearl), Andrew Davidson could now proudly claim that Standard Life was not only a major player in the United Kingdom market for pensions and life assurance but also the largest mutual life office. The credit was entirely his. He had invigorated every part of the enterprise from the moment he returned from serving in the First World War. He had influenced the decision to invest in equities and played a leading part in mechanising business processes. As agency manager he had radically overhauled the sales organisation in the United Kingdom and for the first time had made the whole of the overseas operations directly answerable to the head office. With considerable foresight he realised earlier than most of his contemporaries that home ownership would transform the market for personal savings. Committed to strategic planning, he had realised

A portrait of Andrew Rutherford Davidson on his retirement in 1951 after almost nine years as manager. He, more than anyone else, laid the foundations of the modern company.

that in the changing mood of the mid-twentieth century pensions would become a lucrative and expanding market where mutual offices could compete effectively. Despite those who doubted his vision, he remained steadfast and was rewarded beyond his expectations. His commitment to the company took its toll on his health. He suffered two heart attacks and became increasingly deaf.

At the height of his achievement, he planned to fulfil Dickson's ambition of diversifying into general insurance, by taking over the Caledonian Insurance Company, which had offices on the other side of George Street. He had secured approval from the board in principle to merge with an unnamed London office in 1946;[208] but, never completely at ease with his directors, he had neglected to inform them of the progress of negotiations with either that office or the Caledonian. By 1950 the deal was all but complete and it had even been decided what posts the Caledonian's executives would occupy in the newly merged enterprise. On learning the news, the Standard Life directors refused to endorse the merger[209] and Davidson, in high dudgeon, went south to consult his friend Hugh Recknell, who advised him that without the support of his board he had no alternative but to step down on the genuine grounds of ill health. In paying tribute to him, the chairman, the Hon Sir Archibald Cochrane, made no references to the reason behind his decision to leave early and declared: 'In recent years three things have happened – our business has greatly increased, our financial strength has remained unimpaired, and the team spirit has remained strong throughout the company. Any man retiring from the position of manager in these circumstances has the right to feel that he has done something worth doing and done it well.'[210] At his death 17 years later, the directors were unstinting in their praise: 'To him, as much as to any other single individual, the Company owes its present high position in the world of life assurance.'[211] One commentator has suggested that if William Thomson was the father of Standard Life then Davidson was the mother of the modern business.[212]

CHAPTER SIX

'A MOST REMARKABLE STORY OF SUCCESS': 1951–70

'We have just listened to a most remarkable story of success, a story which is all the more welcome as it is a reflection of the prosperity of British industry. The success of this Company is something of which we should all be proud and in which people from all walks of life can share.'

James C. Stormonth Darling at the annual meeting, 1955.[1]

The Festival of Britain in 1951, designed like the Great Exhibition a century earlier to celebrate the country's achievements, caught the national mood and won instant appeal. The striking architecture and design style became the hallmark of the decade. Tired of the long years of austerity since the slump, people now looked forward hopefully to a prosperous future with secure employment for all. Despite the serious balance-of-payments crisis in the autumn, there was some justification for such optimism. The return of the Conservative Party to power in

October coincided with a recovery in the economy which continued more or less without interruption until the end of the decade. Rising living standards, full employment and the benefits provided by the new welfare state combined to change attitudes towards saving. It was now no longer necessary to save for times of hardship. A survey by the Oxford Institute of Statistics in 1953 found that there was scarcely any saving in whatever form amongst those who earned less than £600 a year, that was the majority of the population.[2] Those with an

Commemorative stamps advertising the Festival of Britain in 1951, a century after the Great Exhibition organised by Prince Albert.

annual income of over £1,000 were also shown to be modifying their investment habits to take advantage of tax concessions on mortgages, building-society interest and life insurance premiums and benefits. Even amongst the better-off the purpose of saving had moved fundamentally towards deferred consumption, financing the purchase of household goods, holidays and cars. These changes made it impractical for the life insurance industry to continue to market whole-life policies unless they were designed to mitigate the high level of death duties. Increasingly popular were endowment policies as collateral for house mortgages. Nevertheless there was plenty of opportunity to sell whole-life policies as was well illustrated in 1957 by the Inland Revenue, which calculated that out of the 60,000 estates paying £800 million in duty just over 2 per cent represented the exempt proceeds of life policies.[3]

With its strong commitment to the provision of pensions, Standard Life should have been more aware of the realignment of the market for life assurance products than most of its competitors. As early as 1952 it was obvious that the ordinary or individual life department 'which before the war contributed the bulk of the business written' was being replaced by what was termed 'specialist business', 'fostered by excessive taxation of the living and the dead' – death-duty policies and endowment pension schemes for company executives. Over 60 per cent of the ordinary department's returns was made up of such business. This was handled by specially trained staff, as ordinary inspectors could not be expected to master the complexities of the tax regime.[4] There were two obstacles to obtaining ordinary business: Standard Life's refusal to cut rates and increase commissions and, more significantly, the lack of tax relief for the self-employed to make pension provision.[5] This last issue had been addressed by a committee (chaired by James Millard Tucker, KC) set up in 1950 by the Labour government to review pensions. The committee took four years to report and failed to recommend a radical overhaul of the existing complex regulations and tax concessions. Since the majority of its members were themselves self-employed, it was not surprising that the committee recommended that the tax relief available under the 1921 Act to members of insurance company schemes should be extended to include the self-employed.[6] Concerned that such a generous concession smacked of the much-abused 'top-hat' schemes, the government in the 1956 Finance Act restricted relief to 10 per cent of earnings with a maximum of £750. Although the industry as a whole reported much less demand for such pensions than had been predicted, Standard Life saw the opportunity to extend its already well-developed links with the professions by negotiating, in the face of stiff competition, a retirement benefits plan based on single-premium policies for the Institute of Chartered Accountants in Scotland and the Law Society of Scotland. It was hoped that these connections would bring more ordinary and personal pension business in their wake.[7] Despite advertising targeted at such self-employed professional groups, this did not happen as the commission of 3 per cent was too low to make it worthwhile for brokers. It was not until the early 1970s when rates were raised as high as 50 per cent of initial premiums that the market took off.

RISE OF HOME OWNERSHIP

The Conservative government's commitment to a 'property-owning democracy' was to transform the character of the business and the fortunes of the ordinary or individual life department. Shortages and controls left over from the war prevented any sustained new private house building until 1953. From then on, however, construction grew at an unprecedented rate until 1970, by which time the proportion of owner-occupied homes had risen from 30 per cent to 50 per cent. During the 1960s home ownership was encouraged by both Conservative and Labour governments, with significant new tax concessions in 1963 and 1965.[8] Most owners of new homes purchased them with the assistance of loans from building societies, which would only make funds available to established depositors whom they considered a good risk. This policy in itself skewed the savings market, drawing funds away from other long-established means of savings towards the building societies. Since demand for mortgages was strong, building societies insisted that the bulk of any loan be repaid in annual instalments, imposing quite heavy charges for early repayment. In addition

to a mortgage over the property, building societies usually insisted that borrowers took out some form of life insurance for the period of the loan.

Standard Life continued to make home loans available through the Heritable as a way of attracting endowment business; but the available cash was restricted to about £2 million a year until 1955 when it was increased to £4.6 million to meet exceptional demand caused by a sharp drop in building-society deposits.[9] Since funds were rationed, they were distributed by

An advertisement for a house-purchase loan from Heritable Securities, a Standard Life subsidiary.

Staff at the Heritable Securities and Mortgage Investment Association Limited on the steps of their office at 76 George Street, Edinburgh. Alex Mackay, the manager, is second from the left in the front row. He was succeeded by Bob Coutts (extreme left).

that the difference would be made up by bonus additions. Home loans through the Heritable continued to play an important role in attracting new ordinary business until 1972, when they were discontinued (see page 278). By then total advances from Standard Life to the Heritable had risen from just under £5 million in 1951 to over £77 million, which included some advances on commercial property.[12]

The main impact of the boom in private housing on the life industry was the rapid growth in sales of mortgage-protection policies where the loan was repayable by instalments and so designed as to provide at death a decreasing sum assured equal to the principal outstanding. These policies were mostly negotiated through small local brokers or lawyers, accountants and bank officials. In 1956 some 37 per cent of new ordinary business came from bank staff, 18 per cent from insurance brokers, 16 per cent from accountants, 3 per cent from solicitors and 26 per cent from other agents including those who represented non-life offices.[13] Competition both on rates and commission was very keen. Standard Life's commission (a flat-rate 1.5 per cent of the sum assured under endowment and whole-life policies or 10 per cent of the premium under term insurance), was recognised as unattractive; but the manager Alec Reid and the agency manager Graeme L. Pullar were reluctant to increase it as long as demand remained strong. They preferred instead in 1955 to improve the benefits to with-profits policy-holders through the introduction of the 'reparticipating com-

quota to the branches – to the frustration of inspectors, who nicknamed the company the 'Irritable'.[10] Unlike the building societies, Standard Life through the Heritable, in common with several other insurance companies which offered this service, was willing to lend on older property and to advance up to 80 per cent of the value of a property.[11] In order to encourage sales of endowment polices the Heritable allowed repayment of a loan at the end of the mortgage period. Although most borrowers took out with-profits endowment policies with a sum equal to the loan, the minimum premium plan was revamped in 1954. Under this plan a sum was assured for less than the loan in the expectation

pound bonus' – a reversionary bonus added to previous bonuses. Its purpose was 'to give steeply increasing rates of bonus to policies of long duration, or, in other words, to benefit particularly those policy-holders who had over the years contributed most to the present prosperity of the Company'.[14] Four years later policy-holders who held their with-profits contracts to maturity were further rewarded with the introduction of a final claims bonus equivalent to 10 per cent of the sum assured and accrued bonuses. These improvements provided a platform for strengthening the sales force from 1954 and revamping the advertising. This was all placed in the hands of John Haddon & Co., London agents, who were to be responsible for the first unified national campaign. They quickly coined the slogan 'Yours for Life' in 1955, accurately reflecting the mindset of the management which, despite all the evidence to the contrary, still believed that 'the basic policy is the whole-life assurance'.[15] The Forth Bridge motif,* introduced in the 1930s, was replaced by the Scottish lion rampant holding a standard with the legend 'Yours for Life'. This was to be used for the next 20 years in a series of campaigns.

Bowing to the inevitable in 1958, brokers' commission was raised to 2 per cent of the sum assured and a sliding scale introduced for agents; but even this was not enough, particularly as several other offices could now match Standard Life's bonus.[16] So serious was the commission war that the Life Offices Association and the Association of Scottish Life Offices reached an agreement early in 1960 to limit commission to 2 per cent of the sum assured. By now it was becoming clear that term assurance was starting to dominate Standard Life's new business, accounting for 26 per cent of all new contracts in 1960 and almost 50 per cent by 1963, and the trend continued as the property-owning democracy multiplied.[17] The company's policies were made more attractive during 1963 with the introduction of the 'convertible term rider'** which provided additional temporary cover at a lower rate of premium and could be converted into permanent cover at any time without further evidence of health.[18] By 1966 Standard Life admitted that 'protection rather than investment is now the order of the day'.[19] The focus of new sales began to move towards endowment policies by the end of the 1960s as building societies began to relax their rules about annual repayments and allowed customers to take out endowment policies to cover final repayment in 25 years' time.

MEETING INFLATION

For all established retail financial institutions the greatest difficulty in coming to terms with

The Standard Life corporate logo in the 1950s and 1960s.

---

* The Forth Bridge was used by many Scottish companies in their advertising as a sign of strength and stability, but was quietly dropped when the warranty expired in the 1950s.

** Rider is an American insurance term for additional benefits to a policy at marginal extra cost.

alterations in people's outlook was the corrosive effect of inflation. Not since the seventeenth century had Europe experienced a period of sustained inflation which had not been followed by deflationary readjustment. After the inflation during the First World War prices did not again reach their 1920 peak until 1951. Conventional wisdom suggested that the strong inflationary pressures in the 1950s would be followed by deflation and sharply lower interest rates. On this assumption the Standard Life actuaries misread the future course of rates and over-priced without-profits policies, leading Reid more or less to abandon this type of contract.[20] The belief that interest rates would fall – which had ramifications for the pricing of all contracts – was not shared by the investment manager, Francis Jamieson, who took the opposite view. As it turned out he was right and inflation continued, albeit at a lower level into the 1960s, rising again at the very end of the decade. Between 1951 and 1970 the cost-of-living index doubled. Against this background, savers, who increasingly had access to a greater range of advice than ever before, looked for investments that would maintain their value, such as houses. With growing access to credit facilities many chose to borrow money to buy consumer goods in the expectation that inflation would reduce the cost of their initial outlay.

UNIT LINKED WITH RELUCTANCE

The performance of the stockmarket throughout the 1950s and 1960s suggested that equities provided a secure hedge against inflation as well as far better returns than cash deposits. Although the majority of savers lacked the expertise to buy shares directly, unit trusts, introduced from America in 1931, became popular towards the end of the 1950s. These allowed investors to have an interest in a range of different securities held on their behalf by managers. M&G in 1957 launched a tax-exempt unit trust designed to appeal to self-administered pension schemes, with impressive results.[21] Established life offices were slow to enter the market for unit-linked life policies, allowing newcomers such as the far-from-progressive Trustee Savings Bank to steal a march. In 1963 Standard Life took defensive action by coming to an arrangement to underwrite the life cover for the Save & Prosper Group's new 'Save-Insure-and-Prosper-Plan'.* This proved popular, contributing £7 million in new group sums assured in its first year and £13.5 million in the second year. Nevertheless, an article in *The Standard Review* in 1967 suggested that this approach to saving was too speculative for most savers and concluded that: 'Unit trusts in recent years have produced some spectacular results as compared with life assurance but it must be borne in mind that the wide spread of a life office's investment portfolio gives a very large degree of flexibility and offers an excellent

* The year before, the Save & Prosper Group had been taken over by a consortium comprising Atlantic Assets Trust (managed by Ivory & Sime), Robert Fleming, Baring Bros and the British Linen Bank Pension Fund.

return for the minimum of speculation.'[22]

During the summer of 1968 Standard Life explored the possibility of taking over the Save & Prosper Group which in that year contributed over £64 million in new group sums assured. When talks broke down the relationship was terminated. The following year, against the advice of David Donald, the actuary, Standard Life launched its unit-linked endowment policy, a year later than the Prudential.[23] In neither company was this new product considered to be part of a wider strategy, and was simply a response to the market. Advertised under the slogan 'Promise and Performance: Risk and Reward' (see page 236), the promotional literature repeated the arguments which had already appeared in *The Standard Review*: 'If the "non-risk" element of your savings is safely invested for the protection of your dependants, the Standard Life Unit Endowment Policy gives you an outstanding opportunity of participation in the risks and rewards of the equity market.'[24] Sales, not surprisingly, were disappointing. Lack of management commitment to this new policy was a serious misjudgement, leaving Standard Life without a range of competitive products throughout the 1970s, apart from the endowment for house purchase. It also allowed newcomers to the industry, such as Allied Dunbar, to capture a large part of the company's traditional market.

DEVELOPING THE SALES STRUCTURE

Reid and Brem Dow, who succeeded him as manager in 1964, can be forgiven for failing to understand the underlying changes in the nature of their market. Ordinary business boomed from the mid-1950s, buoyed up by the growth in home ownership accompanied by a sharp revival in personal saving in the early 1960s, mostly for deposits for house purchases. New sums assured in the ordinary department soared from £11 million in 1951 to over £270 million in 1970, and premium income climbed from £4.5 million to £34 million (see Appendices 2 and 3 on pages 378 and 382). Almost 80 per cent of this growth could be attributed to mortgage business. In these circumstances Reid and Dow naturally put their efforts into expanding the home sales organisation by building on the strong foundations laid by Davidson. In 1953 it was decided to increase progressively the number of inspectors from 59 to 68.[25] All new recruits were trained at the head office in Edinburgh before being sent to their branches. Three years later the promotion prospects of successful resident inspectors and

The Save-Insure-and-Prosper Plan
PROPOSAL FORM

A proposal form for the Save & Prosper Group's Save-Insure-and-Prosper Plan which was profitably underwritten by Standard Life in 1963.

Standard Life announce a new Unit Endowment Policy-

partner to an outstanding With Profit Endowment Policy

Standard Life is the largest British mutual life assurance company. With assets of over £710,000,000, with over 140 years of experience and an outstanding bonus record, Standard Life has long offered one of the best With Profit Endowment Policies available. Their new Unit Endowment Policy therefore provides a valuable new investment channel, with a special appeal to those who have already protected their dependants. By widening the scope of investment opportunity while preserving some of the guarantees and protections of a with profit endowment assurance the Standard Life Unit Endowment Policy will prove a most attractive proposition.

1. Promise and Performance

The Standard Life With Profit Endowment Policy is well known as an exceptionally good investment-with-protection policy. The outstanding bonus record, the additional special bonuses and the record of sound management since 1825 all contribute significantly to the security and investment value of the policy. And Standard Life has the added attraction of being a mutual company.

2. Risk and Reward

Where the non-risk element of savings is prudently invested for the protection of dependants the Standard Life Unit Endowment Policy provides an outstanding opportunity to participate in the risks and rewards of the equity market. The investment element of the premiums of this policy is invested, with the emphasis on equity shares specifically for the benefit of the policy holder. The Standard Life Unit Endowment Policy offers many options and carries a guaranteed minimum death or maturity benefit.

A choice of Standard Nest Eggs!

Should you require more details of either Standard Life policy we shall be happy to help you in any way we can.

'Yours for Life'

⚘ Standard Life
ASSURANCE COMPANY

ESTABLISHED 1825. ASSETS EXCEED £710,000,000
HEAD OFFICE: 3 GEORGE ST., EDINBURGH, 2
LONDON OFFICES: 3 ABCHURCH YARD, CANNON STREET, E.C.4 · 31/32 CURZON STREET, W.1

The advertisement for Standard Life's unit endowment policy which almost guaranteed its failure, 1969. The company adopted an egg motif in nearly all its promotions from 1968 until the late 1970s.

local secretaries were enhanced by giving them the opportunity of taking on an assistant to help develop their area. If results improved they were to be given 'some of the privileges enjoyed by a full branch manager, such as the right *ex officio* to attend Triennial Conferences' and eventually the title of local manager.[26] The results were encouraging. In 1954 only half the 46 inspectors with at least three years' service had achieved their quota of £100,000 of new business; by 1959, in contrast, over 70 per cent had exceeded this target.[27]

Recognising that investors were becoming more sophisticated, in 1961 the districts in Belfast and Manchester were divided to provide a higher standard of service. This reform quickly demonstrated that more regular contact with agents yielded better returns. A further increase in the sales force, especially in Ireland, was approved, and a new branch was established at Coventry, with the possibility of others at Cardiff, Croydon, Nottingham and Watford.[28] The existing branches at Dundee and Sheffield were closed, however, because they were considered to be no longer viable. Unease amongst inspectors that opportunity for promotion was being stifled by such rationalisation resulted in proposals in 1964 for a regional structure modelled on arrangements in the London City branch which covered the south-east of England: 'The regional manager will work within a plan for the development and expansion of his region in consultation with head office and, within the limits of that plan, will have wide

Interior of the new Leeds Office in the Headrow, September 1955.

discretion.' As an experiment, a north-west of England region was formed in Leeds under George McGill, and at the same time George Norman, who was now manager for Dublin, was promoted to be manager for Ireland in anticipation that in due course it would become a region.[29] While the impact of these changes was being evaluated, emphasis was placed on the continuing education of inspectors, who already had 'the reputation of being the best informed in the business'. Regular training sessions on the more technical aspects of life assurance were provided in London to which brokers, 'who are prepared to work with us in this field', were invited.[30]

The adoption of the regional framework was

A group pensions advertisement featuring the Regent Oil Company, a satisfied customer in the 1950s.

A 3,600 gallon Road Tank Waggon is loaded at one of Regent Oil Company's Depots

Regent Oil Company Limited rely on us for Staff Pensions

Regent Oil Company Limited, distributors in the United Kingdom of Regent and Caltex Petroleum Products, is one of the leading organisations whose Staff Pension arrangements we are privileged to administer. With our many years of specialised experience we can work out a scheme to suit every type and size of Company, and the services of our Staff Schemes Superintendents are available in any part of the country.

'Yours for life'

THE STANDARD
LIFE ASSURANCE COMPANY
Established 1825
Head Office : 3 GEORGE STREET, EDINBURGH
London Office : 3 ABCHURCH YARD, CANNON STREET, E.C.4
ASSETS EXCEED £200,000,000

confirmed in 1968 when the midland region was created under Fred Franklin, based in Birmingham, with responsibilities which extended from Worcester to the Wash.[31] The overriding consideration was to achieve greater harmony within the home sales force. Until then branches had tended to think of themselves as autonomous units. This had always been the case in London, and H.R. Crowe, who had been appointed London manager in charge of ordinary business when Reynolds retired in 1962, was no exception. On Crowe's retirement in 1968 Brem Dow, who had earlier dubbed him 'Harry the Crow', paid tribute to his contribution to Standard Life even if 'at times he had turned a blind

eye to signals from head office'. His salesmanship was legendary, telling young inspectors to be 'bubbly bubbly' and to have 'fire in the belly'.[32] His successor, F.E. King, the two regional managers and the manager for Ireland were encouraged to think of themselves as a team under the agency manager and to take a wider view of the ordinary department's performance than just within their own region. To this end they were asked to prepare reports on four topics: productivity of inspectors; early lapses and business 'not proceeded with'; the appointment of agents; and training of inspectors.[33] George Philip, the organisation manager, had independently been developing a training programme for indoor staff. His ideas and those of the regional managers resulted in a more coherent training strategy and the appointment of M.K. Evans from the Newcastle branch as training manager at head office in 1970.[34]

THE COMPETITIVE MARKET FOR PENSIONS

This training initiative came from the ordinary department and did nothing to address the absence of any working relationship with the pensions departments in the regions and branches. In some branches there was open hostility and throughout the whole company there was an assumption that ordinary business was preferable even though pensions accounted for more than 70 per cent of premium income. After 1951 the sale of pension schemes in the United Kingdom grew even more rapidly than

London Office town and country inspectors, *c.*1950

before (see Figure 6.1 on page 240). Pension business was overseen from the head office by the group manager, Ernest Bromfield, rather than the agency manager whose duties only extended to the ordinary department. Much of the increase in new business during the early 1950s reflected inflationary wage rises rather than real growth. Although further contracts were won, competition, even for small contracts, was severe both from life offices outside the agreement and from self-administered private funds managed with independent actuarial advice. Moreover, some brokers refused to place new business with the company until 1953 when the embargo on small

schemes (fewer than 25 members) was lifted.[35]

In this competitive environment the policy of maintaining close contacts with existing schemes paid dividends. This minimised the risk of other life offices poaching business or brokers successfully proposing the reduction in benefits and a switch to a less expensive endowment insurance plan where the commission paid was higher.[36] The Life Offices Association and the Association of Scottish Life Offices extended the group life assurance and pension agreements in 1954 to include uniform rates for retirement endowment schemes. Since Standard Life's commission had been lower than that of most

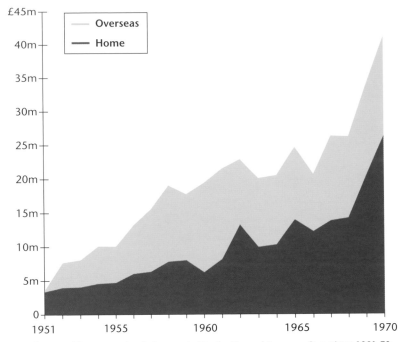

£45m

Overseas

Home

Note: Abstracted from annual statistics reported to the General Purposes Committee 1951-70

FIGURE 6.1
Group deferred annuities
1951–70

other offices, the commission agreement should have strengthened the company's position. Competition intensified, however, as more and more insurance companies and brokers set up pension departments and canvassed possible customers whether they had schemes in place or not. Many of these new entrants preferred to write endowment retirement policies as these were more akin to their existing business than deferred annuities, and were prepared to insure lives for very large sums 'without any evidence of health'. This Standard Life refused to do even if it meant losing business.[37]

The whole pensions market was thrown into confusion in 1956 as a result of the changes in the Finance Act which, apart from providing relief for pensions for the self-employed, allowed the capital content of annuities to be tax-free. It also extended to insurance company schemes concessions on employee contributions and investment income which had been available to self-administered pension schemes since 1921 (see page 200). Despite the recommendation of the Millard Tucker Committee, pensions schemes were refused permission to give tax-free lump sums unlike endowment retirement policies.[38] The immediate consequence was the 'switching of schemes to the type which obtains the maximum tax concessions' and therefore lower premiums. Brokers, particularly Noble Lowndes who specialised in pensions, saw this as an opportunity to persuade schemes to change insurance companies or set up in-house trusts. Unlike some companies, Standard Life responded positively, assisting all their schemes which wished to convert and encouraging them to enhance benefits rather than reduce premiums.[39] This was partly out of self-interest so as to avoid a decline in income with a consequent rise in the expense ratio. In London, where the bulk of the pensions business was handled, G. Peter Glover was transferred from the office to the outdoor staff* to help with the increased workload. Although of a 'studious bearing', 'great things' were expected of him in the future.[40] His promise

* The 'outdoor staff' were the sales staff – the inspectors and superintendents, who had direct contact with customers.

was more than fulfilled when he crossed the divide between the pensions and ordinary department to become agency manager in 1970. It is testimony to the commitment of the superintendents and their supporting office staff that few clients were lost during the late-1950s and that most schemes agreed to improve benefits. As a result both the number of deferred-annuity and endowment contracts rose.

An added complication in 1957 was the proposal to introduce a more ambitious state pension scheme, which was to be hotly debated over the next 20 years. This proposal had its origins in ideas developed by Professor Richard Titmuss and socialist colleagues at the London School of Economics, who were critical of the pension industry's tendency to favour staff rather than works employees, and of inadequate (if not non-existent) transfer rights between employers. They persuaded the Labour Party to support inflation-proof state earnings-related benefits paid for by graduated contributions. Although a general election was some way off, Labour was in the lead in the opinion polls and Harold Macmillan, the new Conservative prime minister, was not yet secure in office. When the Labour Party's plans were announced, many employers delayed 'consideration of new schemes or extension of existing ones', stalling Standard Life's new pension business. The industry immediately proposed to the government that all employees should be compelled to join occupational pension schemes. Considered too radical at the time, this concept was to be revived forty years later

Alexander Robert Reid, manager from 1951 to 1964.

amidst concern about the mounting cost of state provision. Instead, in the spring of 1958, existing state pensions were raised well above the rate of inflation and a state graduated pension scheme, to be introduced the following year, was announced. Members of occupational pension schemes were allowed to contract out of the graduated scheme, and, as an incentive, to pay reduced national insurance.[41] Whilst appreciating that 'things might have been worse', Standard Life's pension department was doubtful about the likely impact of the new system especially on the provision for those on lower incomes.[42] Under the terms of the National Insurance Act of 1959, the state graduated pension scheme was to come into force on 1 April 1961. At the general election in October the Conservatives won a resounding victory, which was taken as endorsement of their pensions policy. The Labour Party, however, gave notice that it was still committed to radical reform and, under Richard Crossman, began discussions with the insurance industry.

In the meantime Standard Life had to address other competitive pressures to defend its pension business which now accounted for 'some 70 per cent of our assets and premium income'.[43] By 1958 the continuing high level of interest rates was leading brokers to recommend with-profits pension plans such as those offered by Legal & General and the Prudential.[44] Brokers also continued to resent Standard Life's insistence on the right 'to contact employers direct and to provide

expert assistance and advice', considering an insurance company should simply be confined to underwriting.[45] This was to be a recurring complaint. The London office reported 32 schemes under 'attack' in 1958, of which five were lost, including Tate & Lyle and Prestige Ltd, and of which in nine cases a decision was still pending.[46] In such circumstances Standard Life had a participating or with-profits deferred-annuity contract to 'defend existing schemes', but this was not available to all customers. In any event the actuaries were not convinced, believing that 'in the end of the day it could be a guaranteed without-profit contract will turn out to have been the better bargain'.[47] They could cite the experience of the Prudential which had switched entirely to with-profit plans in 1951 and found them hard to sell.[48]

Under pressure from the pension superintendents, a with-profits contract was launched in 1959, which even Noble Lowndes was forced to admit was one of the best in the industry.[49] Designed by Ernest Bromfield, the new contract offered the addition of a bonus every three years and net premiums were related to the yield on 2.5 per cent consols (government stock) with annual rebates dependent on the movement of the yield, guaranteed for 20 years.[50] Briefed on the technical details of the National Insurance Act, the superintendents began the formidable task of visiting all customers to discuss the merits of contracting out of the state graduated pension scheme and to introduce the new with-profits contract. Although on balance they advised con-

Workers in the 1980s on the shop floor of the Rover Car Company whose pensions were insured with Standard Life.

tracting in, the company undertook to handle the complex negotiations with the government's registrar for those who wished to contract out.[51] About a quarter of customers decided to contract out; but many, as had been hoped, reconsidered 'the whole basis of their schemes'. Rather than participate in the state scheme, some large clients, such as Alfred Herbert Ltd, the English Steel Corporation and the Rover Company, set up pension schemes for their works employees.[52] The combination of the new with-profits contract and the programme of visits resulted in healthy new business in 1961 and 1962.

With a general election on the horizon, the future was unclear. Hector A. Fraser, now the group pensions manager, warned: 'If Labour were returned to power the diminution in the pension field left to private enterprise might well be serious.' Competition was intense with no fewer than 100 schemes in jeopardy during 1962 and 13 reported casualties. Some fell victim to the appeal of self-administered schemes drawing on the advice of consulting actuaries and encouraged by the buoyant equity market.[53] In some cases the funds were being managed on a fee basis by investment companies, particularly merchant banks such as Warburgs and Helbert, Wagg & Co., which was acquired by Schroders in 1960. Waggs had entered this market in 1946 with the Suez Canal Company's account and at the time of the takeover numbered amongst its large institutional clients the BBC, Boots and Heinz.[54] Stockbrokers, such as Phillips & Drew, also began to offer specialist investment advice

to trustees of pension funds. Although one insurance company had started to provide investment management and limited actuarial advice for pension funds, the senior executives at Standard Life had no doubt that this would be 'a bad example to follow'. Nevertheless, the company's largest clients were repeatedly subjected to direct approaches from merchant banks.[55]

The return of the Labour Party to power in October 1964 cast a shadow over the private pensions industry. By now Standard Life, in common with all pension providers, was convinced that they were 'sailing a little uneasily between Scylla and Charybdis'. There was no doubt that the Labour government, if it remained in office, would introduce an enlarged state scheme, whereas Conservative policy was now to limit state provision to a basic minimum and make it obligatory for employers to provide private pensions with stipulated minimum benefits. Superficially attractive as this proposal was, it would be complicated to administer and held out the real threat of government interference with terms and investment strategies, as had happened elsewhere in the world.[56] When the Labour government was re-elected with a healthy majority in 1966, Richard Crossman, the Minister of Social Security, confirmed that the anticipated legislation would be introduced in the lifetime of the parliament. Until an announcement was made the only growth in business came from existing schemes, which continued to be assailed relentlessly. Premium rates for deferred-annuity business were reduced in 1966 in an effort to

A Standard Life advertisement extolling the virtues of insured pension schemes over managed ones, 1967.

prevent further withdrawals and contributed to record new pension business in the following two years. The publication in 1967 by Standard Life of *The Modern Pension Fund*, which summarised 'the advantage of insured funds against private funds', did nothing to convince one company, Hawker Siddeley, which contributed £400,000 in premium income a year, from converting to a private scheme the following year.[57]

This large loss compelled the executive to examine the potential of unit-linked pensions and to reconsider their attitude to operating managed funds. The Canadian branch had already been forced down this route in 1966 (see page 247). This led to the establishment of Standard Life Pension Funds Ltd in 1969 which, unlike the initiative in Canada, was welcomed by brokers and consulting actuaries. There were two options for schemes – to place their assets either in a pooled equity fund or in a segregated fund. New literature was produced contradicting the advice to be found in *The Modern Pension Fund*. Within a year three large schemes with assets of almost £6 million switched to the pooled equity fund, and Sainsbury's moved their scheme with a transfer value of £8.5 million into a segregated fund.[58]

Despite a large advance in business in 1969 and 1970, mostly attributable to schemes upgrading from average- to final-salary benefits and the winning of the pension contract from the ill-fated Upper Clyde Shipbuilders, the publication in 1969 of the Labour government's white paper on pensions threatened to undermine future provision. Crucially the plans included index-linking, fair provision for widows, and secure transfer rights.[59] Since such terms were technically difficult – if not impossible – for the private sector to provide, the insurance industry protested that it would be misleading for them to recommend their clients to contract out. If this were to happen, they feared a large loss of revenue.[60] While welcoming the Labour government's recognition that the provision of pensions had to be a partnership between the state and the private sector, Standard Life warned that the cost of the proposals would place an intolerable burden on future generations of taxpayers.[61] In the meantime, the Life Offices Association and the newly formed pressure group STOP (Save the Occupational Pension) were negotiating acceptable terms for contracting out of the new scheme. With this in view, the Standard Life actuaries began to examine how final-salary schemes and index-linked benefits might be underwritten in a period of high inflation.[62] So as to provide a better pension service to companies operating in Europe, Standard Life, together with six leading European insurance companies, had formed in 1967 a consortium known as Insurope, covering France, Switzerland, the Benelux countries, Austria, Germany and Italy. Since then the consortium had been strengthened by a programme of visits and study groups.[63]

UNCERTAINTY OVER CANADA

If much of Standard Life's home pension business in the 1960s and 1970s was defensive, overseas expansion was aggressive and rapid. In Canada, as an integral part of a 'programme of vigorous expansion through the building up of older agencies and the opening of new ones', more staff were engaged to cover the whole country. At the time Alec Reid believed, mistakenly as it turned out, that the Canadian business would in the future outgrow that in the United Kingdom.[64] The board were encouraged to accept this view by the spectacular advance in group pension sales stimulated by the reforms in 1945. By 1955 the branch had 302 group pension plans in place, covering 44,000 employees for a total of $6.9 million a year in deferred pensions. A reduction in rates maintained competitiveness, which was reflected in continuing growth, and the branch was soon outperforming its competitors, especially in the provision of pensions – no mean achievement in the hotly contested Canadian market. Standard Life accounted for 25 per cent of all group annuity business in force in the country in 1960 and in that year underwrote no less than 36 per cent of all new contracts. The ordinary market (see Appendix 2 on page 378) behaved in much the same way as in the United Kingdom, with a shift away from whole-life to term assurance, mostly associated with mortgage lending and the withdrawal from without-profits contracts because of the strength of the opposition. Following the example of the Heritable, the Canadian branch attracted new ordinary business by mortgage lending, especially for new home construction under the National Housing

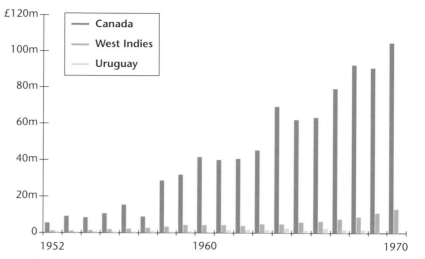

Note: Abstracted from the annual statistics reported to the General Purposes Committee 1952-1970

FIGURE 6.2
Overseas new ordinary business 1952–70

Act. Since Canadian law forbade more than 15 per cent of a life fund being invested in equities and property, proportionally much more capital was devoted to mortgages – some 37 per cent of assets by 1962. Success in Canada was, however, only achieved at a price. There was a deficiency of over $10 million in 'the admissible value of our Canadian assets as compared with the statutory basis for the valuation of our liabilities', which required the deposit of British government securities of equivalent value. Further sums had to be deposited in the 1960s, rising to £37.4 million at the end of the decade.[65]

Lindsay Armstrong, the manager for Canada, died suddenly in 1957 after 47 years' service. A man in Davidson's mould, he laid the foundations for the development of the branch. He was succeeded by his deputy, George Westwater, who

George T. Westwater, manager in Canada from 1957 to 1976.

was equally diligent in promoting Standard Life. In 1961 the chairman of the Canadian local board W.A. 'Dollar Bill' Arbuckle was invited to join the Standard Life board in an attempt to improve liaison between the branch and Edinburgh. The Canadian head office in Sherbrooke Avenue, Montreal, was demolished and rebuilt on the same site between 1960 and 1962 to accommodate the additional staff who were needed to process the growing volume of transactions. Throughout the country, recruiting and retaining well-qualified sales personnel was difficult and at times handicapped development. By January 1966 only 71 of the 136 represen-

tatives employed four years earlier remained with the company. The rest, who had been well trained by Standard Life, were now working for competitors. Although ordinary business continued to advance, the opening of the new Canadian head office in 1962 coincided with a decline in new pension contracts due to growing competition and the refusal of head office to provide with-profits pension products. As in the United Kingdom, a participating or with-profits deferred-annuity scheme could be offered to existing clients who were threatening to withdraw, such as Canadian Oil Companies and Price Bros. Ltd. Competition came from insurance companies such as Manufacturers Life offering better rates and, more significantly, managed funds which had quickly become popular in Canada encouraged by consulting actuaries.[66] As in other parts of the business, Standard Life's rates reflected a pessimistic view about the future trend in interest rates which was not shared by the rest of the industry. Alec Reid was convinced that the with-profits deferred-annuity rates marketed by North American life offices left them 'no possibility of profit'.[67] The Canadian premium rates for deferred annuities, however, were improved in 1962.

With Reid and Dow opposed to Standard Life managing funds (known in North America as deposit administration) for private pension schemes, it was impossible to meet the competition from the trust companies, which now dominated the market. When their pensions became payable, employees in Canada were allowed to choose the best annuity rates available, and employers could withdraw funds at immediate notice, only paying the managers 5 per cent to cover costs. As early as 1955 Reid had argued that such terms were unacceptable and that if Standard Life was forced into deposit administration it would be on American terms whereby employees were required to take out pensions with the insurance company concerned rather than searching the market for the 'best' deal, and an employer could only withdraw a fund over a minimum of five years.[68]

Just as in Britain, the whole pension market was confused after 1963 by the decision of the federal government to introduce a compulsory 'pay-as-you-go' national pension plan. At the same time, in response to the intense challenge from the trusts, the Canadian branch began administering deposits, offering to large plans 'an arrangement whereby up to 50 per cent of a plan can be accepted on a managed-fund basis provided the remainder is insured with us'.[69] Although this reform contributed to an upturn in pension business during 1964, it was

estimated that the government's Canadian Pension Plan, when it came into force on 1 January 1966, would result in the loss of as much as 20 per cent of premium income, quite apart from the costs of altering the terms of existing schemes. Worse was to follow when many schemes on reviewing their terms opted to switch to trust funds. In an effort to retain custom, Standard Life immediately relaxed the rules for participation in its own managed investment fund but further loss of premium income was inevitable. Employees covered by the government scheme also demanded to cash in their existing benefits, which they now regarded as superfluous. The uncertainty was increased by rapid wage inflation during 1965 and the collapse of the North American General Insurance Company, the first failure of a federally registered office for 40 years. Internally the branch compounded the confusion by introducing a new formula for the remuneration of managers and the sales force, which caused dissatisfaction and led several representatives to resign. At the same time a regional structure

Flyers for Canadian Pacific Hotels, whose pension scheme is insured by Standard Life.

James Bremner Dow, manager from 1964 to 1970.

based on the experiment in England and Ireland was adopted, which it was hoped would not only restore morale but help address the profound difficulties in the market for the company's products. As part of this restructuring both Westwater and his deputy Robert Thomson were appointed directors of the Canadian local board, which was still purely advisory and had no executive responsibilities.

With strong support from Ernest Bromfield, the group manager, who visited Canada for five weeks, the 'spirit and effectiveness of the field-force' revived, which was reflected in a record year in 1966 both for new sums assured and pensions. Standard Life took advantage of changes in legislation which allowed for the formation of pooled equity funds with no restrictions on the structure of the portfolio. Consulting actuaries were not impressed and refused to recommend this alternative, damaging new business over the next two years. In response, Westwater planned a campaign to call into question the impartiality of the advice provided by consulting actuaries; before this could be launched, however, Pierre Trudeau's incoming Liberal government in its first budget in October 1968 taxed both the investment income and profits of life companies, along with the capital gains on policies with the exception of proceeds payable at death. Alarmed by this development and the mounting drain on resources, the chairman, Tom Risk, and the manager, Brem Dow, went out to Canada during the following summer to review the future of the branch. Critical of much of what he saw, Dow concluded that management would need to revise 'many of our ideas quite fundamentally' and urged his successors to maintain much closer contact than in the past.[70] At the Standard Life board meeting on 15 July, Dow went further, winning support for a review of the future of the Canadian branch before equity-linked policies were introduced later in the year. The findings were to be discussed at a special board meeting in November.

REVIEWING STRATEGY

In preparing the report, Dow necessarily had to review the 'whole future development of the company'. At a theoretical level he explored the relationship of with- and without-profits contracts from the company's perspective. Although he had no doubts that without-profits policies should not be sold unless a profit to the company could be expected, he was equally convinced that it was not in the interests of existing with-profits policy-holders to dilute their interest by writing 'nothing but new with-profits business'. Having shifted the emphasis at least theoretically back to a balance between both types of contract, he moved on to discuss how much of a mutual company's surplus should be devoted to expansion. Although he admitted there was no general rule, he explained the strategic criteria which he and Reid had adopted:

i. So long as every with-profits policy-holder receives as much or more than his premiums have 'paid for', he cannot claim that his contact has been unsatisfactory.

ii. If the expansion of new business from year to year is reasonably steady so that the cost of financing it also progresses regularly, the effect on successive generations of policy-holders should be reasonably equitable.

iii. There could be held to be an obligation on members to maintain the company as a continuing entity which provides a continuing social service in which each generation receives something from its predecessor and transmits something to its successors.

With these precepts in mind he summarised the reasons for 'the vigorous policy of expansion' after the war:

i. Since insurance business is based on statistics and 'the law of averages', increasing size brings increased stability (e.g. in the emergence of claims) which is in the interests of policy-holders.

ii. Although some of our expenses vary more or less directly with the amount of business written, there are many overhead expenses which do not necessarily increase in proportion to the business in force. Increasing size brings scope for economies in management, which should make the company more efficient and increase profitability.

iii. Life insurance provides a valuable public service both by its protection against disaster of premature death and by the encouragement it gives to national savings. Our past record enables us to claim that the assurance policies of the Standard are amongst the best in the market, and it is natural, therefore, to consider every means of promoting their sale.

Whilst accepting that Standard Life 'has now reached a size where further growth would not materially affect the security it can offer its policy-holders', he calculated that when inflation was discounted new business was growing by only 5 per cent a year.

Dow had no doubt that as a result of increased restrictions and regulations in every country 'the investment advantages of having an international organisation no longer exist' and therefore the continuation of each branch had to be considered on its own merits with no cross subsidies. Analysing Canadian business, he concluded that the changes in taxation posed no real threat; but that a switch of pension funds from fully assured non-participating or without-profits contracts to administered deposits was inevitable, which would materially reduce 'the "gearing" of our ordinary with-profits assurance business'. The only hope in this uncharted territory was that investment management might prove profitable. Recent events in the United Kingdom gave him cause for concern (see page 244). On

The Jamaican staff in 1956 with, in the second row, G.P.S. Macpherson, a director of the company (fourth from left), Alexander Harrison, chairman (sixth from left), and John Hamilton, manager for the West Indies (fourth from right).

these assumptions Dow confessed there was a case for either suspending or substantially curtailing Standard Life's Canadian presence, laying to rest any lingering belief that the branch would outdistance the United Kingdom business. He hesitated, however, to take such a drastic step on the grounds that 'to do so would . . . be an abnegation of the objects of a mutual insurance company which exists to provide a continuing service to the public, to provide a fair return on premiums paid and not to make the maximum profits for any particular generation of policy-holders.'[71] The paper, written as much to educate the directors in the mode of operation of a mutual life company as to articulate future strategy, was endorsed by the special board meeting on 11 November 1969. It was also agreed that the future of operations in the West Indies should be reviewed.[72]

WITHDRAWAL FROM URUGUAY

The background to this review was the decision two years earlier to withdraw from Uruguay. Although the difficulty in recruiting sub-agents in that country continued into the 1950s, Leonard King, the manager, remained confident that prospects were good. There was almost no competition except from the State Insurance Bank which, with a new generation of managers, was moving away from trying to enforce its monopoly towards educating prospective customers, opening new branches and enlisting and training agents. This was the reason Reid gave for Standard Life remaining in Uruguay when he

inspected the branch in 1954.[73] Throughout that decade new business returns were volatile, reflecting as much the well-being of the principal agents as the ups and downs of the turbulent agrarian economy. Dr Arocena, who worked in Montevideo, was 65 in 1953 and beginning to show signs of his age; Don Ramón Paradell, who had secured the majority of new business for some years (see page 224), suffered a heart attack in June 1955 from which he never fully recovered. Their contribution was replaced in part by the efforts of the agent in Buenos Aires, Señor Erenu, who claimed he was an 'intimate friend of everyone in South America of note and fortune, but through his wife (who is a Hapsburg and a relation of the present Queen of England) is in contact with all the high society and big business of Europe'.

With Paradell out of action, King found it easier to begin to penetrate the 'Camp' by sending out into the countryside trusted agents from Montevideo. He was cautious about developing the market in the interior, which would take time and require new staff, until the economic outlook had improved.[74] He reported in 1957: 'I do not think I exaggerate when I say that the country has never, in all its history, been in such a bad situation as it is now, and there is not the slightest evidence or hope that its condition will get anything but worse.'[75] Although King visited Edinburgh during the following year, no one went out to assess the performance of the branch at first hand; had they done so, it would have been closed. Over the next three years his reports grew longer and gloomier, providing an accurate analysis of the rapid deterioration in the fabric of the country. By 1960 there was a hint of desperation: 'I am getting a little tired of writing that the past year has been a critical or a difficult one . . . I should like to mention once more that it is a long while since we had the pleasure of a visit from Edinburgh.'[76]

Although the long-term outlook for the Uruguayan economy remained poor, business improved sharply in the early 1960s due to the introduction of the 'Young Man's Policy' (an endowment contract), the return to work of Señor Erenu, who had been on an extended holiday in Europe, and a strong performance by the agents working the Camp. With prospects seeming brighter the chairman, T.G. (later Sir Thomas) Waterlow, and Ernest Bromfield visited Uruguay in 1962. With the outlook better than for some time, despite a resurgence in the activities of the State Insurance Bank, they encouraged a pessimistic King to expand with the help of Señor Montefiore. His well-organised network of sub-agents now accounted for two thirds of the company's total Uruguayan peso production.[77] With inflation running at about 60 per cent, the exchange rate fell from 50 pesos to the pound in 1963 to 550 four years later, but new business remained surprisingly buoyant as more new agents were taken on. Increasingly, policies were written in Canadian dollars to protect them from escalating inflation and the deteriorating exchange rates throughout Latin America. This was profitable as the resulting commissions and expenses were settled in pesos.[78] Impressed by this performance, Edinburgh ignored King's forebodings of imminent economic collapse. Following the devaluation in 1965 David Donald, the actuary, went out to see for himself and wrote, almost cheerfully, that 'the people gave little impression of a nation on the verge of bankruptcy'. Given that it was impossible for Standard Life to sell the business, he recommended keeping the branch open for at least another year until the trend in exchange rates was clarified.[79] The closure of the branch in 1968 was precipitated not, as might have been expected, by the economic situation, but by a violent dispute between Leonard King and his local directors. In the previous November their chairman resigned, complaining to Dow that he and his colleagues had been treated as ciphers by their manager. Donald returned at once to Montevideo and, although he exonerated King, decided that since the outlook for the economy was so bleak the branch should be shut.[80] By this time the peso had deteriorated to such an extent that the company was able to offer most policy-holders an immediate payment of the sum assured without deduction of future premiums.

FORCED OUT OF THE WEST INDIES

In contrast, the West Indian economy in the 1950s had been both stable and prosperous. With the branch's ordinary business booming and sales of pensions making steady progress, the branch manager, John Hamilton, did not consider it necessary to provide head office with much information – especially as a director and a member of the executive visited at least once every three years during the long Scottish winter.[81] He ran the branch more or less as a separate fiefdom until he retired in 1962. As in the United Kingdom and Canada, much of the new ordinary business came from term insurance linked to mortgage lending including some by Standard Life itself. Competition from Canadian companies, particularly from North American Life and Manufacturer's Life, was strong for all classes of business.[82] The Federation of the West Indies was established in 1958, but strains soon began to emerge and the union collapsed within four years. Anticipating the break up, in 1961 the West Indies branch was divided in two, Trinidad and Tobago under Lieutenant-Colonel A.M. Lamont, previously the deputy manager,[83] and Jamaica, which included the Bahamas, under R.J. Curtis who was sent out from Manchester. From then on their experience differed. In Trinidad and Tobago the incoming government pruned the tax concessions on life assurance, making it a much less profitable form of investment. In the more attractive Jamaican market Canadian and American companies intensified their representation by appointing more full-time agents.[84]

In Trinidad and Tobago Lamont's initial enthusiasm was soon quenched as the changes in taxation, which also contributed to a downturn in the housing market, began to bite. Finding it difficult to meet their quotas, the sales

In the summer of 1960, Trinidad was virtually brought to a standstill by an almost total strike in the oil industry. Standard Life's manager for the West Indies, John Hamilton, used his horse Snowball to beat the traffic chaos in Port-of-Spain, and arrive at work on time. He kept Snowball in what was usually his reserved parking space at Standard Life's building on Marine Square.

force became dispirited. During 1965 new insurance legislation was proposed for Trinidad and Tobago, which would have placed onerous burdens on overseas companies. Francis Jamieson, the investment manager and now an assistant general manager, made representations to the government on behalf of the Life Offices Association and the Fire Offices' Committee, but to little effect.[85] The Trinidad Insurance Act when it came into force in December 1966 required all foreign companies to hold 36 per cent of their Trinidad liabilities in local investments immediately and 60 per cent within five years. Moreover, the Finance Act in the same year withdrew tax relief on all policies which were not written in Trinidad dollars. Ernest Bromfield tried unsuccessfully to persuade the government to continue relief on pension schemes for expatriates, such as the employees of Texaco whose pension scheme was provided in sterling by Standard Life through the London office. With so many commitments in Trinidad, Standard Life in the short term had no alternative but to comply with the investment requirements, particularly as the regulations applied equally to offices which had ceased to write new business.[86] The branch responded by writing record new business over the next four years despite mounting competition from Canadian companies and increasing racial tension. This erupted in the early months of 1970 with serious 'Black Power' riots and a mutiny in the armed forces. A state of emergency was declared in April under Dr Eric Williams, who supported the Black Power movement. He imposed punitive taxation on all foreign companies operating in the country, threatened nationalisation of the insurance industry and later introduced severe exchange controls.[87] Following the review of the Canadian branch, George Philip, one of the assistant general managers, had already started to look at the future of the West Indies branches. His report recommending closure after 125 years of representation was accepted by the board in July 1970.[88]

In Jamaica the new Labour government pursued familiar policies. There were early indications of a move towards economic nationalism by 'looking to see what jobs are held by non-Jamaican citizens and whether Jamaicans could carry out such jobs'.[89] Spencer Marshall, a local inspector, was selected as a possible prospective manager and given more general experience including a spell in Edin-

burgh. This was followed by the expected introduction in 1965 of a compulsory government insurance scheme, which also provided pensions. As in other countries, this innovation, which gave the government wide powers, dented pension sales at the same time as private funds were becoming popular. Although the branch succeeded in increasing custom, it failed to hold its own against American and Canadian companies, as many young Jamaicans, proud of their independence, sought to distance themselves from any connection with the old colonial power.[90] Jamaica Mutual Life Assurance Society, an established local company, remodelled itself on Canadian lines with the help of the London-based consulting actuaries Bacon and Woodrow, and launched an ambitious advertising campaign in both the press and on television. The Standard Life branch was disadvantaged as elsewhere in meeting these challenges by the lack of a with-profits deferred annuity contract which was now generally available from other companies in the market.[91]

As in Uruguay, a decline in the Jamaican economy after 1966 contributed to a sense of isolation, with staff feeling 'that head office is very far away from them'. This impression was reinforced by the summary decision from head office to withdraw from the Bahamas in March 1967 because of political uncertainty.[92] In November 1968 the chairman Sir William Watson and A.C. Stepney, the joint agency manager, visited the country, encouraging the staff and discussing prospects with the new manager, D.J.A. Bennett, and his assistant, Spencer Marshall.[93] Within two months Marshall had been tempted away to work in Grand Cayman, which was beginning to be developed as a tax haven for financial services, and the new office manager, Oscar Hoo, another Jamaican, had left for Jamaica Mutual. It was to Bennett's credit that he succeeded not only in holding the branch together but also increasing business by selling more without-profits policies as collateral for mortgages.[94] With the Black Power movement having taken a grip in Trinidad and Tobago, leading to the decision to close the branch, the executive in Edinburgh were concerned that similar developments might occur in Jamaica. Sir Thomas Waterlow and Brem Dow went out in 1970 to assess the situation. Although they were reassured by the local board about the political and economic situation, they were not convinced that it was in Standard Life's best interests as a British company to comply with the rigorous regulations, similar to those in Trinidad and Tobago, which were to be introduced in new insurance legislation the following year. While in the country they approached Jamaica Mutual with a view to a merger, which was finally agreed in August 1971.[95]

Having been represented around the world at the beginning of the century, Standard Life now had only two overseas branches, Ireland, which was directly managed from the United Kingdom, and Canada. Apart from the withdrawal from Europe during and after the First World War,

decisions to leave a market had been taken reluctantly and were usually the result of legislation designed to encourage local offices and stimulate national economies.

INVESTING IN EQUITIES

With the rapid growth of the company during the 1950s the investment committee and Francis Jamieson had to invest between £15 million and £30 million of new money each year (see Appendix 6 on page 386). At first they continued the policy begun after the war (see page 225) of moving out of fixed-interest securities and into ordinary shares, raising the proportion of all the assets held in this way from 20 per cent in 1952 to a peak of 43 per cent in 1961. The process for authorising purchases by the investment committee was simplified in 1953 when annual mandates for instalment purchases started to be given, and from 1957 no holding was to be less than £50,000 (revised shortly afterwards to £100,000).[96] Under this arrangement, as the name suggests, ordinary shares were bought in instalments throughout the year up to an agreed sum. This ensured that control over investment decisions remained in the hands of the directors and prevented the investment department from moving swiftly to take advantage of market conditions. The directors appear to have had little confidence in the investment department being able to time such interventions correctly.

The portfolio, which was heavily biased towards the United Kingdom financial sector (some 40 per cent, with more than two thirds held in investment trusts),* began to be widened in 1953 when it was agreed to begin investing once more albeit cautiously in the United States, buying at first defensive stocks (mostly utilities).[97] Within a year the investment committee resolved to raise United States investments from 2.5 to 4 per cent of assets by going for growth companies.[98] Although equity yields in the United States were 2 per cent higher than in the United Kingdom, the purchase of such securities on the London market had to be made using investment dollars. This was because United Kingdom investors were not permitted to use sterling to transact net purchases of foreign securities from overseas residents and could only use currency already held by United Kingdom investors. As a consequence, the premium on such investment dollars fluctuated depending on demand.[99] When the premium rose too high during the 1956 Suez crisis, investment in America was suspended, but was quickly resumed when the market fell and stocks appeared cheap. Jamieson, taking the long view, was confident that 'we can, if we confine our investments to equities, afford to ignore fluctuations in rates of exchange'.[100]

The decision to stay with equities when the market reached a historic high in 1955 was influenced by Jamieson's accurate assessment of the long-term pattern of inflation and interest rates. He was heartened by the publication in 1956 of a study by the stockbrokers de Zoete & Gorton with the help of the Economic Intelligence Unit of the result of investing in equities since 1919, which showed an annual return of 9.8 per cent compared with just 3.8 per cent on government stock, and concluded that equity investment alone provided a hedge against inflation. On the basis of the report, Jamieson argued unsuccessfully for a reduction of the flow of funds into the Heritable where the rate of return was 60 per cent less than on equities.[101]

A consequence of the growing consensus that equities provided the best defence against inflation was a decline in yields. Historically, initial yields on equities had been higher than government stock because the risk involved was assumed to be greater. In the United States in 1958, and the following year in the United Kingdom, their relative yields changed so that equities yielded less – the 'reverse yield gap' which persists to this day.[102]

ENTERING THE PROPERTY MARKET

Before this happened Standard Life's investment strategy was revised in 1957 when equity prices

* Many of these holdings dated back to Standard Life's first foray into the equity market in 1925. Their popularity boomed after the Second World War, largely because they represented an effective means of investing in foreign securities. Following the requirement for greater disclosure in the 1948 Companies Act, it became easier for investors to calculate the net asset value (NAV) of investment trust portfolios. This confirmed that shares in investment trusts were traded at a discount to their asset value, partly because a proportion of their income was taken up in management fees (see John Newlands, *Put Not Your Trust in Money: A History of the Investment Trust Industry from 1868 to the Present*, London, 1997 pp.244-7).

were depressed in the aftermath of the Suez crisis. United Kingdom ordinary-share purchases were suspended until the market began to recover in the spring of 1958 and the target for the holding of mortgages over commercial and private property was increased from 5 to 15 per cent. As a result the allocation of new money to the Heritable was raised rather than reduced.[103] At the same time Standard Life considered the potential of entering the property and hire-purchase markets by buying significant holdings in companies such as the City of London Real Property Co., and British Wagon and North Central Wagon, which had cut their teeth in the hire purchase of railway trucks.[104] With many city centres being rebuilt after wartime bomb damage, investment in property and property companies was popular amongst other life insurance companies because yields were much higher than on government stock. Standard Life had held back, largely because none of the directors or members of the still small investment department had any experience of the sector. There were obvious drawbacks as the board, with its long experience of lending over such securities, were well aware. Property was a very illiquid investment. When prices fell they tended to remain depressed for much longer than those of marketable securities. The attraction was the yield which at first appeared higher than it really was, because depreciation was rarely properly accounted for as there was virtually no experience of the likely life-expectancy of modern buildings. In its first transactions

Standard Life calculated returns on the basis of a generous 50 years' depreciation, which was better than many property companies which made no provision whatsoever.[105]

Legal & General had paved the way in property investment with 27 per cent of its assets in property by 1960, followed by Clerical Medical & General with almost 20 per cent, the Yorkshire Insurance Co. with 17.7 per cent and Norwich Union with 16.5 per cent. Standard Life had just 0.6 per cent. The Scottish life company with the largest property portfolio was Scottish Mutual with 4.4 per cent.[106] One of the reasons for this lack of property investment by Scottish life offices was the very slow pace of commercial redevelopment north of the border. No city centre had been blitzed and government policy had been directed towards slum-clearance schemes with no involvement by the private sector.

With most life offices actively engaged in property development, Standard Life had little choice of partner for any joint venture. Hammerson Property & Investment Trust, which had been floated on the stock exchange in 1953, was selected because its prospects were considered to be good. The company had been founded by Lew Hammerson in 1942 and had only started to develop commercial properties in 1948. By this time it was run by Sydney Mason.[107] Towards the end of 1957 D.O.B. Estate Ltd was formed, with Standard Life taking a 25 per cent stake (£1 million in stock and a further £1 million in debentures), to develop part of the Duke of Bedford's estate to the north-west of London's Holborn station. Jamieson and G.P.S. (Phil) Macpherson, a director of Standard Life and of Robert Benson, Lonsdale & Co.,* the merchant bankers, were appointed to the board. Other developments in the same area soon followed. In April 1958 Standard Life made its first acquisition of a large office building when it purchased for £1.5 million the leasehold of the almost complete Castrol House in London from Hammersons.[108] These transactions were the beginning of a long-standing relationship with Hammersons formalised in 1961 when Standard Life took a 15 per cent stake (£1.5 million) in 'A' voting shares and undertook to make £20 million available in debentures secured over specific developments. As a result, Jamieson became a director of Hammersons. At the same time Royal London Mutual Insurance acquired a 10 per cent stake and was also represented on the board.[109]

Having made its debut in the London property market, Standard Life quickly had other suitors seeking capital for large projects. In 1960 an alliance was formed with City Wall Properties Ltd, which was building offices in central London and elsewhere in the south-east of England. City Wall was recommended by Hammersons and Bensons, who 'had been advising them for some time'. Simultaneously, Frank Taylor, chairman of Taylor Woodrow, 'now one of the largest building and civil engineering groups', offered Standard Life the opportunity to enter a joint property development venture on equal terms. The association between the two companies dated back to 1934 when a group pension scheme was negotiated with Taylor Woodrow, then in its infancy. Attracted by this offer, the directors invited Frank Taylor to be their guest at the Edinburgh Festival to discuss the formation of a new company to be known as S.T.W. Development Co. with Phil Macpherson as chairman. Shortly afterwards a similar joint-venture company with Taylor Woodrow, Monarch Investments Ltd, was set up in Canada.[110] As a result of these first initiatives property investments by the end of 1961 had more than doubled to over £5 million or 1.3 per cent of assets.

INVESTMENT STRATEGY

The decision to enlarge Standard Life's property portfolio over the next ten years was conditioned by Jamieson's change of attitude to the long-term performance of equities. On this occasion he was wrong; but with good reason. During the second half of 1961 and well into the following year stock-exchange valuations on both sides of the Atlantic fell steadily, with the worst one-day fall since the Munich crisis of 1938 on Wall Street in May 1962.[111] As the reverse-yield gap narrowed, investment managers looked closely at the disposition of their holdings of various classes of security. Early in

---

* Robert Benson, Lonsdale & Co. merged with Kleinwort Sons & Co. in 1961 to become Kleinwort Benson Ltd. G.P.S. Macpherson continued as a director of the merged company.

1962 the Standard Life investment committee decided to switch to debentures, which yielded 2 to 3 per cent more than government stock until the outlook became clearer. The purchase of equities was reduced to the lower end of the expected range of 20 per cent. In case the markets recovered, the upper limit was left unchanged at 30 per cent. A thorough review in May concluded that the decline on Wall Street was 'merely a temporary shake-out' and that purchases of American securities should be resumed as the dollar premium had fallen to 4 per cent. The same could not be said for the London market for a number of reasons:

Much greater uncertainty prevails about the prospects in this country. Export difficulties, the squeeze on profit margins, the resurgence of inflation and foreign exchange difficulties have frequently been highlighted in the press and elsewhere; there are economic uncertainties, such as the question of throwing in our lot with Europe . . . In the light of all this we have been subjected to many conflicting opinions from our advisers. Some, even among those who have been the most equity-minded in the past, are now advising extreme caution; but this view is by no means universal and others feel that we should not be panicked out of our normal long-term policy in regard to ordinary shares by current uncertainties.[112]

Although the parameters for new equity investment were not altered, the investment com-

mittee, taking a pessimistic view despite a record recovery in the market, only committed 17 per cent of new money to equities in 1963 and withdrew entirely from the American market as the dollar premium was now 12 per cent. Two years later dollar investments were made even more unattractive by the introduction of the '25 per cent surrender scheme' which left only 75 per cent of the premium of the dollar proceeds of any sale available for reinvestment. Taking advantage of rising share prices, the portfolio was restructured during April 1963 by the sale of large quantities of low-yielding sterling equities, particularly those in engineering and iron and steel sectors.[113]

The investment committee regularly revisited the issue of the proportion of new money which should be invested in equities. Although Jamieson was by now well known in the City as a 'notorious bear', he still believed that in the long term a target of 30 per cent was broadly correct.[114] He warned of the dangers of the alternative of investing more in government stock, which of necessity would have to be long-dated or irredeemable 'to secure an adequate "matching" according to the duration of our assets and liabilities'. His main concern was that returns would be much reduced, regardless of evidence to the contrary even during the stockmarket boom of 1963. Some members of the board, particularly Phil Macpherson and Jimmy Gammell, a partner in Ivory & Sime, were on the whole more bullish. Jamieson hit back by pointing out that in the type of business Macpherson and

Gammell were engaged in it was much simpler to switch investments to take advantage of short-term price movements which may be unrelated to long-term fundamentals. He was not seeking greater flexibility but drawing a distinction with the 'greater continuity' required by a policy of instalment purchasing. He observed: 'Its great merit is that it leads one to go on buying at times when the immediate outlook is very uncertain, and it is purchases made at such times in the past that have in the long run turned out most profitable.'[115] This difference in outlook was most obvious after the Labour government imposed a heavy corporation tax in its 1966 budget. Jamieson wished to reduce the parameters for ordinary share investment from 20–30 per cent to 10–20 per cent and raise those for property investment to the same level. He was overruled by the directors, who confirmed the existing 20-30 per cent range because they were reluctant to disturb the balance between equities and fixed-interest securities. Despite a concerted campaign led by Gammell with the support of his fellow director R.F. Scovell to

Churchill Square, Brighton, which Standard Life redeveloped in the mid-1960s and again in the late 1990s.

persuade the executive to achieve this target, the directors' advice was ignored and only 5 per cent of new money was invested in equities during 1966.[116]

BUILDING THE PROPERTY PORTFOLIO

A corollary of this strategy of scaling down investment in equities from 1963 was that 7.5 per cent of new money was allocated to property – with a good spread across the country and in different types of property.[117] A separate property department was set up in 1964 under Gordon Stewart. Over the remainder of the decade Standard Life participated in a number of large city-centre redevelopments, some of which permanently changed the urban landscape of the United Kingdom, such as the Anderston Cross development in Glasgow and Churchill Square in Brighton. These projects were mostly undertaken in partnership with Hammersons, Taylor Woodrow and, from 1964, City Wall. During that year Standard Life acquired that company's convertible loan stock owned by Commercial Union and undertook to make available £15 million in mortgage debentures over the next seven to eight years. The directors were pleased with this proposal as it offered the opportunity for Standard Life to take a 20 per cent stake in City Wall when the loan stock was converted into ordinary shares in three or four years' time.[118] The introduction of corporation tax, however, made such joint ventures unattractive and they were discontinued

after 1965. This did not prevent consideration of the takeover of City Wall, in which Standard Life now had a 25 per cent stake, either alone or jointly with Hammersons in 1969 to frustrate a takeover bid from Star (Great Britain) Holdings Ltd. Although the executive made such a proposal, it was rejected by the board in preference to direct ownership of property which could also be classed as equity investment. News that Standard Life was considering a bid, however, was sufficient to persuade Star to withdraw.[119]* By 1971 Standard Life had an even distribution of property investments amongst offices, shops and industrial premises and warehouses. Not surprisingly the greatest proportion was in London and the southeast with a combined total of almost 60 per cent, followed some way behind by Scotland with 16.2 per cent.[120]

THE CAPITAL FINANCE AFFAIR

When the original suggestion had been made to go into property and hire-purchase, the consensus had been against hire-purchase, even though such an investment could be expected to produce a great deal of new life contracts. As a result, an approach to participate in a rights issue by United Dominions Trust was turned down.[121] This was a lucky escape as UDT was to be one of the principal victims of the secondary banking crisis in the winter of 1973. As the sector expanded following the relaxation of government controls, however, Standard Life was

* City Wall was eventually acquired by the Rank Organisation in 1971.

An advertisement for a Rolls Rapide washing-machine which could be bought on hire purchase with funds made available by Capital Finance. Rolls Razor lost credibility when the free 25-piece kitchenware set failed to be delivered. Capital Finance was rescued by Standard Life in 1965.

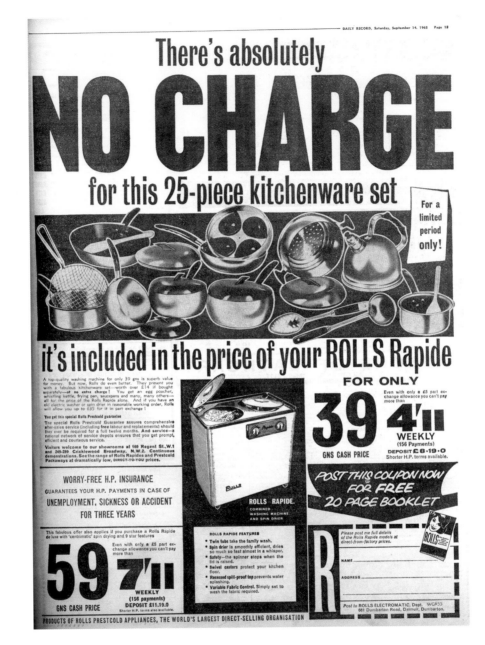

tempted in 1965 to participate in the refinancing of the Edinburgh-based Capital Finance Company Ltd. Founded in the mid-1950s and backed by the merchant bankers Guinness Mahon, the company had introduced in 1960 in collaboration with the Bank of Scotland an innovative hire-purchase scheme 'capital plan for tax relief' designed to take advantage of tax relief then applicable to overdrafts. The bank made £2.25 million available on the understanding that the capital plan could also be marketed through its own hire-purchase company, North West Securities. Boosted by the popularity of the scheme, Capital Finance had gone public in 1962, but suffered a blow to its standing two years later when it came to an agreement to provide hire-purchase facilities for John Bloom's Rolls Razor washing machine company just a few months before it collapsed. At much the same time they reached a similar understanding with Cyril Lord of carpet fame, whose business failed spectacularly in 1968. Both these entanglements resulted in considerable losses to Capital Finance. As serious was the withdrawal at short notice in March 1965 of large deposits held on behalf of the Moscow Narodny Bank. The Bank of Scotland agreed to help fill the gap by extending the overdraft to £3 million.[122] Unfortunately within a year the tax loophole was closed and relief on overdrafts was no longer available. Nevertheless, Capital Finance was reported to be a takeover target, with possible purchasers rumoured to be UDT and Sir Isaac Wolfson's General Guarantee Northern Corporation,

which also provided finance at the time of the withdrawal of the Russian deposit. The directors, however, were determined that the company should remain independent and were looking for a suitable purchaser for the shares held by Guinness Mahon, which had given notice that it could 'no longer provide finance to the extent which Capital Finance requires'.

Francis Jamieson had been engaged in desultory talks with Capital Finance since 1963. He had broken off contact following the understanding with Rolls Razor and only resumed discussions after the collapse. By the late autumn of 1965 he had reached an outline agreement whereby Standard Life would acquire from Guinness Mahon for £750,000 some 25 per cent of Capital Finance's equity and make available £3 million in unsecured loan stock to help reduce the bank overdraft. For its part, the Bank of Scotland undertook not to disclose details of Capital Finance's indebtedness as this 'would lead to withdrawal of deposits . . . with disastrous results'. The Standard Life board, considering Capital Finance an 'interesting recovery share', endorsed the plan in December 1965. Thomas Waterlow, a Standard Life director, joined the Capital Finance board which was chaired by Dr Dunlop, a surgeon and an accountant.[123]

Within months it became clear that the company's financial position was much more serious than had first been assumed, due only in part to the emergency borrowings following the withdrawal of the Russian loan. Hire-purchase instalments had not been collected on time because of the repeated breakdowns of the accounting machines. There had also been large losses on motor trading subsidiaries in London and Northampton and an imprudent investment in Belmont Finance, a housing company, which had gone into receivership. James Dowling, the distinguished Scottish chartered accountant and a partner in Thomson McLintock, was called in to report. With the Bank of Scotland unable to make further funds available because of the government's credit controls, and other financial institutions threatening to withdraw their support, Standard Life came to the rescue in October 1966. It provided short-term funds which were accumulating rapidly because of the decision to reduce equity investments.[124] During 1967 some 29 per cent of all Standard Life's new sterling money was placed on deposit with Capital Finance, totalling over £15 million.[125] A damning report from Dowling was received on 30 March and immediately a special committee of the board was formed to deal with the crisis. All Capital Finance's other outside directors were asked to resign and Jamieson was appointed chairman with George Philip, Standard Life's organisation manager, as deputy chairman and chief executive with instructions to realise the assets 'as speedily as possible'. Tom Risk and J.V. Woolam, chairman of merchant bankers Edward Bates & Sons who had acted for Capital Finance, also joined the board. The Stock Exchange was informed, with the result that the share price fell to 3 shillings and 1½ pence compared to the 10

shillings Standard Life had paid.[126] Publicly Standard Life put a brave face on these untoward events, which were attributed to the problems in the subsidiaries rather than to the hire-purchase business, which was described as sound.[127]

While Philip disentangled the convoluted internal affairs of Capital Finance (which turned out to be more involved than even Dowling had suspected), the Standard Life committee considered how to dispose of the business expeditiously. They were approached at first by Wolfson's General Guarantee Northern Corporation.[128] During the protracted negotiations which followed, the Bank of Scotland made a surprise offer in February 1969 on behalf of its subsidiary North West Securities of just 6 pence per share for the holding of 1.5 million ordinary stock and £1 per share for the £3 million unsecured loan stock. Standard Life's deposits of £15 million were to be repaid in 36 monthly instalments. These terms were accepted. Various subsidiaries, to which no value could be attached, including the motor trading companies and Belmont Finance, were excluded from the deal by Philip and were sold separately.[129] Although Standard Life had written off £6.5 million (representing just 1 per cent of total assets) against the investment in Capital Finance in 1968, most of this sum was eventually recovered by the determined efforts of Philip and his team. The whole affair cast a shadow over Standard Life's reputation as prudent managers of investments, exaggerated by the association of Capital Finance with such bad businessmen as John Bloom and Cyril Lord. The sales force regularly found themselves having to counter criticism fed by competitors who wished to make the most of Standard Life's embarrassment. At the time, the involvement of a leading financial institution with either failure or corporate rescue was unusual.[130] Standard Life's misfortune was to be the first to suffer such a setback. Looking back, this salutary experience deterred both the executive and the directors from making much worse errors in the heady years which led up to the secondary banking crisis of 1973, from which few financial institutions were to escape unscathed.

RECONSIDERING THE EQUITY MARKET

With the crisis behind them and the United Kingdom stockmarket still advancing strongly, the investment committee early in 1968 set a target for investing 60 per cent of new money in equities (40 per cent directly in property* and 20 per cent in ordinary shares). Shortly afterwards, the whole approach to equity investment was reconsidered in the light of the possible decision to launch investment-linked policies and forthcoming legislation requiring the market value of assets to be disclosed in the published balance sheet. Jamieson was cautious, pointing out that since only 52 per cent of Standard Life's contracts were with-profits there was no need to shift the balance any further – at least in the short term. Although he was able to demonstrate that since it was introduced in 1962, Standard Life had beaten

the FT (*Financial Times*)/Actuaries (All Share) Index every year, he still preferred buying property because returns were good and there was a danger of losing out to competitors. By now almost 70 per cent of Legal & General's equity portfolio was held in this way compared with only 21 per cent at Standard Life. There was a heated debate. Gammell, who was a passionate advocate of ordinary shares, wanted an immediate return to 40 per cent and objected strongly to property being classified as equity rather than fixed-interest. Despite a dollar premium of well over 30 per cent, he and Macpherson also called for increases to the United States dollar portfolio, particularly through the purchase of fast-growing Go-Go funds.[131] As a result of these deliberations, the proportion of funds held in ordinary shares was restored to over 40 per cent in 1968.

The following year when the unit endowment policy was launched it was decided that all the proceeds should be invested in investment trusts, 'particularly those with proved management and with a significant stake in the USA'.[132] The timing was unfortunate as the stockmarket on both sides of the Atlantic began to weaken almost immediately. The investment committee switched their strategy for the whole portfolio more decisively to property not only in the United Kingdom but in the United States and Australia where Hammersons were extending their interests.

---

* These property investments were to be made by forming joint companies with Hammersons, Taylor Woodrow and others to handle each development, with Standard Life owning 49 per cent of the equity and with an option over the rest when work was completed.

Francis S. Jamieson, investment manager from 1946 to 1970 and deputy general manager from 1970 to 1972. He was regarded as one of the most astute investment managers of his generation.

CANADIAN INVESTMENTS

Although nominally controlled by the investment committee in Edinburgh, the Canadian assets in practice were managed by the Canadian board and Robert Thomson, the deputy manager. This was largely because until 1966 when it became possible to operate pooled funds with no restriction on assets, life offices were required to invest some 90 per cent of their funds in fixed-interest securities. In Standard Life's case in the 1950s between 65 and 70 per cent of assets were invested in bonds and 20 to 25 per cent in mortgages. During the early 1960s the proportion in mortgages was raised to over 40 per cent.

The Canadian branch financed developments in major cities such as Ottawa, Toronto, Vancouver and Quebec. Prestige projects included the Sir Guy Carleton Buildings in Ottawa, the Civic Centre and Lloyd D. Jackson Square in Hamilton, Ontario, the Canadian National Railway building in London, Ontario, and office blocks with associated shops in Yonge Street, Toronto, in Slater Street, Ottawa, and alongside the Montreal Peel Street metro station. After the change in regulations funds were switched into high-yielding bond issues. There was no substantial investment in equities (common stock and property) until 1969 when a target of 20 per cent was set.[133]

GROWTH AND SUCCESS

Regardless of the highly publicised Capital Finance misadventure, Standard Life's with-profits products outperformed much of the industry in the 20 years after 1951. *The Economist* began publishing comparisons between the returns from whole-life with-profits and 25-year with-profits endowment policies in 1951. Over the next 20 years Standard Life was always amongst the first three – in marked contrast to the poor showing in such ratings at the end of the nineteenth century. This achievement was not matched by any other company.[134] To the wry satisfaction of the senior management, a ten-year endowment policy maturing in 1970 yielded more than an investment-linked policy from any competitor.[135] When reserves were disclosed in the balance sheet for the first

The extension to the head office
in St Andrew Square,
Edinburgh, 1968.

THE COMING OF THE COMPUTER

The ability of Standard Life to transact so much new business in the 1950s depended crucially on the commitment to mechanisation and the extension of the work of the Powers-Samas department (see page 205) into nearly every area of the business. The first electronic computational machines were developed for military purposes during the Second World War and did not become commercially available until the early 1950s. The pioneer of their civil use was the American company IBM. The Canadian branch had been using IBM equipment since the war, although the first real computer was not acquired until 1964.[1] The first British company to develop such a computer was J. Lyons & Co. Ltd, the owners of the well-known chain of cafés, in 1953. Named 'Leo', these machines were expensive, bulky and temperamental. Later the programme-controlled computer (PCC) was developed by Powers-Samas, which was now owned by Vickers, Standard Life's largest pension scheme. At first there was little interest from the business community in the United Kingdom. At Standard Life the machine department was in crisis due to the terminal illness of the manager. The staff were demoralised and there was shortage of machines to deal with the increasing workload. G.C. Philip, a young actuary who had been devising procedures for valuing individual group contracts, took over and was keen to acquire an IBM computer; but the board was reluctant to offend Vickers. As a result, a PCC was purchased in December 1958 shortly before Powers-Samas merged with the British Tabulating Machine Company to form International Computers Ltd. (ICL). Although relatively small, the PCC weighed over two tons and had to be lifted by crane into the head office. It was to be used at first to perform calculations for the declaration of the bonus in 1959; but despite Philip's best efforts it could not be made to work. Eventually the calculations were completed successfully on a PCC at ICL's London head office. The processing, however, took a week rather than the few hours which had been estimated.[2] Disappointed but not deterred, Standard Life decided to switch to the more reliable and powerful Ferranti Pegasus computer and began to develop suitable programmes that were tested in London. On Philip's initiative, a joint company was formed with Scottish Widows, named Edinburgh Computers Ltd, to own and operate a Pegasus, which was installed in May 1961. Philip became mechanisation manager with a wide brief embracing what was to become the organisation and methods department; George Gwilt, a young actuary whose father was manager of Scottish Widows, was appointed computer manager.

One of the driving forces behind this second venture into computing was the pensions department, which was very keen to use the new technology to reduce staff costs.[3] H.A. Fraser, the group manager,

The programme-controlled computer (PCC) being hoisted into Standard Life's office, 1958.

Above left: Schoolboys visit the machine department at 3 George Street, 1955.

The original Pegasus II computer (above right), 1964, and the IBM System 360 computer, 1966 (below).

commented in 1962: 'The transition to computer operation will bring its own difficulties during the next two years, but the end product will be a reduction in the numbers [of staff] required and a major step towards the goal of 100 per cent service.'[4]

During 1963 the records required for the valuation were transferred onto magnetic tape and were soon followed by others. As part of the process of introducing computers, the new organisation and methods department began to standardise forms and procedures and the purchases of new equipment.[5] Within three years Standard Life was fully

committed to using computers throughout the business. It was decided to wind up Edinburgh Computers Ltd and to adopt the Advanced Life Information System (ALIS), which had been developed by IBM for American and Canadian life offices and covered 'every aspect of the record-keeping and updating of a policy from its inception'. New IBM 360 computers were purchased in 1967 for the United Kingdom and Canada and the massive task of entering all policy details began.[6] This undertaking, which involved many employees learning new skills, was approached with considerable forbearance by the staff as ALIS failed to live up to expectations. A cartoon in *The Standard Review* with the caption 'Our Brand New Toy' well illustrated the problem, which was only solved by rewriting most of the programmes.

The changeover to the new system and the related staff training was completed ahead of schedule in 1970. The group manager declared with misplaced enthusiasm: 'The Standard is ahead of most other offices in its comprehensive computer treatment of pension administration and the new system lends itself to further development.'[7]

Ernest Bromfield, deputy general manager from 1964 until his death in 1969.

time in 1969, Standard Life could boast an investment reserve of £70 million, a little under 10 per cent of the assets.[136] Francis Jamieson was widely recognised as a 'commanding presence in the insurance world . . . [who] epitomised the ability that many Scottish investment managers had to take the longer view.'[137] The investment department remained tiny compared with those of other life offices and only began to be strengthened after 1968. There was still no question that Standard Life would try to emulate 'a successful "performance" mutual fund or a successful active investment trust' by regularly switching investments, even if this was what managed funds demanded.[138]

Between 1950 and 1970 Standard Life grew rapidly in size and the number of employees doubled to reach almost 2,000. To accommodate them, the head office in Edinburgh was extended in 1968 and other offices built or refurbished up and down the country. The management structure, in contrast, remained largely unchanged with only a few additions such as a statistician in 1957 and a mechanisation manager in 1959. It was not until 1961 that the secretary and actuary Brem Dow was promoted to be deputy general manager and secretary. At the same time the joint secretary and group manager, Ernest Bromfield, the investment manager, Francis Jamieson, and the agency manager, Graeme Pullar, were given the additional title of assistant general managers.[139] Although they now had wider remits within the executive, there was nothing approximating to an executive group where the various activities of the company could be brought together and reviewed. Throughout the period Standard Life was a sum of its parts and it has been said there were six companies in the United Kingdom alone – 'a life company, a pensions company, an inside staff company, an outside staff company, a head office company and a branch office company'. Nowhere were these tensions more evident than between the ordinary life business and pensions, where there was almost no contact between the staff.[140] This was not unusual in British business at the time and as long as the company continued to prosper, Reid and Dow were not unduly concerned.

Alec Reid, if lacking the charisma of Andrew

Davidson, provided a sure direction which was essential at a time of fast expansion. On his retirement in 1964 Dow commented: 'His quiet and imperturbable temperament, his readiness to consider and accept the views of others, and above all his unfailing friendliness and courtesy, made him an easy and rewarding manager to work for.'[141] He was concerned about staff welfare, persuading the directors to fund the sports societies, particularly the football and golf clubs. He was behind the purchase of Kingsmeadows House in Peebles in January 1952 to act as an emergency head office in the event of war with Russia. A duplicate set of records was stored there and the house equipped with punched-card machines and war-surplus beds and bedding. With the coming of the H bomb this practice was discontinued and the house used to store the increasing volume of records held at the head office. Later Reid instigated the popular holiday cottage scheme for staff at Kingsmeadows.[142]

Brem Dow strengthened the management structure, notably through regionalisation, and placed emphasis on training in an effort to foster a greater sense of homogeneity within the company. He was deeply committed to the concept of mutuality and, taking the opposite view to William Thomson, used every opportunity to emphasise to policy-holders its advantages over proprietary companies. Like Reid he set great store by the welfare of the staff and went out of his way to get to know many of them.[143] Towards the end of his career he realised the need to integrate the Canadian branch much more

closely if it was to remain part of Standard Life. Unfortunately his short time as manager was overshadowed by the tragic death in April 1965 of his eldest son, a talented lecturer in economic history at the University of Glasgow, just days after his marriage. He also felt personally the criticisms of Standard Life's involvement with Capital Finance and was deeply upset by the premature death in 1969 of his deputy and chosen successor Ernest Bromfield, a man of rare abilities and mischievous wit. It was said of him that he 'possessed a capacity for fundamental originality which made his appraisals of existing group business, potential markets, and competitive dangers shrewd and perceptive'. He famously translated the company's motto *Prospice, Aspice, Respice* as 'I decline, I delay, I rate up'.[144]

Reid and Dow complemented each other admirably in much the same way as Dickson and Macnaghten had in an earlier generation. Their achievement in keeping Standard Life amongst

Kingsmeadows House, Peebles, bought in 1952 as an alternative head office should Edinburgh be destroyed in a nuclear attack. It was later used as a store. In 1999, to mark the 175th anniversary, the house was divided into flats for staff holidays.

the leaders of the life offices and principal pension providers at a time of intense competition was considerable. Under their management the company's assets climbed from £113 million in 1952 to over £900 million by 1970. Even allowing for inflation this represented a four-and-a-half-fold increase, dwarfing all their Scottish competitors (see Figure 7.2 on page 317). Scottish Widows was left far behind. Even the Norwich Union life society, which had entered the pension market at much the same time, was overtaken. Standard Life's principal competitor, as Leonard Dickson had foretold before the First World War, was undoubtedly Legal & General. The life industry continued to be dominated by the Prudential, which had become perhaps the largest pension provider, but with Legal & General and Standard Life not far behind.

This accomplishment was not widely recognised within the company, however, because the measure of comparison between offices was customarily new sums assured in the ordinary department, which did not include deferred annuities. More surprisingly, young staff were encouraged to think of Scottish Widows as Standard Life's chief rival, largely in terms of the bonus. This had been the case when most of the senior executives started their careers. The board were largely ignorant of the company's relative standing amongst life offices, as no comparative figures were ever presented even though they were readily available. The perception that Standard Life was still of relatively moderate size

when in fact it was one of the industry leaders had important ramifications for the assessment of the strength and muscle of the competition. It perhaps explains why, on the sales side, new products were often only introduced long after newcomers to the life and pensions business had shown the way. The directors had for some time understood the scale and significance of the assets and enjoyed their direct involvement in investment decisions. It was not until the late 1960s that the directors came to appreciate the sheer size of the enterprise and became more closely involved in shaping future strategy.

The impression of all those who can recall Standard Life during these years was that it was a happy company to work for. Phil Macpherson, who was appointed chairman on Davidson's retirement, summed this up in the language of rugby at which he excelled:

> In this great company which we are privileged to serve we all have the feeling that in our respective spheres our individual efforts have the support and encouragement of a fine team . . . Justified by this team spirit and a confidence well founded on the record of achievements of recent years, to which we have all contributed, we can face the challenge of these uneasy times with cheerful resolution and with the conviction that the company's further prosperity will be assured if we continue to give the community that sound and friendly service which is the tradition of the Standard.[145]

CHAPTER SEVEN

MAKING PROGRESS: 1970–88

*'We made progress against a background of continued political encroachment into our business area . . .
and a decided unrest amongst insurance brokers . . .'*

Peter Glover's agency manager's report, 1975.[1]

When David Donald unexpectedly found himself general manager of Standard Life in March 1970, the prospects for group pension providers were confused. Even though a general election had to take place within a year, the Labour government pressed ahead with its consultations on the future shape of state pension provision. In the event, the election was called in May before legislation could be introduced. The Conservative Party under Edward Heath won a surprise victory and immediately abandoned Labour's plans. Their alternative 'Strategy for Pensions' was announced in a white paper in September which proposed a state reserve scheme for those members of the working population who were not covered by occupational schemes. Life offices were concerned that the money-purchase basis of the proposal was so fundamentally different from their own practice that it made comparison of benefits difficult and might deter many smaller employers from contracting out and setting up their own schemes.[2]

The outlook was further complicated by rising inflation. The government's strategy was to hold down public-sector wages in the hope that the private sector would follow suit. The government's anti-inflationary strategy was in ruins by the spring of 1972. To counter rising unemployment the Chancellor, unwisely as it turned out, introduced a reflationary budget and in the summer allowed the pound to float on the international exchange. This fuelled inflation even further. Having failed to reach agreement with either the CBI or the TUC on a voluntary code of wage restraint, a statutory prices and incomes policy was introduced in November and at the same time measures were taken to curtail the money supply.[3]

The reputation of the whole insurance industry was damaged in June 1971 when the aggressive Vehicle & General Insurance Company (V&G), which had captured 10 per cent of the motor vehicle market, collapsed. Although its small life subsidiary escaped more or less unscathed, there were calls in the wake of the catastrophe for much greater regulation of all aspects of insurance, particularly the 'high-pressure' sales techniques of companies such as V&G and some unit-linked providers.[4] These coincided with concerns in the City that life companies were not subject to the same exacting controls as other financial institutions in marketing their unit-linked products. The financial press called for a wide-ranging enquiry which would address 'the growing overlap between life assurance and investment' and the 'revolution in selling methods' pioneered by newcomers to the industry, notably Mark Weinberg at Hambro Life (later to be renamed Allied Dunbar). The government responded by appointing a committee, chaired by Sir Hilary Scott and which included Brem Dow, with a limited remit 'to look into policies linked to property, equities and similar investments'.[5] In his report two years later, Scott took the view that there was little need for regulation as the life industry was conducted by 'honourable gentlemen'. He recommended a ten-day cooling-off period after new policies were written, improvements in the quality of information given to customers, and much greater disclosure of investments.[6] The report was published too late for its findings to be incorporated in the Insurance Companies Amendment Act of 1973 which, in response to the V&G failure, strengthened the supervisory role of the Department of Trade and Industry (previously the Board of Trade).

DEFENDING GROUP PENSION BUSINESS

Against the unstable economic background it was difficult for Standard Life to plan for the future, believing that 'in current conditions it would be rash to attempt to forecast what the economic future holds for us, how our investment policy may be affected or even the volume and type of new business which we may expect to write in future. One thing is certain and that is without confidence in the stability of our currency, long-term business such as ours cannot be conducted on satisfactory terms.'[7] Donald recognised that Standard Life's mix of business would inevitably change as competition for pension business from brokers and fund managers continued to strengthen. Together with Hector A. Fraser, who had been promoted from group manager to be an assistant general manager in 1969, and A.U. (Drew) Lyburn, who had returned from Canada to help develop pension business, he decided that 'the best tactic was to give ground in the group pensions market as slowly as possible whilst simultaneously investing heavily in a faster build-up of ordinary life new business'.[8] Defending group pension business would inevitably bring Standard Life into direct conflict with the consulting actuaries and national brokers who, increasingly, recommended managed funds rather than insured schemes.

This approach demanded a change in the way the company conducted its business. The efficiency of the pension department in servicing a contracting market share had to be improved and, more fundamentally, there needed to be greater co-ordination between the sales activities of the pension and ordinary departments in the regions. As a preliminary step George Philip, who had just returned from Capital Finance to be assistant general manager and secretary, investigated work practices in re-costing pensions, which was becoming increasingly expensive.[9]

REVIEW OF SALES STRUCTURE

In the meantime David Donald had been working to re-cast the whole sales organisation with Arthur C. Stepney, who had succeeded G.L. Pullar as assistant general manager in charge of ordinary business, Drew Lyburn, and Peter Glover, the new agency manager whose background, unusually, was in pensions. In September 1971 it was decided to introduce a new regional organisation to cover the United Kingdom and the Republic of Ireland. In a major change of direction, the regional managers were also to assume responsibility for 'both pensions and ordinary sales effort within their regions'. All administrative functions were to be removed from the branches and concentrated in regional offices to allow the branch managers to focus on sales and to give 'indoor' staff improved career prospects.[10] Since such a reform would require new regional offices to accommodate administrative staff, it could only be introduced gradually. Productivity was to be raised before any new sales staff were recruited. New style regions were only to be established when the level of new

business justified it. As in the first attempt at regionalisation (see page 237), the north-west region was selected to pioneer the scheme. George McGill, the experienced ordinary business regional manager in Manchester, was appointed 'first overall regional manager'.[11]

David William Alexander Donald, general manager from 1970 to 1979.

Because of their importance, the amalgamation of the London City and West End branches did not await the outcome of this trial. H.W. McLellan (then aged 60), Standard Life's pensions actuary who was based in London, was chosen as the first south regional manager.[12] Shortly afterwards Tom R. King was seconded from head office to the south region and in 1975 McLellan was succeeded by A. Scott Bell. They were joined shortly thereafter by Jim Stretton. The experience they gained in London and the south-east was to be invaluable when they came to manage the whole company after 1988.[13] The new regional structure was extended to the rest of the United Kingdom between 1971 and 1973. G.A.S. Norman retired as manager for Ireland in 1971 after 46 years' service, providing the opportunity to integrate the pensions and ordinary business in the Republic of Ireland under his successor, Harry H. Pearce, who was later to succeed George McGill in Manchester.

RESTRUCTURING INVESTMENT OPERATIONS

At the same time as making these major changes in sales and marketing, the company undertook a radical overhaul of the investment department to improve the dynamics of its operations, particularly in managing pension funds. The staff levels in the department were increased and an economics research department was established under A. David Wilkie.[14] He was sent to gain experience at the Prudential, which had established such a department in 1958 and now employed more economists in macro-economic analysis and forecasting than the Treasury.[15] This new department within Standard Life co-existed uneasily with the investment department, which was more comfortable with the research and information received from stockbrokers. After a few years the two departments were merged and greater emphasis was placed by investment staff on research. This was to provide a solid foundation for the enlarged department post 'Big Bang' in 1986. At an investment conference held at Turnberry in October 1972, the directors agreed to abandon the cumbersome system of granting limited mandates for purchases and to give much greater freedom to the executive, with the investment committee only retaining the power to set the sector distribution. As a result the periodic and time-consuming reviews of individual sectors by the investment committee were discontinued. At the same time it was agreed that the Canadian investment committee should report all transactions directly to the main board.[16]

The Turnberry conference also considered long-term investment strategy. The board supported the view of the executive that the distribution of investments of the free fund (those assets not subject to investment constraints) between fixed-interest securities (40 per cent) and equities including property (60 per cent) was broadly correct. With the memory of Capital Finance fresh in the minds of senior executives, diversification into other financial services, such as banking,

The atrium in the Brent Cross shopping complex in north London. This was Britain's first out-of-town retail centre and attracted a great deal of interest.

'Buying your own home' brochure.

insurance broking, hire purchase and leasing or the acquisition of a property development company, were firmly rejected. This meant that, unlike the Prudential and Legal & General, Standard Life had no exposure to the secondary banking crisis of a year later. Additionally, the maximum proportion of equities in the free fund which could be held in overseas securities was raised to 25 per cent. New investments in foreign markets were only to be made when the opportunity arose, with the bulk still to be in the United States but with a greater emphasis on Europe, Japan and emerging Far Eastern markets.[17] The existing strategy of indirect investment in property in association with property companies, such as Hammersons and Capital and Counties, was to be redressed in favour of greater direct investment.[18] Nevertheless, a commitment of £25 million was made to Hammersons for the development of the innovative Brent Cross shopping complex, strategically placed on London's North Circular Road.[19]

It had already been decided that the Heritable Securities and Mortgage Investment Association would cease to transact new mortgage business after May 1972; the investment return was no longer attractive and the proportion of new home ordinary business such loans contributed had fallen to 3 per cent compared with 27 per cent in 1955. The Heritable would in future only transact loans for members of staff, and commercial and farm loans on fixed terms. In the Republic of Ireland it would also continue to grant home loans secured against endowment policies. This was to comply with a 'gentlemen's agreement' with the government, as at that time the building societies there would only countenance repayment mortgages.[20]

With hindsight the conference seriously underestimated competition from merchant banks, such as Schroders and Warburgs, which 'it was felt . . . treated fund management as a "loss leader", and gave poor service for too low fees. Our fees were higher than many others, and our policy should be to compete on performance, and to charge enough to support the costs of a knowledgeable and skilled investment department.'[21]

SALES PROGRESS

Along with the decision to withdraw the Heritable from the house purchase market, contact was established with major building societies to maintain a continued flow of new mortgage-related business. With every sign that the building societies were seeking to become their own insurance brokers so as to retain commissions, the development of such relationships was vital. In a limited experiment, the Leeds Permanent Building Society was invited to offer loan and savings schemes to certain Standard Life pension customers on the understanding that Standard Life got all of the collateral business. Likewise Standard Life was included in a small panel of life offices to which the Nationwide Building Society directed enquiries for loans 'which would otherwise be written on a capital and interest mortgage repayment basis'.[22] Such connections were expected to yield a large volume of house purchase business cheaply and with little effort, leaving inspectors more time to build up other business. By 1974 the proportion of other new business had been raised to almost 50 per cent, which Peter Glover was confident provided a 'solid base . . . from which we can continue to expand our efforts to diversify and to sell more non-committed life assurance'.[23]

Although new pension premium income barely kept pace with inflation (see Appendix 4 on page 384), results were better than expected in the face of mounting competition from merchant banks and against the background of changes in government policy. New schemes were negotiated for Scott-Lithgows Ltd, the recently formed Clyde shipbuilding group, its associate Lithgows Ltd, the merged Glenlivet & Glen Grant Distilleries and the Territorial and Volunteer Reserve Association.[24] When schemes decided to switch to managed funds, most of Standard Life's contracts opted to move to Standard Life Pension Funds (SLPF), including May & Baker and Bristol Siddeley in 1973 and Vickers in 1974.[25] This was a considerable achievement against strong opposition from other insurers and merchant banks.[26]

INSUROPE

Membership of Insurope, which Standard Life had joined in 1967 as the United Kingdom representative, initially brought pension business mainly from the European subsidiaries of American companies. By 1973 Standard Life had secured 20 plans with a total premium income of £150,000 and could claim to be the leading United Kingdom company in the multinational market.[27] Although predominantly a European association with its office in Brussels, Insurope's international connections were strengthened by agreements with insurance companies through-

Strathisla Distillery in Keith, the home of Chivas Regal whisky, which belonged in 1973 to Glenlivet & Glen Grant Distilleries.

out the world and by the opening of a further office in New York.[28] By 1978 it was able to offer multinational clients facilities in the 'most important countries in all five continents'.[29] Seven years later Insurope provided 139 pension schemes for multinationals in which Standard Life participated in the United Kingdom, Ireland and Canada with a premium income of £7.1 million along with £2.2 million in managed funds.[30]

FIGHTING FOR PENSION BUSINESS

Under the terms of Sir Keith Joseph's Social Security Act, which became law in 1973, the Occupational Pensions Board (OPB) was established to register schemes and ensure they were adequately funded. Only registered schemes, which met the criteria and also provided benefit for widows, were entitled to contract out of the terms of the Act, which was to come into force in 1975.[31] Standard Life introduced the Stanplan range of pension products tailored to meet the requirements of the new Act and incorporating trustee facilities if required. These plans, designed by Andrew McLeish, the pensions legal

manager, were praised by brokers for their sheer simplicity and flexibility.[32] In the meantime, existing schemes hurried to comply with the new legislation, bringing a welcome increase in premium business from existing contracts.

Pension business was completely disrupted in May 1974 by the announcement from Barbara Castle, the Secretary of State for Social Security in the new Labour government (elected in February), that the terms of the Conservative legislation were to be scrapped in favour of 'better pensions fully protected against inflation', designed to bring to an end dependence on supplementary benefit.[33] The only feature of the Conservatives' plan to be retained was the OPB which was to have extended functions under Labour. As a result only a few Stanplan contracts were completed during 1974.[34] For the first time ever Standard Life flexed its muscles and, under Drew Lyburn, now pensions manager, led the attack on the Castle proposals, pointing out that they did nothing for 'existing pensioners and not enough for future lower-paid employees', and that the index-linked terms for contracting out

were so onerous as to require 'a guarantee against inflation'. Frightened of the possible consequences of such outspoken criticism, other life companies were not prepared to follow this lead. Behind the scenes, George Gwilt, the pensions actuary and a gifted musician, established good relations with Brian O'Malley, Barbara Castle's junior minister, who represented the Musicians' Union in parliament and was prepared to listen to the industry's concerns.[35]

The Labour government went to considerable lengths to obtain cross-party support before introducing the Social Security Pensions Act (SSPA) in 1975. This provided for the ambitious index-linked state earnings-related pension scheme (SERPS) to come into effect in 1978. As Standard Life had suggested, significant concessions were made to occupational pension schemes by limiting the guarantee against inflation. Having achieved the changes which it wanted, Standard Life withdrew from the Campaign for Company Pension Schemes. This had been set up in 1973 on the initiative of Legal & General and the Prudential, both of which were irritated by Standard Life's decision to break ranks.[36]

On a wider plane, however, Standard Life joined forces with the rest of the industry the following autumn to condemn left-wing proposals to nationalise the banking and insurance industry, which had been approved by Labour's National Executive. David Donald took the novel step of writing to every policy-holder, firmly rejecting allegations that the company had failed to invest in British industry.[37]

A LARGER STAFF AND HEAD OFFICE

While all these changes were taking place, a search for a site in Edinburgh for a new head office to house 2,000 staff had been in progress. Various possibilities were considered between June 1970 and March 1971, including the site in Lothian Road where Standard Life House was later to be built (see page 328). Eventually outline planning permission was sought for a building in Dundas Street. This was rejected as unsuitable and the Lord Provost of Edinburgh suggested South Gyle as an alternative. Although acceptable to Standard Life, prolonged wrangles

The narrative sculpture by Gerald Ogilvie Laing of the parable of the wise and foolish virgins on the extension to the head office. The figures on the left are the Wise Virgins, who have prepared themselves for death through their faith in God; those on the right are the Foolish Virgins, who have failed to do this and instead are caught up in various mundane preoccupations.

followed between Edinburgh town council, the Scottish Development Department and the owners, Mactaggart & Mickel. By July 1973 almost no progress had been made and Donald was not above threatening the council that the company would move from the city if the matter was not resolved in the near future.[38] In the event numbers 7–13 George Street and the existing head office itself were redeveloped in 1976. The number of staff rose from just over 1,500 in 1968 to more than 2,300 by 1974 but declined thereafter as more and more tasks were mechanised.

With so many changes taking place within the company, it was essential that communication between the management and the staff be improved. In 1972, following recommendations from the Industrial Society, a series of consultative committees to promote good staff relations were established in the branches and at head office, with one overall national consultative body.[39] These arrangements allowed Standard Life to comply with the Industrial Relations Act's code of practice without becoming a closed shop, and provided a mechanism for addressing staff concerns. At first this consultative structure was used by the management to implement alterations in the working environment rather than to encourage participation in decision-making. Attitudes began to change in the late 1970s with consultations on such topics as the reorganisation of the branches and the regional structure, the length of the working day, pensions and terms and conditions for agents.

THE STOCKMARKET COLLAPSE

At the end of 1974 the Labour government (re-elected in October) failed to introduce an effective policy to tackle escalating inflation. The stockmarket crashed, leaving all financial institutions seriously exposed.[40] By the end of the year the FT Actuaries index had fallen 54 per cent. The market had been weakening steadily for almost a year, driven down by rising oil prices and, with interest rates rising, gilts had also suffered.[41] In the midst of the crisis Standard Life tactically switched investment of new money into completed properties by raising the allocation from £22 million to almost £33 million. Peter Henwood, a property expert who had joined the company in 1972 from Legal & General as Gordon Stewart's successor as property investment manager, recognised the risks. For the next four years he directed purchases of completed properties away from central London where rents had fallen sharply as a consequence of the secondary banking crisis. With building costs rising at between 25 and 30 per cent per annum, the strategy paid off, particularly as the passing of the Community Land and the Development Land Tax Acts in 1976 made building new properties prohibitively expensive.[42]

The impact of the stockmarket crash was profound. Financial institutions were still reeling from the effects of the secondary banking collapse earlier in the year which had forced many hire-purchase and property companies to the wall.[43] Within days of the crash seven relatively small life insurance companies in England were reported to be in difficulties. Five of these were quickly taken over by other life offices, including the Investment Annuity and Life Assurance Co. (IALA) which was acquired by Lifeguard. The affairs of the remaining two life offices in difficulties, London Indemnity & General and Nation Life, were too tangled to allow them to be rescued in this way and became the subject of protracted negotiations.[44] At the time of the crisis, in an effort to head off criticism, the Life Offices Association (LOA) urgently sought to set up a fund to guarantee the benefits of its members' policy-holders and those of the Association of Scottish Life Offices (ASLO). The Scottish offices refused to participate unless policy-holders were indemnified for only 90 per cent rather than all of their benefits, since imprudent practices might otherwise result. To mitigate the effect of disasters, the Policy-holders Protection Act of 1975 formally established the Policy-holders Protection Board (PPB) to supervise a permanent guarantee fund raised from a levy of a maximum of 1 per cent of premium income.[45] In April 1976 Standard Life agreed to join a consortium led by Norwich Union to preserve most of the policy-holders' rights in IALA after its new parent company Lifeguard had got into difficulties as a result of the secondary banking crisis. This was a less costly alternative to using the mechanism of the PPB.[46]

News that several life offices were in difficulties during 1974 hampered sales of conventional products at a time when the personal savings ratio was at a record level of 12 per cent of disposable income.[47] Since interest rates were high (although negative in real terms), much of these savings went to the building societies, which as a result were able to increase lending. At Standard Life the consequent rise in mortgage endowment business compensated in large measure for the decline in sales of other contracts.[48]

At the height of the stockmarket crisis the Governor of the Bank of England, Gordon Richardson, summoned the chairmen and managers of Scottish Amicable, Scottish Provident, Scottish Widows and Standard Life along with representatives of English insurance companies to a meeting at the Bank in November 1974 to discuss a proposal that the leading life offices 'should consider lending part of their funds [a total of about £1,000 million over six years] to Finance for Industry to enable that organisation to perform effectively an enlarged role'. He argued that the announcement of such a scheme would 'have a beneficial effect on the market, and therefore on the financial affairs of large collective investors'. The Bank's difficulty, which the Governor did not report, was that the lifeboat launched earlier in the year to rescue the secondary banks was rapidly approaching its capacity of £1,200 million.[49] Tom Risk, the chairman, and George Philip (recently promoted to be deputy general manager and secretary on Jamieson's retirement), represented Standard Life at the meeting and, after discussions with their colleagues,

his scheme, tried once more to obtain Standard Life's support. In the private knowledge that without help several major financial institutions would have collapsed, he warned of the possible damage to the value of Standard Life's portfolio in the long term. He again met with a firm rebuttal: 'For Standard Life to attempt to meet such short-term demand on any worthwhile scale would require mismatching of our funds and liabilities to a point where not only would it impose unacceptable risks on our policy-holders and pension clients, but also would seriously impair our ability either now or in due course to provide the long-term or permanent finance upon which we both recognise a true recovery of industry will ultimately depend.'[51]

An outcome of the Bank of England's proposal was an invitation from the Prudential to a meeting on 16 December 1974 to agree a progressive programme of aggressive buying of equities to a total of about £20 million. This concerted action undoubtedly contributed to a turn in the market early in the new year. Having decided that it was for the government to take action to reduce inflation, Standard Life refused to play any part in the plan.[52] Although equities recovered strongly during 1975, they did not return to their 1972 levels until the autumn of 1977. This left all insurance companies with the serious problem of how to present their balance sheets. In addition there were doubts as to whether many pension funds could meet their liabilities, and a large number of firms were

rejected the proposal on the grounds that an '"artificial" recovery engineered in this way would not address the underlying cause of the lack of corporate profitability, which could only be solved by government action'. Within a week the Standard Life board had agreed that during 1975 all new money (some £75 million) would be invested in government stock where future asset values could be guaranteed and returns were high, albeit less than inflation.[50] With the Bank of England being forced towards the end of December to draw on its own reserves to keep the financial system intact, the Governor, having recruited some insurance companies to

obliged to increase their rates of contribution.[53]

At the close of the financial year on 15 November 1974 it was estimated that the value of Standard Life's assets was some £250 million (25 per cent) less than the ledger value and £400 million (40 per cent) less than the market value at the beginning of the year. As a result the excess of assets over the net actuarial liability had collapsed from 36 per cent in 1972 to just 3.5 per cent. Although insurance companies were not required to show market values, Standard Life had done so for five years and to change this policy would only serve to draw attention to the problem. Instead, following tax concessions introduced by the Inland Revenue, the value of the liabilities was reduced 'by increasing the assumed rates of interest to something closer to the rates our funds are actually earning', which allowed just under £244 million to be transferred to the investment reserve. This was only possible because for the past fifty years Standard Life had used a very stringent basis in valuing liabilities. As a result in the published balance sheet the value of the assets was shown to have declined only by some £150 million rather than £400 million.[54]

At the end of July 1975, with no sign of inflation abating, an attempt was made to plan ahead. It was recognised that if wage costs continued to escalate with no corresponding increase in interest rates, 'we might have to consider ceasing to write new business altogether'.[55] Overall emphasis was to continue to be placed on developing life assurance business 'which is less vulnerable to political pressures than our pension business'.[56]

In the wake of the financial difficulties of the smaller life offices and the practices of brokers during 1974, the LOA decided – against fierce opposition from the brokers – that the basis on which commission was calculated should be changed from a percentage of the sum assured to a percentage of premium income. This was a significant reform in the interest of the customer.[57] The change reduced the market for whole-life policies, since compared with other products premiums and commissions were low, but it encouraged the design of savings policies giving better value for money and the sale of self-employed personal pension policies.

ENTERING THE INVESTMENT-LINKED MARKET

Between 1975 and 1980 sales had continued to be seriously affected by inflation, which, although it had fallen from its peak in 1975, still remained higher than in most other developed countries. The launch in June 1975 of index-linked national savings schemes provided an attractive and seemingly more secure outlet for personal investment, and the only real growth in new business for Standard Life came from mortgage-related contracts and the rapid development of tax-efficient personal pension schemes encouraged by large increases in the rate of commission.[58] More and more, mortgage business came directly from building societies, which were now energetically seeking to raise

A Standard nest egg
is a treasured possession

Standard Life policies are protected by the accumulated
assets of Britain's largest mutual life assurance company.

A Standard Life with profits policy is rewarded by
outstanding bonus distributions, the product of 145 years of
experience and expert management.

Your Standard Life policy is a nest egg well worth treasuring.

'Yours for Life'

Standard Life
ASSURANCE COMPANY

Established 1825. Assets exceed £700,000,000
Head Office: 3 George Street, Edinburgh.
Branches throughout the United Kingdom
and the Republic of Ireland.

One of Standard Life's series of
'nest egg' advertisements from
1973, promoting with-profits
policies.

'the total amount of commissions earned by the acceptance of endowment assurance policies for collateral purposes'.[59]

By 1977, although Standard Life was holding its own in the sale of conventional products, traditional with-profits policies were losing their appeal to investment-linked products, which were growing faster than any other type of life insurance or personal pension contracts.[60] Accordingly, it was decided to enter the market by introducing a capital investment bond during 1979, followed a few months after that by a regular investment bond and a year later by personal pension bonds. Unlike the previous attempt to enter this market in 1969 (see page 235), the management was now committed. Alex Shedden devoted much time and effort to the design of these new products, particularly the development of appropriate computer systems. A subsidiary, Standard Life Investment Funds Ltd (SLIF), was established for the unit-linked investments.[61] The new investment-linked policies were welcomed by the industry. One commentator, aware of previous hostility within Standard Life, exclaimed: 'The walls of Jericho have fallen down,' and Mark Weinberg declared that Standard Life had 'given respectability' to unit-linked insurance.[62] The new products quickly lived up to expectations with an increase in price of the equity fund of 55 per cent in the first year compared with an overall stockmarket rise of 26 per cent. Within two years these bonds accounted for over 75 per cent of new single premiums (£36 million) and for 10 per cent of new annual premiums (£27 million).[63] Additionally, in 1982 the company was the first significant life office to add a unitised with-profits fund to its range of products.[64]

THE BATTLE FOR GROUP PENSIONS

In the face of the uncertainties surrounding the implementation of the Social Security Pensions Act (SSPA) in 1978 and strong competition, pension sales remained more buoyant than anticipated and SLPF continued to attract funds, particularly into its pooled mixed fund. Legal & General dominated the life offices' share of managed funds with a colossal 40 per cent. Standard Life had 8 per cent, behind Scottish Widows with 9 per cent and the Prudential with 16 per cent.[65] The real winners in the battle for pension fund management were, however, the merchant banks, such as Schroders and Warburgs.

FIGURE 7.1
Group pension business
1971–86

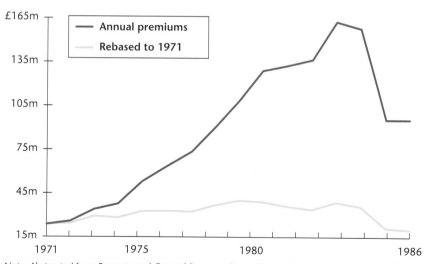

Note: Abstracted from Property and General Purposes Committee and Home branch reports 1971-87

Most of the effort of the whole pensions industry was concentrated on ensuring that schemes complied with the terms of the SSPA regulations, which were only finally agreed in the spring of 1977. Standard Life was the first pension provider to obtain approval for a scheme from the Occupational Pension Board (OPB). During that year, for the first time for some years, there was real growth in the com-pany's pension business, with 316 new insured schemes (mainly Stanplan) contributing a total premium income of almost £10 million (see Figure 7.1 on page 287).[66] Although this perfor-mance was sustained in the following year, the overall impression was that Standard Life was struggling in the total group insured pension market to maintain its position in third place after Legal & General and the Prudential, with

The widely acclaimed Cutler's Gardens development in London, which was completed in 1982.

Sun Life, Norwich Union and Scottish Widows only a short way behind.[67]

RETURN TO EQUITIES

Since the crash in 1974 Standard Life had raised its investment income from £65 million to over £103 million in 1979 by buying fixed-interest securities, but chose to return to investing in equities in strength both at home and overseas where the real rate of return was forecast to be higher than on other securities.[68] At the same time A.D. Wilkie wrote to the *Financial Times* in November proposing that the recently elected Conservative government should show its commitment to defeating inflation by issuing long-dated index-linked bonds, which would be an ideal investment for life companies. Moreover they would allow pension providers to sell index-linked annuities, offering money-purchase schemes (mostly personal pension plans) some measure of protection against inflation.[69] When this proposal was criticised by the Prudential, Wilkie and George Gwilt, who had recently succeeded Simon Keppie as assistant general manager (finance), lobbied ministers and Treasury officials. Their efforts contributed to the issue of index-linked gilts in 1981, exclusively for pension funds in the first year.[70]

Standard Life's property investment had only been temporarily disrupted by the events of 1974 and had recommenced with an allocation of £20 million during 1977. In October of that year Peter Henwood encouraged the board to

purchase the historic Port of London warehouses in Cutler Street which were lying derelict. The architects R. Seifert & Partners had obtained planning permission to develop the site, preserving half the historic buildings, as a new home for the Baltic Exchange. Work had begun on the site in July 1976 but the developers had subsequently been forced into liquidation. For Standard Life an additional attraction of the site was that since planning permission had already been granted, development land tax was not applicable.[71] When completed in 1982 the development, now known as Cutler's Gardens, won acclaim for setting new standards in building

The new Taunton shopping centre in 1981. After the success of Brent Cross, Standard Life invested in a number of such centres.

conservation.[72] With the allocation of £120 million for property investment over four years from November 1978 to 1982, other projects quickly followed, including the redevelopment of Stafford and Taunton town centres and the construction of industrial parks at Abingdon, Basingstoke and Watford.[73]

THE FUTURE OF CANADA

The Canadian branch was challenged by the rise during the late 1960s of the Parti Québécois, which demanded independence for French-speaking Québec. English-speaking Canadians across the whole country were understandably nervous about these ambitions. In the Québec provincial elections of April 1970 there was genuine concern that the separatists would secure a resounding mandate.[74] In the event the Liberal Party, led by the forceful Robert Bourassa, won the election. For the moment the danger had passed; but Standard Life started to plan for a Francophone environment.[75] During 1971 the federal government led by Pierre Trudeau introduced a reflationary budget and revealed its programme for tax reform in an effort to reduce the very high levels of unemployment in Québec, one of the principal grievances of the separatists. These measures, particularly the incentives for retirement savings programmes, contributed directly to record new business for Standard Life.[76]

Just as in the United Kingdom, during 1973 Canada experienced 'continued inflation, unsettled stockmarkets, generally high long-term interest rates . . . and growing discontent among consumers with the apparently uncontrolled rise in costs'. Despite the loss of some pension schemes to competing managed funds, new business remained buoyant, encouraged by a further victory for Bourassa on a platform of economic recovery. By this time the Canadian branch was considered to be the market leader in segregated funds. Altogether assets in Canada totalled over $1 billion, of which $166 million were in segregated funds.[77] This progress was tempered by the passing of the Foreign Investment Review Act by the federal government which restricted the acquisition or control of a Canadian business by persons other than Canadians and prohibited businesses already operating in Canada from establishing new ventures unrelated to their existing activities. George T. Westwater, the general manager for Canada, warned the executive in Edinburgh of the threat of economic nationalism which lay behind the legislation.[78] There was more cause for concern during the following year when Canada bore the full brunt of the economic crisis and the provincial government in Québec threatened to compel life insurance companies to invest a proportion of their assets locally to aid recovery. Westwater was less troubled by the adoption of French as the official language in the Province and decided that the company should seek to qualify for a Certificate of Francisation.[79]

W.A. Arbuckle stood down as chairman of the Canadian advisory board in November 1975 and was succeeded by Lucien G. Rolland who, like his predecessor, was appointed to the main Standard Life board.[80] George Westwater retired as general manager the following June and was replaced by his deputy John C. Burns, then aged 61, who was given the North American-style title of president, Canadian operations.[81] When these appointments had been confirmed the deputy chairman A.M. (Sandy) Hodge and the deputy general manager George Philip visited Canada to review once again the future of the branch, primarily because the individual life business was losing money.[82] Before they left for Canada Tom Risk, the chairman, had written privately to Rolland explaining that he hoped the Canadian branch would in future function 'as if it were, *de facto*, a subsidiary', with the chairman and president coming to Edinburgh three times a year to report progress. This was welcomed in Canada, providing the branch was given greater autonomy.[83]

A year later René Lévesque's Parti Québécois won a landslide victory in the provincial elections on 15 November 1976 with a separatist socialist agenda. In line with many other Canadian businesses, the Canadian executive recommended moving the head office as soon as possible out of Québec.[84] Worried by the political situation, Donald responded by asking John Burns to review the future of Standard Life's interests in the country, particularly as in his view there had been no improvement in the profitability of the individual life business. He outlined various scenarios in a letter to Burns, including restricting new sales to pensions and,

Standard Life's Sherbrooke Street office in Montreal, which was completed in 1962.

as a worst case, complete closure: 'This would be sad in the extreme, but would not necessarily involve our policy-holders in a loss.'[85] Believing spending money on a costly removal would not be in the best interests of either the Canadian or United Kingdom with-profits policy-holders, he asked Burns and Rolland to be prepared to review all the possibilities, including remaining in Montreal, at the meeting of the main board in Edinburgh in January 1977.[86] At the same time, to add to Donald's concern, the federal government introduced changes to the Canadian and British Insurance Companies Act and to the taxation of life assurance premiums and matured policies.[87]

John Burns, president, Canadian operations, from 1976 to 1980.

Discussions about the possibility of moving offices continued throughout 1977, with visits to Canada by the chairman, two directors, Sir Thomas Waterlow and John Trott, and Donald. There was increasing anxiety in Edinburgh that 'if conditions in Québec, including possibly separation, make it impossible to work from Montreal, is it going to be desirable, or even possible, to continue to do business in Canada?'.[88] The members of the Canadian board, who mostly had Québec attachments, were reluctant to contemplate moving the office, hoping that the political situation would resolve itself.[89] This attitude simply fuelled uncertainty when able staff were already leaving and morale was low. Burns for his part was convinced that Donald was taking too narrow a view and failing to appreciate either the efforts he was making to raise productivity or the highly charged atmosphere of life in Québec under Lévesque.[90] In these circumstances it was to Burns' credit that Standard Life increased its sales of individual life business by 20 per cent in 1976[91] and attracted more new business than its immediate competitors in Canada during the following year, albeit with the largest sales force ever employed. Burns reported that there was a prospect that staff numbers would fall with the completion of the installation of new computer systems.[92] Donald remained unconvinced.[93]

As it happened, Donald was by this time in discussions with Manufacturers Life about the possible sale of the branch. He had been approached in August on their behalf by a

London actuary.[94] Negotiations did not begin in
earnest until towards the end of the year but
without at this stage involving either the
Canadian board or executive.[95] In January a
meeting of the main board, at which Rolland
was present, authorised discussions to proceed.[96]
Burns, who had also come to Edinburgh, was
told; but he and Rolland were 'instructed not to
discuss the matter with anyone else in
Canada'.[97] Given the sensitivity of the issues this
was hardly surprising but it was, nevertheless,
an error.

THE BID FOR CANADA

David Donald was faced with perhaps the most
difficult decision of his career. Despite his
obvious frustration with Canada, he tried to set
out objectively the advantages and disadvantages of continuing to write business in the
country. He had no doubt that the business was
sound, 'running at an overall profit thanks to
our pension business, but unable as at present
organised to be self-supporting so far as its
assurance business is concerned'. He concluded
that it was in the interests of the with-profits
policy-holders to take the offer seriously.[98]
Supported by the board, the executive started
the complex task of setting a value on the
Canadian business. During March 1978 Alex
Shedden visited Canada to negotiate a price with
Manufacturers Life but with instructions from
Donald that he was not to involve Burns in the

STANDARD
LIFE

A Canadian portfolio

Annual review 1976

Annual review published
by the Canadian board in
1977 to explain the
branch's business; and
press comment on the sale
of Standard Life's Canadian
branch to ManuLife in
1978.

discussions.[99] After a price of $250 million had been agreed, Donald, who was inclined to 'take the cash and let the credit go', made it plain to his directors that if the deal fell through some hard decisions would need to be taken, leading either to the closure or total reorganisation of the unprofitable ordinary life business.[100] Although the main board was persuaded in mid-April that the sale to Manufacturers Life (about to be renamed ManuLife) was for the best, Rolland threatened to resign at once if the decision was taken without consulting the other members of the Canadian local board,* who still knew nothing about the proposal.[101] Hodge and Donald flew out immediately to explain the decision to the local directors. At their meeting on 17 April, the Canadian directors unanimously refused to endorse the proposal, believing that it was not in the interests of the Canadian policy-holders as it was intended to transfer to the United Kingdom surplus balances which were deemed not to belong to them. As Rolland explained: 'The Canadian board consider themselves as trustees in Canada for the policy-holders and, rightly or wrongly, in coming to their conclusion, went beyond the actuarial aspects of the problem and looked at their moral obligation to secure the best possible back-up behind every policy issued in Canada.'[102] Donald was upset by this turn of events, believing that the Canadian local directors were

questioning his professional actuarial judgement.[103]

Unpersuaded by Rolland's point of view, Donald replied at considerable length, rehearsing his reasons for continuing the negotiations with ManuLife, but adding that Waterlow would come out to Canada once more to discuss the local board's concerns and talk to ManuLife.[104] Waterlow, wrongly, gained the impression that the objections were largely political but, more accurately, also reflected a genuine concern for the staff, many of whom would inevitably lose their jobs in the merged business.[105] The local board remained intransigent.[106] Although ManuLife had made it clear that any sale would require approval from the federal and provincial governments, it was not believed that this presented a serious obstacle. Waterlow agreed with ManuLife that if 'the answer was no, complete confidentiality should be maintained for ever and the book closed'.[107] On receiving his report, the Standard Life board on 9 May confirmed the decision to proceed.[108] Within days Donald returned again to Canada to meet the federal minister of finance, Jean Chrétien, and Dick Humphries, federal superintendent of insurance. There was no indication at this stage that there would be federal opposition or significant delay.[109] In the meantime, at their meeting on 16 May, the Canadian local directors reaffirmed their opposition to the deal, adding that it was in the

---

* At the time the Canadian local board comprised Lucien G. Rolland (chairman), G. Drummond Birks, Donald S. Harvie, Harry W. Macdonell, D.R. McMaster, W.D. (Bill) Mulholland, A. Blaikie Purvis, R.T. Riley and J.C. Burns (president, Canadian operations).

interests of neither the staff nor the policy-holders, and warning that there might be repercussions from the Québec government.[110] Discussions with the federal government continued over the next ten weeks and involved the prime minister's office and Jacques Parizeau, the minister of finance in Québec.[111]

After Chrétien's permission had been received Standard Life and ManuLife announced on 25 July the sale of the branch and, as required by federal law, appointed an independent actuary to review the interests of the policy-holders.[112] The English-speaking press was on the whole sympathetic while the French newspapers were hostile. The headline in *Le Devoir* read *'une mutuelle québécoise farouchment anglophone'* – a Québec mutual fiercely English-speaking.[113] Meeting a month later, the whole Canadian board asked to be allowed to resign (and Rolland stood down as a director of Standard Life) on the grounds that they could no longer represent the interests of the local policy-holders.[114] At the same time it became clear that 'the question of the release of liability of Standard Life under its policies [was] a matter which falls to be determined by the laws of each province in which the policies were made' and was not a matter solely for the federal government. Since provincial law did not allow for such release, every policy-holder would need to agree to the sale or legislation would have to be promoted in every province.[115] As either course would have been both time-consuming and expensive, each was dismissed as impractical and early in

October Donald was advised that the only solution was for Standard Life, in the unlikely event of ManuLife going into liquidation, to continue to carry the large resultant liability on the balance sheet until the death of the last policy-holder.[116] Attempts were made in London to seek insurance for these liabilities. It is unclear whether Donald was really aware of this issue before this turn of events. He certainly should have been. In the event it was to prove the final stumbling block.

Additionally, two lawyers, one of whom earlier in the year had failed to prevent Sun Life moving its Canadian office from Montreal to Toronto, announced their intention of opposing the merger both in the federal and provincial courts and called for support from policy-holders and the Canadian board. On 19 October under the headline 'Battle lines drawn over transfer of Standard's business to ManuLife', *The Globe and Mail* carried a full report of the Canadian board's opposition.[117] The prospect of protracted legal action and negotiations in the full glare of publicity and political scrutiny alarmed the directors in Edinburgh. Their fears were fuelled by concern that the recommendations of the independent actuary, who had been conducting a careful scrutiny of the terms of the merger, would not be 'financially acceptable to Standard Life' as he wanted the policy-holders to have greater protection.[118]

At the end of October it became clear that it would not be possible to insure the large contingent liability.[119] Deeply troubled by this news,

Donald went back to Canada to review the situation, and on his return advised the board to cancel the deal.[120] This decision was made public on 20 November.[121] In the meantime, following the announcement of the merger, ManuLife had been making contact with the Standard Life sales force. On learning the news that the deal was off, three branch managers and 40 of the fieldforce left, the majority to join ManuLife.[122]

This sequence of events cast a long shadow across Donald's last years as manager. There were clearly misunderstandings on both sides, which were very reminiscent of the bitter dispute between the Edinburgh board and the London board over a century before. Once the approach from ManuLife had been made, however, the Standard Life board had to take the offer seriously, but matters would not have gone so far had it been appreciated earlier that, under provincial law, the company would have retained a large outstanding contingent liability.

REBUILDING THE CANADIAN BRANCH
Donald was now convinced that the Canadian branch needed to be completely reorganised 'in such a way that it could reasonably stand on its own without the backing of the company's other resources'. He at once instructed John Burns to take action in four areas:

a) an examination of the terms of compensation of representatives and branch managers;
b) a method of assessment of the costs of running individual branches as compared with the

Alastair Fernie, president, Canadian operations, from 1980 to 1993.

income they generated to meet those costs;
c) arising from b), plans for expansion in profitable areas and contraction in others;
d) a method of control of expenses, particularly of staff numbers and standards of accommodation.

From now on there was to be no Canadian local board and the president of the Canadian organisation was to report directly to the general manager in Edinburgh. At the same time all Canadian managers would continue to report to Burns, but all policy documents were to be made available to the appropriate assistant general manager in Edinburgh. In future there was to be no suggestion that the assets invested in Canada (other than those required by law) were independent of the total portfolio.[123] With this strategy in place Tom Risk agreed to go out to Canada to offer four former members of the Canadian board seats on the Standard Life board on the understanding they attended at least four meetings annually, particularly those at the beginning of the year when the results were discussed. Following this fence-mending visit Lucien Rolland rejoined the board and Harry Macdonell QC, a lawyer in Toronto, and Bill Mulholland, president of the Bank of Montreal, became directors of Standard Life.[124] Drummond Birks at first declined, but eventually became a director in 1984.[125]

For the first time at the January meeting in 1979, the whole Standard Life board considered full reports on all aspects of the Canadian business. In the circumstances it was not surprising that new ordinary sums assured had dropped by 18 per cent and that premium income had fallen by 23 per cent. Group life contracts had only increased because of wage rises after the removal of anti-inflation controls; but, remarkably, pension business held up. With Donald's four points very much in mind, Burns outlined the measures he had taken to improve productivity, reduce costs and promote profitable products.[126] By the time Donald visited Montreal in April, the senior executives in Canada were committed to improving the performance of the branch; but the middle ranks remained deeply suspicious of Edinburgh's intentions.[127] The most critical problem was to

identify a successor to Burns, who would retire in 1980. Unusually for Standard Life, the search was extended outside the company. Eventually one of Burns' deputies, Alastair Fernie, was promoted to the position, allaying fears that an external appointment would be a prelude to another attempted merger.[128]

DONALD'S CONTRIBUTION

In October 1979 David Donald retired as manager of Standard Life after 47 years' service. Although not the easiest person to work with, he was much respected because he gave a clear lead on the issues which confronted the company. Under him Standard Life had changed. The sales side in the United Kingdom had become more focused and the financial strength of the company was regained after the stockmarket crash. His policy of shifting the balance of business away from pensions and mortgage-related contracts towards other savings and non-profits contracts had been handicapped by the rising tide of inflation, although sales of individual pension policies were beginning to grow. Since Standard Life was founded, except in time of war, no other manager had been buffeted by so many external pressures, from rampant inflation to the growth in regulation. As the son of a managing editor of the newspaper publishers D.C. Thomson of Dundee, he naturally encouraged the staff for the first time to speak publicly about matters of policy and to brief politicians and civil servants. At times his views were out of step with those of the Prudential and Legal &

General, the other two industry leaders; but as the manager of the largest mutual he refused to be browbeaten by these two proprietary companies which inevitably had different objectives. A man with wide-ranging interests including the Faculty of Actuaries, the territorial army, the theatre, opera, golf and fine wine and food, he had persuaded the board to begin sponsoring sports and the arts. When he proposed that the first sponsored opera should be *Die Meistersinger*, one director complained: 'Does it have to be Wagner?' Donald replied: 'You get more notes for your money.'[129] To the amusement of his deputy George Philip he categorised staff in the same way as port – vintage, tawny, grocer and so on. He was succeeded by George Gwilt, the assistant general manager (finance), whose previous experience had been in computing and pensions.

THE THATCHER ERA

Prospects in 1979 were in some ways more settled than at the beginning of the decade. The election of the Conservative government led by Margaret Thatcher in May, with a mandate to defeat inflation and 'roll back the boundaries of the public sector', did not, at least in the short term, raise the spectre of another round of pension legislation.[130] The Conservative government found it much more difficult to reduce inflation than had been anticipated. During its first year in office inflation increased steadily to reach nearly 22 per cent, almost the height it had attained in 1975.[131] In these circumstances

interest rates rose and the stockmarket weakened, pushing Standard Life's investment strategy back towards fixed-interest securities in the United Kingdom and overseas equities. Well before the 1979 general election the dollar premium had fallen in the expectation that a Conservative government would abolish exchange controls. The market was taken by surprise, however, when all restrictions on outward investment and on portfolio investment in securities in EEC countries were summarily removed on 18 July 1979.[132] The investment department formed the view that the proportion of the free fund held overseas should now be 15 per cent; up to 40 per cent of the investment in the United States could be in oil and other natural resources; and up to 35 per cent of that in Japan in technology. This was a more adventurous approach to portfolio management and bore the hallmark of George Gwilt and Scott Bell, who had followed him as assistant general manager (finance).[133]

FIRST STEPS TO REGULATION

Despite its non-interventionist stance, the Conservative government was concerned about allegations of mis-selling of financial products. During 1980 some of the larger life offices took action by setting up the insurance ombudsman with advice from Sir Gordon Borrie, the director general of fair trading. At his suggestion a voluntary ten-day cooling-off period for regular premium policies was introduced and efforts were made to improve the quality of information available to policy-holders. The British Insurance Association, with Standard Life's support, objected that there was no need for such a semi-official appointment and established its own personal insurance arbitration service.[134] These initiatives were not enough, however, to prevent the government from appointing a committee in 1981 chaired by Professor L.C.B. Gower to review investor protection. In a final report published in 1984 he called for better safeguards for the 'prudent man' through the establishment of a set of self-regulatory agencies, themselves to be responsible to a new government authority.[135] This conclusion, which overturned the findings of the Scott committee ten years earlier, was the prelude to radical changes in the regulatory environment for all financial services.[136]

Some of the newer insurance companies selling the increasingly popular unit-linked products had never been members of the Life Offices Association (LOA) and were free to pay commission at whatever rate they chose.[137] The concern of the LOA continued to be that some brokers would recommend products which paid them higher commission rather than those which were in the best interests of the customer. The brokers responded to this criticism by pointing out that, as matters stood, the direct sales forces of the life offices were completely unregulated. As a last resort the LOA appealed to the government for support for the commission agreements. During 1982 there was a spate of defections from the LOA, including Abbey Life, Crown Life and Scottish Equitable. M&G, Save &

Prosper and Scottish Amicable threatened to leave if no solution was forthcoming.[138] Standard Life, believing a commission war was in the interests of neither the customer nor the industry, worked hard to try to save the agreements. When the government refused to legislate, the commission agreements were terminated on 1 January 1983.[139] Subsequently the Association of Scottish Life Offices (ASLO) in collaboration with some English offices tried to maintain a limited agreement, but without success.[140] Sir Gordon Borrie told the annual meeting of the British Insurance Brokers' Association at Peebles in 1983 that the whole insurance industry must put its house in order by establishing an effective self-regulatory authority.[141] On the collapse of the commission agreement, Standard Life immediately became a member of the Insurance Ombudsman Bureau, 'giving the public added protection'.[142]

PLANNING IN A COMPETITIVE MARKET

Meanwhile George Gwilt with the help of Alex Shedden, assistant general manager and actuary, had been pondering the future direction of the company. He presented his findings to the directors' conference at Ballathie in May 1981. Alarmingly, he showed that 97 per cent of new contracts in the United Kingdom during 1979 were with-profits. The balance was only redressed by the 75 per cent of without-profits (mostly pension) business written in Canada, which reduced the proportion of with-profits business for the company as a whole to 80 per cent. Gwilt reiterated Davidson's warning – given fifty years earlier at a time when there was no inflation – that writing too much with-profits business spelled eventual disaster. The solution in the long term was to increase the sales of the new investment-linked products whilst recognising that the margins would be considerably lower than on more traditional products, such as term assurance and immediate annuities. In the meantime Gwilt concluded: 'We *must* operate at the smallest cost practical, otherwise the bonus will begin to suffer.' Efforts had to continue to be made to reduce overheads by raising the productivity of the fieldforce, which Peter Glover had been doing for some time, and by deploying computer technology to administer the business to its best advantage.[143]

A CHANGING BUSINESS ENVIRONMENT

In 1983 mortgage tax relief began to be given at source under a new scheme called MIRAS (mortgage interest relief at source). This had the unforeseen effect of making endowment mortgages even more attractive than the repayment method. Standard Life's endowment mortgage business quadrupled to £53 million during the year, causing chaos in the offices as staff tried to cope with the unprecedented demand. At the same time the building societies and the banks made determined efforts to increase their commission earnings from insurance by selling more endowment policies themselves and so cutting out the insurance advisers.[144] Even after life assurance premium relief (LAPR) was with-

George David Gwilt, general manager (later managing director) from 1979 to 1988.

drawn in the 1984 budget, Standard Life was convinced that its outstanding bonus record still made an endowment policy the most attractive means of mortgage repayment.[145] This proved to be the case and, by 1987, over 80 per cent of all new mortgages were to be repaid in

The Castle Pension Series group plan brochure.

this way, with Standard Life taking 14 per cent of the market through the strong links with the building societies which Peter Glover had cultivated.[146]

The abolition of LAPR did not affect tax relief on personal pensions, which could include limited life assurance cover. This was a growing market. In November 1984 Standard Life launched the Castle Pension Series, a comprehensive range of money-purchase pension plans for directors and employees.[147] The Castle personal pensions were an instant success. Despite the uncertainty caused by the government's proposals for a radical reappraisal of pensions, sales of new group pension plans were greater than at any time since the surge in demand when the Social Security and Pensions Act came into force in 1978. Total premium income was, however, depressed by some group schemes switching to managed funds with competitors and a lack of growth in others. After allowing for inflation total premiums were much lower than their 1979 peak (see Figure 7.1 on page 287). Worryingly, Standard Life was now markedly failing to attract managed funds due to poor investment performance. Its position in the league of funds under management by insurance companies fell from fourth to seventh in 1984 and by early 1985 the company had dropped out of the top ten.[148]

CONSERVATIVE CHALLENGE TO PENSIONS

Although the rules for contracting out of SSPA were not to be reviewed until 1983, the industry, through the Occupational Schemes Joint Working Group,* began discussions with the Department of Health and Social Security (DHSS) in 1981.[149] When the *Report on Greater Security for the Rights and Expectations of Members of Occupational Pension Schemes* was published on 19 October 1982, it was evident that the Conservative government was not interested in extending the consensus achieved by Barbara Castle in 1978. This report, which was accepted by the Secretary of State for Social Security, Norman Fowler, recommended greater disclosure to members, tougher rules for solvency, improvements in preserved benefits and better options on leaving service.[150] In 1983 the right-wing Centre for Policy Studies published *Personal and Portable Pensions for All*, which proposed solving at one stroke the problem of early leavers by giving everyone a personal pension contract.[151] The pension industry reacted angrily to this concept. Standard Life, while welcoming the suggested improvements to final-salary schemes, warned:

Allowing individuals the choice of buying their own personal pensions would initially benefit insurance companies since many would choose

* The group comprised the Association of Consulting Actuaries, LOA, ASLO, the National Association of Pension Funds, and the Society of Pension Consultants.

mum pension and thereafter to increase in line with inflation up to a maximum of 5 per cent per annum.[159] With the government actively encouraging personal pension plans, Standard Life immediately launched a new range of products and set up 'Strategy Eighty-Eight' – 'an exercise in communication to ensure that our existing pension scheme clients and our agents are fully aware of the implications for them of the changes brought about by the Act'.[160] As a sales effort Strategy Eighty-Eight was a success but this in itself was to lead to administrative problems. At the same time the building societies and banks were given permission to enter the pensions market. The Social Security Act of 1986 was the genesis of the mis-selling controversy which was to cause the insurance industry so much grief in the 1990s.

NEW INVESTMENT OPPORTUNITIES

After the Conservative government's uneasy start in the fight against inflation, the battle began to be won. This was as much a worldwide phenomenon as the outcome of any deliberate government policy. Declining inflation combined with economic expansion to produce a sustained rise in equity prices both in the United Kingdom and overseas.[161] By March 1982 the expected return on equities had improved to such an extent that it was decided to stop all further free fund investment in fixed-interest securities. At the same time the overseas portfolio was raised from 15 to 20 per cent of the free fund.[162] In extending its foreign investments

STRATEGY Eighty Eight.

The Strategy Eighty-Eight logo.

the company increased the resources devoted to this area.[163] Although purchases of shares in investment trusts continued, largely because they remained at a discount of up to 30 per cent of their asset value, the investment department adopted a more active role towards these investments, supporting proposals for unitisation or liquidation.[164] A characteristic of the management of fixed-interest securities during these years was a much greater emphasis on switching stock to maintain or add value to the portfolio.[165] Late in 1982 the investment department began trading on the newly formed London International Financial Futures Exchange (LIFFE) with an initial investment of £10 million. As well as providing a mechanism for arbitrage between the gilt market and futures contracts, LIFFE also enabled the temporary sale of equities without incurring capital gains tax. After the success of the first year of trading the ceiling was raised and Standard Life became a determined player in the market.[166]

BIG BANG

In July 1983 the chairman of the London Stock Exchange, Nicholas Goodison, reached an agreement with the Secretary of State for Trade and Industry, Cecil Parkinson, that the minimum commission on dealing in securities would be abolished by the end of 1986. Although inevitable if London were to continue to be a major international financial centre, the end of fixed commission meant that in future the relationship of institutional investors, such as Standard Life, with the stockmarket would change.[167] Most stockbroking firms believed that the only way forward was for themselves to become market makers by acquiring firms of stockjobbers, which previously had not been permitted under stock exchange rules. Successful market making required large capital resources and, as a result, over the next two years many stockbroking firms were taken over by the banks.[168] With the financial world changing rapidly, Standard Life looked at various means of strengthening its investment department. Associations with other investment houses were considered[169] but in the event it was agreed that to ensure it remained competitive the company would increase the compensation for investment staff to reflect more closely the wider investment market.

At the same time a small team was created to deal direct with the market makers but it was decided to continue to place half the investment business with agency brokers whose advice was valued. The research team was enlarged, however, as there was concern that financial pressures, conflicts of interest and changing personnel might contribute to a decline in the 'quantity and quality of research' provided by stockbrokers, particularly on ordinary shares in smaller companies.[170] Already the investment department had built up good working relations with those companies in which Standard Life had a large shareholding.[171] The effectiveness of these strategies was reflected in improved performance and a consequent increase in annual deposits with SLPF.[172]

PROPERTY

With rents on city-centre properties being squeezed in the early 1980s, attention was also given to small-town shopping centres, as in Kidderminster, and estates on the periphery of large cities where there was potential for developing business parks, as at Basingstoke and Watford. This policy did not preclude major city-centre developments, such as the flagship Whiteley's store in Bayswater built at a cost of £75 million. The opportunity was taken to rationalise joint ventures with Hammersons which resulted in Standard Life taking over some properties completely.[173] The improvement in the equity market and the privatisation of nationalised industries resulted in some investors moving out of property. This provided Standard Life with the opportunity of making sound purchases of London offices on the correct assumption that businesses would continue to be located in city centres. However, with weakening yields in 1985 and allowing for the first time for realistic depreciation, investment was restricted.[174] Although there was a substan-

The famous Whiteley's department store in Bayswater, which was built in 1909 to rival Harrods. It was refurbished as a shopping complex by Standard Life in the 1980s.

tial programme of development and refurbishment in the coming year, future investment of some £500 million between 1986 and 1990 was in doubt until the consequences of Big Bang became clearer.[175]

THE BANK OF SCOTLAND

Towards the close of 1984 in this changing market for financial services Standard Life received an unexpected chance to form an alliance with retail banking. In September the Governor of the Bank of Scotland, Sir Thomas Risk, who was also a director of Barclays Bank and Standard Life, was informed by the chairman of Barclays that its 35 per cent holding in the Bank of Scotland was to be sold. Risk asked for a month's grace to find a buyer and immediately approached Robert Smith, the well-known Glasgow accountant who was now chairman of Standard Life, with a view to purchase. The Bank had been Standard Life's principal Scottish banker since 1846 and in recent years had sold more Standard Life products north of the border than any other bank.[176] The announcement in January 1985 of the acquisition of this holding for £182 million with Bank of England approval surprised the City and brought some criticism from policy-holders.[177] Although the investment was evidently opportunistic, as Tom King, then general manager marketing, explained, 'the value of the link with Bank of Scotland would come primarily from new ideas and not "special treatment" so far as business from the bank is concerned'.[178] Subsequently Robert Smith and

George Gwilt joined the Bank of Scotland board and Bruce Pattullo, treasurer and general manager of the Bank of Scotland, became a director of Standard Life. At the same time, following the fashion set by other life companies, the acquisition of estate agents was examined but prudently rejected.

THE NEW REGULATORY REGIME

The Financial Services Act (FSA), designed to implement the findings of the Gower report, was passed in 1986 and was due to come into force in 1988. It seemed likely that under the terms of the regulations a distinction would be drawn between 'tied agents' who sold insurance products on behalf of one provider and those independent advisers 'who have a duty to advise on the choice of insurance company'.[179] Without a direct sales force, Standard Life put its weight behind the independents to set up the campaign for independent financial advice (CAMIFA), which quickly coined the term 'independent financial adviser' (IFA) in an effort to reinforce their sense of identity.[180] So as to continue to provide a level playing field where IFAs could be seen to be recommending products on merit rather than on commission earnings, Standard Life, along with other life offices using this distribution channel, wished to reinstate the commission agreement. This was to be done through a new body known as the Registry of Life Assurance Commission (ROLAC), which would be supervised by the Life Assurance and Unit-Trust Regulatory Organisation (LAUTRO) provided for in the FSA.[181]* Peter Glover, now Standard Life's general manager (sales), was a member of ROLAC from its inception and was appointed to the steering committee preparatory to the formation of LAUTRO. He later joined the LAUTRO board and became chairman of the Selling Practices Committee responsible for drawing up rules of conduct for life office sales staff. Although ROLAC was acceptable to the Securities and Investment Board (the overall regulatory authority), the Office of Fair Trading ruled against it – a decision which was to result in a bidding up of commission rates as companies vied for market share in the new environment.[182]

THE UKPI AFFAIR

During 1986 confidence in life offices was dealt a serious blow by the announcement that the old-established and respected mutual United Kingdom Provident Institution (UKPI) would be forced to cut its bonus due to a sharp fall in the value of its reserves. This had come about because UKPI had pursued an inappropriate investment policy for a life company, holding over 10 per cent of its funds in unquoted situations where the risks were unacceptably high having regard to its liabilities. In the competitive market for with-profits business, it was feared that this news would lead to a collapse in new business. Friends' Provi-

dent, another mutual, came to the rescue and acquired the business. An additional cause of UKPI's problems was over-expansion of its with-profits business based on unrealistic predictions of likely future bonus rates. The life insurance council of the ABI immediately issued new guidelines for such quotations and the DTI gave notice that actuarial scrutiny of the accounts of life offices would be more rigorous.[183]

CHANGING THE MANAGEMENT STRUCTURE

By 1985 the coming revolution in financial services demanded further changes in the way in which Standard Life was directed and managed. Since 1825 there had been a division between the board and the executive, with most of the power in the hands of the executive. The non-executive board was treated by successive general managers as a necessary evil rather than as integral to the decision-making process. The relationship began to improve while Tom Risk was chairman from 1969 to 1977 – the first chairman to serve for more than three consecutive years. After the successful conferences at St Andrews and Turnberry, further conferences allowed the directors and executive to share their views on all aspects of the business. George Gwilt declined the offer of a seat on the board on his appointment as manager in 1979. Following

* The FSA established two other regulatory authorities which would have an impact on life offices – the Investment Managers Regulatory Organisation (IMRO) and the Financial Intermediaries Managers and Brokers Regulatory Authority (FIMBRA). All these regulatory authorities were to be supervised by the Securities and Investment Board (SIB).

The new management group in 1985 with (left to right) at the front George Gwilt and Alex Shedden, and behind Iain Lumsden, Scott Bell, Drew Lyburn, Peter Glover, Tom King and Jim Stretton.

the lead of other Scottish mutuals he agreed, however, in 1984 to be the first manager to become a director of Standard Life while in office, with the new title of managing director and actuary.[184]

This was the prelude to a review of executive responsibilities, which led to the creation of a management group in 1985 with the appointment of Alex Shedden as deputy chief executive and secretary, and six general managers – Drew Lyburn (administration), Peter Glover (sales), Scott Bell (finance), Iain Lumsden (actuarial), Jim Stretton (operations) and Tom King, agency manager (marketing).[185] With the expanding range of products and associated services, it was essential that there was greater understanding at

the level of the executive of investment policy and the actuarial balance of the company. Above all, in a much more competitive world, it was important that a distinction be drawn between sales and marketing. Peter Glover as agency manager had always stressed the significance of marketing 'Standard Life' as a brand, to which research and product development was critical. It was therefore decided to divide the responsibilities for sales and marketing.[186] At the same time the life and pensions sales forces were amalgamated together with their administrative support. These reforms were designed largely to ensure that a better distribution of business flowed from the new product range.

UNIT TRUSTS

The results for 1985 were encouraging, with a substantial growth in investment-linked business. Personal pensions was the fastest-growing section of the pensions market, fuelled by a pre-budget scare (unfounded, as it turned out) that tax privileges would be withdrawn. Standard Life's Castle Series comfortably outperformed the industry.[187] In May 1986 the company's unit-linked portfolio was significantly extended with the launch of eight unit trusts,[188]* designed to capture a large share of this growing market and in so doing help shift the balance of the United Kingdom business back towards without-profits contracts.[189] To the annoyance of other unit-trust companies, Standard Life resigned from the Unit Trust Association to enable it to pay the same rates of commission to all its insurance brokers and agents.[190] The launch was *too* successful, taking over £200 million of new investment in six weeks – four times the estimate – and overwhelming the company's administration. The number of enquiries was so great that more than 500 new clerical staff had to be recruited in Edinburgh and, to make full use of computer capacity, shift working was introduced. The staff consultative procedures put in place in 1972 ensured that this large expansion and change in working practices progressed smoothly. The marketing campaign for the year was cancelled in an effort to stem the tide. The future was, however, unpredictable.[191]

PROGRESS IN CANADA

The forging of a much closer relationship with the Canadian operations after the abandoning of the merger with ManuLife was initially more successful than could have been anticipated. In 1980 the branch contributed a record 40 per cent of Standard Life's new insured premium income, which, even allowing for the prevailing exchange rate, was higher than at any time in the previous twenty years. This achievement reflected Gwilt's decision to release Canada from the actuarial requirement to balance its business, which made it possible to write more profitable annuity contracts through brokers.[192] This was a growing segment of the market but required substantial investment in technology to be successful. At the same time older staff were deliberately replaced with young recruits, whose ideas and perceptions could more easily be moulded to the new approach of the branch through a management development programme. A corporate advertising campaign with the theme 'Standard Life Salute to Local Sport', to counter the adverse press comment at the time of the proposed merger, made the company better known. Moreover, gains in sales were at last matched by a rise in productivity.

The political situation had improved with the defeat of the separatists in a referendum in Québec in March 1980, but the worldwide economic downturn was affecting Canada more than most other developed countries.[193] Addi-

Standard Life launched unit trusts in 1986. This brochure was part of a suite of product literature.

---

* A new subsidiary, Standard Life Trust Management Ltd, formed in 1982, was to manage the expanding unit-trust business.

Canada's first Prime Minister created an estate with the stroke of a pen — and the help of Standard Life

tional problems were caused for Standard Life by the resignation during 1981 of five senior investment managers, who left to set up their own business as investment counsellors. They took some of their clients with them, resulting in both a loss of schemes and of managed funds. This had a damaging effect on morale in the investment department, where remuneration and incentives lagged behind the competition.[194]

As in the United Kingdom, the government during the early 1980s pressed for more flexible pension provision, compounding the difficulties caused for Standard Life by the country's continuing economic problems. Although the slow-down in sales of group pensions was more than compensated for by a growth in individual business, particularly personal pension plans, even here there was uncertainty due to proposed changes in legislation and taxation. Moreover, the management in Edinburgh were reluctant to allow the creation of segregated funds for this purpose because, unlike in the United Kingdom, they had to include guarantees to be saleable.[195]

In 1983 Standard Life celebrated its 150th anniversary in Canada with a number of events. These included in Montreal a meeting of the board and the launch of the Standard Life marathon, which quickly became a popular annual event.[196] During the year Standard Life Alliance Services (SAS) was formed with Alliance Mutual, an old-established but small Canadian insurer, to develop and market a complete range of group life, accident and health insurance contracts. Without such additional products it was extremely difficult for Standard Life to compete effectively for group business. This was an important milestone, as never before had Standard Life sold anything other than life and pension products. SAS started cautiously, seeking new business at first only in Québec and then in Toronto. Early results were encouraging.[197] During 1986 Alliance Mutual merged with Industrial Life and SAS was renamed Standard Industrielle Alliance Services (SIAS).[198] Two years later Industrial Alliance acquired Nation Life and as a result the joint venture was terminated.

Pierre Trudeau stepped down as prime minister and leader of the Liberal Party in 1984

Standard Life Centre in King
Street West, Toronto, 1986.

The Montreal Marathon in 1997. This annual fund-raising event was established in 1983 as part of Standard Life's 150th anniversary celebrations in Canada.

and in the subsequent general elections the Conservatives, led by Brian Mulroney, were swept to power with an agenda similar to that of Margaret Thatcher. The new government began a reappraisal of pension provision to give consumers greater choice and flexibilty. This had the inevitable consequence of shifting the emphasis away from defined benefits towards defined contribution (money purchase) plans. As in the United Kingdom, Standard Life adopted a high profile in pressing for amendments to the legislation 'in order that people can reach retirement age with adequate pension

arrangements',[199] while at the same time selling a record number of personal pensions. A registered retirement income fund (RRIF), enabling clients to take advantage of guaranteed or variable returns with capital repayment of at least 75 per cent on maturity or 100 per cent on death (complying with recent legislation), was at first unsuccessful because the terms and conditions were too complicated. When these were simplified and made more flexible, it proved popular, attracting over $60 million in new premiums in 1987. Group insured pension business boomed in 1985 and 1986 and only slackened in the following year because competitors were willing to make more generous mortality assumptions to secure business. The market for ordinary life products was depressed because Standard Life's commission rates were unattractive to brokers and the company withdrew largely from that part of the brokerage market. New products were introduced in 1985 and 1986 in an attempt to revive interest in conventional life assurance.[200] As a result of continuing concern with the disappointing results from the individual life business, consultants were retained to examine its overall cost effectiveness and to recommend a future organisational structure which 'would maximise efficiency and increase performance levels'.[201]

Standard Life continued to hold the bulk of its assets in Canada in fixed-interest securities to match guaranteed liabilities. An increasing proportion, however, was invested in equities and property. The largest developments in Canada during this period were the Standard Life Centre in Hamilton, Ontario (the final commercial stage of the Lloyd D. Jackson Urban Renewal Scheme), completed in 1983, and the Standard Life Centre in Toronto, a 26-storey office and commercial complex in the heart of the financial district, completed in 1986.[202] Nevertheless, Standard Life's portfolio management was still not considered to be sufficiently aggressive to stem the loss of insured pension schemes to specialist fund managers.[203]

REPUBLIC OF IRELAND

In 1984 Standard Life celebrated 150 years of business in Ireland.[204] This event provided an opportunity to give the Irish business greater autonomy. Since the difficulties experienced in Ireland at the end of the nineteenth century, the Irish branches had shared the same status as those in the United Kingdom even though the characteristics of the market were different. This had begun to change under David Donald with the new approach to regionalisation. At the end of the 1970s the total business was in the order of £75 million new premium income a year. As an interim measure to provide a product for the market, Standard Life introduced very competitive guaranteed income and growth bonds which had a beneficial tax position because of the worldwide business mix.[205] These attracted over £500 million in investments in the early 1980s before the government in the Republic changed the tax regulations.[206] Shortly after their introduction in the United Kingdom, unitised

pension and then investment products were also made available and, as the guaranteed products matured, much of the proceeds were re-invested in these vehicles.[207] The manager in Ireland at this time was the well-known Bertie R. O'Hanlon, a legendary rugby player who became an equally successful salesman. On one occasion, he went into hospital for a private operation and paid for it by selling policies to members of the medical staff.[208]

The rise in Irish business allowed further diversification from the traditional whole-life with-profits contracts which had always been popular there. The mortgage contract (MC) house purchase plan launched in 1984 through

Bertie O'Hanlon, manager for the Republic of Ireland from 1976 to 1988.

The new Standard Life head office in the Republic of Ireland, at St Stephen's Green, which opened in 1984. The Green was given to the people of Dublin by Lord Ardilaun, to whom Standard Life had sold Muckross House in 1899.

the Irish Nationwide Building Society introduced a wider Irish market to the attraction of repaying loans by way of endowment policies.[209] The growth in activity prompted a review of the overall business as O'Hanlon approached retirement. Ireland became an overseas branch with its own general manager. The offices in Dublin moved from cramped premises in Dawson Street to a handsome building on St Stephen's Green. New offices were also acquired in Limerick, Sligo and Waterford, whilst the original home of the Irish branch on South Mall in Cork was refurbished.[210]

GWILT'S LEGACY

In September 1987, George Gwilt agreed with the directors that he should retire at the AGM in 1988 at the age of 60 along with his deputy, Alex Shedden.[211] Since he had taken over from David Donald in 1979 Gwilt had seen Standard Life become a serious player in the investment-bond and unit-trust markets and adapt to the changes in pension regulations and the growth in sales of personal pensions. He had witnessed the political consensus on pensions policy, which he had done much to foster, swept away and replaced by a more doctrinaire approach with which he had little sympathy. He had also to grapple with the Conservative government's commitment to abolishing long-established practices within financial services while at the same time attempting to offer consumers greater protection through a complex edifice of self-regulation. Proud of Standard Life's achieve-

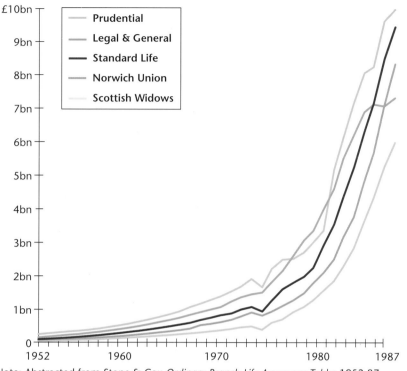

Note: Abstracted from Stone & Cox *Ordinary Branch Life Assurance Tables* 1952-87.

ments and service, he considered these reforms unnecessary and frustrating, diverting his attention away from the time-honoured task of managing with actuarial prudence one of the most successful life offices. On the sales side he encouraged Peter Glover to expand the business and in investment he gave his whole-hearted support to equities rather than bonds. It was under his management that in 1985 Standard Life's long-term assets for the first time overtook those of Legal & General to reach almost £10 billion (Figure 7.2 above). The increase in assets by two-and-a-half-fold in real terms between 1971 and 1987 (see Appendix 7 on page 390) was

FIGURE 7.2
Long-term assets of major competitors 1952–87

no mean achievement during a period of such unprecedented change in financial services. In the United Kingdom growth had come largely from mortgage-related endowment policies and, latterly, personal pensions (see Appendices 3 and 4 on pages 382 and 384). Likewise, in Canada, the drawbacks and opportunities to do business had been conditioned by government.

Writing in the *Money Observer* in February 1987 under the headline 'A Standard triumph', Helen Pridham paid tribute to the reputation of Standard Life's products: 'Over a decade [its with-profits endowment policies] have appeared in the top ten in every survey of past performance. And the unit-linked funds have been equally impressive.'[212]

CHAPTER EIGHT

AIMING FOR EXCELLENCE: 1988–2000

We are one of the world's leading mutual financial services companies operating in a number of countries.

We will aim for excellence by providing quality products, a level of financial security and performance and a quality of service which fully meets the needs of our customers, while at all times being ethical and compliant and maintaining the financial strength of the group.

For specific markets, products and services, we will expand our business if it would be in the long-term interests of our policy-holders.

Group Mission Statement 1998.

At the annual meeting in March 1988 Scott Bell became managing director and actuary of Standard Life, with Jim Stretton, who also joined the board, as his deputy. At the same time Norman Lessels became chairman, serving for the next ten years, to be succeeded in 1998 by John Trott. As the report for the year readily admitted, there were 'major uncertainties facing new business development in all areas'.[1] Recognising that success in this changing environment depended on agreement on clear objectives, Bell and Stretton started to hold regular meetings of the senior executive team. Apart from the managing director and his deputy, the executive team at the time comprised A.M. (Sandy) Crombie, who had succeeded Stretton as general manager (operations); Peter Glover, Tom King, Iain Lumsden, Drew Lyburn; David M.

Simpson, general manager (investment) and secretary; David M. Potter, deputy general manager (marketing); A.M. (Sandy) Skinner, deputy general manager (administration); Alastair Fernie, president, Canadian operations; and Claude Garcia and Roy Naudie, executive vice-presidents, Canadian operations.[2] Peter Glover retired early in July to become chief executive of the Campaign for Independent Financial Advice (CAMIFA) and his post was amalgamated with that of marketing under Tom King.[3]

OBJECTIVES

From the outset the executive team devoted a great deal of time to discussing corporate objectives and in 'formulating a framework of strategies within which to operate over the next few years'. To advance the discussion, a team was

The management team in the entrance hall at Tanfield in 1992.
From left to right: Norrie McLeod, David Potter, Claude Garcia,
Jim Stretton, Scott Bell, Iain Lumsden, Tom King, David Simpson,
Sandy Skinner and Sandy Crombie.

set up consisting of Scott Bell, Jim Stretton, Iain Lumsden, Tom King and Alan Forbes, who was in charge of a newly created research and planning department.[4] After considerable debate it was finally agreed that the central objective was 'to ensure that the company provides . . . with-profits contracts on which the ultimate returns will be consistently greater than those available on comparable policies of other life offices, and to do so in the maximum volume consequently possible without detriment to the maintenance of an appropriate level of financial strength'.[5] Demanding but achievable targets were to be set for all the main variables. From the outset it was agreed that this could only be achieved if the proportion of new without-profits contracts was significantly increased, otherwise the capital requirements associated with ever increasing volumes of with-profits business would impose unacceptably severe investment constraints.[6] This was a problem for the industry as a whole and Standard Life was determined it would not expose itself to the risk of inadequate capital which was subsequently to lead to the takeovers of both the Scottish Equitable and Scottish Amicable.[7]

Considerable emphasis was therefore given to the importance of maintaining the company's financial strength. The intention was to achieve appropriate strength relative to the industry as a whole, providing of course that solvency would be maintained in all conceivable circumstances. A business model was developed based on the ability to withstand 'worst case' investment

Jim Stretton, deputy managing director (later chief executive UK operations) since 1988.

scenarios – prescribed falls in income from equities and property, adverse currency movements, and so on. The 'Black Monday' stock-market collapse of the previous October had reinforced the necessity of such prudence, but it was the more significant 1974 bear market which lay behind much of this thinking. Although it took over two years to refine the model and four years to devise appropriate controls, the principal tenets were in place by the end of 1988.[8] Iain Lumsden, who was responsible for much of this work, was appointed group finance director in 1989 with a seat on the board.

A second important objective was to seek to broaden the company's activities, both within

Iain Lumsden, group finance director since 1989.

the UK through an extension of its core product range, and overseas, by investing heavily in the established operations in Canada and Ireland, and by considering profitable new markets in which to operate. This was to lead later to the purchase or creation of healthcare, banking and investment-management subsidiaries. It was also to result in the setting up of insurance operations in Spain and Germany and in the initiatives which it was hoped would enable Standard Life to operate eventually in both India and China.

PLANNING

At the same time, a formal planning process was put in place in the UK, informed by various initiatives to develop and improve the business, culminating in a full discussion at a senior management conference in November 1990. This was accompanied by an experimental project of continuous improvement in service within the financial administration department. This took as its point of departure the strategic value – 'simplicity from the customer's point of view'. The success of this project led to the addition of other values, with the purpose of developing indicators to form a control system to provide management with the necessary information to allow the process to be continuous.[9]

The core elements of the corporate plan (including the corporate objective, the mission statement, the business model, marketing strategy, diversification and the all-important recommendations on the criteria for financial strength) were discussed at two board meetings in January and February 1991.[10] Following agreement, the plan was outlined to assistant general managers who were then asked to co-ordinate the drafting of divisional plans. These were discussed at a major senior staff conference at St Andrews in June at which the level and quality of service were debated. These had been much criticised in the United Kingdom in the wake of Strategy Eighty-Eight.[11] It was noted that members of the Financial Intermediaries Managers and Brokers Regulatory Authority (FIMBRA) felt that, although Standard Life's products performed well, their servicing left much to be desired. It was agreed that service clearly added significant value to products and therefore the means of enhancing service needed to be thoroughly and speedily investigated.[12] One resulting initiative was a study tour by members of the executive to companies in North America which had embraced total quality management (TQM). Learning from American experience, the planning cycle was adjusted in the autumn of 1991 to ensure that all staff were so engaged in identifying strategic values and output measurements that they were not only aware of but subscribed to the long-term objective.[13]

By the spring of 1992 this first attempt at coherent planning was complete. At the end of May, Scott Bell wrote to all staff in the United Kingdom and the Republic of Ireland outlining the organisational and procedural changes, notably the need to shorten chains of communication, to prevent unnecessary duplication, and to move towards 'one stop' processing now common in other sectors. Consequently the processing of all new business was to become the responsibility of the sales and marketing division under Tom King who, at the same time, became a director of the company. Scott Bell was confident that the changes would alter fundamentally the way in which business was handled and enable Standard Life to operate in 'a much more efficient and effective way'.[14] As part of these organisational changes, his own job was redefined as group managing director and Jim Stretton became chief executive of UK operations. At the same time, consultants were commissioned to produce a new visual identity

Extract from Scott Bell's letter to staff in May 1992 regarding the forthcoming reorganisation of the business in the United Kingdom and the Republic of Ireland.

by the beginning of the new financial year which would project a clear image to customers of 'what Standard Life stands for'.[15] The first operational plan for 1992–93 summarised concisely all the thinking of the previous four years. The goal was to achieve a better with-profit:without-profit mix in the United Kingdom by putting marketing effort behind without-

In August 1993, Standard Life launched its latest UK television advertising campaign. By featuring a number of people, each of whom lead very different lives, the advertisement aimed to show that regardless of the kind of life you lead, you can benefit by investing with Standard Life.

Financial products have historically been difficult to advertise successfully, so to make clear to the viewer the range of services and products we offer, the advertisement also featured this scroll effect which picks out key words.

Standard Life's Group Managing Director, Scott Bell, said: "The reaction to the campaign has been very positive. Our main aim was to build name awareness, and we have exceeded our most optimistic projections."

An advertisement from 1994 incorporating in a scroll effect the key words used to support the Standard Life brand.

profits contracts particularly investment-linked products. This was in keeping with the spirit of the times which was seeing greater consumer choice and self-determination. Within the strategic framework, emphasis was placed on human resources, now the responsibility of Norrie McLeod, who had succeeded Drew Lyburn on his retirement a year earlier. Greater attention was to be given to training and creating mechanisms for matching people to jobs, ensuring the best fit. Already senior managers had been sent on courses at business schools in the United Kingdom and the United States.[16]

A number of additional structural changes were made during 1992, including the separation once more of marketing from sales, which remained the responsibility of Tom King, and the establishment of a corporate development department under David Potter. Five new cross-divisional standing committees were established, covering customers, processes, people, planning and results.[17] One of the first responsibilities of the new marketing division under John Hylands was a major television advertising campaign to build name awareness. This featured a number of people from different walks of life. The aim was to show that 'regardless of the kind of life you lead, you can benefit by investing with Standard Life'. Every advertisement incorporated a scroll effect with key words to be associated with the brand – saving, income, pensions, planning, protection and confidence.[18]

After substantial progress had been made in

achieving the initial strategic goals, the corporate plan was further revised in 1995 with greater emphasis on customer needs so that Standard Life would naturally be 'first choice as a personal financial partner'. These needs were identified for the business in the United Kingdom as investment, protection against lifetime events, saving, regular income, borrowing, advice on tax planning, and education on financial affairs. Standard Life provided some but not all of these services and, as opportunities arose, new activities such as health insurance and banking would be added to the portfolio. In a very competitive marketplace, Standard Life's advantages were to be integrity, strength and security, investment performance, ease and simplicity of dealings, value for money, an integrated flexible product range and education. These were to be supported by a bias towards action and innovation, the competence and loyalty of staff, a compliant corporate culture and the appropriate use of technology. Performance was to continue to be measured against leading with-profits companies by comparing relative financial strength, costs, business growth, and with-profits returns.[19] Outcomes along with the financial results showing the main elements of profits and other objective measures of performance were summarised in a 'balanced scorecard', introduced at that time and produced regularly thereafter. This benchmarking was to be widely distributed and used to direct attention to performance throughout the United Kingdom operations.[20]

MUTUALITY

Fundamental to Standard Life's vision of the future was mutuality. The concept of mutuality within the financial sector had been under threat for some time, fuelled in part by immediate windfall gains paid to investors on the demutualisation of building societies. The number of mutual life offices taking this course of action had been increasing. Scottish Mutual, which had been struggling for new business, demutualised in 1992 when it was acquired by Abbey National Bank. Scottish Equitable followed suit in 1993 as did Provident Mutual on its takeover by General Accident in 1995 and Scottish Amicable when it was acquired by Prudential in 1997. During 1995 Norwich Union, one of the largest mutual insurance companies, announced its intention to demutualise. There was speculation that other large mutuals might convert to proprietary status either to raise more capital or to be acquired themselves. Standard Life had no such intention, declaring that it was more than able 'to finance all likely future developments'. Scott Bell, in his annual review in 1996, was unequivocal in his commitment to mutuality for Standard Life: 'We believe strongly that a well-run mutual company should provide better returns to its policy-holders than a proprietary company.'[21]

The advantage of mutuality was, as it always had been, that all the profits were available for distribution to the with-profits policy-holders, who owned the business, whereas in a proprietary company they had to be divided with the shareholders. Since the 1890s it had become customary for this division to be in the ratio of 9:1; but this was not a hard and fast rule.[22] The advantage of a proprietary company, as William Thomson (the manager from 1837 to 1874) had argued in his bitter quarrel with Scottish Widows (see page 86), was that it had access to more capital and was therefore less constrained in its investment policies. For Standard Life, although this was the case in the mid-nineteenth century, it was certainly not at all so at the end of the twentieth century with the company being one of a handful of life assurance companies in the world with a triple A credit rating for financial strength from both Moody's and Standard and Poor's.

INVESTMENT

A survey of IFAs in the autumn of 1988 had confirmed the executive's impression that the perception of Standard Life's administration was poor and that there was a belief that the managed and equity funds had underperformed over the last few years.[23] Unless such attitudes changed there was little chance of promoting Standard Life as a competitive brand or substantially increasing sales of investment-linked products. Returns on investment-linked products had been affected by the company's strong commitment to the equity market, which had been in retreat since October 1987.[24]

With almost the entire free fund now held in equities or property, much of the effort of the investment division was concentrated on deve-

loping better knowledge of the companies in which investments might be held through regular contacts and a programme of visits.[25] In January 1989 defensive action was taken by increasing the holding in Hammersons, the property company (see page 257), to almost 28 per cent to prevent a hostile takeover by Rodamco (the property investment trust arm of the Dutch Robeco group). This was done primarily because it was considered that it would be very difficult to replace the high-quality property owned through this investment. Following the defeat of the Rodamco bid, Standard Life took steps to strengthen Hammersons' board and to rationalise further the joint interests.[26]

During the autumn of 1989 a series of seminars for staff and IFAs, marking the tenth anniversary of the launch of the investment bonds, was held to promote sales of retail products, which were more profitable than wholesale pension fund management. These highlighted Standard Life's outstanding returns on its property portfolio and its success in outperforming the equity market through good stock selection and sector distribution.[27] The presentations resulted in a surge in demand for investment bonds and invitations to take part in 'beauty parades' for corporate pension funds.[28] The company had long since ceased to be a major player in this market which was dominated by Mercury Asset Management, Phillips & Drew Fund Management (PDFM), Barclays de Zoete Wedd (BZW) and Schroders. The only insurance company in contention with the leaders was the Prudential and even it was falling behind.[29]

The London equity market recovered during 1989, peaking in January 1990. It then once more became unsettled because of political uncertainty and the threat of recession with the accompanying danger of the return of inflation leading to higher interest rates. Although share prices in world markets remained erratic for the next four years for a variety of reasons, the Standard Life executive was unwavering in support of holding the bulk of the free fund in equities as providing the highest likely long-term return. Holdings in the unquoted securities market were increased and Standard Life played a secondary role in management buyouts.[30] In 1991, as a consequence of the continuing emphasis on the importance of the company's financial strength, investment constraints were imposed whereby 4 per cent of the free fund was to be held in long-dated fixed-interest securities and 2.5 per cent in cash to ensure the company could withstand the most demanding worst-case scenarios.[31] The immediate consequence was that more than 30 per cent of new money in the coming year was placed in gilts.[32] After a further analysis of the product mix and investment behaviour of the company and its major competitors in 1992, and taking into account declining yields on equities, the proportion of fixed-interest assets was raised to 12 per cent in the coming year.[33] Such adjustments were now integral to setting investment targets, and the models on which they were based steadily became more sophisticated. The objective was always to continue to be able to hold as much of the free fund as prudent in equities. Despite the change in investment policy, by the end of 1992 Standard Life still had more of its free fund invested in equities than all but one of its major competitors.[34]

High interest rates in the United Kingdom had the intended effect of taking the heat out of the domestic economy to such an extent that during 1991 the commercial property market suffered its largest annual fall since the secondary banking crisis in 1973–74. As a result, all the book gains on Standard Life's property portfolio recorded in 1988 and 1989 were lost. In

'Cnihtengild', outside Standard Life's London offices in Cutler's Gardens, 1992. Mounted on a turntable, the horse and rider turned one degree every day, thus completing an entire revolution during a year. This impressive sculpture by Denys Mitchell was part of a commitment to contemporary art by Standard Life. It was unveiled in November 1990.

STANDARD LIFE'S NEW BUILDINGS

By the mid-1980s the company had long since outgrown No. 3 George Street and staff were scattered across 19 different buildings, some of which were cramped and uncomfortable. George Street itself had been steadily extended and enlarged and now comprised nine separate buildings, all linked together. Before George Gwilt retired in 1988 it had already been agreed to build new offices and a data-processing centre at Tanfield on the site of the church where the ministers and elders who walked out of the General Assembly of the Church of Scotland at the Disruption in 1843 first met. These new buildings were designed by the Michael Laird Partnership to blend with their historic surroundings and incorporated many novel features which provide an excellent modern working environment on two main office floors. At the time of its completion in 1990 the office had the largest floor plate of any office in Europe, allowing for easy communication. As part of a programme to support the visual arts in all its developments, Standard Life commissioned Axis Mundi or the Apotheosis of the Wise Virgins from the sculptor Gerald Ogilvie Laing.

With the company growing so quickly, the development at Tanfield did nothing to relieve pressure on existing offices and in fact further premises had to be acquired. It was decided in September 1991 to accommodate head office staff in three major offices, namely 3 George Street, Tanfield and a new head office at the foot of Lothian Road close to the city centre.

The new building, named Standard Life House, was occupied in September 1996 and houses over 1,700 staff. The architects were once again the Michael Laird Partnership. Although the building is clad in sandstone in keeping with its surroundings, the design is far from traditional with flexible space allowing moves and changes to take place quickly and economically. In addition staff can control their own working environment by adjusting temperature and light levels. The building also incorporates many architecturally striking features. In 1999 a series of fine illuminated panels were installed in the entrance hall, depicting a fresh interpretation of the parable of the wise and foolish virgins by Gerald Ogilvie Laing.

Her Majesty the Queen and Scott Bell at the official opening of Tanfield in 1991.

Right: an artist's impression of Standard Life House, 1996.

Below right: HRH the Princess Royal at the opening of the building with Norman Lessels and Scott Bell.

Below: lights and railings designed by Jane Kelly.

The old head office at No. 3 George Street was subsequently refurbished and now provides a home for Standard Life Investments. The objective was to retain the character of this important landmark building while at the same time bringing the working conditions up to the highest standard. Standard Life's commitment to supporting the visual arts was carried a stage further by commissioning objects from contemporary Scottish artists and designers including handmade glass objects and silver and glass clocks. Renamed No. 1 George Street, it was officially re-opened in October 1999. At the same time 52 Annandale Street was converted to accommodate Standard Life Bank's mortgage centre and other premises were taken on elsewhere in Edinburgh. Another new building, Exchange Crescent, across the Western Approach Road from Standard Life House, will open in 2000 and house a further 1,700 staff. Not since the turn of the century has Standard Life built so many new offices.

every property sector there was over-supply and rents fell to historic lows. There was little improvement until the last quarter of 1993 when the confidence of investors began to return, and during 1994 the number of unlet premises declined, with the strongest demand in the retail sector. Having invested for some time in quality offices and shopping centres, Standard Life benefited more quickly than its competitors from the recovery. In the circumstances the proportion of new money placed in property was reduced in 1992 and 1993 but raised thereafter.[35]

In the spring of 1994 David Simpson relinquished his dual responsibilities as secretary and general manager (investment) and Sandy Crombie became general manager (investment and development). He continued to address the long-term challenges confronting the investment department, namely its low profile within the company and the need to respond to the ever-increasing competition from fund managers. After internal consultation the department was reorganised in December to provide better service for customers and improved performance. This was done by building on its reputation for in-depth research at all levels to gain an 'information advantage' over competitors and thereby beat them and the markets. Economic forecasts for all international equity markets were to be brought together in a house view, which would underpin decision-making and drive stock selection and asset mix. Each market was to be ranked as 'very heavy, heavy, light and very light', leaving no room for

neutrality. As in all other parts of Standard Life's business, the process was to be continuous, with daily reviews by the decision-making group comprising senior investment managers from the client fund management and asset class management teams.[36] When the first house view was compiled in January 1995 it was welcomed as providing 'a more complete view of policy than previously'.[37] At the same time board resolutions covering derivatives, stock lending, and so on were rationalised in a single statement on group investment and lending policies which, it was anticipated, would give greater freedom in managing the main life fund.[38]

With these changes in place, Sandy Crombie and his team were keen to use improved performance to renew the attack on the market for managed funds. The response was disappointing, with prospective clients questioning whether 'a life company could ever be a premier investment manager'. Many believed that fund managers were much more committed to developing their capability, because they were dedicated to just one business, and favoured them when placing mandates.[39] As a result the gap between the leading fund managers and insurance companies had widened even further. PDFM, the market leader in 1996, managed pension funds in the United Kingdom alone of over £40 billion, whereas the Prudential, still the leading insurance company, managed only £10 billion and Standard Life just £2 billion of external funds.[40] Although remuneration packages had been further improved, Standard Life still had difficulty in recruiting staff in a very competitive market in which it was perceived to be more rewarding to work for fund managers.

BANK OF SCOTLAND

Early in 1996 the board, after a strategic review, decided to reduce Standard Life's 32 per cent stake in the Bank of Scotland, then worth £900 million, to a more realistic market weight. There had been growing concern about the size of the investment and about the responsibilities associated with such a large holding in the banking sector. In addition any anticipated additional advantage of this investment had long since failed to materialise. The Bank's governor, Sir Bruce Pattullo, who had been on the Standard Life board since 1985, was informed and invited to suggest how the stock might be placed. Concerned that the sale of such a sizeable holding would trigger an unwelcome takeover bid at the end of the Bank's well-publicised tercentennial year, he asked for the stock to be split amongst a number of share-holders. On Sunday 13 May the proposed sale was reported in the Sunday newspapers and the situation quickly polarised around the issue of the future independence of Scotland's financial institutions. Much of the discussion was emotional and ill-informed and failed to recognise that financial institutions were rapidly globalising, leaving fewer and fewer niche players. In a highly charged debate Sir Bruce Pattullo resigned from the Standard Life board. Over the next three weeks with the help of its advisers

Standard Life attempted but failed to sell its stake to any single institution. This was not at all unexpected by the company as no approach to purchase the holding had been made since it had been acquired. The entire holding therefore was put on the market in a book-building exercise. The placing was handled by BZW and Lazards with a syndicate of merchant banks. When it was completed in July Scott Bell resigned from the Bank of Scotland board. Norman Lessels, Standard Life's chairman, tendered his resignation, but was invited by Pattullo to remain a director in a personal capacity.[41] There was a book loss to Standard Life's with-profits policy-holders in the short-term because, although holdings in other bank stocks were immediately increased, the portfolio, nonetheless, had now less weight overall in the banking sector which in the short term outperformed the market. The loss was, however, quickly recouped over the next few years by good stock selection in the bull market.

STANDARD LIFE INVESTMENTS

By this time Scott Bell and Sandy Crombie were seriously considering the most appropriate structure for Standard Life's investment activities to meet customer needs. Among their ideas was the possibility of developing a separate brand.[42] After considerable discussion it was decided in January 1998 to create within the Standard Life group a separate company to manage virtually all of the group's assets and market a range of investment products and services.[43] In Canada a

Philosophy and Style
Recourses
Process and Structure
Products and Services
Performance
Risk Control

STANDARD LIFE INVESTMENTS

Profit from our knowledge

our one aim is to maximise our clients' returns within the risk profile they select

separate investment company had already been formed and this was to become an integral part of this new venture. Collective investment as a method of saving was becoming increasingly popular, being seen as a flexible alternative to pensions and life assurance. As importantly, it was hoped that this initiative would improve Standard Life's ability to compete in the profitable market for managed funds which other insurance companies were also trying to break into. For example, as a result of successful marketing of tracker funds, Legal & General's assets under management for the first time for more than a decade overtook those of Standard Life in 1998 (see Figure 8.1 on page 334).[44]

Standard Life launched its new company, Standard Life Investments Limited, on 16 November 1998. The new company, which initially managed funds of £60 billion, adopted as its motto 'Profit from our Knowledge' to remind clients of Standard Life Investments' total commitment to in-depth research and recruiting, rewarding and retaining 'only the best' people. Ambitious targets were set including the doubling of Standard Life's market share in institutional fund management within five years. To draw a clear distinction from the life company Standard Life Investments moved in July 1999 to the old principal office at 3 George Street, now redesignated No. 1 George

'Profit from our Knowledge' promotion from the launch of Standard Life Investments in October 1999. This banner was displayed outside the refurbished George Street premises.

The official opening of the head office of Standard Life Investments at No. 1 George Street in November 1999 by Howard Davies, chairman of the Financial Services Authority (centre), Sandy Crombie, chief executive, Standard Life Investments (right), and Scott Bell (left).

Street (see page 329). In September 1998 the nine existing unit-trusts had been converted into open-ended investment companies (OEICs) which made for greater flexibility and simpler pricing. They were also easier for customers to understand and were more acceptable in Europe and by extension elsewhere in the world. To mark the inauguration of Standard Life Investments in November 1998 five new OEICs were launched.[45]

Shortly afterwards it was announced that a private equity* fund of funds with investments mostly in Europe would be launched in the coming year. This offered the potential for greater returns than quoted markets in the medium to long term and was designed to appeal to investors in the United States (particularly state and corporate pension funds), Europe and, to a lesser extent, the Middle East.[46] Additionally, a joint-venture agreement was signed in October 1999 with the Housing Development Finance Corporation Ltd (HDFC) to establish an asset management company and enter the growing Indian mutual fund industry. The new venture will offer a wide range of investment products to both retail and institutional investors in the sub-continent, drawing on HDFC's large client base and its strong brand image (see page 366).

Standard Life Investments more than matched expectations, winning some £1.3 billion of new investment business in its first year of operation, with a significant proportion coming from Canada.

THE UNITED KINGDOM MARKET

In the United Kingdom the challenge was to translate the corporate objectives into practical strategies at a time when the whole industry was in a state of upheaval due to the 1986 Financial Services Act (FSA) coming into force on 29 April 1988. This made it illegal for anyone to give investment advice (including advice on life assurance and pension business) unless authorised directly by the Securities and Investment

FIGURE 8.1
Long-term assets of major competitors 1988–98

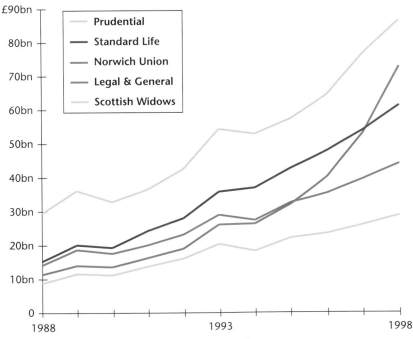

Note: Abstracted from annual reports of individual companies

* Private equity was the field of finance previously known as 'venture capital', including management buy-outs, buy-ins and so on, and related to companies not listed on recognised stock exchanges.

Board (SIB) or one of the regulatory bodies established for the purpose such as the Life Assurance and Unit-Trust Regulatory Organisation (LAUTRO) or the Financial Intermediaries, Managers and Brokers Regulatory Authority (FIMBRA). All the regulatory bodies were required to conduct periodic inspection visits (PIVs) to ensure companies' practices and procedures complied with the regulations. Under the LAUTRO regulations advisers were required either to be 'appointed representatives' (tied agents) of one life company selling only its products or 'independent financial advisers' (IFAs) who were able to select the most suitable products from those available from all life companies. This polarisation was to change the nature of the market for life insurance products.[47]

Standard Life was committed to supporting IFAs and Scott Bell had encouraged Peter Glover to become chief executive of CAMIFA in 1988. There was concern, however, that the effect of the Act would be to erode the company's market share. Key account managers were therefore appointed to maintain contact with the largest IFAs and consideration was given to the purchase of a general insurer so as to increase penetration of intermediaries' total business. The purchase of a direct-sales life office and that of a building society were investigated but eventually rejected.[48] A closer relationship with a building society was, however, pursued vigorously when it became clear in the autumn of 1988 that most were 'moving towards ties or joint marketing ventures with life assurance companies'. Under pressure CAMIFA, which represented the majority of leading life offices relying on IFAs for their distribution with the slogan 'independent advice is the best advice', was forced to modify its opposition to tied agencies.[49] Standard Life, with the largest slice of the endowment mortgage market, had most to lose from such alliances and during the summer it held talks with a few of the leading societies with a view to forming its own alliance. This was a difficult course of action for Scott Bell and his team as they were concerned about how IFAs might react. To maintain good relations, Scott Bell wrote to them in January 1989 to reassure them of Standard Life's continued support but offered them the opportunity to tie if they so wished.[50]

LINK WITH THE HALIFAX

The following month it was announced that the Halifax Building Society was to become a tied agent of Standard Life. Additionally a joint venture would be set up to handle unit-linked and investment business.[51] It was anticipated that the Halifax would contribute some 20 per cent of Standard Life's new business. It took a year to finalise the details of the joint venture and to establish Halifax Standard Trust Management Ltd, which would market unit-trusts and personal equity plans (PEPs).[52]* The joint venture was finally launched on 26 September 1990.[53]

The logo of CAMIFA, which coined the phrase 'Independent Financial Adviser'. It was established in 1988 by a number of leading insurance companies to promote impartial advice for customers.

* PEPs had been introduced in the 1986 budget to encourage, through tax incentives, equity investment by small investors.

The launch in 1990 of the joint venture with the Halifax, with (on the left) Peter Roney and Jim Birrell of the Halifax and Scott Bell and Hamish Simpson of Standard Life.

60 other tied agents. The task of training agents and installing the necessary technology was complex and time-consuming. In December it was decided to increase the number of tied agents with a target of 300 in the coming year. This was to prove difficult as competition was intense.[55]

At the same time customer service consultants (CSCs) were appointed to area offices to look after orphan policy-holders (those without independent financial advisers). Providing Standard Life with the rudiments of a direct sales organisation, it was thought that they might produce a significant proportion of new business by the end of the decade. Some of them were recruited from amongst the ranks of the smaller IFAs.[56]

Since Standard Life had been perceived by IFAs as the most supportive member of CAMIFA, these changes of direction needed to be handled sensitively. With the termination of the LAUTRO commissions agreement in April 1989 it was possible for the first time in almost 30 years for life offices to set their own terms. Standard Life increased commission rates for all IFAs by 10 per cent in recognition of the extra costs they would incur in implementing the requirements of the Financial Services Act. Additional commission was to be paid to those IFAs who agreed to the provision of quotations on-line and there were further additions based on real savings. Although these terms were in line with those of Scottish Widows and Norwich Union, they fell far short of those

Under the terms of the agreement, if either party wished to withdraw, the other had the right to acquire the whole of the joint venture. During the summer the Bank of Scotland had also become a tied agent because under LAUTRO rules the size of the Standard Life shareholding would have prevented it from selling the company's products had it continued as an IFA.[54]

By the end of 1989 all the building societies, except for the Bradford & Bingley, the Bristol & West and the Yorkshire, and the majority of banks had either tied or set up their own insurance subsidiaries. Regulatory pressures also forced many of the smaller intermediaries to seek equivalent relationships with life offices. Altogether during the year Standard Life appointed

offered by Scottish Amicable and most English offices. As a result during 1990 Standard Life lost custom from the small to medium-sized IFAs – its traditional base – but gained business from the national IFAs, who were consolidating their own position in the wake of the Act.[57]

In the short term the link with the Halifax filled the gap in the market left by the loss of business from other building societies and the smaller IFAs, but it did nothing to address the aim of shifting the balance of new business away from with-profits contracts which remained the most popular method of mortgage repayment.[58] Moreover it could do nothing to lessen the administrative problems which had resulted from a doubling in demand for personal pensions – an outcome of Strategy Eighty-Eight – and the new products introduced to provide the greater freedom of individual choice under the terms of the 1988 Social Security and Pensions Act. Although all life offices were experiencing similar difficulties, Standard Life, as one of the largest providers of personal pensions, was very exposed and much criticised for long delays in processing applications. There was no easy solution in the short term except better monitoring of progress and improving productivity.[59] Scott Bell felt it necessary to apologise for the poor level of service in his annual review in February 1989.[60]

Within two months there was evidence that these initiatives were being reflected in a more positive attitude to the company amongst IFAs.[61] Encouraged by this news, efforts to clear the

'Axis Mundi', by Gerald Ogilvie Laing, commissioned in 1991 to complement the new Tanfield building. It is a sequel to the sculptor's Ten Virgins bas-relief. It represents the tree of life from birth to death and rebirth.

pension backlog were redoubled. By September there was sufficient breathing space to allow for additional training and the inauguration of a client help desk from 15 November 1989.[62]

FINANCIAL SERVICES ACT

The implementation of the Financial Services Act in 1988 led to many changes in the way business was transacted. There had been growing frustration with the new system of regulation, which the financial sector found burdensome and yet consumers considered it did not give them sufficient protection. Consumer organisations and the press felt that customers were entitled to know what proportion of their premiums were taken up by expenses. Although life offices came to accept that customers were entitled to this information, they mistakenly resisted the separate disclosure of commissions. The press latched on to this issue, equating high initial commissions with bad early surrender values. These accusations, together with the high-profile collapse in 1990 of the Levitt Group, one of the largest IFAs, damaged the reputation of the whole industry. Encouraged by sensational press coverage of such failures, the public came increasingly to believe that the regulators should protect them even if they made a foolhardy investment based on adequate disclosure, such as investing all their assets in a speculative project offering unrealistic rates of return.[63] LAUTRO responded by introducing new rules during 1990 for the disclosure of expenses associated with individual life insurance con-

tracts and the Securities and Investment Board (SIB) required all offices to publish 'with-profits guides' providing details of expenses. Believing these provisions did not go far enough, the Department of Trade and Industry told the SIB to undertake a wide-ranging review of retail regulation. A series of discussion papers was published during 1991, reaffirming the need for a clear distinction between IFAs and tied agents and the benefits to consumers of the 'competitive pressures exerted on companies as a result of a strong independent sector'. While Standard Life welcomed these developments, the company was now becoming concerned that the complex hierarchy of regulatory bodies each taking a distinctive approach was both costly and confusing.[64]

During 1992 the image of the whole life assurance industry was tarnished by further allegations of poor selling practices, big commissions, high lapse rates and inequitable surrender values.[65] LAUTRO issued guidance and companies were required to adjust their practices and procedures.[66] Subsequent investigations by the regulator resulted in spiralling fines and closure of IFAs found guilty of mis-selling. This in turn increased distrust of the industry by the consumer organisations and the press. Standard Life took the view that regulation was being driven by the need to police selling at the lower end of the market with no allowance made for companies which had adopted their own high standards and procedures. This all-embracing approach to regulation was adding considerably to costs for the industry as a whole at a time when consumers were already complaining that administrative charges were too high.[67]

A FAVOURABLE MARKET

By the summer of 1993 there were clear signs of a sustained recovery in the United Kingdom economy. After sterling's traumatic escape from the straitjacket of the European Exchange Rate Mechanism the previous September, the Conservative government switched its economic policy away from curbing inflation towards promoting growth. Interest rates were cut and sterling was devalued. This was a far more favourable economic climate in which to effect change than that of the previous five years. Sales could be expected to grow, providing consumers had confidence in Standard Life as a market leader. Although surveys suggested that the company's standing was improving,[68] much still needed to be done to raise quality and to convince IFAs that it was committed to a high level of after-sales service.

Convinced by now that quality was an essential ingredient in effective marketing as customers now expected much higher levels of service,[69] the senior executive developed their own approach to total quality management (known as total customer satisfaction – TCS). Their personal commitment contributed directly to the success of the programme, which embraced all staff. By May 1993 divisional quality managers had been appointed to commence the initial assessment phase.[70] The programme was

divided into five areas of activity – improvement initiatives, teamwork, direction, implementation and customer – each with its own management team.[71]

Preparatory training began in the autumn and the results were presented at a workshop in January 1994. Before the official launch in April, a booklet, *Putting Customers First*, was distributed to all staff.[72] TCS sessions were held in Edinburgh throughout the year in groups of 100 drawn from across divisions and involving altogether 16,000 training days. An important purpose of the TCS programme was to stress throughout the whole enterprise the inevitability of continuous change and improvement to match the needs and expectations of customers. This was to be achieved by convincing every member of staff

Standard Life sponsored the Princes Street Mile wheelchair race in 1993 as part of its continuing involvement in the wider community.

A workshop session in Standard Life's Total Customer Satisfaction (TCS) programme, 1994. This was a company-wide initiative to improve the quality and level of service.

that they had a contribution to make to this process.[73]

The programme was judged such a success by both staff and customers that it was followed two years later by the 'helping change happen initiative' (HCH).[74] An outcome of TCS was a review and simplification of systems throughout the company, for example for processing new business and handling telephone calls, and the conversion of all letters, forms and policies to a style which was easier to understand. Although an external evaluation early in 1995 showed that there was now much greater alignment of effort towards meeting customers' requirements, there was still a need for the executive to have a higher profile within the industry as a whole, to be more visible and to articulate their vision for the long-term direction of the group and the future of the financial services sector.[75] Evidence of the impact of TCS was an improved position in the perceptions of the market, with Standard Life taking first place in industry-wide surveys for good after-sales service, responding to queries, rapid settlement of claims, and prompt premium collection.[76]

UNITED KINGDOM SALES

Although the level of new business in the United Kingdom during 1993 and 1994 was disappointing, Standard Life performed far better than most of its competitors, many of whom recorded substantial falls in new business. Additionally, there was a significant shift, as had been planned, away from with-profits to without-profits contracts, which climbed from 35 per cent to over 60 per cent of new premium income between 1991 and 1994. This was due partly to the decline in popularity of endowment mortgages as a means of house purchase as inflation and bonuses fell, but more importantly also to the marketing emphasis given to investment-linked contracts. Scottish Amicable and Scottish Equitable pursued similar strategies.[77] The fall in endowment mortgage business at Standard Life was accelerated during 1994 by the decision of the Halifax not to renew its tied sales agreement when it expired in January of the following year. The Halifax had hoped to establish with Standard Life a jointly owned life assurance company. Standard Life rejected this proposal as the resulting demands on its resources would have hampered the development of its other businesses.[78] Accordingly Standard Life exercised its option, well before the termination date, of purchasing the whole of the unit-trust joint venture which in future was to trade under the name of Standard Life Fund Management.[79]

The termination of the arrangement with the Halifax, which had contributed some 25 per cent of sales, led Standard Life to review its

STANDARD LIFE

Key features of the Free-Standing Additional Voluntary Contributions Plan

Before you enter any financial contract, it is important that you understand what the product is, how it works, the risks involved and what a decision to buy could mean for you. We recommend that you read this document and the enclosed Personal Illustration before you purchase.

IMPORTANT
Please read and keep for future reference

An advertisement for Standard Life's free-standing additional voluntary pensions contribution plan (AVCs), designed to appeal to the generation born just after the Second World War.

future distribution strategy to replace the loss of business. Since the Financial Services Act was implemented in 1988 there had been a marked decline in the market share of IFAs, dropping from over 50 per cent to 34 per cent. In the circumstances it was considered impossible to replace all the Halifax business by enlarging IFA sales. Standard Life recognised that it was now overly dependent on this single distribution channel. The idea of buying a building society was again investigated but quickly rejected. Instead it was decided to use the platform of the 300 customer service consultants (CSCs) and the 700,000 orphaned policy-holders inherited from the Halifax to build over the next six years a large directly employed sales force. It was anticipated this would generate £50 million additional premium income a year. The sales personnel – to be known as financial planning consultants – who had previously largely reacted to customer enquiries were now expected to generate much of their own sales. The focus was to be on the quality of business produced and remuneration was to be based not just on volume but also on such measures as persistency and on excellence of advice.[80] This was not without its problems. The 'best advice' requirements of the regulatory authorities required that the direct sales force be trained in the whole product range; and it was proving difficult to recruit CSCs. Moreover, in entering the direct selling market, Standard Life would need to acquire new distribution skills, particularly in the use of rapidly evolving electronic channels which were being exploited with great success by newcomers to the market.[81]

REGULATION

Meanwhile, the SIB had become increasingly concerned that FIMBRA members lacked the capital to implement the new regulations and services expected by their customers. Likewise, many providers had come to the view that there was no need for two regulatory bodies (LAUTRO and FIMBRA) to police selling practices in the IFA market. Consequently during 1993 FIMBRA's functions were merged by the SIB with those of LAUTRO into the Personal Investment Authority (PIA) which was to take over officially on 1 January 1995.[82] This merger was not a seamless process, as all existing members of FIMBRA and LAUTRO had to apply to become members of the PIA. Also, from the same date, customers had to be informed of the cost of each product, the level of commission paid to the IFA, and the likely impact of future charges on the expected return.

Although Jim Stretton became a board member of the PIA, he, along with others in the industry, was critical of the change of direction when it became clear that membership of the PIA board in future would effectively comprise a majority of those from outside the industry. Such a move was against the spirit of self-regulation enshrined in the Financial Services Act and suggested that the whole system of self-regulation should be revisited. Stretton's resignation in January 1994 was widely supported.[83]

Stretton had in any event come to the view that the then objectives of the SIB were largely unachievable since complete protection of the customer could not be guaranteed no matter what controls and requirements were imposed on sales personnel. He preferred a different regulatory goal, one which would allow customers and providers of financial services to transact business together with confidence in an open market.[85] At the time, however, this reasonable suggestion found little support outside the industry as press interest was focused on the failure of the regulators to prevent the mis-selling of personal pensions following the opt-out provisions in the SSPA. Since 1988 employees could opt out of joining or being a member of their occupational pension scheme and the exercise of this option was encouraged by a government campaign. However, the full blame (rightly in some cases) and subsequent costs were laid at the door of companies selling personal pension products on the grounds that they had not fully alerted customers to the possible consequences of opting out.

No other country had such stringent requirements. Insurance companies could in theory choose whether to be regulated by the PIA or directly by the SIB. With the exception of the Prudential, all life companies chose the PIA.[84] In a bold move, which was to change the industry, Standard Life responded to the demand for the disclosure of commissions by spreading all the costs (including commissions) over the term of its contracts and improving both early surrender and transfer values.

In December 1993 the SIB announced a far-reaching investigation into the sales of personal pensions. This was to fall into two categories: 'those where only a transfer value has been paid, rather than leaving benefits in a previous scheme' and 'those who have opted out of occupational schemes in favour of a personal pension, and are paying regular contributions'. Customers, who could prove they had been ill-advised, were to be entitled to redress, but in the event providers were required to compensate all policy-holders where a loss might be anticipated. Standard Life set in place procedures to co-ordinate the response to customers and to the SIB/LAUTRO. It was recognised from the outset that it would be necessary to scrutinise a large number of sales and that it would be difficult to identify all those who could be affected. Moreover Standard Life only held the necessary documentation for their own CSCs and tied agents.[86] In October 1994 the SIB announced a review of all previous personal pension transfers and opt-outs to identify cases of mis-selling and make provision for those who were considered to have lost money. Although Standard Life was convinced that the number of cases of mis-selling would be very small, the process of examining every contract would require considerable effort over several years and would be expensive. Subsequently questionnaires were sent out to all the 70,000 personal pension customers initially concerned.[87]

There is no doubt that many people were

Wey House, Guildford, Prime Health's head office building in Surrey. Standard Life acquired this company in 1994.

wrongly advised to transfer existing benefits to a personal pension or to take out a personal pension in preference to their occupational scheme. The groups most affected (miners, teachers, nurses and so on) could have been identified and compensated rapidly. However, the review was extended to those who had never joined an occupational scheme and eventually included all those who might conceivably have lost money by having taken out a personal pension. Since some of these cases did involve genuine mis-selling, the industry was in a weak position in trying to limit the scope of the review and the eventual compensation.

Confidence in life assurance and pension products was badly damaged by these events. In the first quarter of 1995 sales of regular premium pensions and individual life products by the whole insurance industry in the United Kingdom plunged by 20 per cent compared with the first quarter of 1994, itself a poor year. Several companies sold their life assurance interests and a few life offices were forced to find protection through amalgamation. Many financial commentators believed further takeovers were inevitable, seeing these as the only means of reducing overheads and improving returns.[88] The reputation of the whole financial services sector was dealt a further blow by the sudden collapse of Baring Brothers, one of the most respected merchant banks in the City, in January 1995. It was evident that there had been a total failure in the internal compliance mechanisms within Barings and some weakness in the Bank of England's review procedures. This catastrophe was to accelerate a compete overhaul of the regulatory system, leading to the Financial Services and Markets Bill of 1999.

In these difficult circumstances, Standard Life managed to maintain the volume of new pension business and to stabilise the decline in life contracts. Overall total sales fell by almost 26 per cent, most of which could be attributed to the loss of the link with the Halifax. The proportion of business through IFAs increased significantly, with personal pensions accounting for the majority of sales.[89]

COMPETITIVE PRESSURES

During 1994 Standard Life had seized the opportunity to extend its product range in the United Kingdom by acquiring Prime Health from the troubled Municipal Mutual Insurance Group. Prime Health had been established in 1988 to concentrate on the profitable personal segment of the medical insurance market which was expanding rapidly thanks to tax incentives for those over 60 years of age. Prime Health had a 20 per cent share of the personal market, although only a 4 per cent share of the total health market, and was fifth largest player after the large Provident Associations and Norwich Union.[90]

Poor volumes combined with the introduction of the new disclosure rules in 1995 were to drive up the life industry's costs. London Life, which closed its doors to new business in May, was reported by the DTI to have spent £200 for every £100 of new regular premiums. Even the largest offices were showing signs of strain. Bacon & Woodrow, the consulting actuaries, estimated that only one life office in ten was cost competitive. Moreover, competition was becoming even fiercer, with the announcement that Virgin Direct was intending to offer a range of cut-price life products when it launched its successful PEPs in May. Retail chains with a reputation for reliability and integrity, such as Marks & Spencer, were extending their activities into financial services. Not surprisingly, the industry continued to concentrate. Standard Life made very tentative approaches to potential targets, but concluded that there would be little to gain through acquisitions in the UK.

PENSIONS

A new Pensions Act in 1995, an ill-thought-through reaction to the misuse of pension funds by Robert Maxwell, established the Occupational Pensions Regulatory Authority (OPRA). While welcomed by the industry and enjoying broad cross-party support, the legislation, on the eve of a general election, rekindled the debate about future pension provision.[91] Standard Life was already engaged in dialogue with members of parliament and opinion-makers within the Labour Party about proposed reforms in pensions and savings. For some time the Labour Party had been reconsidering its approach to welfare. Frank Field, the shadow social services minister, had already dubbed occupational pension schemes 'one of the great welfare successes post Beveridge' and declared that 'universalism should come from the private not the public sector'. He believed all employees should be members of an occupational money-purchase scheme (which would replace defined benefit schemes), contributing at least 4 per cent of their earnings which would be matched by 6 per cent from their employers. He had reservations about tax relief on both capital gains and contributions as they represented an inequitable and regressive subsidy to the better-off.[92] As might have been expected, these views were not shared by the whole Labour Party. The Conservative Party on the other hand remained wedded to personal pensions. On balance it was believed that tax concessions were necessary to encourage providence even amongst the prudent. If tax relief on capital accumulation was abolished, it was argued that a necessary consequence must be the removal of restrictions on withdrawing the whole capital sum on retirement, otherwise benefits would be taxed twice.[93] With a Labour victory almost guaranteed at the election there could be no doubt that there would be further changes in legislation. The concept of universal pensions provided by the private sector, whilst attractive, would be expensive to administer because of the relatively small sums involved at the lower end of the income scale.

STAKEHOLDER PENSIONS

Despite its large majority after the election, the Labour government found it more difficult than expected to push through radical welfare reforms. During 1998 Frank Field resigned as social service minister when it became clear that his proposals would not be acceptable. The government actuary, Christopher Daykin, pointed out that according to OECD surveys the United Kingdom had much less exposure to unfunded state benefits than most other European countries. He cast doubt on the wisdom of funding, which he suggested might 'simply have the effect of forcing up prices in stock markets, if there are too many investors chasing a finite volume of financial instruments, unless the availability of investment monies leads to new investment projects being pursued which would otherwise not have taken place'. He condemned 'as a great mistake' proposals which would result in the termination of defined benefit schemes and defended tax concessions for savers. He warned: 'Our challenge in the United Kingdom is to ensure that we do not destroy that which we already have which is good, and to make better those elements of the current system which are not working as well as they should'.[94]

Disregarding this advice the government came forward with proposals for 'a new contract for welfare – partnership in pensions', whereby the existing state pension would continue but with decreasing benefits, and a second state pension to replace SERPS would be introduced for those earning between £9,000 and £18,500. Embedded within the second state pension would be incentives to join an occupational scheme or take out a money-purchase stakeholder pension to be introduced in 2001. These were to be provided by the private sector at low cost and with flexible contracts. Since total charges, including commissions, were to be restricted, it was unclear whether IFAs would be willing to distribute such products unless they were offered strong support by providers or whether providers could sell such products profitably.[95]

In the spring of 1999 the government started to put some flesh on the previously ill-defined concept of the 'stakeholder pension'. As the consultation papers were published it became evident that the intention was to put pressure on the industry to improve the value for money offered to customers and to simplify the decisions they would have to take. The motivation behind the changes was that the government needed to engage the private sector much more fully in funding provision for the growing numbers of the elderly. It was vital to the providers that the structure ultimately agreed should enable them to operate profitably.

THE CHANGING MARKET PLACE

With the rapid changes taking place within the financial services sector, Standard Life reviewed the future servicing of IFAs and the future of direct sales.[96] In the wake of mis-selling, customers might be expected to have more confi-

dence in reputable IFAs than in a direct sales force. The trend towards more sophisticated products such as pensions (including new retirement options) and investment products also favoured IFAs who had become better qualified to give advice. Moreover, the costs of a direct sales force with the accompanying compliance risks resulted in the larger direct-selling companies cutting back their numbers severely. Standard Life devoted a good deal of time to these issues during 1996 and there were further study tours to the United States. An important consideration was how far the Standard Life brand could support the envisaged range of activities, including investment and direct

Tom King, director and general manager (sales), holding the trophy awarded at the Personal Investment Marketing Show to Standard Life as the life and pensions company of the year, 1996. The company went on to win this award again in 1997, 1998 and 1999.

During the 1990s Standard Life became the largest provider of personal pensions, and this advertisement outlined the key features of the company's plan.

*Key features
of the Standard Life
Personal Pension Plan*

Before you enter any
financial contract,
it is important that you
understand what the
product is, how it works,
the risks involved and
what a decision to buy
could mean for you.
We recommend that
you read this document
and the enclosed
Personal Illustration
before you purchase.

business. Much effort was concentrated on refining and improving the corporate scorecard detailing every aspect of the company's performance, an essential ingredient in monitoring the impact of the brand and the effectiveness of the different channels of distribution.[97] Encouragement came in June 1996 when Standard Life was awarded the accolade of 'PIMS Company of the year' at the tenth Personal Investment Marketing Show, replacing Sun Life which had held the position for three years. In November Standard Life was voted top life office in the IFA awards and 'Best Service Provider' in a survey by the

Financial Adviser magazine.[98] These awards showed just how far the company had come in providing a high quality of service for IFAs and their clients in the few years since the TCS programme was launched.

Business improved during 1996 with strong sales growth of personal pensions where demand was strong because of the new regulations on contracting out in the 1995 Pensions Act. There was also concern that the Labour government would reduce or withdraw tax concessions. Speculation was intense in the weeks before Gordon Brown, the new chancellor of the exchequer, introduced his first budget in July 1997, driving up sales to record levels. By the end of that year sales of life and investment products has also begun to recover but not to the level they had reached during 1994. During the subsequent three years, overall sales through IFAs increased significantly and accounted for 84 per cent of Standard Life's new business. The company's market share (excluding unit-trusts) in this sector rose from 9.5 per cent to almost 12 per cent.[99]

This success reflected to some extent outstanding investment performance due to the remarkable boom in the equity market from July 1996 which continued almost without interruption for the next two years.[100] This contributed to excellent returns on Standard Life products. A typical 25-year endowment policy maturing in 1999 provided an average return of 13.5 per cent per annum after charges and tax, while equivalent pension policies provided an average return of 16 per cent per annum.

After the abolition of tax credits on dividends for pension funds by Gordon Brown in his first budget, the future returns on all pension products were reduced. Many commentators assumed he had cynically chosen this vehicle to raise revenue as pension policy-holders were unlikely to understand the effect until it was too late to complain. Although there had been speculation that the abolition of tax credit would lead to a sharp drop in the stockmarket, this did not happen.[101] Market sentiment had been influenced by the earlier decision to grant independence to the Bank of England and to transfer its supervisory role to the new Financial Services Authority.

In his first budget Gordon Brown also abolished tax relief on private health insurance for those over 60. This doctrinaire attack had an immediate effect on the market which was already troubled by higher-than-anticipated claims frequency and costs. This had an immediate and negative effect on Prime Health. Steps had already been taken to increase productivity through the introduction of improved working practices supported by new computer systems. Immediately tax relief was removed many low or no-claims customers did not renew their policies putting further pressures on the remaining business.

With the political debate about the future funding of the National Health Service unresolved, the short-term outlook for private medical insurance in the United Kingdom was uncertain. Standard Life, however, remained convinced that prospects for health insurance in the long term were good and to underline this confidence Prime Health was renamed Standard Life Healthcare under its managing director, Mike Hall.[102]

STANDARD LIFE BANK

Standard Life decided in 1997 to open a bank. This was a natural extension of its product range and a sensible use of the company's existing distribution, its customer base and of course its brand. In 1996 Scottish Widows and the Prudential had established banks. Jim Spowart, who had been developing banking services for Direct Line, the Royal Bank of Scotland subsidiary, was appointed managing director of Standard Life Bank Limited in January 1997. The concept of a telephone banking facility with simple easy-to-understand products fitted precisely with Standard Life's thinking about the future. The strategy was to sell savings accounts to private customers, mostly through IFAs, and to institutions, such as charities and legal practices, using telesales techniques. From previous experience it was known that there was considerable inertia in the market, with customers leaving their accounts with the same bank or building society for years. By offering keen rates supported by well-targeted marketing, it would be possible to capture a good deal of business from existing providers. Mortgages would be sold direct and distributed through IFAs who controlled 50 per cent of the market. The aim would be to attract more savings and sell more mortgages at lower

Top: an advertisement to mark the £1 billion in deposits secured by Standard Life Bank in its first year of trading, 1998.

Bottom: one of the company's mortgage advertisements, 1999.

Baby James, a precocious child with an uncanny knowledge of financial affairs, who featured in Standard Life's television advertising in the late 1990s.

attracted £1.3 billion. This was followed by a 50-day notice account and together they were being used by 140,000 clients within the year.[107] There were also business savings accounts. Mortgages were introduced in January 1999 and by July Standard Life had captured over 17 per cent of new mortgage lending, outstripping such well-known names as the Halifax, Abbey National and Cheltenham & Gloucester. Spowart resigned in October and was replaced as managing director by Neil Ross. By November the bank had 250,000 customers with deposits of almost £3.8 billion and had completed £3.3 billion in mortgages.

BUILDING THE BRAND

The bank's impact was reinforced during 1998 by renewed brand building for the whole group under Tom King, now director of corporate affairs, through advertising in the media and the visibility of the senior executive team. Standard Life's view was that, in the future, companies which were perceived to be 'big' would take a greater share of the market as consumers made more investment decisions for themselves. The television campaign used as its central motif 'Baby James', who had an appetite for asking searching questions. New opportunities for sponsorship were explored where the Standard Life name would be evident in coverage worldwide. The flagship event was the annual Standard Life Loch Lomond golf tournament in July at the new Loch Lomond golf course in a beautiful setting across the water from Ben Lomond. The tournament

costs than the major players in the market as quickly as possible. With no branch network and a well-trained and motivated telesales force, Standard Life would have a clear competitive advantage given the reputation of its products and services with IFAs.[103]

A feasibility study was presented to the board in April 1997[104] and in a little over six months the Bank of England had given preliminary approval.[105] Standard Life Bank was launched on 1 January 1998. It was an instant success. Like its products, its logo (of a hand forming the shape of a telephone) was as simple as it was ingenious and quickly caught the public imagination.[106] The initial product was a direct access savings account which, by the end of its first year, had

The beautiful Loch Lomond course at Luss in Dumbartonshire. The club house, which is in the distance, was formerly Rossdhu House, the home of the Colqhouns of Luss. It is said that, to prove their manhood, members of Clan Macgregor had to swim across the loch from the promontory and climb Ben Lomond on the opposite shore. Today, competition is confined to the fairways and greens in one of the most beautiful locations in Scotland.

provided an excellent venue for corporate hospitality and reached a television audience in the United Kingdom and overseas of over a million viewers. In Canada the brand was supported through the now well-established Standard Life Marathon in Montreal and by increasing advertising on television and later in the press. Without continuing attention to the quality and level of service, such corporate promotion would have failed. The TCS programme, which was revisited in 1997 with further training and consultation, will be reviewed again in 2000.

CANADA

Fundamental to Scott Bell's vision of the future development of the group was the expansion of the Canadian branch which was experiencing equivalent deregulation of the market for financial services. Consultants, who had been retained to recommend a future organisational structure for the branch late in 1986, finally reported in 1988. As a result during the summer a managed matrix structure was adopted which it was anticipated would increase productivity, enhance the ability to implement corporate strategies, and flatten the management structure. The corporate structure was reorganised into two divisions under Alastair Fernie: operations, including marketing and product administration under Claude Garcia and corporate, including investment, accounts, and corporate administration under Roy Naudie.[108] This structure was abandoned within three years when Naudie retired and Garcia became chief operating officer

and executive vice-president. Unusually, Garcia had been recruited from outside Standard Life and had experience in government service and as a consulting actuary.

As part of the process of reorganisation and following the termination of the joint venture with Industrial Alliance, the balance of the shareholding in Standard Industrielle Alliance Services was acquired (see page 312) and its group life, accident and health insurance products integrated within the organisation. Most of the clients came to Standard Life.[109]

Already sales of both group and individual products had improved. During 1988 total premium income increased sharply. Individual sales were dominated by registered retirement savings plans (RRSP). Standard Life's registered retirement income fund (RRIF) had stolen a march on the competition when it was introduced in 1986. Simple, well administered and fully guaranteed, this product had quickly become popular with brokers and by 1988 was the acknowledged market leader. Money purchase defined contribution and group RRSP plans were gaining popularity over defined benefit pension schemes. Confidence in investment-linked products seemed at first to return more quickly in Canada than in the United Kingdom; Standard Life's ideal capital accumulator (ICA) enjoyed spectacular growth, with the bulk of sales to better-off customers.[110]

This performance was, however, not sustained in 1989 due to the monetary policy pursued by the Bank of Canada. Additionally demand for investment-linked products was hampered by a poor investment performance the previous year.[111]

Business recovered in 1990 with a sharp advance in premium income. The strongest demand was for group insurance and individual savings and retirement products, notably ICAs and RRIFs, allowing Standard Life to regain market share. Building on this success it was planned to expand sales further by transferring during 1991 the responsibility for the sale of individual money products to group offices in smaller cities.[112] At the same time, new computer software was rolled out to give better product and sales support to representatives and brokers. By the spring of that year, restructuring of the Canadian branch was complete, with an organisation aligned to the management of different product ranges and the appropriate technology in place.[113]

SOVEREIGN LIFE

The opportunity in October 1992 to acquire the sales force of the Calgary-based Sovereign Life provided an attractive alternative to recruiting a large number of new agents. Sovereign Life was in severe financial difficulties, a casualty of the recession and the recently introduced tougher regulatory environment.[114] It was not until May 1993 that Standard Life's bid was accepted on condition that the majority of the sales force joined the company.[115] By 1 July some 100 agents, sales and branch managers had been won over and early the following month the acquisition of the portfolio of life and annuity funds was completed. The former head office was converted into Standard Life's Calgary regional office with 75 staff to administer the acquired policies.[116]

The Canadian economy remained depressed throughout 1993, with high unemployment, stagnant disposable incomes and falling interest

Standard Life's Group Pension Office (Toronto) developed a group scheme for K-mart employees across Canada in 1989. Here, Bob Coyle of Standard Life (centre) is photographed with members of the K-mart workforce.

 rates all affecting insurance business. These adverse conditions accelerated the concentration and reconstructing of the whole financial services industry, leading to more intense competition and heightening customers' expectations. Despite the launch in January 1993 of four mutual funds, Standard Life's sales of individual annuity and savings products fell. This was offset by continued growth in the individual life market and by a sharp recovery in group pension sales and associated group life and health products.[117] The economic depression undermined the property market with many properties in the company's portfolio unlet at the end of the year and a growing number of foreclosures on those unable to meet their mortgage interest payments.[118]

QUALITY AND DIVERSIFICATION

In June 1993 Alastair Fernie retired as president, Canadian operations. He was succeeded by Claude Garcia whose first task was to grapple with the mounting tide of defaults on mortgages and consequent foreclosures, which reached a high-water mark two years later. Substantial provisions had to be made to cover the losses, but there were signs that the property market was recovering with a decline in the number of unlet premises. Standard Life's Canadian business was far more exposed to commercial mortgages than the rest of the industry since they represented nearly 60 per cent of the assets at the end of 1993. Garcia decided to increase the proportion of corporate bonds and private placements and gradually to reduce the share held by commercial mortgages. At the end of 1999, private placements represented 4 per cent of the assets in Canada, other bonds 34 per cent (as against 22 per cent in 1993) and commercial mortgages stood at 42 per cent.

At the same time Garcia and his team were active in shaping the business for the future. An important element of this strategy was the design and introduction of new individual life products to meet customers' needs, particularly 'Perspecta', a non-participating universal life policy offering guaranteed long-term insurance protection and tax-sheltered savings. As in the United Kingdom quality was paramount and a TCS programme was implemented in the autumn of 1994, which it was anticipated would significantly improve customer satisfaction.

With the market moving towards investment-linked products due to lower interest rates and younger less risk-averse savers, sales of the four mutual funds took off during 1994. As a result, six new mutual funds were added to the portfolio and in 1995 several third party fund arrangements were concluded with some of Canada's leading mutual fund managers allowing Standard Life to deal in their products.[119]

THE 'SLX' PRODUCT

A new range of group savings and retirement products, launched in May 1994, was well received. In 1992, the executive committee had

Confederation Square, on Ottawa's historic waterfront, which was restored and developed by Standard Life in 1994.

LIVE175 – STANDARD LIFE IN THE COMMUNITY

To mark its 175th anniversary in 2000, Standard Life launched an anniversary appeal in 1999 with the aim of generating up to £2 million for charities across the United Kingdom and Ireland. The company agreed to match pound for pound up to £1 million sums raised by staff taking part in all kinds of fund-raising events. The charities to benefit were in the general area of health and wellbeing, including the Standard Life Centre for Pregnancy, Wellbeing and Development at the new Edinburgh Royal Infirmary. The appeal built on the commitment of the staff and the company to the wider community over many years through work with charities, schools and colleges and other organisations. For almost the whole of its 175-year history members of staff have given of their time and expertise to voluntary activities, at first to the churches, hospitals, schools and the University of Edinburgh and then later to numerous charities.

Standard Life adopted its first co-ordinated community involvement policy in September 1992, focusing on health, homelessness, older people, education and training and the local environment. It was the first Scottish financial services company to adopt such a targeted policy. Staff were encouraged to become involved in charity work with appropriate paid time off and in some cases were seconded to specific projects of value to local communities and charitable organisations. By 1999 40 staff had been on secondment, spending time with such organisations as Children First, Edinburgh Cyrenians, and the Edinburgh and Lothians Council on Alcohol. By that time the Community Involvement Department had started to sponsor a number of events such as the Edinburgh International Science Festival, the Children's Classic Concerts and

Below left: the foyer of the Simpson Memorial Maternity Hospital which was refurbished in 1999.

Below right: Malcolm Russell of new business development spent time with underprivileged young people while he was on secondment at the Cyrenians Farm, November 1997.

Fred MacAulay and Shauna Lowry, the celebrity publicists of the Live175 appeal.

Right: The award-winning 'life: outlined'™ literature, giving customers unbiased and comprehensive information on key life events such as planning for retirement.

the Lothian & Borders Police Children's Road Safety Campaign.

Likewise, in Canada, Standard Life's employees earned a reputation for generosity through their direct involvement in fund-raising campaigns, particularly for health and education. The proceeds from the Montreal Marathon, which totalled over $4 million in 16 years, were donated to the city's two children's hospitals (Montreal Children's and Saint-Justine), and the Centre Hospitalier de l'Université Laval in Québec City. In 1992 Standard Life donated premises in its Vancouver office to the Red Cross for use as the Standard Life Blood Donor Clinic.

Since 1990 Standard Life has placed particular emphasis on education and training by raising the company's profile in centres of education and helping to improve the skills of those at school. This has been achieved through a spread of activities from mentoring at secondary schools in socially disadvantaged areas to running management training sessions at universities. Standard Life's engagement with education is widely respected

and by 2000 the company was in a position to influence education policy throughout the United Kingdom. In Canada Standard Life focused its support for education on universities where there was demand for long-term sponsorship of capital projects, renovation of physical plant, research programmes and specialised professorships.

decided to make a major investment to obtain a much greater share of the growing deferred contribution and group RRSP market. A new computer system based on client server technology, a first at the branch, was developed.[120] The newly introduced 'SLX' product, with state-of-the-art features, soon became popular with customers. Standard Life secured a number of large group pension plans as a result of product advantage, a strong investment performance and the growing reputation of the company's services.[121] Premium and deposits for this product rose from $250 million in 1995 to over $1.1 billion in 1999.

One of the principal reasons for this success was the creation of the Client Communication and Education Services (CCES) in November 1995. A larger number of pension plan sponsors were changing their pension arrangements from defined benefit plans to defined contributions or group RRSP schemes. This meant that the investment risk and the responsibility for investment decisions were transferred from the employer to the employee. CCES was created to take advantage of the opportunity to provide education to employees so that they could make informed investment decisions with some confidence. CCES offered seminars at the workplace to new members and telephone advice to them at all times.[122]

Market acceptance of the 'SLX' product was confirmed by a national survey among pension brokers and consultants conducted by Brendon Wood International, which rated Standard Life as the number one provider of group retirement services in both 1997 and 1999.[123]

1997 STRATEGIC REVIEW

A major strategic review in 1997 concluded that the Canadian operation should focus on two complementary but distinct activities – wealth management and managed care – aimed directly at higher income groups. The main objective in wealth management was to build assets under management through mutual funds, individual and group savings vehicles and individual life products. In managed care the aim was to achieve critical mass in the group life and health markets in which Standard Life then had less than a 2 per cent market share. To ensure the

The Canadian executive team in 1999 with (from left to right) Jean Guay, senior vice-president (customer services), Christian Martineau, senior vice-president (finance), Carole Briard, senior vice-president (information and technology), Claude Garcia, president, Canadian operations, Peter Hill, president, Standard Life Portfolio Management, Perla Kessous, senior vice-president (human resources and quality), Denis Lussier, senior vice-president (sales) and Alain Brunet, senior vice-president (marketing).

implementation of this new strategy, a significant reorganisation took place. The marketing division was split into a sales division and a new marketing division, which took responsibility for product development. The finance division became responsible for the property portfolio and for defining the investment mandate of the stock and bond portfolio. At the same time, partly in response to a revival of the separatist debate in Québec, it was decided to adopt a regional decentralised structure in an effort to strengthen the branch's presence in Ontario and Western Canada.[124]

Sales more than doubled during the next three years, with the balance shifting decidedly towards investment products. In 1996, 60 per cent of sales were in guaranteed income products whereas by 1999 two thirds were investment-linked. Four new segregated funds were launched under the 'Ideal Solutions' banner, providing customers with the right balance between the performance of investment funds and the security of guaranteed investments. Performa Financial Group Limited was created to deal in the 500 mutual funds offered through Standard Life to meet the needs of even the most sophisticated investor.

AN INVESTMENT SUBSIDIARY

Following the reorganisation in 1988, the investment department was strengthened with the introduction of new systems and disciplines, particularly a greater emphasis on research leading to better stock selection. When this was

An advertisement for the Canadian Standard Life Portfolio Management, 1999.

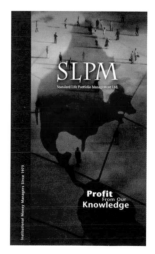

Year	United Kingdom £m	Canada £m	Ireland £m	Germany £m	Spain £m	Total £m
1988	711.2	290.5	70.3	-	-	1,072.0
1989	1,365.6	328.6	119.2	-	-	1,813.4
1990	1,242.9	412.1	100.1	-	-	1,755.1
1991	1,474.6	584.7	22.7	-	-	2,082.0
1992	1,729.5	615.9	24.6	-	-	2,370.0
1993	2,078.0	669.5	21.0	-	0.6	2,769.1
1994	2,094.4	501.8	31.5	-	4.9	2,632.6
1995	1,389.7	620.2	29.6	-	5.2	2,044.7
1996	2,008.4	630.7	109.1	4.8	8.0	2,761.0
1997	2,343.3	854.9	159.2	11.0	9.3	3,377.7
1998	2,602.3	804.8	157.9	13.5	11.9	3,590.4
1999	2,880.9	985.9	94.9	39.0	14.1	4,014.8

Note: abstracted from Standard Life archives

FIGURE 8.2
New premiums 1988–99

reflected in improved investment performance, attention shifted to marketing retail and wholesale investment services. Investment marketing specialists were hired in Montreal and Toronto. In addition, a new Euro-Pacific Equity Fund was launched, managed from Edinburgh but marketed by the Canadian organisation to local clients.[125] During the summer of 1997 Standard Life Portfolio Management (SLPM) was given a measure of independence to allow the investment activity to gain recognition as an independent fund manager. In November of the same year and to avoid duplication of effort, Sandy Crombie, who was head of investment operations in the UK, assumed overall responsibility for SLPM. Additionally the management of all United States assets was moved to Montreal and the Edinburgh US equity desk closed. Some £2 billion of assets were transferred to Canada, attracting favourable comment in the financial press.[126] On the launch of Standard Life Investments the following year SLPM became one of its major subsidiaries and will change its name to Standard Life Investments in 2001. In the two years since its formation, SLPM has become a significant player, winning an increasing proportion of the mandates for which it has been shortlisted and accumulating an impressive client list.

DISTRIBUTION STRATEGY FOR INDIVIDUAL BUSINESS

The life insurance product of choice in the Canadian individual financial planning and wealth management markets is 'Universal Life' because it offers the flexibility and investment choices which consumers demand. The sources of premium income for Universal Life in 1997 showed that more than 55 per cent of the premium income the top ten providers received came through general agents (GAs). In addition general agents were increasing their share of Standard Life's traditionally strong individual savings product line. It was therefore agreed that they must be included in any future distribution strategy for individual products if this segment of the market was to continue to be developed.

In 1999 a new structure was introduced with regional offices in Montreal, Ottawa, Toronto, Hamilton, Calgary, and Vancouver. The mandate of each regional office was to develop life insurance and money business from individual producers (including former IFS representatives and current brokers) and from GAs. They were also to service at a local level national accounts. To underpin this strategy, a new sales support centre was established to advise producers on an increasingly wide range of issues from technical product questions to specialised quotations. In addition, Tel Insurance (life insurance application by telephone) and Tel Invest (application for money business by telephone) were introduced to make it simpler to do business with Standard Life. Early indications are that this strategy will be successful since total new premiums in 1999 were significantly more than in the previous year.

In 1999 Canada exceeded its sales and performance targets and contributed some 25 per cent of the Standard Life Group's total new premium income (Figure 8.2 on page 360). This achievement was the result of the substantial investment made in the branch, particularly in new systems, over the last five years and of the success of the clear and focused strategies adopted in Canada in recent years.

REPUBLIC OF IRELAND

In 1988 Alan Ashe succeeded the legendary Bertie O'Hanlon as general manager for the Republic of Ireland. Between 1989 and 1993 the market there was more stable than that of either the United Kingdom or Canada. It was much less badly affected by the stockmarket crash of 1987 and as a result the confidence of investors did not suffer to the same extent. During 1988–89

sales of investment products were remarkable, with I£117.5 million of new money which represented growth of nearly 70 per cent.[127] This success was not sustained as new investors were deterred by the erratic performance of the stockmarket. In 1990 a new universal life plan was introduced.[128] The lack of an index-linked fund and a with-profits element hampered sales. During 1993 a government initiative to encourage savings by providing tax relief on special cash deposit accounts skewed the whole savings market away from life assurance products. Subsequent government action fell short of restoring a level playing field between competing savings vehicles.[129]

The Tower pension series (the Irish equivalent of the Castle plan) performed well. As in the United Kingdom endowment-mortgage business, in which Standard Life was the market leader, was depressed by high interest rates and increased competition following the entry of

This witty advertisement directed at the self-employed appeared on hoardings in the Republic of Ireland in January 1996.

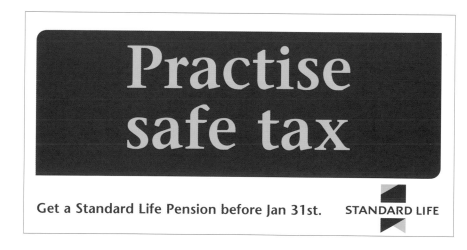

Practise safe tax

Get a Standard Life Pension before Jan 31st. STANDARD LIFE

Irish Life into the market during 1989.[130] With mounting press criticism of levels of commission, mis-selling and low standards, demand for this method of house purchase continued to fall away. During 1993 Standard Life mounted an extensive media campaign to put the opposing point of view in the debate but to little avail.[131] At that time the Irish branch was given a considerable degree of autonomy as part of international operations, allowing services and products to be tailored more precisely to the needs of the market, which now clearly differed from that of the United Kingdom. At first most processing was transferred from Edinburgh to Dublin and later product design and other functions followed.

Sales in Ireland were almost exclusively through intermediaries. Since the commission agreements still operated in Ireland, there was little advantage in intermediaries becoming tied agents.[132] However, with high interest rates and turmoil in the currency markets, demand was changing with a trend away from investment products, in which Standard Life was traditionally strong, towards protection policies and savings vehicles with a high guaranteed return. Efforts by the government to encourage thrift favoured the banks and building societies, and even when concessions were made to life offices these were not sufficiently attractive.

The recovery of the Irish economy from 1994 was impressive and saw an unprecedented rise in living standards over the next five years. Standard Life supported the Irish Insurance Federation's new agreement with the Irish Brokers Association. This restricted levels of commission on savings products in 1994 and introduced in 1995 greater disclosure of product terms and minimum standards of competency for sales personnel. Systems had already begun to be put in place to provide better support for customers through greater transparency in the terms of products. Over the next four years Standard Life doubled sales and outperformed its competitors. During 1998 key brokers were offered a higher level of attention and service as part of a strategy to enhance the image of the Standard Life brand.[133]

RETURN TO EUROPE

From the time he assumed office in 1988, Scott Bell was determined that Standard Life should actively seek to broaden its business base through diversification. He and his team recognised that, although operations would remain largely focused on the UK and Canadian markets, it would nonetheless be important in future to operate more diversely and in particular to seek to enter new and potentially profitable markets. This was of course clearly an available option for Standard Life, given its huge financial strength.

The advent of the European Community's life services directive facilitated entry into the European markets and extensive studies of the German, Dutch, Italian, French and Spanish markets were conducted.[134] Holland, Italy and France were discarded at the time because their markets were either overcrowded or culturally constrained.[135]* There was a clear preference to enter Spain and Germany. In the former case the market was relatively under-developed and very fragmented, with no foreign life company controlling more than 1.5 per cent of the market, thus providing the potential for acquisition. The choice of Germany was more predictable, with a large and relatively prosperous buying public providing the opportunity to market successfully well-designed equity backed products.[136]

SPAIN

In the spring of 1993 the company made its first European investment by the purchase of the small Spanish life office, Prosperity SA, which like Prime Health belonged to the troubled Municipal Mutual Insurance Group (MMI). Prosperity SA had been established in 1989 with a head office in Barcelona. The managing director, Tomas Soler, who had previously worked for Allianz-Ras, joined in 1990 and the company had commenced trading the following year. Prosperity's strategy was to sell through smaller agents who were willing to accept lower rates of commission. However, to survive they sold a wide range of products from a variety of companies. So as to broaden the business to be an all-round financial service provider, Prosperity Financial Services SA was set up in June

1991 to sell a range of UK investment-linked products, provided by Prosperity UK. Later in the year the life portfolio of Union de Mutuas Aseguradoras (UMA) was acquired. By 1993, with its head office still in Barcelona, Prosperity had some 20 branches spread throughout the country but the network was not yet complete. There were some 1,000 agents selling Prosperity products. In recent months sales had been adversely affected by the problems of MMI, which had been well publicised in Spain, and Prosperity SA urgently needed to find a new backer to restore confidence. The attraction for Standard Life was the quality of the management of Prosperity SA with its emphasis on simplicity of products and quality of service and the fact that as a relatively new company it had none of the problems of its older competitors.[137] Although it was not until 1998 that Prosperity SA became profitable, the growth in premium income was very encouraging (see Figure 8.2 on page 360). The Spanish market remained fragmented but the regulator was unofficially promoting mergers as many small companies were known to be struggling. Standard Life remained on the lookout for potential acquisitions, particularly a general company offering motor and home insurance and small business cover, both to establish critical mass and to increase its attractiveness to potential agents.[138]

---

* At the time the European market was concentrating rapidly around six key players, Allianz in Germany, Assicurazioni Generali in Italy, Axa and Compagnie UAP in France and Aegon and Internationale Nederlanden Groep (ING) in the Netherlands. By 1997 Axa and UAP had merged to form the largest insurance company in the world with assets of over $407 billion. Allianz was in third place with assets of $293 billion. Standard Life was ranked 27th with assets of $92 billion.

Torre Tarragona, the new head office in Barcelona for Prosperity SA, the Spanish arm of Standard Life, purchased in 1999.

GERMANY

During 1995 a distribution agreement was signed with Marschollek, Lautenschläger und Partner AG (MLP), the largest independent insurance broker in Germany. Founded in 1970 MLP concentrated sales to high-income professional groups.[139] Having obtained a licence to do business in Germany, Standard Life opened an office in Frankfurt in February 1996 with Bertram Valentin as general manager. During the year a number of new products designed specifically for the German market were introduced. As elsewhere in the world the market was changing, with new business volumes in traditional life products stagnating in favour of alternative, more flexible savings products. Financial services were also concentrating, rapidly blurring the distinction between banks, investment houses and insurance companies, as Germany's largest companies sought to become major European players after monetary union in 1999. In this environment MLP continued to develop a successful business, bundling many of its products under the title Vorsorgemanagement, to which Standard Life began to subscribe in April 1998.[140]

At the same time Standard Life began to raise awareness of its products more generally in Germany through an initial publicity campaign in three major economic and political magazines and by building relationships with brokers in an effort to broaden its distribution base. Business developed very quickly and in 1999, after just three years of operation, new business premiums amounted to some DM130 million (see Figure 8.2 on page 360). By this time the company was dealing with more than 900 brokers in Germany and Austria. Furthermore, towards the end of the year Standard Life was in discussions with a large potential partner with the prospect of quickly building an even greater presence in Germany through a joint-venture arrangement.[141]

INDIA

The company also investigated the possibility of re-entering the Indian market through a joint-venture arrangement with the Indian company Housing Development Finance Corporation (HDFC), the largest private-sector housing finance company in the developing world. The government had been pursuing a programme of economic reform and there was a prospect that private companies would be able to enter the insurance market. In the spring of 1995 the finance minister indicated that an insurance regulatory body would be set up and new insurance legislation introduced. Although 75 per cent of the population lived below the poverty line, there was a rapidly growing middle class with a very high savings ratio, accounting for some 25 per cent of GDP. The savings market was forecast to grow strongly, making it very attractive to western investors. Since life assurance accounted for only 4 per cent of savings, there was ample room for expansion providing products were kept simple. With 32,000 part-time brokers and some 300,000 borrowers and 200,000 depositors HDFC was

German marketing literature, 1999.

ideally placed to distribute Standard Life products. HDFC enjoyed a considerable reputation and was rated as one of India's few 'genuinely blue chip companies'. The company's standing was confirmed by Scott Bell during a visit when he met senior figures in the financial services sector, including the governor of the Reserve Bank of India and the chairman of the nationalised Life Insurance Corporation of India. While waiting for the necessary legislation, preparatory work was to be undertaken to research the needs of customers and to set up a new life assurance company.[142] Standard Life took a 5 per cent stake in HDFC when the joint venture was

Signing the joint-venture agreement with the Housing Development Finance Corporation of India in 1994, with (seated) Deepak Parekh, chairman of HDFC, and Scott Bell.

made public in the autumn of 1995.[143] Standard Life announced that it planned to operate in the country through a joint-venture company in conjunction with HDFC. It would contribute its expertise in customer service and product knowledge, while HDFC would provide its knowledge of the market, its strong brand, a branch network and its large customer base. A joint-venture asset-management company was set up with HDFC four years later in October 1999 (see page 334). In December, the Indian government opened the insurance market to foreign companies. Standard Life believed that the long-term potential offered by the Indian insurance market was enormous, and was determined to be one of the first foreign companies to enter the market.[144]

CHINA

Much the same thinking lay behind the decision in May 1995 to return to China. During the previous decade the country had enjoyed impressive growth rates and the indications were that it would be one of the world's leading economies in the coming century. Unlike India the savings market was small, but demand for life assurance was growing rapidly, satisfied largely by the nationalised People's Insurance Company of China (shortly afterwards renamed China Life). Two foreign companies were licensed to operate in the Shanghai insurance market, but the process of obtaining the necessary sanction was lengthy. Before an application could be made, a representative office had to be open in the country for at least two years. A representative office was prohibited from engaging in profit-making activities and was only allowed to undertake market research and develop contacts. Already 40 foreign companies had opened representative offices.[145] Encouraged by the regulatory authorities in Beijing that a request for an operating licence might be well received because of its mutual status, financial strength and reputation, Standard Life re-opened an office in Shanghai and appointed Robbie Knight as general manager (Pacific region) in April 1996.[146] The objective was to contribute to the development of the Chinese life assurance industry through the training of local personnel both in Shanghai and in Edinburgh. A second office was opened in Beijing in 1997. Efforts were made to build trust with key decision makers in the

The Novel building in Shanghai (third from left) which houses Standard Life's representative office in 1999. Standard Life has had a presence in China since 1847. At the end of the nineteenth century its office was on the waterfront at No. 2 Bund (left), next door to the French Embassy. The Standard Life branch in Shanghai closed in 1922, although business continued until after the Second World War.

Scott Bell signing the joint-venture agreement with Geoffrey Cohen, chairman of HIH, and Liu Ming Kang, chairman of China Everbright, in Hong Kong, December 1999.

government and the financial institutions.[147] In December 1999 an agreement was signed between HIH (Asia) Limited and China Everbright (CEL) to establish a joint venture in Hong Kong to offer term assurance and investment-linked savings policies. HIH (Asia) Limited is a subsidiary of HIH (Australia), the largest general insurer in that country, and CEL is the listed Hong Kong-based arm of China Everbright Holdings (CEHL), a state-owned investment company and one of the few Chinese corporations able to do business with foreign companies. It was anticipated that the experience of this joint venture would provide an excellent platform for eventual entry into the Chinese market.[148]

EPILOGUE

Looking back over 175 years Standard Life achieved its dominant position in the life assurance industry as a result of good judgement and far-sighted management. In its early years under William Thomas Thomson the company grew more rapidly than its competitors, largely by acquisition and the adventurous entry into overseas markets through the establishment of Colonial Life. This advantage was squandered in ill-considered and headlong expansion overseas in the late nineteenth century, which almost brought the business to its knees in 1904. Thereafter Leonard Dickson courageously saved the business, re-established its financial strength and developed a clear strategy for future development. His ambition to extend into

The senior executive team in 1999 with (seated) Jim Stretton, chief executive (UK operations), Scott Bell, group managing director, and Iain Lumsden, group finance director, and (standing) from left to right Sandy Skinner, general manager (international), Alan Maxwell, group audit and compliance manager, Norrie Arthur, general manager (sales), Mike Hall, managing director, Standard Life Healthcare, Alan Forbes, general manager (customer services), Sandy Crombie, chief executive, Standard Life Investments, Neil Ross, managing director, Standard Life Bank, John Hylands, general manager (marketing), Marcia Campbell, general manager (corporate services) and secretary, Norrie Macleod, general manager (personnel), and Shaun Doherty, general manager (information systems).

general insurance was thwarted by his untimely death. Next, Steuart Macnaghten converted Standard Life into a mutual office, invested in equities and completed the withdrawal from unpromising overseas markets. Andrew Davidson brought new rigour to the control of the branches and developed the very profitable pension business. Under him Standard Life became for the first time the largest Scottish life office and the largest mutual life assurance company in the United Kingdom. During the next forty years a succession of managers built on these achievements and consolidated Standard Life's position as a leading life office. Without their contributions, the company would not have had the size or the resources to refocus its corporate objectives in the last decade of the twentieth century.

Since 1988 under the leadership of Scott Bell and his executive team the business has been transformed, with a well-developed corporate strategy, mirroring that put in place by Dickson eighty years before. As in his time, preserving Standard Life's financial strength under Scott Bell's leadership has been a central objective, so that by its 175th anniversary the Standard Life group could claim to be among the strongest financial institutions in the world and one of the few life offices with a triple A credit rating from both Moody's and Standard and Poor's.

With its very significant presence, influence and reputation in the UK life and pensions marketplace, the company is well positioned to increase its share of the financial services market in the years ahead. In addition, the launch of Standard Life Bank in 1998 was an outstanding success, winning a large share of the market for deposit banking and the outlook for Standard Life Investments, formed in 1999, is encouraging. Substantial investments have been made in Canada and Ireland, allowing those branch operations with their increased autonomy to expand strongly. Standard Life has returned to mainland Europe and has prepared to re-establish branches in India and China. Throughout the group, management has become much more participative with everyone within the company having a clear sense of the objectives and performance criteria. Standard Life as a brand, with its distinctive blue and gold livery, has been well established in the minds of customers in the company's major markets, respected for excellent returns and quality service. Testimony to the scale of this success was the growth of Standard Life's assets under management from £15 billion in 1988 to some £78 billion in 1999. The key to all these achievements lay in the clarity of the vision and common sense of purpose of Scott Bell and his executives. Although medium sized by European standards, there is a determination that Standard Life will continue to expand and diversify from within its own resources and it looks to the future with great confidence. Scott Bell is a worthy successor to William Thomas Thomson, the founding father of Standard Life, to Leonard Dickson, its saviour, and to Andrew Davidson, the mother of the modern company.

INVENTIONS	WORLD EVENTS
Morse Code invented	The Reform Act
	Victoria became Queen
	Irish Famine (1845–48)
	Repeal of the Corn Laws
Joseph Lister introduced antiseptic surgery	American Civil War (1861–65)
Alexander Graham Bell invented the telephone	
Swan and Eddison invented the electric light bulb	Economic crisis, collapse of the City of Glasgow Bank
Waterman invented the fountain pen	
Judson invented the zip fastener	
Vaaler invented paper clips	Boxer Rebellion in China
	Edward VII became King

DATE	STANDARD LIFE
1903	
1904	Office opened in Barcelona
1905	Bonus passed
1909	
1910	First group pension scheme
1914–18	
1920	Vickers group pension scheme; Spanish branch closed to new business
1922	Shanghai branch closed
1924	Hungarian branch closed to new business
1925	Mutualisation
1928	
1929	South African branch closed to new business
1930	Egyptian branch closed to new business
1934	Heritable Securities and Mortgage Investment Association Ltd acquired
1936	
1937	Business in China ceased
1938	Indian branch closed to new business
1939–45	
1941	London office bombed during the Blitz
1952	South African business transferred to the South African Life Assurance Co.
1966	Insurope established
1968	New business in Uruguay ceased
1973	Business in Jamaica transferred to Jamaica Mutual
1979	Unit-linked products launched
1986	Launch of Unit Trusts
1988	Financial Services Act
1993	Prosperity SA acquired
1994	Prime Health acquired
1995	Joint venture in India
1996	Offices opened in Frankfurt and Shanghai
1997	Standard Life Bank formed; Beijing office opened
1998	Standard Life Investments launched
1999	Indian market opened; joint venture signed in Hong Kong

INVENTIONS	WORLD EVENTS
Wright brothers' first flight	
	Russo-Japanese war
Bleriot made the first flight across the English Channel	Old-age pensions introduced in Britain
	George V became King
	First World War
'2LO' first radio station	
John Logie Baird invented television	
Fleming discovered penicillin	Women in Britain got the vote
	World economic slump
Cats' eyes invented	Launch of the *Queen Mary*, signalling the end of the recession
	Edward VIII became King, and abdicated George VI became King
	Second World War
	Elizabeth II became Queen
	Martin Luther King shot
	Pensions Act
	CAMIFA coined the term Independent Financial Adviser
	Gulf War
	Scottish Parliament re-established

APPENDIX 1: ANNUAL REVENUE (£s) 1844–1970

Abstracted from Standard Life archives. Retail price index has been used for all rebased figures.

Year	Annual Revenue	Annual Revenue Rebased to 1844	Year	Annual Revenue	Annual Revenue Rebased to 1844	Year	Annual Revenue	Annual Revenue Rebased to 1844
1844	60,000	60,000	1887	915,925	1,145,834	1930	2,861,223	1,946,755
1845	103,371	100,641	1888	929,939	1,129,081	1931	3,492,000	2,488,307
1846	120,816	113,932	1889	974,948	1,165,412	1932	3,853,000	2,841,543
1847	131,317	110,019	1890	991,957	1,186,891	1933	3,364,000	2,480,911
1848	136,130	134,965	1891	1,006,720	1,163,990	1934	3,194,000	2,339,178
1849	145,838	160,047	1892	1,022,610	1,250,194	1935	3,529,000	2,531,776
1850	169,152	186,642	1893	1,036,672	1,289,062	1936	3,304,000	2,307,569
1851	180,177	207,546	1894	1,055,992	1,395,945	1937	3,638,000	2,397,917
1852	192,929	215,142	1895	1,119,108	1,525,050	1938	3,916,513	2,647,682
1853	205,035	191,896	1896	1,093,884	1,532,924	1939	4,081,494	2,488,078
1854	218,969	183,624	1897	1,123,013	1,540,563	1940	4,382,387	2,370,103
1855	237,410	199,088	1898	1,168,368	1,549,469	1941	4,096,777	2,149,499
1856	254,484	215,127	1899	1,198,171	1,606,228	1942	4,452,898	2,348,032
1857	265,370	219,031	1900	1,242,518	1,562,313	1943	4,647,307	2,462,857
1858	275,990	260,632	1901	1,313,795	1,682,749	1944	4,995,625	2,621,106
1859	289,232	263,637	1902	1,339,962	1,714,487	1945	5,637,852	2,928,930
1860	304,162	265,693	1903	1,390,196	1,762,342	1946	7,022,518	3,630,394
1861	314,498	286,667	1904	1,431,234	1,806,953	1947	10,356,372	5,173,316
1862	322,897	282,058	1905	1,464,777	1,825,066	1948	12,860,286	6,129,416
1863	336,960	291,911	1906	1,494,125	1,786,014	1949	14,803,284	6,805,728
1864	437,380	385,275	1907	1,513,962	1,790,676	1950	16,760,803	7,506,405
1865	661,195	592,380	1908	1,511,849	1,805,454	1951	17,986,753	7,187,941
1866	675,267	589,862	1909	1,522,248	1,768,325	1952	20,814,002	7,835,587
1867	693,895	616,408	1910	1,541,812	1,746,731	1953	23,218,463	8,615,896
1868	703,451	641,199	1911	1,555,245	1,714,796	1954	26,503,979	9,495,938
1869	710,429	695,974	1912	1,580,506	1,688,425	1955	29,637,632	9,998,105
1870	720,199	686,304	1913	1,598,758	1,691,838	1956	33,951,119	11,149,029
1871	729,969	665,371	1914	1,591,071	1,525,416	1957	40,546,066	12,724,041
1872	700,609	596,386	1915	1,561,649	1,317,541	1958	42,220,533	13,009,049
1873	724,301	589,360	1916	1,560,287	997,268	1959	47,395,209	14,603,478
1874	733,112	616,832	1917	1,588,206	905,370	1960	55,057,280	16,661,938
1875	769,943	677,813	1918	1,670,913	800,982	1961	61,968,757	17,968,820
1876	770,249	694,404	1919	1,663,196	779,564	1962	67,107,115	18,956,528
1877	787,688	693,435	1920	1,746,527	684,722	1963	73,479,517	20,378,130
1878	806,910	760,749	1921	1,682,470	891,631	1964	80,643,151	21,340,790
1879	796,460	787,540	1922	1,710,876	1,002,391	1965	89,462,953	22,658,087
1880	809,995	776,090	1923	1,756,807	1,046,748	1966	91,667,614	22,392,215
1881	838,467	818,598	1924	1,934,839	1,127,347	1967	103,455,638	24,667,058
1882	876,893	848,741	1925	2,158,715	1,286,215	1968	117,312,072	26,402,408
1883	870,082	854,187	1926	2,194,892	1,293,158	1969	127,728,606	27,463,425
1884	883,884	957,478	1927	2,409,923	1,503,861	1970	147,121,200	29,320,613
1885	897,870	1,037,165	1928	2,559,614	1,606,779			
1886	904,757	1,107,208	1929	2,579,638	1,629,047			

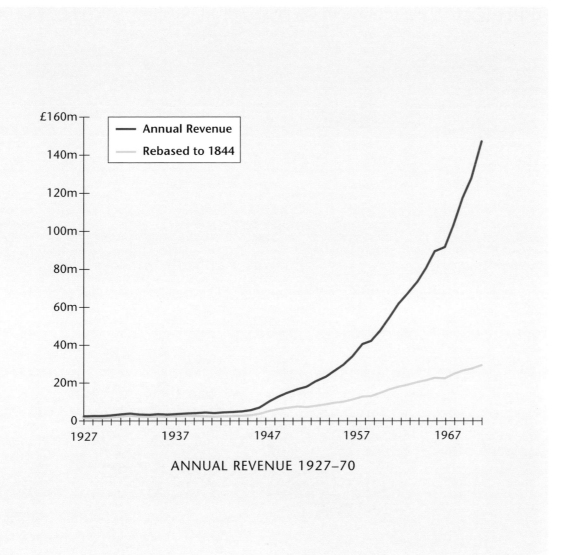

ANNUAL REVENUE 1927–70

APPENDIX 2: NEW LIFE ASSURANCE BUSINESS (£s) 1825–1970

Abstracted from Standard Life archives. Retail price index has been used for all rebased figures.

Year	Total	Total Rebased to 1825	Year	Total	Total Rebased to 1825	Year	Total	Total Rebased to 1825
1825	12,099	12,099	1843	348,136	493,593	1861	503,854	639,914
1826	36,190	40,895	1844	387,381	539,754	1862	506,120	616,007
1827	28,475	32,404	1845	446,027	605,055	1863	643,960	777,298
1828	57,009	66,826	1846	368,679	484,427	1864	805,980	989,217
1829	45,763	53,979	1847	443,578	517,813	1865	974,194	1,216,113
1830	35,322	42,237	1848	395,865	546,854	1866	1,190,282	1,448,713
1831	40,920	48,520	1849	429,372	656,549	1867	1,127,520	1,395,584
1832	80,890	99,897	1850	509,148	782,771	1868	1,104,265	1,402,458
1833	75,501	96,294	1851	467,499	750,333	1869	1,110,347	1,515,614
1834	44,260	57,819	1852	455,799	708,206	1870	1,181,399	1,568,621
1835	92,116	123,184	1853	455,249	593,670	1871	1,041,097	1,322,232
1836	92,762	110,106	1854	515,117	601,880	1872	1,190,453	1,411,957
1837	81,446	97,597	1855	609,323	711,953	1873	1,218,619	1,381,614
1838	112,084	129,504	1856	516,351	608,188	1874	1,088,666	1,276,288
1839	213,153	230,933	1857	574,839	661,084	1875	1,509,528	1,851,613
1840	163,079	179,784	1858	507,522	667,800	1876	1,176,096	1,477,344
1841	196,667	227,465	1859	510,845	648,792			
1842	252,411	321,199	1860	705,897	859,160			

Year	LIFE			PENSIONS				
	Home	Overseas	Total	Home	Overseas	Total	Total	Total Rebased to 1825
1880	815,304	450,763	1,266,067				1,266,067	1,690,222
1881	743,609	510,235	1,253,844				1,253,844	1,705,633
1882	794,150	591,521	1,385,671				1,385,671	1,868,728
1883	674,211	537,676	1,211,887				1,211,887	1,657,724
1884	612,593	553,524	1,166,117				1,166,177	1,760,082
1885	680,559	535,073	1,215,632				1,215,632	1,956,564
1886	540,309	583,560	1,123,869				1,123,689	1,916,330
1887	653,546	596,867	1,250,413				1,250,413	2,179,579
1888	679,765	708,729	1,388,494				1,388,494	2,348,941
1889	685,204	662,587	1,347,791				1,347,791	2,244,801
1890	792,236	747,944	1,540,180				1,540,180	2,567,716
1891	779,265	688,299	1,467,564				1,467,564	2,364,259
1892	836,173	855,258	1,691,431				1,691,431	2,881,238
1893	811,897	826,433	1,638,330				1,638,330	2,838,515
1894	724,375	984,620	1,708,995				1,708,995	3,147,790
1895	727,660	1,128,815	1,856,475				1,856,475	3,524,996
1896	692,036	1,001,415	1,693,451				1,693,451	3,306,583
1897	649,727	1,104,696	1,754,423				1,754,423	3,353,408
1898	701,969	1,236,429	1,938,398				1,938,398	3,581,819
1899	626,028	1,504,155	2,130,183				2,130,183	3,978,897
1900	582,812	1,440,972	2,023,784				2,023,784	3,545,576
1901	622,881	1,301,366	1,924,247				1,924,247	3,434,076
1902	809,607	1,396,234	2,205,841				2,205,841	3,932,542
1903	767,828	1,560,351	2,328,179				2,328,179	4,122,331
1904	749,951	1,564,439	2,314,390				2,314,390	4,071,272
1905	679,446	1,679,709	2,359,155				2,359,155	4,095,632
1906	550,245	1,730,407	2,280,652				2,280,652	3,798,519
1907	564,225	1,436,724	2,000,949				2,000,949	3,297,581
1908	582,345	1,259,601	1,841,946				1,841,946	3,064,872
1909	519,757	1,434,666	1,954,423				1,954,423	3,163,389
1910	531,682	1,318,962	1,850,664				1,850,644	2,921,292
1911	500,354	1,431,414	1,931,768				1,931,768	2,967,741
1912	582,000	1,470,218	2,052,218				2,052,218	3,054,685
1913	682,400	1,506,924	2,189,324				2,189,324	3,228,074
1914	586,126	1,127,520	1,713,646				1,713,646	2,289,166
1915	400,767	649,326	1,050,093				1,050,093	1,234,428
1916	601,605	479,921	1,081,526				1,081,526	963,168
1917	527,880	375,369	903,249				903,249	717,438
1918	684,781	485,624	1,170,405				1,170,405	781,740
1919	1,098,636	861,197	1,959,833				1,959,833	1,279,926
1920	1,203,681	1,307,116	2,510,797				2,510,797	1,371,538
1921	900,868	1,133,963	2,034,831				2,034,831	1,502,532
1922	905,567	1,117,928	2,023,495				2,023,495	1,651,878
1923	861,992	1,115,105	1,977,097				1,977,097	1,641,359
1924	969,813	1,044,246	2,014,059				2,014,059	1,635,092
1925	1,075,892	902,875	1,978,767				1,978,767	1,642,745

	LIFE			PENSIONS				
Year	Home	Overseas	Total	Home	Overseas	Total	Total	Total Rebased to 1825
1926	1,213,056	1,029,144	2,242,200				2,242,200	1,840,645
1927	1,649,203	1,351,637	3,000,840				3,000,840	2,609,184
1928	1,705,527	1,284,239	2,989,766				2,989,766	2,615,027
1929	1,541,778	1,258,693	2,800,471				2,800,417	2,464,128
1930	1,855,191	1,198,999	3,084,190			57,011	3,141,201	2,977,918
1931	1,525,623	976,075	2,501,698			262,294	2,763,992	2,744,251
1932	1,892,741	835,839	2,728,580			86,168	2,814,748	2,892,359
1933	2,169,967	1,020,038	3,190,005			350,544	3,540,549	3,638,172
1934	2,420,734	1,067,961	3,488,695			1,760,627	5,249,322	5,356,596
1935	2,619,353	1,291,255	3,910,608			468,672	4,379,280	4,377,577
1936	2,585,489	1,488,557	4,074,046			502,030	4,576,076	4,453,129
1937	2,932,374	1,408,800	4,341,174			788,800	5,129,974	4,711,335
1938	3,101,371	1,548,168	4,649,539			1,816,720	6,466,259	6,090,834
1939	2,548,613	1,123,645	3,672,258			358,150	4,030,408	3,423,350
1940	1,332,854	814,959	2,147,813			97,100	2,244,913	1,691,662
1941	1,217,417	769,365	1,986,782			17,850	2,004,632	1,465,504
1942	1,613,297	1,043,685	2,656,982			344,050	3,001,032	2,204,902
1943	1,741,294	1,106,695	2,847,989			694,250	3,542,239	2,615,611
1944	1,591,935	1,289,034	2,880,969			224,500	3,105,469	2,270,280
1945	1,899,894	1,079,679	2,979,573			970,275	3,949,848	2,859,125
1946	4,035,644	1,545,174	5,580,818			3,115,515	8,696,333	6,264,039
1947	7,401,052	2,225,921	9,626,973	6,666,953	151,261	6,818,214	16,445,187	11,446,102
1948	8,100,246	2,391,380	10,491,626	8,007,860	83,002	8,090,882	18,582,508	12,340,428
1949	8,877,431	3,803,805	12,681,236	9,169,116	362,643	9,531,759	22,212,995	14,229,218
1950	10,041,683	4,530,647	14,572,330	8,528,376	284,209	8,812,585	23,384,915	14,592,523
1951	11,054,239	5,342,427	16,396,666	11,021,698	1,432,492	12,454,190	28,850,856	16,064,523
1952	13,587,093	6,173,551	19,760,644	13,780,333	508,429	14,288,762	34,049,406	17,860,059
1953	10,141,534	8,126,848	18,268,382	14,306,966	3,025,593	17,332,559	35,600,941	18,407,121
1954	12,726,895	10,166,260	22,893,155	15,636,345	1,047,068	16,683,413	39,576,568	19,757,060
1955	15,448,578	12,808,706	28,257,284	17,213,977	844,797	18,058,774	46,316,058	21,770,240
1956	15,452,685	16,722,525	32,175,210	20,234,459	2,055,762	22,290,221	54,465,431	24,920,761
1957	16,364,297	20,601,398	36,965,695	23,516,491	2,602,086	26,118,577	63,084,272	27,583,848
1958	19,863,647	26,339,067	46,202,714	30,100,231	6,754,827	36,855,058	83,057,772	35,658,209
1959	21,734,953	33,385,998	55,120,951	29,137,944	4,088,174	33,226,118	88,347,069	37,929,001
1960	28,333,012	37,405,882	65,738,894	25,832,689	9,457,192	35,289,881	101,028,775	42,600,360
1961	35,280,724	39,518,856	74,799,580	36,675,642	6,782,743	43,458,385	118,257,965	47,778,727
1962	41,702,506	41,587,555	83,290,061	60,964,618	5,214,665	66,179,283	149,469,344	58,830,124
1963	56,974,373	46,485,477	103,459,850	47,864,422	5,786,756	53,651,178	157,111,028	60,710,262
1964	71,291,232	52,254,787	123,546,019	64,140,391	24,885,897	89,026,288	212,572,307	78,380,332
1965	83,341,662	55,739,306	139,080,968	67,556,531	14,052,679	81,609,210	220,690,178	77,879,012
1966	108,390,936	56,789,766	165,180,702	79,067,511	15,535,061	94,602,572	259,783,274	88,419,840
1967	136,018,107	67,748,175	203,766,282	100,129,476	21,439,720	121,569,196	325,335,478	108,081,666
1968	171,771,830	83,994,799	255,766,629	147,542,637	17,532,727	165,075,364	420,841,993	131,970,634
1969	211,688,695	87,786,779	299,475,474	147,865,315	27,920,989	175,786,304	475,261,778	142,382,569
1970	271,459,455	98,872,985	370,332,440	129,349,852	40,546,086	169,895,938	540,228,378	150,014,277

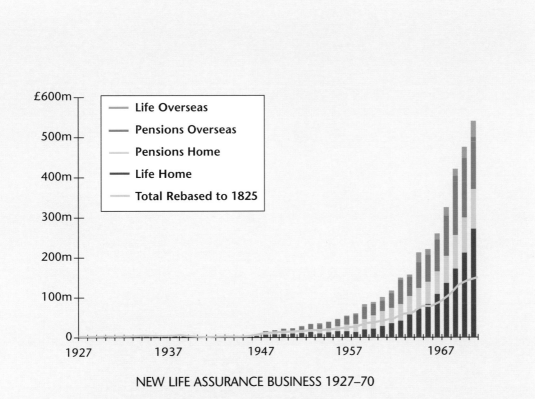

£600m

500m

400m

300m

200m

100m

0

1927   1937   1947   1957   1967

— Life Overseas
— Pensions Overseas
— Pensions Home
— Life Home
— Total Rebased to 1825

NEW LIFE ASSURANCE BUSINESS 1927–70

APPENDIX 3: PREMIUM INCOME (£s) 1927–70

Abstracted from Standard Life archives. Retail price index has been used for all rebased figures.

Year	Life	Pensions	Total	Total Rebased to 1927
1927	1,109,414	42,860	1,152,274	1,152,274
1928	1,119,851	47,004	1,166,855	1,173,800
1929	1,054,421	53,810	1,108,231	1,121,504
1930	1,165,220	66,531	1,231,751	1,343,006
1931	1,099,146	88,627	1,187,773	1,356,309
1932	1,135,845	98,797	1,234,642	1,459,123
1933	1,154,852	116,807	1,271,659	1,502,870
1934	1,250,275	222,863	1,473,138	1,728,889
1935	1,334,097	329,299	1,633,396	1,912,339
1936	1,400,342	384,024	1,784,366	1,977,073
1937	1,550,519	465,374	2,015,893	2,129,288
1938	1,699,310	677,385	2,346,695	2,542,251
1939	1,763,044	779,169	2,542,213	2,483,432
1940	1,747,993	821,698	2,569,691	2,227,065
1941	1,657,644	830,336	2,487,980	2,091,882
1942	1,705,849	896,404	2,602,253	2,198,904
1943	1,760,028	1,033,818	2,793,846	2,372,662
1944	1,804,222	1,281,779	3,086,001	2,594,695
1945	1,869,098	1,525,275	3,394,373	2,825,858
1946	2,076,593	2,337,888	4,414,481	3,657,093
1947	2,436,477	3,470,953	5,907,430	4,728,849
1948	2,848,331	4,646,886	7,495,217	5,724,640
1949	3,242,372	6,375,632	9,618,004	7,085,931
1950	3,905,661	7,351,583	11,257,244	8,079,133
1951	4,522,875	8,372,361	12,895,236	8,258,031
1952	5,331,036	10,174,592	15,505,628	9,354,074
1953	5,866,917	11,706,675	17,573,592	10,450,161
1954	6,460,305	13,472,629	19,932,934	11,444,412
1955	7,166,354	14,650,186	21,816,540	11,793,849
1956	7,805,094	16,463,398	24,268,492	12,770,892
1957	8,585,150	17,876,222	26,461,372	13,307,123
1958	9,438,274	20,373,397	29,811,671	14,719,859
1959	10,254,180	22,584,630	32,838,810	16,214,544
1960	11,310,997	24,268,322	35,579,319	17,254,560
1961	12,414,216	26,746,493	39,160,709	18,196,707
1962	13,334,474	28,461,343	41,795,817	18,919,887
1963	14,767,221	30,817,379	45,584,600	20,258,704
1964	16,088,135	32,517,486	48,605,621	20,612,230
1965	18,263,449	35,671,933	53,935,382	21,890,177
1966	20,157,513	33,844,620	54,002,133	21,139,151
1967	22,335,081	37,090,847	59,425,928	22,705,687
1968	26,224,485	39,931,489	66,155,974	23,859,722
1969	29,545,669	42,295,246	71,840,915	24,753,343
1970	34,267,906	45,263,737	79,531,643	25,399,972

Note: The figures are annual premiums.

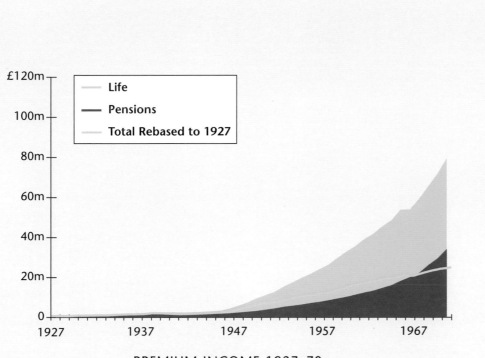

£120m

100m

80m

60m

40m

20m

0

— Life
— Pensions
— Total Rebased to 1927

1927   1937   1947   1957   1967

PREMIUM INCOME 1927–70

APPENDIX 4: PREMIUM INCOME (£m) 1970–99

Abstracted from Standard Life archives. Retail price index has been used for all rebased figures.

Year	Total	Total Rebased to 1970	Year	Total	Total Rebased to 1970	Year	Total	Total Rebased to 1970
1970	91	91	1980	386	106	1990	3,051	450
1971	106	97	1981	463	113	1991	3,327	470
1972	130	111	1982	525	122	1992	3,876	534
1973	111	86	1983	660	146	1993	4,829	652
1974	132	85	1984	867	183	1994	4,240	557
1975	166	86	1985	1,104	220	1995	3,772	480
1976	204	92	1986	1,307	251	1996	4,280	531
1977	216	87	1987	1,627	302	1997	4,832	579
1978	252	93	1988	1,822	317	1998	4,959	578
1979	296	93	1989	2,880	465	1999	5,600	646

Note: Total includes annual and single premiums. Figures for 1999 are estimates.

APPENDIX 5: NEW BUSINESS (£m) 1970–99

Abstracted from Standard Life archives. Retail price index has been used for all rebased figures.

Year	Premiums	Total Rebased to 1970	Year	Premiums	Total Rebased to 1970	Year	Premiums	Total Rebased to 1970
1970	22	22	1980	124	34	1990	1,755	259
1971	23	21	1981	158	39	1991	2,082	294
1972	41	35	1982	130	30	1992	2,370	326
1973	33	25	1983	242	53	1993	2,769	374
1974	39	25	1984	382	81	1994	2,633	346
1975	55	28	1985	556	111	1995	2,045	260
1976	77	35	1986	923	178	1996	2,761	343
1977	84	34	1987	1,029	191	1997	3,378	405
1978	90	33	1988	1,072	186	1998	3,590	418
1979	109	34	1989	1,813	292	1999	4,015	464

Note: From 1986 the figures include the whole group's business. Figures for 1999 are estimates.

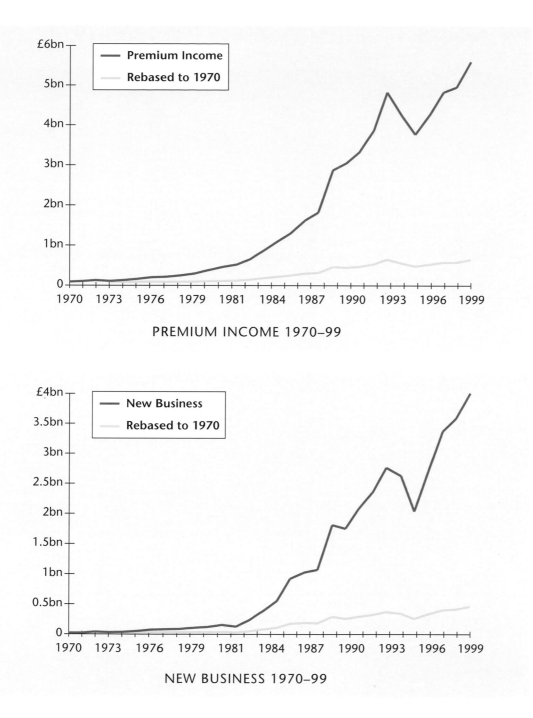

PREMIUM INCOME 1970–99

NEW BUSINESS 1970–99

APPENDIX 6: LONG-TERM ASSETS (£s) 1869–1970

Abstracted from Standard Life archives. Retail price index has been used for all rebased figures.

Year	Gifts & UK Municipal	%	Foreign Government	%	Debenture & Preference	%	Ordinary	%	UK Mortgages	%	Overseas Mortgages	%	Property	%	Cash & Loans	%	Total	Total Rebased to 1825
1869	57,933	1.5	49,069	1.3	277,349	7.2	24,154	0.6	2,632,336	68.6	36,742	1.0	353,703	9.2	407,332	10.6	3,838,618	5,239,682
1870	79,060	1.8	72,630	1.6	225,495	5.1	28,032	0.6	2,769,730	62.1	35,816	0.8	918,230	20.6	333,815	7.5	4,462,808	5,925,564
1871	75,961	1.9	89,193	2.2	152,109	3.8	28,032	0.7	2,913,691	72.1	38,877	1.0	334,901	8.3	408,483	10.1	4,041,247	5,132,536
1872	45,486	1.1	191,967	4.8	218,688	5.4	28,032	0.7	3,062,096	75.9	38,877	1.0	164,808	4.1	286,518	7.1	4,036,472	4,787,526
1873	42,976	1.0	188,905	4.3	246,521	5.7	28,032	0.6	3,273,444	75.1	43,367	1.0	167,214	3.8	368,386	8.5	4,358,845	4,941,856
1874	41,169	0.9	157,126	3.3	91,509	1.9	34,083	0.7	3,595,344	75.6	81,311	1.7	207,017	4.4	548,282	11.5	4,755,841	5,575,467
1875	41,169	0.9	157,126	3.3	91,779	1.9	34,803	0.7	3,595,344	75.8	81,311	1.7	146,272	3.1	592,277	12.5	4,740,081	5,814,264
1876	39,991	0.8	215,416	4.4	50,636	1.0	35,571	0.7	3,821,029	78.2	80,777	1.7	179,768	3.7	465,311	9.5	4,888,499	6,140,650
1877	39,510	0.8	237,524	4.7	50,334	1.0	35,571	0.7	4,028,434	79.5	78,118	1.5	180,263	3.6	419,205	8.3	5,068,959	6,217,671
1878	39,185	0.8	273,143	5.3	50,000	1.0	38,215	0.7	4,075,276	79.4	86,587	1.7	180,815	3.5	391,348	7.6	5,134,569	6,744,937
1879	39,067	0.7	222,535	4.3	50,000	1.0	38,215	0.7	4,096,411	78.2	187,398	3.6	183,641	3.5	418,482	8.0	5,235,749	7,213,476
1880	38,242	0.7	286,993	5.2	36,059	1.0	36,059	0.7	4,077,396	73.6	221,048	4.0	205,446	3.7	640,064	11.6	5,541,307	7,397,742
1881	38,217	0.7	319,375	5.7	47,680	0.8	47,680	0.8	4,052,273	72.1	269,868	4.8	191,760	3.4	650,683	11.6	5,617,536	7,641,663
1882	38,217	0.7	381,669	6.6	44,060	0.8	92,388	1.6	4,017,524	69.6	282,231	4.9	196,953	3.4	717,077	12.4	5,770,119	7,781,631
1883	38,217	0.6	429,349	7.2	118,733	2.0	92,388	1.5	3,896,565	65.3	388,984	6.5	257,980	4.3	747,379	12.5	5,969,595	8,165,728
1884	38,217	0.6	514,268	8.3	193,894	3.1	92,388	1.5	3,844,139	62.1	456,867	7.4	287,600	4.6	758,401	12.3	6,185,774	9,336,516
1885	39,810	0.6	641,575	10.2	110,827	1.8	60,265	1.0	3,914,561	62.4	505,075	8.1	306,612	4.9	693,991	11.1	6,272,716	10,095,957
1886	39,810	0.6	632,542	9.4	461,974	6.9	22,884	0.3	3,874,587	57.5	693,085	10.3	314,287	4.7	699,223	10.4	6,738,392	11,489,759
1887	39,810	0.6	717,756	11.1	156,531	2.4	22,884	0.4	3,645,044	56.3	776,143	12.0	317,607	4.9	795,345	12.3	6,471,120	11,279,729
1888	39,779	0.6	770,883	11.6	166,729	2.5	22,884	0.3	3,528,231	53.1	928,219	14.0	364,512	5.5	819,594	12.3	6,640,831	11,234,419
1889	39,779	0.6	786,180	11.3	197,499	2.8	20,898	0.3	3,524,832	50.5	1,082,495	15.5	407,378	5.8	917,070	13.1	6,976,131	11,619,032
1890	37,790	0.5	860,459	12.1	208,365	2.9	26,253	0.4	3,341,143	47.0	1,279,530	18.0	467,041	6.6	894,682	12.6	7,115,263	11,862,234
1891	37,790	0.5	851,464	11.6	158,926	2.2	12,641	0.2	3,311,497	45.0	1,495,880	20.3	584,274	7.9	900,028	12.2	7,352,500	11,844,943
1892	26,032	0.4	873,552	11.9	151,784	2.1	12,641	0.2	3,219,909	43.7	1,699,864	23.1	607,717	8.3	774,183	10.5	7,365,682	12,546,940
1893	26,032	0.3	903,104	12.1	179,916	2.4	12,641	0.2	2,941,208	39.3	1,927,999	25.8	620,759	8.3	863,543	11.6	7,475,202	12,951,280
1894	26,032	0.3	792,633	10.2	205,870	2.7	12,641	0.2	2,637,679	34.1	2,414,697	31.2	671,687	8.7	977,906	12.6	7,739,145	14,254,696
1895	29,218	0.4	607,537	7.8	331,142	4.3	12,641	0.2	2,537,088	32.7	2,632,685	33.9	748,585	9.6	870,868	11.2	7,769,764	14,752,898
1896	30,824	0.4	548,961	6.8	783,707	9.7	12,641	0.2	2,097,292	26.0	2,753,014	34.1	809,121	10.0	1,028,939	12.8	8,064,499	15,746,507
1897	30,548	0.4	609,780	7.4	849,491	10.2	12,641	0.2	2,151,458	25.9	2,959,826	35.7	842,028	10.2	838,916	10.1	8,294,715	15,854,536
1898	88,701	1.0	633,747	7.2	918,850	10.4	12,641	0.1	2,054,431	23.4	3,219,727	36.6	959,324	10.9	909,614	10.3	8,797,035	16,255,375
1899	88,701	1.0	2,409,678	26.4	1,051,574	11.5	12,641	0.1	2,005,771	22.0	1,550,995	17.0	1,066,182	11.7	929,048	10.2	9,114,590	17,024,834
1900	80,638	0.8	2,468,497	25.9	1,022,086	10.7	13,370	0.1	2,089,873	21.9	1,670,367	17.5	1,159,384	12.2	1,037,602	10.9	9,541,817	16,716,817
1901	158,675	1.6	2,275,985	23.1	1,309,436	13.3	13,370	0.1	2,033,873	20.6	1,803,365	18.3	1,135,804	11.5	1,140,801	11.6	9,871,309	17,616,309
1902	202,926	2.0	2,334,323	22.8	1,471,145	14.4	13,370	0.1	2,158,276	21.1	1,863,744	18.2	1,128,967	11.0	1,067,766	10.4	10,240,766	18,256,650
1903	208,782	2.0	2,311,540	22.3	1,643,729	15.9	13,370	0.1	2,200,471	21.5	1,900,991	18.4	1,123,146	10.9	929,329	9.0	10,351,358	18,283,906
1904	204,140	1.9	2,376,719	21.8	1,669,566	15.3	13,370	0.1	2,248,725	20.7	2,181,167	20.0	1,113,457	10.2	1,078,462	9.9	10,885,606	19,149,002
1905	191,058	1.7	2,305,005	20.6	1,923,744	17.2		0.0	1,871,771	16.8	2,257,671	20.2	1,156,845	10.4	1,460,408	13.1	11,166,502	19,385,706
1906	190,097	1.7	2,343,900	20.4	2,348,257	20.4		0.0	1,734,182	15.1	2,259,710	19.6	1,180,034	10.3	1,450,463	12.6	11,506,643	19,164,785
1907	165,164	1.4	2,261,040	19.3	2,527,227	21.6		0.0	1,730,057	14.8	2,547,045	21.8	1,080,623	9.2	1,388,271	11.9	11,699,427	19,280,757
1908	163,315	1.3	2,412,107	19.9	2,649,921	21.9		0.0	1,599,333	13.2	2,561,209	21.1	1,077,490	8.9	1,662,653	13.7	12,126,028	20,126,882
1909	164,118	1.3	2,490,751	20.0	2,800,771	22.5		0.0	1,566,554	12.6	2,598,388	20.9	1,057,122	8.5	1,773,778	14.2	12,451,482	20,153,713
1910	157,822	1.2	2,457,264	19.3	2,987,485	23.5	48,128	0.4	1,311,587	10.3	2,645,555	20.8	1,034,639	8.1	2,080,679	16.4	12,723,159	20,083,851

Year	Gifts & UK Municipal	%	Foreign Government	%	Debenture & Preference	%	Ordinary	%	UK Mortgages	%	Overseas Mortgages	%	Property	%	Cash & Loans	%	Total	Total Rebased to 1825
1911	131,967	1.0	2,294,491	17.9	3,572,577	27.8	46,640	0.4	1,275,696	9.9	2,695,143	21.0	843,644	6.6	1,975,068	15.4	12,835,226	19,718,528
1912	83,345	0.6	2,246,424	16.9	3,704,454	27.8	63,405	0.5	1,134,256	8.5	3,178,201	23.9	1,001,248	7.5	1,890,373	14.2	13,301,706	19,799,323
1913	50,637	0.4	2,161,395	15.9	3,761,375	27.7	58,005	0.4	1,073,612	7.9	3,299,975	24.3	962,867	7.1	2,192,459	16.2	13,560,325	19,994,177
1914	34,703	0.3	1,924,824	14.0	3,865,261	28.1	71,924	0.5	1,025,193	7.4	3,279,322	23.8	974,916	7.1	2,588,823	18.8	13,764,966	18,387,865
1915	1,984,402	14.5	1,795,538	13.1	2,061,364	15.1	59,540	0.4	905,767	6.6	3,134,810	22.9	1,022,489	7.5	2,727,557	19.9	13,691,467	16,094,894
1916	2,965,238	21.5	1,787,956	12.9	1,778,684	12.9	60,467	0.4	906,183	6.6	2,882,707	20.9	1,044,573	7.6	2,389,780	17.3	13,815,588	12,303,659
1917	4,227,003	33.7	865,104	6.9	1,414,722	11.3	56,833	0.5	819,229	6.5	2,326,912	18.5	1,049,426	8.4	1,785,928	14.2	12,545,157	9,964,438
1918	5,481,691	38.7	1,982,123	14.0	1,331,607	9.4	57,352	0.4	731,087	5.2	1,629,548	11.5	1,036,856	7.3	1,920,063	13.5	14,170,327	9,464,683
1919	6,100,525	43.4	1,995,028	14.2	1,340,076	9.5	65,018	0.5	575,126	4.1	1,333,314	9.5	1,065,922	7.6	1,565,577	11.2	14,040,586	9,169,615
1920	6,443,259	47.5	1,295,908	9.6	1,062,059	7.8	62,426	0.5	532,807	3.9	1,138,605	8.4	857,463	6.3	2,166,162	16.0	13,558,689	7,406,517
1921	6,453,259	49.4	1,053,484	8.1	1,061,969	8.1	62,426	0.5	532,087	4.1	1,138,605	8.7	887,463	6.8	1,866,668	14.3	13,055,961	9,640,602
1922	7,583,455	54.9	1,893,846	13.7	1,059,989	7.7	104,252	0.8	448,471	3.2	805,190	5.8	491,376	3.6	1,427,185	10.3	13,813,764	11,276,853
1923	7,036,104	52.9	1,564,066	11.7	1,655,009	12.4	134,147	1.0	391,311	2.9	854,071	6.4	333,719	2.5	1,344,381	10.1	13,312,808	11,052,112
1924	6,964,774	47.2	2,233,549	15.1	2,337,561	15.9	188,437	1.3	368,387	2.5	938,016	6.4	340,706	2.3	1,374,591	9.3	14,746,021	11,971,400
1925	5,904,970	36.7	2,571,492	16.0	3,838,032	23.9	270,724	1.7	334,659	2.1	1,138,217	7.1	558,526	3.5	1,461,898	9.1	16,078,518	13,348,167
1926	5,539,927	29.5	3,141,469	16.8	4,791,424	25.6	1,173,398	6.3	382,987	2.0	1,369,720	7.3	498,698	2.7	1,852,556	9.9	18,750,179	15,392,216
1927	5,728,696	29.0	2,316,176	11.7	5,490,455	27.8	1,889,615	9.6	349,615	1.8	1,501,048	7.6	501,976	2.5	2,006,394	10.1	19,783,966	17,201,865
1928	5,562,937	26.0	2,126,292	9.9	6,737,352	31.5	2,411,898	11.3	459,919	2.2	1,549,575	7.2	508,851	2.4	2,022,214	9.5	21,379,038	18,699,380
1929	4,196,195	19.8	1,787,461	8.4	7,259,762	34.2	3,334,635	15.7	545,127	2.6	1,480,781	7.0	521,083	2.5	2,107,929	9.9	21,232,973	18,682,848
1930	4,672,694	20.6	2,056,470	9.0	7,945,561	35.0	3,371,777	14.8	515,829	2.3	1,290,913	5.7	498,997	2.2	2,377,786	10.5	22,730,027	21,548,496
1931	5,014,082	22.7	1,699,359	7.7	7,678,698	34.7	3,076,858	13.9	495,356	2.2	1,242,270	5.6	498,780	2.3	2,407,004	10.9	22,112,407	21,954,476
1932	6,849,770	26.0	2,532,465	9.6	8,947,021	33.9	3,328,135	12.6	532,453	2.0	1,230,380	4.7	502,323	1.9	2,438,580	9.3	26,361,127	27,087,980
1933	7,116,290	24.8	3,123,104	10.9	10,297,833	35.8	3,748,749	13.0	409,463	1.4	1,169,794	4.1	507,743	1.8	2,377,860	8.3	28,750,836	29,543,581
1934	7,790,846	24.7	3,847,859	12.2	11,508,858	36.4	4,353,315	13.8	400,550	1.3	1,088,816	3.4	510,012	1.6	2,095,655	6.6	31,595,911	32,241,601
1935	7,631,572	22.7	4,214,787	12.5	12,054,982	35.8	5,644,790	16.8	474,119	1.4	1,015,684	3.0	502,135	1.5	2,124,162	6.3	33,662,231	33,649,142
1936	7,398,688	20.6	3,991,245	11.1	12,723,236	35.3	7,341,532	20.4	1,050,166	2.9	988,455	2.7	503,502	1.4	1,995,567	5.5	35,992,391	35,025,370
1937	7,230,630	20.4	3,836,602	10.8	12,738,126	35.9	6,999,300	19.7	1,362,788	3.8	943,824	2.7	493,691	1.4	1,855,998	5.2	35,460,959	32,567,115
1938	6,946,851	19.2	3,755,475	10.4	13,123,579	36.3	6,855,680	19.0	1,267,127	3.5	896,298	2.5	492,871	1.4	2,809,687	7.8	36,147,568	34,048,874
1939	6,670,152	18.9	3,253,087	9.2	12,974,832	36.8	5,989,373	17.0	1,490,873	4.2	833,220	2.4	500,693	1.4	3,529,284	10.0	35,241,514	29,933,456
1940	8,707,679	23.8	3,129,313	8.5	13,147,711	35.9	5,210,798	14.2	1,755,584	4.8	775,689	2.1	529,392	1.4	3,529,284	9.2	36,616,160	27,592,228
1941	10,868,015	27.4	3,305,548	8.3	13,575,312	34.2	5,656,770	14.2	1,697,769	4.3	749,569	1.9	497,779	1.3	3,352,128	8.4	39,702,890	29,025,142
1942	13,023,529	30.7	3,454,335	8.2	13,803,596	32.6	6,189,165	14.6	1,650,010	3.9	680,203	1.6	497,127	1.2	3,071,822	7.3	42,369,787	31,129,699
1943	15,363,145	33.2	4,611,622	10.0	13,659,149	29.5	7,160,107	15.5	1,573,369	3.4	645,653	1.4	614,751	1.3	2,647,881	5.7	46,275,677	34,170,245
1944	17,796,464	35.7	4,920,201	9.9	13,604,926	27.3	8,475,218	17.0	1,521,437	3.1	562,864	1.1	563,413	1.1	2,371,432	4.8	49,815,955	36,418,386
1945	21,637,869	39.7	5,134,659	9.4	14,108,448	25.9	9,036,155	16.6	1,401,912	2.6	579,020	1.1	554,139	1.0	2,038,987	3.7	54,491,189	39,443,827
1946	24,165,188	38.3	5,986,589	9.5	15,286,995	24.2	11,644,115	18.4	1,433,709	2.3	744,167	1.2	594,512	0.9	3,271,723	5.2	63,126,998	45,470,887
1947	20,338,541	31.4	5,945,298	9.2	19,665,287	30.4	13,317,693	20.6	1,756,413	2.7	739,575	1.1	429,227	0.7	2,493,142	3.9	64,685,176	45,021,874
1948	26,135,994	35.3	6,101,455	8.2	20,069,049	27.1	14,464,324	19.5	3,291,599	4.4	916,461	1.2	498,261	0.7	2,604,879	3.5	74,082,022	49,197,011
1949	23,610,570	29.4	9,583,385	11.9	23,545,883	29.3	14,420,207	17.9	4,296,238	5.3	1,634,969	2.0	560,593	0.7	2,735,958	3.4	80,387,803	51,494,883
1950	26,476,837	27.8	10,772,717	11.3	29,038,878	30.5	18,301,456	19.2	5,044,074	5.3	2,299,110	2.4	623,669	0.7	2,706,828	2.8	95,263,569	59,445,838
1951	25,048,778	24.6	10,680,085	10.5	31,886,201	31.3	21,960,097	21.5	5,618,574	5.5	3,495,912	3.4	637,675	0.6	2,688,012	2.6	102,015,334	56,803,434
1952	27,367,565	24.2	11,926,458	10.6	33,170,237	29.3	22,622,591	20.0	7,131,462	6.3	6,079,351	5.4	769,045	0.7	3,966,694	3.5	113,033,403	59,289,822

Year	Gifts & UK Municipal	%	Foreign Government	%	Debenture & Preference	%	Ordinary	%	UK Mortgages	%	Overseas Mortgages	%	Property	%	Cash & Loans	%	Total	Total Rebased to 1825
1953	31,711,609	23.5	11,521,667	8.5	38,069,518	28.2	30,827,507	22.9	8,234,029	6.1	9,132,481	6.8	874,793	0.6	4,423,795	3.3	134,795,399	69,694,652
1954	35,320,135	20.8	13,392,991	7.9	49,101,511	28.9	47,803,621	28.1	9,191,263	5.4	9,795,104	5.8	1,329,092	0.8	4,115,560	2.4	170,049,277	84,890,477
1955	29,253,696	15.9	13,926,910	7.6	54,083,854	29.4	57,436,607	31.2	11,469,001	6.2	12,355,605	6.7	1,480,150	0.8	4,046,000	2.2	184,051,823	86,511,082
1956	26,283,924	13.5	13,721,893	7.0	55,876,521	28.6	62,525,812	32.0	14,536,733	7.4	15,600,078	8.0	1,553,351	0.8	5,240,039	2.7	195,338,351	89,377,432
1957	23,442,977	11.0	14,735,787	6.9	66,231,536	31.0	65,721,011	30.8	16,323,445	7.6	19,010,210	8.9	1,678,996	0.8	6,307,315	3.0	213,451,277	93,332,415
1958	26,434,477	10.0	16,967,012	6.4	80,509,498	30.4	91,865,123	34.7	19,334,224	7.3	21,352,776	8.1	1,721,848	0.6	6,868,872	2.6	265,053,830	113,792,421
1959	26,147,370	7.9	19,552,180	5.9	92,829,094	28.1	136,801,952	41.5	20,173,557	6.1	25,013,732	7.6	1,935,144	0.6	7,449,923	2.3	329,902,952	141,633,327
1960	24,868,300	6.8	23,658,026	6.5	99,423,096	27.3	150,884,171	41.5	23,793,229	6.5	29,889,961	8.2	3,578,194	1.0	7,907,331	2.2	364,002,308	153,487,255
1961	22,601,900	5.5	24,598,141	6.0	105,567,900	25.8	176,902,809	43.3	26,628,277	6.5	38,257,324	9.4	5,109,502	1.3	8,770,210	2.1	408,436,153	165,016,871
1962	33,789,159	7.6	25,576,603	5.8	117,176,730	26.5	175,140,180	39.6	29,210,385	6.6	44,472,785	10.1	6,990,310	1.6	9,428,310	2.1	441,784,342	173,883,332
1963	38,793,530	7.6	30,503,045	6.0	133,137,076	26.0	205,290,823	40.1	32,102,038	6.3	52,888,310	10.3	8,415,805	1.6	10,255,554	2.0	511,386,181	197,607,955
1964	38,401,149	6.9	33,192,498	6.0	142,695,837	25.6	220,359,594	39.6	37,218,219	6.7	62,577,188	11.2	11,352,261	2.0	11,251,273	2.0	557,048,019	205,396,505
1965	37,735,937	6.2	32,420,475	5.3	155,385,352	25.5	230,828,015	37.9	45,328,913	7.4	76,204,076	12.5	13,803,901	12.5	16,793,329	2.8	608,499,998	214,732,613
1966	38,416,051	6.3	30,034,982	4.9	163,457,385	26.7	203,571,102	33.3	51,539,101	8.4	84,479,445	13.8	22,722,173	3.7	17,282,844	2.8	611,503,083	208,131,202
1967	67,114,784	9.2	32,616,116	4.5	160,737,969	22.1	256,990,377	35.4	55,107,451	7.6	88,995,263	12.2	33,908,657	4.7	31,205,699	4.3	726,676,316	241,413,532
1968	59,173,987	6.7	38,778,763	4.4	176,282,178	20.0	356,181,730	40.3	62,716,393	7.1	112,547,722	12.7	43,184,438	4.9	34,164,047	3.9	883,029,258	276,906,614
1969	53,722,105	6.3	35,325,520	4.1	172,381,863	20.1	319,061,887	37.3	73,605,436	8.6	119,502,857	14.0	53,877,391	6.3	28,077,056	3.3	855,554,115	256,313,464
1970	54,216,643	5.9	55,123,768	6.0	171,723,341	18.6	338,231,170	36.7	79,505,657	8.6	116,452,602	12.6	78,686,424	8.5	27,170,887	2.9	921,110,492	255,780,204

Note: All figures are ledger values, not market values.

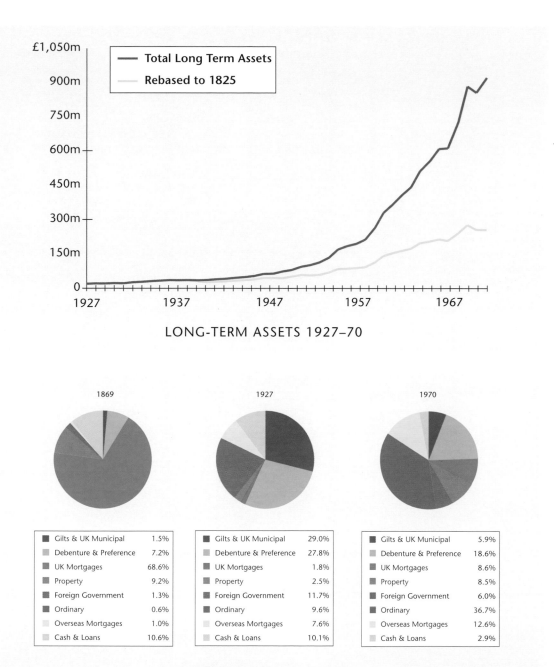

LONG-TERM ASSETS 1927–70

1869		1927		1970	
Gilts & UK Municipal	1.5%	Gilts & UK Municipal	29.0%	Gilts & UK Municipal	5.9%
Debenture & Preference	7.2%	Debenture & Preference	27.8%	Debenture & Preference	18.6%
UK Mortgages	68.6%	UK Mortgages	1.8%	UK Mortgages	8.6%
Property	9.2%	Property	2.5%	Property	8.5%
Foreign Government	1.3%	Foreign Government	11.7%	Foreign Government	6.0%
Ordinary	0.6%	Ordinary	9.6%	Ordinary	36.7%
Overseas Mortgages	1.0%	Overseas Mortgages	7.6%	Overseas Mortgages	12.6%
Cash & Loans	10.6%	Cash & Loans	10.1%	Cash & Loans	2.9%

DISTRIBUTION OF ASSETS

APPENDIX 7: ASSETS MANAGED (£m) 1971–99

Abstracted from Standard Life archives. Retail price index has been used for all rebased figures.

Year	Main Fund	SLIF	Various	Owned	SLPF/SLPM & SLIMS	Unit Trust	SL Bank	Total	Total rebased to 1971
1971	1,064.0	-	36.5	1,100.5	-	-	-	1,100.5	1,100.5
1972	1,270.9	-	71.2	1,342.1	2.4	-	-	1,344.5	1,248.9
1973	1,215.6	-	96.6	1,312.2	7.4	-	-	1,319.6	1,108.5
1974	941.7	-	109.8	1,051.5	15.0	-	-	1,066.5	752.0
1975	1,300.0	-	177.4	1,477.4	35.0	-	-	1,512.4	853.9
1976	1,583.2	-	281.6	1,864.8	92.0	-	-	1,956.8	960.1
1977	1,994.8	-	321.8	2,316.6	111.0	-	-	2,427.6	1,062.1
1978	2,127.3	-	385.4	2,512.7	125.0	-	-	2,637.7	1,064.8
1979	2,315.5	1.3	442.6	2,759.4	156.0	-	-	2,915.4	1,003.8
1980	2,938.3	17.7	598.3	3,554.3	201.0	-	-	3,755.3	1,123.2
1981	3,314.5	38.4	688.2	4,041.1	319.0	-	-	4,360.1	1,163.9
1982	4,615.9	66.1	943.2	5,625.2	402.0	-	-	6,027.2	1,526.3
1983	5,598.8	130.5	1,106.4	6,835.7	531.0	-	-	7,366.7	1,771.4
1984	6,829.6	208.4	1,178.0	8,216.0	607.0	-	-	8,823.0	2,028.7
1985	7,964.3	663.0	913.1	9,540.4	521.0	-	-	10,061.4	2,188.9
1986	9,642.1	1,231.7	636.2	11,510.0	598.0	145.0	-	12,253.0	2,570.0
1987	10,321.9	1,474.4	457.0	12,253.3	627.1	136.4	-	13,016.8	2,632.9
1988	12,462.8	1,712.4	459.4	14,634.6	573.7	124.0	-	15,332.3	2,904.5
1989	16,826.1	2,214.4	258.7	19,299.2	745.0	131.4	-	20,175.6	3,548.5
1990	16,035.8	2,248.5	199.9	18,484.2	687.8	104.8	-	19,276.8	3,100.7
1991	20,752.9	2,838.3	250.5	23,841.7	845.3	151.2	-	24,838.2	3,824.5
1992	23,805.4	3,440.0	282.2	27,527.6	880.4	212.5	-	28,620.5	4,296.1
1993	29,764.5	4,799.0	393.9	34,957.4	1,049.3	354.0	-	36,360.7	5,354.1
1994	30,237.0	5,755.3	469.2	36,461.5	1,022.9	485.0	-	37,969.4	5,434.0
1995	35,427.4	6,486.8	535.1	42,449.3	882.1	569.9	-	43,901.3	6,087.0
1996	39,259.3	7,424.9	773.6	47,457.8	942.4	674.9	-	49,075.1	6,641.3
1997	44,593.2	8,562.3	1,080.4	54,235.9	1,180.6	896.1	-	56,312.6	7,354.0
1998	49,744.0	10,238.7	1,156.5	61,139.2	1,547.8	1,040.5	1,593.4	65,320.9	8,302.1
1999	55,244.3	13,268.9	1,560.4	70,073.6	1,950.3	1,397.3	4,018.7	77,439.9	9,724.1

Note: Figures for 1999 are estimates.

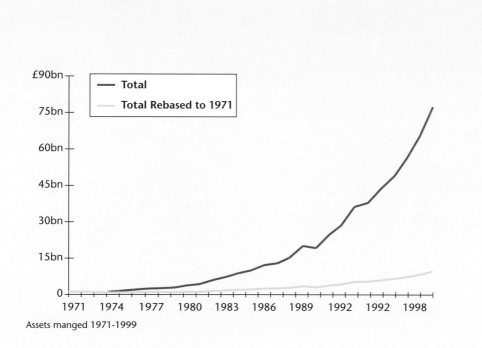

Assets manged 1971-1999

REFERENCES

NOTE: All references prefixed by SLA are to records held in the archives of Standard Life. Other commonly used abbreviations include: PRO (Public Records Office), ASLO (Association of Scottish Life Offices), GPC (General Purposes Committee), PGPCM (Property and General Purposes Committee Meeting), GCA (Glasgow City Archives)

CHAPTER 1: 'WITH CAUTION AND PRUDENCE': 1825–45.

1   SLA A1/1/1 minute 18 October 1830.
2   SRO GD 354/1/1 minute book of the Insurance Company of Scotland.
3   James L. Anderson, *The Story of the Commercial Bank of Scotland Limited During Its Hundred Years from 1810 to 1910, Edinburgh*, 1910, pp.1–24.
4   Henry Cockburn, *Memorials of His Time, 1779–1830*, Edinburgh, 1856, pp.238–9.
5   C.W. Munn, *The Scottish Provincial Banking Companies 1747–1864*, Edinburgh, 1981, p.65.
6   SRO GD 354/1/1, op. cit., minute May 1822.
7   Ibid., minute 11 June 1823.
8   John Anderson, *A History of Edinburgh from the earliest period*, Edinburgh and London, 1856, pp.375–7.
9   SRO GD 354/1/1, op. cit., minutes 9 and 22 February 1825.
10 Clive Trebilcock, *Phoenix Assurance & the development of British Insurance*, vol.1 1782–1870, Cambridge, 1985, pp.469–71.
11 GCA TD 446/5/1 North British Insurance Co. minute book no.1, minutes of 6 and 20 December 1822 and 22 January 1823.
12 Edinburgh Post Office Directory, 1824.
13 R.C. Michie, *Money, Mania and Markets – Investment, Company Formation and the Stock Exchange in Nineteenth-Century Scotland*, Edinburgh, 1981, pp.32 and 39.
14 H.A.L. Cockerell & Edwin Green, *The British Insurance Business – A Guide to its History & Records*, second edition, Sheffield, 1994, pp.57–61.
15 M.E. Ogborn, *Equitable Assurances – The Story of Life Assurance in the Experience of the Equitable Life Assurance Society, 1762–1962*, London, 1962, pp.32–3 and 104.
16 Sir William Schooling, *The Standard Life Assurance Company 1825–1925*, London, 1925, pp.23–4.
17 *Encyclopaedia Britannica*, Edinburgh 1810, vol. 11 pp.289–90 and 7th ed. 1852 pp.310–17 (reputedly contributed by W.T. Thomson).
18 William Wallace, *The Law of Bankruptcy in Scotland*, Edinburgh, second edition, 1914, pp.384–9.
19 SRO GD 354/1/1, op. cit., minutes 9 February and 23 March 1825.
20 Trebilcock, op. cit., pp.523–4.
21 Jonathan Mantle, *Norwich Union – The First 200 Years*, London, 1997, p.16.
22 P.G.M. Dickson, *The Sun Insurance Office 1710–1960*, London, 1960, pp.100–9.
23 SLA A1/1/1 minute 30 March 1825.
24 Ibid. meeting 21 April 1825.
25 Ibid. meeting 13 May 1825.
26 Edinburgh Post Office Directory, 1824.
27 Ibid. 1826 and SLA A1/1/1 meeting of 17 August 1825.
28 SRO SC70/1/37 folio 537 inventory of the estate of Lt. Col. John Munro died 3 September 1827.
29 SLA Contract of co-partnery, 1825.
30 quoted in Schooling, op. cit., pp.8–9.
31 SLA Contract of co-partnery, 1825.
32 Ibid.
33 Ogborn, op. cit., pp.108–9.
34 Ibid. pp.189–92.
35 SLA A1/1/1 meetings 11 and 25 July and 8 August 1825.
36 Ibid. meeting of 7 and 29 August 1825.
37 Ibid. meeting of 12 September 1825.
38 Ibid. meeting of 19 September 1825.
39 Ibid. meeting of 12 September 1825.
40 Ibid.
41 Ibid. meeting of 19 September 1825.
42 Ibid. meeting of 24 October 1825.
43 Ibid. meetings of 28 October and 5 December 1825 and Paisley Trade Directories, 1814–26.
44 Ibid. meetings of 5 and 19 December 1825.
45 Paisley Trade Directory, 1829.
46 SLA A1/1/1 meetings of 19 September and 3 October 1825.
47 Ibid. meeting of 5 June 1826.
48 Ibid. meetings of 17 July, 9 October 1826 and 16 April 1827.
49 Ibid. meeting of 6 October 1828 and SRO GD 124/15/1774.1 Mar letter book 1826–32.
50 Ibid. meetings of 16 February 1829 and 2 January 1830.
51 *Scottish Revised Reports Court of Session 1st series* vol. 4 Shaw vols. 9–11 1830–3, Edinburgh 1901, pp.569–80.
52 SLA A1/1/2 meetings of 2 January, 25 June, 22 October and 12 November 1832.
53 Ibid. AGM 15 December 1826.
54 abstracted from SLA A5/1/1.
55 SLA A1/1/1 meeting of 31 March, 1828.
56 Ibid. meetings of 6 September and 8 November 1830.
57 Ibid. meeting of 25 October 1830.
58 Ibid. meeting of 21 December 1829.

59 Ibid. meeting 15 November 1830.
60 Ibid. meeting 20 November 1826.
61 This issue is discussed in Trebilcock, op. cit., pp.616–7.
62 SLA A1/1/1 meeting 3 July 1828.
63 SRO SC70/1/60 folio 71 inventory of the estate of David Clyne, died 1 November 1833.
64 SLA A1/1/1 meeting of 5 January 1829.
65 SRO GD354/1/2 Insurance Company of Scotland minute book no 2 minute 7 August 1829.
66 SLA A1/1/1 meeting of 21 December 1829.
67 SRO GD354/1/2 op cit. AGMs 1827 and 1830.
68 Ibid. meeting of 30 June 1830.
69 SLA A1/1/1 meeting of 16 August 1830.
70 Ibid. meeting of 20 September 1830.
71 Ibid. meeting of 18 October 1830.
72 Ibid. meetings of 25 October and 29 November 1830.
73 Ibid. meeting of 6 December 1830.
74 Ibid. meeting of 22 November 1830.
75 SLA A1/1/2 minutes of 21 and 24 January 1831.
76 Ibid. meeting of 27 January 1831.
77 Ibid. meeting of 4 February 1831.
78 Ibid. meeting of 18 February 1831 and Edinburgh Post Office Directories, 1825–30.
79 Ibid. meeting of 28 February 1831.
80 SRO GD354/1/2 op. cit. meeting of 20 April 1831, Court of Session minute book, vol.51, pp.404 and 453 and CS 46/27 minute book of sequestered estate of W.H. Kerr, 1832–4.
81 SRO GD354/1/2 op. cit. meeting of 28 July 1831.
82 SLA A1/1/2 meeting of 1 August 1831.
83 SRO GD354/1/3 AGM 1832.
84 SLA A1/1/2 meeting of 28 February 1831 and SRO SC70/1/60 folio 71 inventory of the estate of David Clyne, died 1 November 1833.
85 SRO GD354/1/3.
86 SLA A1/1/2 meeting of 7 March 1831.
87 Charles Colquhoun McInroy, *Scottish Equitable Landmarks – Our First 150*

*years 1831–1981,*Edinburgh, 1981.
88 SLA A1/1/2 meeting of 4 July 1831.
89 Ibid. meetings of 1 July 15 August, 31 October and 21 November 1831.
90 Ibid. meeting of 12 November 1831.
91 Ibid. meetings of 27 June and 1 July 1831.
92 Ibid. meeting of 19 March, 16 and 30 April and 12 November 1831.
93 Ibid. meetings of 5 and 19 March and 16 July 1831.
94 Ibid. meeting of 3 February 1834.
95 Ibid. meeting of 27 October 1831 and SRO CS235 A1/43 sequestration of Robert Adams, Carron and ironmonger, 1831.
96 Ibid. meeting of 19 December 1831.
97 Ibid. meeting of 23 April 1832.
98 *An Act to enable the Standard Life Assurance Company to sue and be sued in the Name of their Manager; for confirming the Rules and Regulations of the said Company; and for other Purposes relating thereto,* 6 June 1832.
99 John Habakkuk, *Marriage, Debt, and the Estates System – English Landownership 1650–1950*, Oxford, 1994, pp.243–358.
100 Trebilcock, op. cit., pp.633–43.
101 Ibid. p.640.
102 SLA A1/1/2 meeting 17 December 1832.
103 Ibid. meeting of 26 September 1831.
104 Ibid. meeting of 28 November 1831.
105 Ibid. meeting of 6 February 1832 and Rev. David Macrae, *Notes about Gourock*, Edinburgh 1880.
106 Ibid. meeting of 12 November 1832.
107 Ibid. meetings of 13 and 27 February, 21 May, 11 June, 30 July and 17 December 1832.
108 Ruthven's expenditure is detailed in SRO SC49/59/28–35, Perthshire registers for improvements to entailed estates, 1827–40.
109 SLA A1/1/2 meetings of 18 March 1833 and 5 May 1834.
110 SLA A1/1/3 meetings of 1 and 22 June 1835.
111 SLA A1/1/2 meeting of 8 October 1832.

112 Ibid. meeting of 6 August 1832.
113 Ibid. meeting of 19 August 1833.
114 Trebilcock, op. cit., 659–61.
115 SLA A1/1/2 meeting of 15 July 1833.
116 Ibid. meetings of 19 August and 23 December 1833.
117 SLA 1/1/3 meetings of 17 and 24 August 1835.
118 Ibid. meeting of 2 January 1837.
119 Ibid. meeting of 6 March 1837.
120 SLA A1/1/7 meeting of 19 February 1844.
121 SLA A1/1/3 meeting of 23 March 1835.
122 Ibid. meetings of 5 September 1836 and 27 March 1838.
123 SLA A1/1/5 meeting of 24 February 1840.
124 SLA A1/1/3 meeting of 8 June 1835.
125 Ibid. meeting of 11 April 1836.
126 SLA A1/1/2 meeting of 1 February 1832 and G.A.S. Norman, *The Overseas History of The Standard Life Assurance Company*, Volumes 1 & 2, Edinburgh, 1950, vol.1, p.9.
127 Ibid. meeting of 11 July 1834.
128 SLA A1/1/2 meetings of 29 and 30 September 1834.
129 Norman, op. cit., vol.1, pp.13–15.
130 SLA A1/1/3 meetings of 12 and 26 September and 17 October 1836.
131 Ibid. meeting of 14 November 1836.
132 SLA A7/1/1 investigation papers 1835.
133 SLA A1/1/3 meeting of 14 March 1836.
134 Ibid. meeting of 4 July 1836.
135 Ibid. meeting of 22 February 1836 and John Rankine, *A Treatise on the Rights and Borders incipient to the Ownership of Lands and Heritages in Scotland*, fourth edition, Edinburgh, 1909, pp.688–92.
136 Ibid. meetings of 17 April, 15 May, 31 July, 11 September, 23 October and 22 November 1837.
137 Ibid. meeting of 8 February 1836 and James Hunter, *The Making of the Crofting Community*, Edinburgh, 1976, pp.35–6.
138 SRO CS 236/M/53/9 sequestration papers of Macneil of Barra, 1836–42.
139 SLA A1/1/5 meeting of 10 and 17 May 1841.

140 SLA A1/1/3 meeting of 11 January and 10 October 1836.
141 Ibid. meeting of 31 October 1836 and 14 August 1837.
142 Ibid. meeting of 16 May 1836.
143 Ibid. meetings of 31 October and 12 December 1836.
144 see Ian Anstruther, *The Knight and the Umbrella: An Account of the Eglinton Tournament 1839*, London, 1963.
145 SLA A1/1/3 meeting of 7 November 1836.
146 Ibid. meeting of 6 November 1837.
147 SLA A1/1/6 meeting of 24 October 1842 and 13 March 1843.
148 SLA A1/3/1 meetings of 16 and 30 October 1837.
149 SLA A1/1/3 meetings of 13 November 1837 and 18 January and 9 July 1838.
150 SLA A1/1/4 meeting of 5 March 1838.
151 Ibid. meeting of 28 January 1839.
152 SLA A1/1/3 meetings of 27 November and 4 and 11 December 1837 and A1/1/4 meeting of 16 April and 1 October 1838.
153 SLA. Bundle of unlisted papers relating to sculpture frieze, 1837–39.
154 SLA A1/1/4 meeting 8 June 1839.
155 SLA A1/1/4 meetings of 14 May and 17 December 1838.
156 Ibid. meeting of 31 December 1838 and 21 January 1839.
157 Ibid. meeting of 27 August 1828.
158 SLA A1/1/5 meeting of 6 April 1840.
159 Ibid. meeting of 4 May 1840.
160 Ibid. meetings of 27 August and 15 October 1838.
161 SLA A1/1/3 meeting of 9 February 1838.
162 SLA A1/1/4 meetings of 19 and 26 March, and 7 May 1838.
163 G.A.S. Norman, *The History of the London City Offices and the Early English Branches of Standard Life*, Edinburgh, 1962, pp.1–2.
164 SLA A1/1/3 meeting of 19 March 1838.
165 SLA A1/1/4 meeting of 4 March 1839.
166 SLA A1/1/5 meeting of 26 October 1840.
167 Ibid. meeting of 3 March 1841 and

Ogborn, op. cit., pp.198–9.
168 Ibid. and A7/1/1 investigation papers 1840.
169 SLA investigation report 1840.
170 SLA A1/1/4 25 meeting of February 1839.
171 SLA A1/1/7 meeting of 27 January 1845 and A1/1/8 meeting of 10 February 1845.
172 SLA A1/1/6 meeting of 6 December 1841.
173 Ibid. meeting of 1 November 1841 and 31 January 1842.
174 SLA A1/1/5 meeting of 24 August 1840 and 4 and 11 January 1841.
175 SLA A1/1/4 21 May 1838.
176 SLA A1/1/6 meeting of 15 November 1841.
177 Ibid. meeting of 27 December 1841.
178 SLA A1/1/3 meeting of 19 June 1837.
179 SLA A1/1/4 meeting of 4 March 1839.
180 Ibid. meeting of 23 September 1839.
181 SLA A1/1/5 meeting of 3 September 1840.
182 SLA A1/1/7 meetings of 14 August 1843 and 8 July 1844.
183 Ibid. meeting of 28 August 1841.
184 H.W. Andras, *Historical Review of Life Assurance in Great Britain and Ireland*, 1912, p.46.
185 W.M. Thackeray, *The History of Samuel Titmarsh and the Great Hoggarty Diamond*, London, 1895, p.91.
186 SLA A1/1/5 meetings of 11 January and 9 August 1841 and A1/1/6 meetings of 27 September and 22 November 1841.
187 SLA A7/1/1 valuation of City of Glasgow Assurance Co., 1841.
188 SLA A1/1/6 meeting of 27 December 1841.
189 Ibid. meeting of 17 January 1842.
190 Ibid. meeting of 21 March 1842.
191 Ibid. meeting of 16 May 1842.
192 Ibid. meeting of 8 August 1842.
193 Ibid. meeting of 12 August 1842.
194 Ibid. meetings of 5, 19, and 26 December 1842.
195 SLA A1/1/7 meetings of 2 and 29 January, 12 February, and 4, 13, and 29 March 1844 and A7/1/2 York and London valuation papers.

196 SLA A1/1/8 meeting of 15 December 1845.
197 SLA A7/1/1 investigation papers, 1845, and investigation report 1845.
198 SLA A1/1/6 meetings of 7 September and 8 August 1842, A1/1/7 meeting of 26 June 1843. See also SRO CS244/1483 case papers George Udny v John Henry Udny and SC19/65/2–6 registers of improvements to entailed estates in Wigtonshire, 1814–45.
199 See for example SLA A1/1/8 meeting of 10 February 1845.
200 Ibid. meeting of 17 March 1845 and James S. Donelly Jr, *The Land and the People of Nineteenth-Century Cork*, London and Boston, 1975, pp.203–4.
201 SLA A7/1/1 investigation papers, 1845.
202 SLA A1/1/7 meeting of 1 May 1843.
203 SLA A1/1/6 meetings of 30 January and 9 October 1843.
204 SLA A7/1/1 investigation papers, 1845.

Feature: 'Dealing with landed families' (p.18)
1 G.E. Mingay, *The Agrarian History of England and Wales, vol.6 1750–1850*, Cambridge, 1989, pp.545–640.
2 John Habakkuk, *Marriage, Debt and the Estates System: English Landownership 1650–1950*, Oxford, 1994, pp.1–76.
3 John Rankine, *A Treatise on the Rights and Burdens Incident to the Ownership of Lands and Heritages in Scotland*, fourth edn, Edinburgh, 1909, pp.1043–56.
4 Ibid., pp.689–94.
5 Habakkuk, op. cit., pp.522–9; Clive Trebilcuk, *Phoenix Assurance and the Development of British Insurance, vol.1, 1782–1870*, Cambridge, 1985, pp.624–9; Barry Supple, *The Royal Exchange Assurance: A History of British Insurance, 1720–1970*, Cambridge, 1970, pp.312–13.
6 Clive Trebilcock, op. cit., pp.526–7 and 631–7.
7 Josiah W. Smith, *The Law of Real and Personal Property*, London, 1855, p.6.

8   G.D. Beaumont, *The Law of Fire and Life Insurance*, London, 1846, p.46, fn a.

9   H.H.L. Bellott and R. James Williams, *The Law Relating to Unconscionable Bargains with Money Lenders*, 1897, pp.27–8.

10 Rankine, op. cit., p.1046.

11 Bellott and Williams, op. cit., p.705.

12 See for example George Rae, *The Country Banker: His Clients, Cares and Work from an Experience of Forty Years*, privately printed, London, 1976, pp.111–12.

13 Habakkuk, op. cit., pp.146–8.

14 Rankine, op. cit., pp.1056–64.

CHAPTER 2: A 'FIRST CLASS' BUSINESS: 1846–1874

1   SLA report of investigation committee, 1866.

2   SLA A1/1/8 meeting of 2 March 1846.

3   Ibid. meetings of 30 June and 21 July 1845.

4   Ibid. meeting of 20 November 1845.

5   G.A.S. Norman, *The Overseas History of The Standard Life Assurance Company*, Volumes 1 & 2, Edinburgh, 1950, vol.1, pp.21–4. At the time of writing this book, the first five volumes of minutes for Colonial Life, which Norman had consulted, had been mislaid.

6   SLA Contract of co-partnery Colonial Life Assurance Co., 1845.

7   Norman, op. cit., vol.1, pp.24–5.

8   SLA A5/11/1 policy no.1.

9   Norman, op. cit., vol.1, p.24 and SLA Colonial Life prospectus 1846.

10 SLA A1/1/8 meeting of 2 March 1846.

11 SLA A1/1/7 meetings of 13 May and 3 June 1844.

12 SLA A1/1/8 meeting of 2 and 14 April 1845.

13 Ibid. meeting of 13 October 1845.

14 Ibid. meeting of 2 June 1846.

15 SLA A1/3/1 p.151 and A1/1/8 meeting of 5 October 1846.

16 Ibid. p.157.

17 Ibid. pp.186–94.

18 Ibid. pp.196–9.

19 Ibid. pp.222–33.

20 Ibid. pp.234–62.

21 Ibid. p.288.

22 SLA A1/1/8 meetings of 18 May and 6 July 1846 and A7/1/2 valuation of Commercial Life.

23 SLA A3/1/1 pp.307–13.

24 S.G. Checkland, *Scottish Banking – A History, 1695–1973*, Glasgow and London, 1975, pp.327–8.

25 SLA A1/1/10 meeting of 18 September 1848.

26 Norman, op. cit., vol.1, p.27 and SLA Colonial Life almanac 1848.

27 Ibid. pp.26–8 and 38–43.

28 Ibid. pp.49–52.

29 Ibid. p.53.

30 Norman, op. cit., vol.2, pp.255–66.

31 Ibid. pp.266–7.

32 Ibid. pp.268–76.

33 Norman, op. cit., vol.1, pp.68–9.

34 SLA A2/2/1 letter Thomson to A. Duncan, Castle Menzies, 27 August 1853, p.43.

35 SLA Colonial Life annual reports 1848–54.

36 Norman, op. cit., vol.1, p.85.

37 SLA A1/1/8 meeting of 5 October 1846 and A1/1/9 meeting of 5 May 1846.

38 SLA A1/1/9 meetings of 2 and 23 August 1847.

39 SLA A1/1/10 meetings of 9 October 1848 and 30 July 1849.

40 SLA A1/1/12 p.260.

41 Ibid. p.408–9.

42 SLA A1/1/3 meeting of 16 January 1854.

43 Clive Trebilcock, *Phoenix Assurance and the Development of British Insurance*, vol.1, Cambridge, 1985, p.642.

44 John Habakkuk, *Marriage, Debt, and the Estates System – English Landownership 1650–1950*, Oxford, 1994, pp.339–41.

45 *Scottish Land – The Report of the Scottish Land Enquiry Committee*, London, 1914, p.22.

46 John Rankine, *A Treatise on the Rights and Burdens incident to the Ownership of Lands and heritages in Scotland*, fourth edition, Edinburgh, 1909, pp.1073–1103.

47 William Thomas Thomson, *Notes on the pecuniary interests of heirs of entail, with calculations regarding such interests in reference to acts of parliament affecting entails and tables showing the values of liferent interests*, Edinburgh, 1849.

48 SLA A1/1//10 p.359.

49 SLA A1/1/11 meeting of 11 November 1850.

50 SLA A1/1/10 p.611.

51 SLA A1/1/11 pp.233–4.

52 SLA A1/1/13 pp.391–2.

53 SLA A1/1/15 pp.238 and 258–9.

54 SLA A1/1/14 p.75.

55 SLA A1/1/21 p.237.

56 Ibid. p.23.

57 Ibid. p.276.

58 Ibid. p.443 and SLA A1/1/22 pp.446–50.

59 *Insurance Spectator*, 1882, p.134.

60 SLA A1/1/11 p.326.

61 SLA A1/1/15 p.215.

62 SLA A1/1/17 p.118.

63 SLA A1/1/20 pp.174–5.

64 SLA A1/1/18 pp.468–9 and 478.

65 SLA A1/1/16 p.512 and A1/1/18 p.470.

66 SLA A1/1/20 p.592.

67 SLA A1/1/21 pp.79–80.

68 SLA A1/1/12 meeting of 15 February 1853.

69 These events are recorded in SLA A1/15/5.

70 SLA A1/1/22 p.84 and A1/1/22 p.109.

71 SLA A1/4/1 pp.93–4 and A6/2/1 Colonial Life Ledger 1847–54, entry for Trinity estate.

72 SLA A1/1/14 pp.304 and 326.

73 SLA A1/1/21 pp.250 and 472 and Peter Michael Scott, *Financial Institutions and the British Property Investment Market 1850–1980*, University of Oxford D.Phil thesis, 1992, p.18.

74 Ibid. p.544 and SLA A1/1/22 p.1.

75 SLA A1/1/8 meeting of 14 September 1846.

76 SLA A1/1/9 meetings of 16 February and 1,2, and 8 March 1847.

77 SLA A1/1/10 pp.540, 607 and 611.

78 Ibid. pp.475 and 572 and SLA A1/1/13 p.209.

79 SLA A1/1/6 pp.1 and 394 and L.S. Pressnell & John Orbell, *A Guide to the Historical Records of British Banking*, London, 1985, p.83.

80 SLA A1/1/16 pp.25–7.

81 see for example SLA A1/1/20 p.540.

82 SLA A1/1/11 p.224.

83 Ibid. pp.249 and 274.
84 SLA A1/1/13 pp.148–50.
85 SLA A1/1/15 p.116 and SLA A1/1/20 p.479.
86 SLA A1/1/16 p.272.
87 SLA A1/1/17 pp.303 and 351.
88 SLA A1/1/19 pp.234 and 277.
89 SLA A1/1/21 p.268.
90 SLA A1/1/22 p.90.
91 SLA A1/4/1 pp.209 and 287.
92 Ibid. pp.362–4 and 372.
93 SLA A1/3/4 p.382.
94 SLA A1/1/10 p.501.
95 Ibid. p.629.
96 Ibid. p.512. He was the great grandfather of the author.
97 Checkland, op. cit., pp.466–9.
98 SLA A1/3/2 p.34.
99 G.A.S. Norman, *The History of the London City Offices and the Early English Branches of Standard Life*, Edinburgh, 1962, pp.4–5.
100 SLA A1/3/2 pp.176–9, A1/1/7 p.201 and Charles Colqhoun McInroy, *Scottish Equitable Landmarks – Our First 150 years 1831–1981*, Edinburgh, 1981, p.6.
101 SLA A1/1/17 p.201.
102 Ibid. p.180.
103 Ibid. p.235.
104 SLA A1/3/4 pp.25 et seq.
105 SLA A1/1/14 pp.529–31.
106 SLA A1/1/13 p.390.
107 SLA A2/1/1 p.264.
108 SLA A1/1/13 p.587.
109 SLA A1/3/2 p.268.
110 Ibid. p.291.
111 For a discussion of competition see Barry Supple, *The Royal Exchange Assurance – A History of British Insurance 1720–1970*, Cambridge, 1970, pp.130–45.
112 SLA A1/1/14 p.493.
113 Trebilcock, op. cit., p.572.
114 SLA A1/3/2 p.49 et seq.
115 SLA A1/1/10 pp.565–6.
116 SLA D1/1/1 minute book of the Experience Life Assurance Co., 1843–48.
117 Sir William Schooling, *The Standard Life Assurance Company 1825–1925*, London, 1925, p.43.
118 SLA 1/1/11 pp.281–2.
119 Faculty of Actuaries Association of Scottish Life Offices (ASLO) 1/1/2/1, p.171.

120 SLA A2/2/1 p.29.
121 L.H. Humpherson, *The First Hundred Years of the Marine and General Mutual Life Assurance Society*, London, 1952, pp.12–13.
122 Schooling, op. cit., pp.44–5.
123 SLA A2/4/1 p.209.
124 SLA A1/3/4 p.162.
125 Schooling, op. cit., p.45 and J. Butt and J.H. Treble, *History of Standard Life, 1825–1975* (unpublished), 1975, p.28.
126 SLA A1/1/16 pp.297–8 and *An Act for making further provisions with respect to the Standard Life Assurance Company*, 19 April 1859.
127 SLA A1/1/14 p.262.
128 Ibid. p.264.
129 SLA A3/1/4 p.25 et seq.
130 The pamphlets can mostly be found in the Faculty of Actuaries Library, *Edinburgh Assurance pamphlets*, 1863.
131 SLA A1/3/2 pp.365–6.
132 SLA A1/1/15 p.370.
133 SLA A1/1/17 p.99 et seq.
134 SLA A1/3/2 pp.391 et seq. and 402.
135 SLA A1/1/18 pp.412, and 447, and A1/1/19 pp.79–80.
136 SLA A1/3/4 pp.55–70.
137 Ibid. pp.111–13.
138 SLA A1/1/12 p.357.
139 see for example Ibid. pp.104 and 115.
140 SLA A1/1/19 pp.176 and 548.
141 SLA A1/1/18 p.540.
142 SLA A1/4/1 pp.215–6 and 266–7.
143 SLA A1/4/1 pp.101–2.
144 SLA A2/2/1 pp.75–7.
145 SLA A2/4/1 pp.103, 109, 127–8, and 151–2.
146 Norman, op. cit., vol.1, pp.72–4.
147 SLA A2/4/1 p.161.
148 Norman, op. cit., vol.1, pp.74–5 and 104.
149 Ibid. pp.103–6.
150 Norman, op. cit., vol.1, pp.78–9 and 81.
151 Ibid. pp.108–11 and SLA A1/4/2 p.155.
152 Ibid. pp.276–8 and SLA A2/4/1 p.93.
153 Ibid. p.279–80.
154 An account of O'Hagan's journey is to be found in Norman op. cit., vol.1, pp.82–5.

155 SLA A1/4/1 pp.309–10, 331–4, and 433–6.
156 Ibid. p.583.
157 Ibid. p.328.
158 SLA A1/1/19 p.380.
159 Ibid. pp.430, 517 and 602 and A1/3/4 p.52 and Schooling, op. cit., p.45.
160 SLA A1/1/19 p.22.
161 SLA A1/4/4 p.144.
162 Ibid. pp.144 and 157.
163 Schooling, op. cit., pp.38–9.
164 SLA A1/15/1–2 and A10/5/1–2.
165 SLA A1/1/14 pp.356–83.
166 SLA A1/1/18 pp.149 et seq.
167 SLA A1/1/19 pp.220 and 228 et seq.
168 SLA A1/1/24 p.237.
169 SLA A1/3/4 p.230.
170 Ibid. p.273.
171 Ibid. p.237.
172 Ibid. p.252.
173 Ibid. pp.315–9.
174 Supple, op. cit., pp.326–8.
175 SLA A1/1/20 p.168.
176 Ibid. p.340.
177 Ibid. p.540.
178 Ibid. p.576.
179 SLA A1/1/21 pp.265, 427 and 559.
180 SLA A1/3/4 p.117.
181 SLA A1/6/4 p.333.
182 SLA A1/1/20 p.350.
183 SLA A1/1/19 p.555.
184 SLA A1/1/22 p.248.
185 Ibid. p.474.
186 SLA A1/1/22 p.70.
187 Ibid. pp.405 and 450.
188 SLA A1/1/21 p.475.
189 SLA A1/1/22 p.250.
190 Ibid. p.11.
191 SLA A1/1/21 p.201.
192 SLA A1/1/22 p.86.
193 SLA A1/1/21 p.425.
194 SLA A1/1/22 p.60.
195 SLA A7/1/16 Investigation report 1875.
196 SLA A1/6/4 pp.505–11.
197 SLA 1/3/4 pp.304, 331–2 and 338.
198 Cockerell & Green, op. cit., p.106.
199 SLA A1/3/4 p.403.
200 Ibid. p.393.
201 SLA A1/6/4 pp.469–71 and 505–11.
202 SLA A1/1/21 pp.122 et seq.
203 Ibid. pp.104 et seq.
204 SLA A1/1/20 p.440.
205 SLA A1/1/21 pp.557 et seq.
206 see for example SLA A1/1/22 p.122.

207 SLA A1/6/4 p.444.
208 Ibid. pp.505–11.
209 SLA annual report 1870.
210 Norman, op. cit., vol.2, pp.281–5 and SLA A1/4/2 pp.512–15.
211 SLA A1/4/2 pp.511–12.
212 Butt and Treble, op. cit., chapter 3 p.33.
213 SLA A1/4/3 p.112.
214 Ibid. pp.243–4.
215 Norman, op. cit., vol.1, pp.117–18.
216 SLA A2/1/3 p.292.
217 SLA A1/4/3 p.150 and Norman, op. cit., vol.1, pp.118–19.
218 SLA 1/3/5 pp.419 et seq.
219 SLA A1/1/11 p.193 and SLA A1/1/19 pp.92 and 182.
220 SLA A1/1/19 p.430.
221 Faculty of Actuaries ASLO 1/1/2/2 meeting of 22 January 1867.
222 Ibid. 1867–70 passim.
223 *Post Magazine*, vol.34 1873, p.244.
224 SLA report of investigation committee, 1866.
225 SLA A1/3/5 pp.40–1.
226 Reginald C. Simmonds, *The Institute of Actuaries 1848–1948*, Cambridge, 1948, p.6; Andrew Rutherford Davidson, *The History of the Faculty of Actuaries in Scotland 1856–1956*, Edinburgh, 1956, pp.23–8.
227 These actuarial reports are held in the library of the Faculty of Actuaries in Edinburgh.
228 William Thomas Thomson, *Further suggestions with reference to the amendment of the Joint Stock Companies Registration Act as regards life assurance institutions*, Edinburgh, 1852.

Feature: 'Medical officers' (p.58)
1 SLA A1/1/9 meeting of 8 February 1847.
2 R. Christison, *Suggestions to Medical References for the Examination of Persons Proposing Life Assurance*, Edinburgh, 1847.
3 *Dictionary of National Biography*, vol.4, 1901, pp.290–1.
4 This section is based on Marguerite Dupree, 'Other Than Healing: Medical Practitioners and the Business of Life Assurance during the Nineteenth and Early-Twentieth Centuries', in *Social History of Medicine*, 1997, pp.79–103.
5 *Dictionary of National Biography: 1912–21*, Oxford, 1927, pp.198–9.
6 *Standard Quarterly*, December 1946, no.71, p.9.
7 SLA annual reports 1978 and 1979.

Feature: 'Sport and Standard Life' (p.74)
1 G.P. Glover, *Standard Life Assurance Company*, unpublished, 1996, p.5.

CHAPTER 3: SITTING ON THE SAFETY VALVE: 1875–1904
1 contained in SLA A4/2/1.
2 SLA A1/6/9 pp.110 et seq.
3 SLA A1/1/24 pp.60 and 283.
4 SLA A1/1/23 p.503.
5 SLA A1/1/24 p.262 and A1/6/5 pp.93 et seq.
6 SLA A1/1/25 p.72.
7 Ibid. pp.124–5.
8 Ibid. p.126.
9 SLA A2/1/4 p.721.
10 SLA A1/1/25 p.135.
11 Ibid. pp.247–8.
12 SLA A2/1/3 p.742.
13 SLA A1/1/25 pp.410–15.
14 SLA A1/1/26 pp.191–3.
15 SLA A1/1/27 pp.378 and 539.
16 SLA A1/1/31 p.98.
17 SLA A1/1/29 p.141.
18 Ibid. p.631.
19 *Post Magazine* 14 July 1888 p.481 and 15 August 1891 p.569.
20 SLA A1/1/26 pp.360, 398 and 525.
21 SLA A1/1/26 pp.514 and 573, A1/1/27 p.34 and information supplied by Major Donald Galbraith.
22 SLA A1/1/28 p.639.
23 SLA A1/1/27 pp.44 and 247.
24 see for example Ibid. p.352 where Herbert of Muckross was allowed just £75 per annum from the rents.
25 R.H. Campbell, *Owners and Occupiers – Changes in Rural Society in South-West Scotland before 1914*, Aberdeen, 1991, p.170.
26 SLA A1/1/27 pp.45 and 47.
27 SLA A1/1/28 p.106.
28 Ibid. p.37.
29 SLA A1/1/29 p.260.
30 SLA A1/1/24 p.363.
31 Ibid. p.512.
32 Ibid. pp.42 and 68
33 Ibid. p.85.
34 Ibid. p.305–6.
35 SLA A1/1/25 p.385.
36 Ibid. p.261.
37 S.G. Checkland, *Scottish Banking – A History, 1695–1973*, Glasgow and London, 1975, pp.469–77.
38 SLA A1/1/25 pp.291 and 326.
39 Ibid. pp.302–3.
40 Ibid. p.525.
41 SLA A1/126 p.244.
42 Ibid. p.444.
43 Sir Herbert Eustace Maxwell, 7th Bart., *Annals of the Scottish Widows' Fund Life Assurance Society, 1815–1914*, Edinburgh, 1914, p.116.
44 SLA A1/1/25 p.574.
45 SLA A1/1/28 pp.38 and 85.
46 see for example Ibid. p.138.
47 SLA A1/1/30 p.138.
48 Ibid. p.261 and p.271.
49 SLA A1/1/31 p.268.
50 SLA A1/1/30 p.600.
51 SLA A1/1/25 p.387.
52 Ibid. p.361.
53 SLA A1/1/26 pp.122 and 129–30.
54 SLA A1/1/30 p.29.
55 SLA A1/1/25 pp.434 and 496.
56 SLA A1/1/29 p.123.
57 W.R. Lawson, *The Scottish Investors' Manual*, Edinburgh, 1884, pp.27–46.
58 SLA A1/1/27 p.433.
59 SLA A1/1/27–29 passim.
60 SLA A1/1/28 p.109.
61 Ibid. p.63.
62 Ibid. p.495.
63 SLA A1/1/29 p.177.
64 SLA A1/1/30 p.138.
65 SLA A1/1/31 p.480.
66 SLA A1/1/30 p.254 and paper read by Professor Ernest W. Sullivan II, 'Joseph Conrad tries to prove who he is – life insurance as a form of autobiography', 1991.
67 SLA A2/1/3 p.292.
68 Ibid.
69 SLA A1/1/24 p.63.
70 SLA A2/1/3 p.311.
71 SLA A1/6/5 p.13.
72 SLA 1/1/23 pp.312–13.
73 Ibid. pp.481–2 and A1/6/5 p.78.
74 SLA investigation report 1875.
75 See for example Charles Cox, *Facts & fallacies of life insurance*, London, 1904, p.10.
76 see for example T. Terloc, *Life*

Assurance as it is and as it should be, 1888.

77 SLA A7/1/7 Valuation papers 1880.

78 see for example SLA A2/1/3 pp.331–2.

79 Ibid. pp.880–6 and A1/3/5 pp.143–4.

80 SLA valuation report 1880.

81 SLA A1/3/5 pp.124 et seq.

82 SLA A1/6/5 p.78 et seq.

83 SLA A1/1/24 pp.513, 522, and 534.

84 SLA A1/3/5 p.97.

85 SLA A1/1/24 p.534.

86 SLA A1/1/25 p.68.

87 Ibid. p.168.

88 SLA A1/6/4 pp.121–2.

89 SLA A2/1/3 p.707.

90 SLA A1/1/26 p.5; SLA A2/1/3 p.967.

91 Peter Michael Scott, *Financial Institutions and the British Property Investment Market 1850–1980*, University of Oxford D.Phil thesis, 1992, p.40.

92 SLA A2/1/3 p.786.

93 SLA A1/6/5 p.134.

94 SLA 1/3/5 pp.152 and 155.

95 SLA annual report 1882.

96 SLA A1/6/5 p.149.

97 SLA A2/1/4 p.16.

98 Joseph Allen, *An inquiry concerning all the life insurance offices . . . having agencies in the United Kingdom*. [On cover *Where shall I get the most for my money?*] 10th ed., London, 1883.

99 William Bourne, *Expenses Ratios of Life Offices*, Liverpool, 1886

100 Laurie Dennet, *A Sense of Security: 150 Years of Prudential*, Cambridge, 1998, pp.114–15.

101 *Insurance Spectator of London*, 16 March 1885, p.99.

102 Birmingham Archives department MS1605/1 AGM Beacon Insurance 1885.

103 SLA A2/1/4 p.82.

104 Oliver M. Westall, *The Provincial Insurance Company 1903–38: Family, markets and competitive growth*, Manchester, 1992, p.33.

105 Norman, op. cit., vol.1, pp.118–19.

106 J. Butt and J.H. Treble, *History of Standard Life* (unpublished), 1975, chapter 5, p.28.

107 Norman, op. cit., vol.1, p.119.

108 Butt and Treble, op. cit., ch.2 pp.28–9.

109 SLA A1/4/4 pp.24–30.

110 SLA A1/4/3 meeting of 4 May 1877.

111 Norman, op. cit., vol.1, p.120.

112 SLA A1/4/3 meeting of 30 April 1878.

113 SLA A1/4/4 meeting of 18 December 1882.

114 Norman, op. cit., vol.1, p.120.

115 Figures compiled by Butt and Treble, op. cit., chapter 5, p.33.

116 Ibid. p.34.

117 SLA A7/1/8 Valuation papers 1895 bundle b.

118 SLA A3/3/4 report of visit to Canada 1900 pp.37–70.

119 SLA valuation report 1875.

120 Report of visit to Bombay by George Kemp, 10 March 1876, SLA A1/3/8 pp.8–18.

121 SLA A1/3/8 pp.23–40.

122 SLA A1/4/3 meeting of 16 September 1880.

123 SLA A1/4/4 pp.172–6.

124 Ibid. meetings of 2 August and 4 October 1881.

125 Ibid. pp.96 and 116.

126 SLA A3/3/1 pp.102–3.

127 Norman, op. cit., vol.2, pp.294–5.

128 Ibid. pp.353–4.

129 SLA A7/1/8 Valuation papers bundle b.

130 SLA A1/3/5 p.252.

131 SLA A1/4/4 p.510.

132 Norman, op. cit., vol.2, p.294.

133 Ibid. pp.295–8.

134 SLA A1/3/5 p.283.

135 Ibid. p.275.

136 SLA A1/4/4 pp.509–13.

137 Ibid. meetings of 23 and 11 April 1889.

138 SLA A3/3/1 p.104.

139 Ibid. pp.104–7.

140 SLA A1/3/6 p.46.

141 Memorandum by the manager for the investigation committee, 1896, SLA 7/1/8 bundle f.

142 SLA A3/3/1 p.106.

143 Ibid. pp.110–19.

144 SLA London letters Thomson to Kemp 24 January 1902.

145 SLA A1/3/6 p.156.

146 SLA A3/1/43 annual reports, Shanghai, 1900–3.

147 SLA A1/4/5 pp.75–80 and Norman, op. cit., vol.2, pp.188–9.

148 Norman, op. cit., vol.2, p.191.

149 SLA A2/1/5 p.287.

150 SLA A1/1/31 p.346 and A3/3/2 p.160.

151 Norman, op. cit., vol.2, pp.228–9.

152 SLA A3/3/1 reports on European branches, and A1/1/27 p.292.

153 SLA A1/1/27 pp.495–6.

154 SLA A1/1/28 pp.439 and 535.

155 SLA A1/1/29 p.244.

156 SLA A2/1/4 letter Thomson to Thalbitzer 7 January 1893.

157 SLA A2/1/5 p.304.

158 SLA A3/1/5 p.304.

159 SLA A1/3/6 pp.191–3.

160 SLA A2/1/5 p.602.

161 SLA A1/3/6 p.222.

162 SLA A1/1/28 p.620.

163 SLA A3/1/9 and A3/3/1 pp.156–63.

164 SLA A2/1/5 p.553.

165 SLA A2/1/6 letter Thomson to Szilagyi 23 October 1903.

166 SLA A1/3/5 p.206 and SLA A1/1/30 p.414.

167 Norman, op. cit., vol.2, pp.238–9 and 247.

168 Abstracted from Bourne's *Handy Insurance Manual*, Liverpool, 1886 and 1896.

169 Insurance Policy-holders' Mutual Protection League Ltd., *Profit or plunder? In respect to life insurance &c.*, London, 1888, p.23.

170 *Post Magazine*, 30 May 1896, p.383 and SLA annual report 1896.

171 SLA A1/1/26 p.210.

172 Ibid.

173 SLA annual report 1885.

174 SLA A1/3/5 p.198.

175 SLA A1/3/5 p.259.

176 SLA annual reports 1889 and 1890.

177 SLA annual report 1900.

178 SLA A1/3/5 pp.275, 283 and 287.

179 SLA A1/1/27 pp.210 et seq.

180 SLA A1/3/5 pp.317 et seq.

181 SLA A2/1/4 p.296.

182 SLA A1/3/5 pp.317 et seq.

183 SLA A2/1/4 p.331.

184 SLA A1/3/5 p.362.

185 Ibid. p.392.

186 Ibid. pp.399–400.

187 SLA A1/3/6 p.53.

188 SLA London correspondence 1895–1904.

189 Ibid. Thomson to Rolland 30 March, 11 April and 18 June 1895.

190 SLA A2/1/4 p.682.

191 Ibid. p.785.
192 SLA A2/1/5 p.82.
193 SLA London letters Thomson to Rolland 30 March 1895.
194 Ibid. Thomson to Rolland 30 July 1896.
195 Ibid. Thomson to Rolland 29 June 1896 and SLA A1/3/6 pp.85 and 87.
196 See for example E. Colqhoun, *Notes on Life Assurance*, 1883 ,and W.A. Teasdale, *How to distinguish the safest and most profitable life offices*, 1898.
197 A.A.M., *Life Insurance Up-to-Date*, Edinburgh, 1890.
198 C. Spensley, *A thousand tips about Life Assurance Offices*, Sheffield, 1893.
199 Charles Cox, *How and where to insure*, London, 1903.
200 *Bourne's Handy Insurance Manual*, op. cit., 1886 and 1890
201 SLA London letters Thomson to Rolland 26 June 1897.
202 Ibid. Thomson to Rolland 30 March 1899.
203 SLA A2/1/5 p.464.
204 SLA London letters Thomson to Rolland 1 December 1902.
205 SLA A1/3/6 p.232.
206 *Post Magazine*, 15 August 1891, p.569.
207 Reginald C. Simmonds, *The Institute of Actuaries 1848–1948*, Cambridge, 1948 pp.291 et seq.
208 *Bourne's Handy Insurance Manual*, op. cit., 1901.
209 SLA annual report 1891.
210 SLA annual report, 1895.
211 SLA A7/1/8 Valuation papers 1895 bundle g.
212 SLA A7/1/9 Valuation papers 1900 bundle c.
213 see for example SLA A7/1/8 Valuation papers 1895 bundle g correspondence between S.C. Thomson and G.A. Jamieson.
214 *Bourne's Handy Insurance Manual*, op. cit., 1901–4.
215 SLA A1/3/6 p.239.
216 Ibid. p.254.
217 SLA A3/3/1 pp.99–139.
218 SLA A1/1/31 p.216.
219 Ibid. p.342.
220 SLA A1/3/6 p.253.
221 Ibid. p.310.

CHAPTER 4: 'TO IMPROVE OUR BASIS OF VALUATION': 1904–19

1 SLA A2/1/6 p.516.
2 Quoted in Barry Supple, *The Royal Exchange Assurance – A History of British Insurance 1720–1970*, Cambridge, 1970, p 299.
3 SLA A2/1/6 pp.127 and 142.
4 Ibid. p.125.
5 Ibid. p.119.
6 Ibid. p.305.
7 SLA A1/1/32 p.113.
8 SLA A3/3/1 p.106.
9 SLA A1/3/6 p.305.
10 Ibid. p.274 and SLA A1/1/31 p.572.
11 SLA A3/1/4 minutes of meeting of the Establishment Committee, 1904.
12 Ibid. Budapest report, 1906.
13 SLA A1/3/6 p.322 and SLA A3/3/1 pp.140.
14 SLA A3/3/1 p.172.
15 SLA A3/1/37.
16 Ibid.
17 SLA 2/1/6 p.253 and SLA A1/1/31 p.623.
18 SLA A7/6/17 statement of affairs 1900–5.
19 SLA A1/2/6 p.383.
20 Ibid. p.516.
21 Ibid. p.159.
22 SLA A2/1/7 pp.331.
23 R. Cook Watson, *Life Assurance Premiums Charged by Various Companies*, Newcastle upon Tyne, 1900–15.
24 SLA annual report 1905.
25 SLA A7/1/9a Investigation papers 1905.
26 SLA A2/1/7 p.249.
27 SLA A1/3/6 p.310.
28 SLA 15th quinquennial investigation report 1905.
29 Charles Cox, *How and where to insure*, London, 1903, p.16.
30 SLA 15th quinquennial investigation report 1905.
31 SLA A2/1/7 pp.257 and 265.
32 *Post Magazine*, 1906.
33 SLA A4/2/15 p.28.
34 Laurie Dennet, *A Sense of Security: 150 Years of Prudential*, Cambridge, 1998 pp.179–83.
35 SLA A4/2/15 pp.27–29.
36 SLA A2/2/1, p.90.
37 SLA A1/3/7 p.12.

38 SLA A2/3/2 pp.359–60
39 Ibid. p.506.
40 Ibid. p.419 and SLA A2/1/7 p.589.
41 SLA A1/1/33 p.31.
42 SLA A1/3/7 p.26.
43 SLA A1/3/7 p.33 and A2/1/8 p.3.
44 SLA A8/4/2–5 Barlein case papers 1907–8.
45 SLA A8/4/1 Larsen case papers, 1906–8.
46 *Standard Life Assurance Company Act*, 1910
47 SLA annual reports 1907–10.
48 *Bourne's Handy Insurance Manual*, Liverpool, 1905–8.
49 SLA A2/1/7 p.436.
50 SLA A2/2/5 pp.17–19.
51 SLA A2/4/1 p.39.
52 SLA A2/2/1 pp.127–8.
53 SLA A3/2/2 West End branch annual report 1908.
54 see for example SLA A3/3/1 p.215.
55 see for example SLA A3/1/42 Blount to Søderberg 13 April 1911.
56 see for example SLA A2/1/8 p.743.
57 Supple, op. cit., p.221.
58 SLA new product brochures 1906–11.
59 SLA A1/1/33 p.276.
60 Supple, op. cit., p.115 and Clive Trebilcock , *Phoenix Assurance & the development of British Insurance, vol.1 1782–1870*, Cambridge, 1985, p.604.
61 Supple, op. cit., pp.223 and 255–7.
62 SLA new product brochures 1906–14.
63 *Bourne's Handy Insurance Manual*, op. cit., 1907–19.
64 SLA A3/2/2 London West End branch annual reports, 1908.
65 A.H. Swain, *The War and Life Insurance, with-profit policy-holders' precarious position*, Leicester, 1915, pp.6–24.
66 see E. Piercy Henderson, *Insurance Questions Plainly Treated for Plain People*, London, 1906, and *Latest Supplement to Insurance Questions Plainly Treated for Plain People*, London, 1910.
67 SLA A2/1/7 p.470.
68 SLA A3/2/2 London West End branch annual reports, 1905.
69 SLA A3/1/4 report on the Budapest branch and SLA A1/3/7 p.38 et seq.

70 SLA A1/3/7 p.116.
71 SLA A3/1/4 report on the Budapest branch, 1913, p.15.
72 SLA A1/3/7 p.217.
73 SLA A3/1/4 report on the Budapest branch, 1913, p.1.
74 SLA A1/1/35 pp.368 and 393–4 and G.A.S. Norman, *The Overseas History of The Standard Life Assurance Company*, Volumes 1 & 2, Edinburgh, 1950, vol.2. pp.243–4.
75 SLA A1/3/7 pp.281–2.
76 Norman, op. cit., vol.2, pp.245–7.
77 SLA A1/1/36 p.628 and A1/1/37, pp.230, 306, and 430.
78 Norman, op. cit., vol.2, p.247,
79 SLA A3/3/2 report by accountant (Mr Wilson) upon his visit to Copenhagen and investigation into defalcation, 1909
80 SLA A3/3/2 reports by Mr Blount upon his visits to Scandinavia, 1909 and 1910.
81 SLA A3/1/42 Scandinavia annual report, 1917.
82 SLA annual report 1922.
83 SLA A1/1/36 meetings of 31 December 1918 and 28 January 1919 and A1/3/8 meeting of 14 January 1930.
84 SLA A3/3/2 pp.91–124.
85 SLA A3/3/2 first memorandum by manager upon fluctuation of the peseta and investment of peseta reserves, 1910.
86 SLA A1/1/37 meeting of 1 June 1920.
87 *Standard Newsletter* no.23 , December 1929 and SLA annual report 1929.
88 SLA A2/2/1 p 119.
89 SLA A3/1/22 Canada and United States – report by manager upon his visit 1909.
90 SLA A2/2/1 letters 1906–9 passim.
91 SLA A2/2/1 p.202.
92 SLA A3/1/21 Canada and the United States – report by Charles F. Whigham upon his visit, 1908.
93 SLA A2/2/1 p.346.
94 SLA A3/1/23 Canada and United States – report by manager upon his visit 1912.
95 SLA A3/1/24 Canada and United States – report by manager upon his visit 1909.

96 Norman, op. cit., vol.1, pp.153–4.
97 SLA A2/2/2 Private letters No 2 – Canada, letters p.197 Dickson to Greenshields 19 January 1917.
98 SLA A2/3/2 Dickson to Angus 8 August 1917.
99 SLA A2/1/7 pp.44–7.
100 Norman, op. cit., vol.2, p.313.
101 Ibid. p.313.
102 Ibid. pp.313–5.
103 SLA A2/3/5 Dickson to Prevost and Hill 26 April 1906.
104 *Standard Quarterly,* March 1953, pp.8–9.
105 SLA A2/3/5 p.930.
106 SLA A1/3/7 p.250 and A2/3/6 p.282.
107 A2/3/6 p.270.
108 SLA A2/2/5 p.843.
109 Norman, op. cit., vol.2, p.315 and SLA A3/1/5 India, report by Mr Macnaghten on his visit, 1922–23.
110 SLA A3/3/2 report by Mr. Blount upon his visit to Montevideo, 1911.
111 SLA A2/2/7 p.182.
112 Norman, op. cit., vol.2, pp.191–2.
113 SLA A3/3/2 report by Mr. Blount upon his visit to Cairo, 1909.
114 SLA A3/1/44 Cairo annual report, 1924.
115 SLA A2/2/7 p.74.
116 SLA A3/3/2 report by Mr Blount upon his visit to Montevideo, 1911.
117 SLA A3/3/4 pp.89–142.
118 Norman, op. cit., vol.2, p.232.
119 SLA A2/2/8 p.304.
120 Norman, op. cit., vol.1, p.232.
121 SLA A2/4/2 p.255.
122 Ibid. p.930.
123 Ibid. p.932.
124 SLA annual report 1912.
125 SLA A3/3/2 report by Mr. Blount upon his visit to the north of England branches, January 1912.
126 SLA A2/1/8 p.473 et seq.
127 *Standard Newsletter* 1938 two articles on group schemes.
128 see for example Michael Moss and Iain Russell, *An Invaluable Treasure: A History of the TSB*, London, 1994, pp.122–7.
129 see for example Lloyd George's introduction to R.D. Morris, *Life Assurance from the National and Personal standpoint*, London, 1909.
130 SLA A1/1/35 pp.81 and 109.
131 SLA A2/4/3 p.248.

132 SLA A2/1/8 p.505.
133 SLA A2/4/3 pp.110 and 220.
134 Ibid. pp.248 and 466.
135 *Bourne's Handy Insurance Manual*, op. cit., 1906–14.
136 SLA A2/1/8 p.722.
137 SLA annual report 1904.
138 Ibid. 1906.
139 SLA A1/1/32 p.53.
140 Peter Pugh, *Number One Charlotte Square*, Edinburgh, 1987, pp.15–16.
141 SLA A1/1/33 p.241.
142 SLA A3/1/24 Canada and United States – report by manager upon his visit 1909.
143 Information supplied by Dickson's granddaughter, Mrs Cunningham.
144 SLA A3/3/2 report by investment clerk (Mr Peat) upon his visit to Canada and United States, 1911.
145 SLA A3/3/3 report by investment superintendent upon visit to Canada and United States, 1913.
146 *Bourne's Handy Insurance Manual*, op. cit., 1908.
147 SLA A3/3/4 reports by G.M. Forman and T.D. Peat on Argentine mortgages, 1914.
148 SLA A1/1/32 p.448.
149 SLA A1/1/33 p.214.
150 SLA A1/1/36 p.150.
151 SLA A1/1/36 p.647.
152 SLA A1/1/37 pp.63, 120, and 129.
153 Ibid. p.520.
154 SLA A1/1/34 p.123.
155 Ibid. p.635.
156 SLA A1/1/33 p.329
157 SLA A1/1/35 p.9.
158 SLA A1/1/33 pp.382 and 426.
159 SLA A1/1/35 p.293
160 SLA A3/3/4 pp.1–14.
161 SLA A1/1/35 p.67.
162 A.W. Kirkaldy, ed., *British Finance during and after the war, 1914–21*, London, 1921, pp.342–6.
163 SLA A1/1/36 p.652 and A1/1/37 pp.45 and 57.
164 Faculty of Actuaries, Association of Scottish Life Offices (ASLO) 1/1/2/4 pp.307–24.
165 Public Record Office (PRO) T1/11926/11806/16*.
166 Eric Street, ed. by Richard Glen, *The History of the National Mutual Insurance Society*, London, 1980, pp.9–21 and Geoffrey Marks

obituary, *Journal of the Institute of Actuaries*, vol.19 pp.223–5.

167 Robert Skidelsky, *John Maynard Keynes – The Economist as Saviour, 1920–37*, London, 1992, pp.25–6.

168 Street, op. cit., and Oliver M. Westall, *The Provincial Insurance Company 1903–38: Family, markets and competitive growth*, Manchester, 1992, pp.376–83.

169 SLA A2/1/8 p.834.

170 W.R. Lawson, *British War Finance 1914–15*, London, 1915, pp.17–53.

171 Ibid. pp.54–81 and Sir William Beveridge et al., *War & Insurance*, London, 1927, pp.147–50.

172 Ibid. pp 233–47.

173 Kirkaldy, op. cit., pp.329–32.

174 Faculty of Actuaries ASLO 1/1/2/4 pp.328, 332 and 335 and 1/1/2/5 passim pp.17–40.

175 SLA A2/1/8 p.877.

176 Faculty of Actuaries ASLO 1/1/2/5 passim 1915–16 and SLA A1/2/8 p.941.

177 PRO T172/490.

178 R.S. Sayers, *The Bank of England 1891–1944*, Cambridge, 1976, p.91.

179 SLA A1/1/35 pp.559–66.

180 Kathy Burke, *Morgan Grenfell 1838–1938*, London, 1989, p.75 and Sayers, op. cit., p.86.

181 Kirkaldy, op. cit., p.184.

182 PRO T172/221 and Faculty of Actuaries ASLO 1/1/2/5 pp.23, 51 and 69.

183 SLA A2/1/9 p.33.

184 Faculty of Actuaries ASLO 1/1/2/5 p.83.

185 E.V. Morgan, *Studies in British Financial Policy 1914–25*, London, 1952, pp.326–31 and see also PRO T170/99 and T172/418A.

186 PRO T172/625.

187 Faculty of Actuaries ASLO 1/1/2/5 pp.71–8.

188 Ibid. pp.73–189 passim.

189 Ibid. p.120.

190 Lawson, *British War Finance*, op. cit., pp 296–303.

191 Beveridge, op. cit., pp.124–5.

192 Beveridge, op. cit., pp.145–6.

193 Guildhall Library, Life Offices Association minutes MS 28375.8 passim and Faculty of Actuaries ASLO 1/1/2/5 pp.1–75.

194 Beveridge, op. cit., p.125.

195 Faculty of Actuaries ASLO 1/1/2/4 pp.319–28.

196 SLA A2/1/9 pp.18 and 31.

197 SLA A2/1/8 p.968.

198 Ibid. p.38.

199 SLA A7/1/13 Valuation papers 1915.

200 SLA A2/4/2 p.255.

201 *Insurance Record*, 28 February 1919, p.66.

202 *An Act to confirm a Provisional Order under the Private Legislation Procedure (Scotland) Act 1899 relating to the Standard Life Assurance Company*, 16 April 1919.

203 Richard Saville, *Bank of Scotland: A History 1695–1995*, Edinburgh, 1996 p.560.

204 SLA *Memoir of Leonard Dickson*, 1919.

205 *Bourne's Handy Insurance Manual*, op. cit., 1919.

CHAPTER 5: 'A LONG-TERM POLICY': 1919–51

1 SLA report by the manager and actuary upon the development of the company since mutualisation in 1925, 1946.

2 SLA annual report 1919.

3 G.A.S. Norman, *The Overseas History of The Standard Life Assurance Company*, Volumes 1 & 2, Edinburgh, 1950, vol.1, pp.140–1, and SLA annual reports 1880–95.

4 'Memoir of Albert Edward King', *Journal of the Institute of Actuaries*, vol.71, pp.453–5; R.C. Simmonds, *The Faculty of Actuaries 1848–1948*, Cambridge, 1948, pp.205–6; A.R. Davidson, *The History of the Faculty of Actuaries in Scotland 1856–1956*, Edinburgh, 1956, p.105.

5 SLA A11/1/2 Macnaghten to Elderton 14 July 1942.

6 Ibid. memorandum by manager, 5 December 1921.

7 SLA annual report 1919.

8 SLA A4/2/31 p.43.

9 SLA Quinquennial valuation report 1920.

10 SLA A4/2/3 p.111 and *Standard Newsletter*, 1923, pp.50–1.

11 G.A.S. Norman, *The History of the London City Offices and the Early English Branches of Standard Life*, Edinburgh, 1962, pp.14–15.

12 SLA *Standard Newsletter*, 1922.

13 Ibid. 1923, p.75.

14 *Bourne's Handy Insurance Manual*, Liverpool, 1924.

15 SLA A/1/3/7 p.397.

16 G.A.S. Norman, *Overseas History*, op. cit., vol.1, pp.155–6.

17 SLA A2/3/8 pp.304–5.

18 Norman, *Overseas History*, op. cit., vol.2, p.233.

19 SLA A3/1/4 Buenos Aires and Montevideo: report by Mr Blount, agency manager, 1920.

20 SLA A3/1/31 India: report by Mr Macnaghten upon his visit, 1922–3.

21 SLA annual report 1921.

22 SLA Triennial investigation report 1923.

23 SLA *Standard Newsletter*, March 1924, pp.71–2.

24 Ibid. p.72.

25 SLA A4/2/4 p.233.

26 SLA *Standard Newsletter*, March 1927, p.73.

27 SLA A1/3/9 p.75 and Sir William Schooling, T*he Standard Life Assurance Company 1825–1925*, London, 1925.

28 William Thomas Thomson, *Answers to observations by the Scottish Widows Fund on the comparative merits of Life Assurance Companies and Mutual Assurance Societies*, Edinburgh, 1863.

29 SLA A11/1/2 memorandum from manager 5 December 1921.

30 Ibid. letter Wallace to Macnaghten 14 April 1924.

31 Ibid. memorandum from the manager 13 May 1924.

32 See for example James O'Shea et al., *Special Report on Demutualisation*, London, 1966.

33 SLA A11/1/2 memorandum from the manager 13 May 1924.

34 Ibid. these papers are to be found on this file.

35 Ibid. actuarial opinion 4 July 1924.

36 Ibid. notes of 16 July 1924.

37 SLA A11/1/3 chairman's speech at mutualisation meeting, February 1925.

38 SLA annual report, 1925.

39 See Guildhall Library North British & Mercantile minutes (MS14040/6) p.362.

40 SLA A1/1/37 p.650.
41 Information supplied by the Davidson family.
42 Robert Skidelsky, *John Maynard Keynes – The Economist as Saviour, 1920–37*, London, 1992, pp.25–6.
43 SLA A1/1/38 pp.111–12.
44 John Newlands, *Put Not Your Trust in Money – a history of the Investment Trust Industry from 1868 to the present*, London, 1997, p.175.
45 SLA A1/1/39 p.55.
46 SLA General Investment Committee (GIC) unlisted files, 1927.
47 SLA A1/3/9 pp.153–6.
48 SLA A/7/5/17-19 annual investigation files, 1927–29.
49 SLA A1/1/40 p.289.
50 SLA A1/1/43 p.284.
51 SLA 7/12a/3 p.5.
52 GIC unlisted files, 27 July 1928.
53 Ibid.
54 Ibid. 4 September 1928.
55 Ibid. 30 June 1931.
56 SLA A7/9/25.
57 SLA A1/3/9, p.154.
58 Susan Howson, *Domestic Monetary Management in Britain 1919–38*, Cambridge, 1975, pp.86–9.
59 R.S. Sayers, *The Bank of England 1891–1944*, Cambridge, 1976, pp.443–6.
60 SLA A7/9/16.
61 for a general discussion of these problems see Archibald M. Woodruff Jr, *Farm Mortgage Loans of Life Insurance Companies*, London, 1937.
62 SLA A7/1/14 valuation papers 1920 and A 7/1/16 valuation papers 1926.
63 SLA A1/1/37 p.120 and A1/1/38 p.324.
64 SLA A1/1/38 p.182.
65 SLA A1/1/37 p.371.
66 SLA A1/1/38 p.314.
67 SLA A1/1/40 p.280.
68 SLA *Standard Newsletter* 1933, p.588.
69 SLA General Investment Committee (GIC) unlisted files, 1933.
70 SLA HS2/1/3/1/9 meeting of 30 April 1934.
71 SLA notes compiled by J.B. Dow for the centenary of the Heritable, 1962.
72 SLA HS2/1/1/9 meeting of 11 July 1934.

73 SLA *Standard Quarterly*, 1935, p.103.
74 SLA A1/1/37 p.62.
75 SLA *Standard Review*, 1930 pp.419–20.
76 SLA A5/24/1.
77 E. Gore-Brown, *Glyn Mills & Co.*, London, 1933.
78 Information supplied by the late Col. Terrence Maxwell.
79 SLA Group scheme brochures 1927.
80 SLA *Standard Review* 1930 pp.419–20.
81 SLA A1/5/3 p.207.
82 SLA Group scheme brochures, 1929.
83 SLA *Standard Quarterly*, 1935, p.102.
84 SLA A1/3/9 p.78.
85 Ibid. p.93.
86 SLA annual report 1927.
87 *Bourne's Handy Insurance Manual*, op. cit., 1931.
88 SLA report by the manager and actuary upon the development of the company since mutualisation in 1925, 1946.
89 *Bourne's Handy Insurance Manual*, op. cit., 1931.
90 SLA report by the manager and actuary upon the development of the company since mutualisation in 1925, 1946.
91 Percy Arnold, *Bankers of London*, London, 1938, section on Glyn Mills.
92 SLA *Standard Quarterly*, 1937, pp.77–8.
93 Obituary of E.M. Beilby, *The Accountants' Magazine*, 1944, p.71.
94 SLA report by the manager and actuary upon the development of the company since mutualisation in 1925, 1946.
95 SLA *Standard Review* 1930 pp.419–20.
96 SLA A1/5/3 p.207.
97 SLA *Standard Quarterly*, 1935, pp.102–3.
98 Guildhall Library LOA files MS 28375/24 minute 14 September 1928.
99 Guildhall Library LOA files MS 28375/25 agreement 13 June 1931.
100 SLA A1/3/9 pp.153 and 163.
101 SLA *Standard Review*, 1968, no.139 p.9.
102 G.P. Glover, *Standard Life Assurance Company – a story* (unpublished), 1996, pp.94–6.

103 SLA A1/5/1.
104 Ibid. pp.300, 674 and 747.
105 SLA Group scheme booklets 1933–34.
106 Ibid. 1936.
107 SLA A1/5/3 pp.402–4.
108 SLA Group scheme brochures, 1931–39.
109 Guildhall Library LOA files MS 28375/26, passim.
110 SLA *Standard Quarterly*, March 1933, p.545.
111 SLA A1/5/3 p.346.
112 SLA *Standard Quarterly*, December 1935, p.83.
113 Barry Supple, *The Royal Exchange Assurance – A History of British Insurance 1720–1970*, Cambridge, 1970, p.450.
114 SLA A1/5/3 p.388.
115 See for example SLA A1/5/2 p.328.
116 SLA A3/1/3 South Africa reports by the manager and agency manager.
117 Norman, *Overseas History*, op. cit., vol.2, p.233.
118 Ibid. pp.233–5.
119 Ibid. pp.239–40.
120 SLA A3/1/33 India report by Mr T.J. Christie, 1930.
121 SLA A1/5/1 p.791.
122 SLA A1/5/2 pp.402–9 and 625–6.
123 'Standard in India', *Standard Quarterly* 1937.
124 SLA A1/5/3 pp.180–2 and 'Not Only Prime Ministers', *Standard Quarterly*, 1938, p.146.
125 Norman, *Overseas History*, op. cit., vol.2, pp.320 and 330.
126 Ibid. pp.330 and 333–4.
127 SLA A1/5/1 p.223.
128 Ibid. pp.480 and 753.
129 Ibid. pp.757–8.
130 SLA A1/5/3 p.398.
131 SLA A3/1/6 West Indies and Montevideo: report on Mr Marshall's visit, 1929–30.
132 SLA A1/5/1 p.253.
133 SLA A1/5/5 GPC 1948 4th meeting pp.13–14.
134 Ibid. p.495.
135 SLA A1/5/1 p.778.
136 Ibid. p.253.
137 SLA A1/5/2 p.388.
138 SLA A1/5/3 p.431.
139 SLA A1/5/1 pp.196,468, and 767, and A1/5/2 pp.135,377 and 634.

140 *Committee on Industrial Assurance and Assurance on lives of children under ten years of age* [Cohen Committee] Cmd. 4376 1932–33.

141 *Bourne's Handy Insurance Manual*, op. cit., 1918–38.

142 SLA A1/3/10 minute of 16 December 1952.

143 J. Butt and J.H. Treble *History of Standard Life 1825–1975* (unpublished), 1975, chapter 6, pp.8–9; *Stock Exchange Year Book*, 1938; 'Memoir of Albert Edward King', *Journal of the Institute of Actuaries*, vol.71, pp.454-6.

144 SLA A1/3/9 p.300 and information supplied by the Davidson family.

145 SLA annual report 1942.

146 SLA A1/5/3 p.453.

147 SLA A1/5/4 GPC 1940, 1st meeting p.18 and GPC 1941 1st meeting p.11.

148 *Standard Quarterly* 1950, p.294.

149 SLA 1/5/4 GPC 1940, 1st meeting, p.1.

150 Ibid. pp.2–3.

151 Ibid. GPC 1941 1st meeting p.2.

152 Ibid. GPC 1940 1st meeting p.3.

153 Ibid. GPC 1942 1st meeting p.1.

154 Ibid. GPC 1944 2nd meeting, Canadian report pp.3–4.

155 Ibid. GPC 1945 2nd meeting, Canadian report pp.2–5.

156 SLA A3/1/25 Canada: visits and reports, 1946–59, report 1946.

157 SLA A1/5/4 . GPC 1943 2nd meeting, Uruguayan report, p.21.

158 Ibid. GPC 1945 2nd meeting, pp.14–18.

159 Ibid. GPC 1944 2nd meeting, p.23.

160 SLA A7/12a/1 meeting of 13 January 1942.

161 R.S. Sayers, *Financial Policy 1939–45*, London, 1956, pp.178 and 363–6.

162 Ibid. p.174.

163 SLA annual report, 1941.

164 SLA A7/12a/1 meeting of 13 January 1942.

165 Ibid. meeting of 12 May 1942.

166 Sayers, op. cit., p.513 and Guildhall Library LOA minutes MS 28375.39 passim.

167 Guildhall Library LOA minutes MS 28375.26 passim.

168 Sir William Beveridge, *Report on Social Insurance and Allied Services*, 1942.

169 Guildhall Library LOA minutes MS 28375.44 evidence to the Beveridge committee.

170 Beveridge Report, op. cit.,

171 Alan Sked and Chris Cook, *Post-War Britain*, (2nd ed.), London, 1984, pp.39–40.

172 Guildhall Library LOA minutes MS 28375.44 passim.

173 SLA A1/5/5 GPC 1947 3rd meeting pp.33–4.

174 SLA annual report 1946.

175 SLA A7/12/ Investment committee files, 1946.

176 SLA report by the manager and actuary upon the development of the company since its mutualisation in 1925, 1946.

177 see for example SLA A1/5/5 1948 3rd meeting p.42.

178 Ibid. 1949 4th meeting, p.23.

179 SLA A1/5/7.

180 SLA A1/5/6 GPC 3rd meeting p.34.

181 SLA A1/5/5 GPC 1947 3rd meeting p.34 and 'Pension schemes as a source of ordinary business' *Standard Review* 1947.

182 Stone & Cox, *Ordinary Branch Life Assurance Tables*, 1951.

183 SLA A1/5/4 GPC 1945 1st meeting pp.1–2.

184 SLA A1/5/5 GPC 1948 1st meeting pp.2.

185 see for example SLA A1/5/5 3rd meeting p.9.

186 SLA A1/5/5 GPC 1948 4th meeting p.23.

187 Ibid. GPC 1949 5th meeting pp.2–3.

188 SLA A1/5/6 GPC 1951 3rd meeting pp.14–15.

189 SLA A3/1/25 Canada: visits and reports, 1946–59.

190 SLA A5/1/4 GPC 1946 3rd meeting, p.14.

191 SLA A3/1/10.

192 SLA A1/5/5 GPC 1948 4th meeting p.14.

193 Ibid. GPC 1949 4th meeting p.32.

194 Ibid. and SLA A1/5/6 GPC 1950 4th meeting pp.60–3.

195 SLA A3/1/9 West Indies visits and reports, 4 February 1946.

196 SLA A3/1/25.

197 SLA A3/1/9 1952 p.14.

198 Ibid.

199 Susan Howson, *British Monetary Policy 1945–1951*, Oxford, 1993, pp.117–18.

200 Ibid. pp.193–7 and *Standard Review*, December 1947, pp.70–2.

201 Butt and Treble, op. cit., chapter 8, p.65 interview with F.S. Jamieson.

202 J.C.R. Dow, *The Management of the British Economy*, Cambridge, 1964, pp.242–4.

203 SLA A7/12a/3–4.

204 SLA A7/12a/3 meeting of 21 March 1950 and 2/12a/4 meeting of 9 December 1951.

205 SLA A3/1/25 1949, p.3.

206 SLA A7/12a/3 meeting of 21 March 1950.

207 SLA A1/6/8 meeting of 8 November 1949.

208 SLA A1/3/10 p.18.

209 Information supplied by the late J.S. Gammell.

210 *Standard Review*, 1951 p.561.

211 SLA A1/3/10 p.334.

212 G.P. Glover, op. cit., p.95.

Feature: 'Pension schemes and the Inland Revenue' (p.200)

1 For a discussion of the issues, see Leslie Hannah, *Inventing Retirement: The Development of Occupational Pensions in Britain*, Cambridge, 1986, pp.47–50.

2 'Group Schemes', *Standard Quarterly*, 1938, pp.192–7.

3 H. Dougharty, *Pensions, Endowment and Life Assurance Schemes*, London, 1927, pp.6–7.

4 Bernard Robertson and H. Samuels, *Pension and Superannuation Funds*, London, 1928, p.12.

CHAPTER 6: 'A MOST REMARKABLE STORY OF SUCCESS': 1951–70.

1 SLA annual report, 1968.

2 L.R. Klieg 'Patterns of Saving – The Surveys of 1953 and 1854', *Bulletin Oxford Institute of Statistics*, May, 1955.

3 SLA quoted in annual report 1957, p.10.

4 SLA A1/5/6 General Purposes Committee (G.P.C.) 1952 1st meeting p.1.

5 SLA A1/5/7 G.P.C. 1953 1st meeting p.1.

6 *Report of the Committee on the*

Taxation Treatment of Provisions for Retirement Cmd 9063, 1954. For a discussion of the report see L. Hannah, *Inventing Retirement – The development of occupational pensions*, London, 1986, pp.49–50.

7   SLA A1/5/8 GPC 1957 1st meeting p.1.
8   Rodney Lowe, *The Welfare State in Britain since 1945*, 1998, p.254 and M.J. Daunton *A Property-owning democracy*, 1987, p.78.
9   SLA A1/5/8 G.P.C. 1st meeting p.4.
10 G.P. Glover, *Standard Life Assurance Company – A Story* (unpublished), 1996, p.108.
11 Information supplied by Bob Coutts.
12 SLA annual reports 1951 and 1971.
13 J. Butt and J.H. Treble, *History of Standard Life 1825–1975* (unpublished), chapter 8 p.44.
14 SLA annual report, 1955 1st meeting pp.10–11.
15 SLA A/1/5/7 GPC 1954 1st meeting p.2, information supplied by G.P. Glover, and annual report 1957, p.11.
16 SLA A1/5/8 GPC 1958 1st meeting pp.2 and 24.
17 SLA A1/5/9 GPC 1960 1st meeting p.1 and A1/5/10 GPC 1962 1st meeting p.1; GPC 1963 1st meeting p.1.
18 SLA A1/5/10 GPC 1963 1st meeting p.1.
19 SLA A1/5/11 GPC 1966 1st meeting p.1.
20 SLA A1/5/8 GPC 1958 1st meeting p.2.
21 John Newlands, *Put Not Your Trust in Money – A history of the Investment Trust Industry from 1868 to the present day*, London, 1997, pp.211–12 and Hannah, op. cit., p.75.
22 *Standard Review*, 1967, pp.15–16.
23 SLA A1/5/12 1969 1st meeting pp.2–3.
24 SLA A1/4/6 Advertising guard book p.21.
25 SLA A1/5/7 GPC 1953 1st meeting p.1.
26 SLA A1/5/8 GPC 1956 1st meeting p.1.
27 SLA A1/5/9 GPC 1959 1st meeting p.1.

28 SLA A1/5/9 GPC 1961 1st meeting pp.1–2.
29 SLA A1/5/10 GPC 1964 1st meeting pp.1–3.
30 SLA A1/5/11 GPC 1965 1st meeting p.3 and 1966 first meeting pp.2–3.
31 SLA A1/5/12 GPC 1968 1st meeting p.6.
32 SLA A/1/5/12 GPC 1968 1st meeting p.11 and Glover, op. cit., p.105.
33 SLA A1/5/12 GPC 1969 1st meeting pp.4–5.
34 SLA A1/5/12 GPC 1970 1st meeting p.4.
35 SLA A1/5/6 GPC 1952 2nd meeting p.48 and A1/5/7 GPC 1953 2nd meeting p.46.
36 SLA A1/5/7 GPC 1953 2nd meeting p.47 and GPC 1954 2nd meeting p.39.
37 SLA A1/5/7 GPC 1955 2nd meeting p.40.
38 Leslie Hannah, *Inventing Retirement: The Development of Occupational Pensions in Britain*, Cambridge, 1986, p.50
39 SLA A1/5/8 GPC 1956 2nd meeting pp.41–2, 1957 2nd meeting pp.42–4 and 1958 2nd meeting p.26.
40 SLA A1/5/8 GPC 1956 2nd meeting p.43.
41 Hannah, op. cit., pp.55–6.
42 SLA A1/5/8 GPC 1958 2nd meeting p.45–6.
43 Memorandum on pension business by Ernest Bromfield, 1959, cited in Butt and Treble, op. cit., chapter 8 p.56.
44 Dennett, op. cit., pp.346–7.
45 SLA A1/5/8 GPC 2nd meeting 1958 p.46.
46 Ibid. p.26.
47 Ibid. p.45.
48 Dennett, op. cit., p.347.
49 SLA A1/5/9 GPC 1960 2nd meeting pp.30–1.
50 Information supplied by T.W.N. MacCallum cited in Butt and Treble, op. cit., p.56.
51 SLA A1/5/9 GPC 1960 second meeting pp.30–1.
52 Ibid. GPC 1961 2nd meeting pp.32–3.
53 SLA A1/5/10 GPC 1962 2nd meeting pp.26–7.
54 Richard Roberts, *Schroders –*

Merchants & Bankers, London, 1992, pp.410–11.
55 SLA A1/5/10 GPC 1964 2nd meeting p 66.
56 SLA A1/5/11 GPC 1965 2nd meeting pp.2–3.
57 Ibid. GPC 1966 2nd meeting pp.47–8.
58 SLA A1/5/12 GPC 1969 1st meeting pp.68–9.
59 *National Superannuation and Social Insurance: Proposals for Earnings Related Social Security*, Cmd 3883, 1969.
60 SLA A1/5/12 GPC 1st meeting p.68.
61 SLA annual report 1969 p.17.
62 Hannah, op. cit., p.60.
63 *Standard Review*, 1968 pp.67–8.
64 Information supplied by the late J.S. Gammell.
65 SLAC board papers 1974–79, paper 'Canada', 25 April 1978.
66 SLA A/1/3/21 encl. 36 Summary of report by the group manager on his visit to Canada, July 1955, p 2, and A1/3/24 encl. 75 report by directors on their visit to Canada, Autumn 1962, p.12.
67 SLA A/1/3/21 encl. 36, op. cit., p.3.
68 Ibid., pp.3–4, 6.
69 SLA A1/5/10 report from Canada 1963, p.13.
70 SLA A1/3/26 encl. 146 report to the directors by the general manger on his visit to Canada, June 1969, p.15.
71 SLA A1/3/26 encl. 158 report to the directors by the general manager on the future of the Canadian branch, 1969.
72 SLA A1/3/10 private minute book, no.10, p.369.
73 SLA A1/3/21 encl. 29 report to the directors by the general manager on his visit to Uruguay, 1954.
74 SLA A1/5/7 GPC 1953 4th meeting pp.70–3, 1954, 4th meeting pp.81–4, 1955 4th meeting pp.85–8, and SLA A1/5/8 GPC 1956 4th meeting pp.93–8.
75 SLA A1/5/8 GPC 1957 4th meeting p.111.
76 SLA A1/5/9 GPC 1960 3rd meeting p.57.
77 SLA A1/5/10 GPC 1962 3rd meeting pp.70–1.

78 SLA A1/5/10 GPC 1964 3rd meeting pp.61–5.

79 SLA A1/3/24 encl. 95 report by the actuary on his visit to Uruguay, 4 November 1965.

80 SLA A1/3/25 encl. 120 memorandum by the general manager on the Uruguayan branch, 15 December 1967.

81 SLA A3/1/9 Visits and reports to the West Indies 1946–71.

82 SLA A1/5/9 GPC 1961 3rd meeting p.40.

83 J.E. Newbolt, the secretary in Trinidad, was appointed manager but died suddenly before he took up the post.

84 SLA A1/5/9 GPC 1961 3rd meeting pp.32–43.

85 SLA A1/5/11 GPC 1965 3rd meeting p.53.

86 SLA A1/3/25 encl. 101 report by A.E. Bromfield on a visit to Trinidad in August 1966.

87 SLA A1/5/12 GPC 1968 3rd meeting pp.35–6, 1969 3rd meeting pp.63–6.

88 SLA A1//3/26 encl. 176 memorandum on Trinidad, 25 June 1970.

89 SLA A1/5/10 GPC 1963 3rd meeting p.59.

90 SLA A1/5/11 GPC 1965 3rd meeting pp.44–5.

91 SLA A1/5/11 GPC 1966 3rd meeting pp.56–8.

92 SLA A1/5/11 GPC 1967 3rd meeting pp.49–51.

93 SLA A3/1/9 Visits and reports to the West Indies 1946–71, report by Joint agency manager on his visit to the West Indies, October/November 1968.

94 SLA A1/5/12 GPC 1969 3rd meeting pp.58–60.

95 SLA A1/3/26 encl. 185 report on visit to Canada and Jamaica of the chairman, Sir Thomas Waterlow and the general manager, October 1970.

96 SLA A7/12a/6 investment file 1953 and A7 /12a/10 investment file, 1957.

97 SLA A7/12a/8 investment file 1955.

98 SLA A7/12a/9 investment file 1956.

99 F.T. Blackaby, *British Economic Policy 1960–74*, London, 1978, pp 326–7.

100 SLA A7/12a/9 and 10 investment file 1956 and 1957.

101 SLA A7/12a/9 investment file 1956. The de Zoete & Gorton *Equity-Gilt Study* has been published every year since 1956 and is now published by Barclays Capital.

102 George G. Blakey, *The Post-War History of the London Stock Market – Fifty years of business, politics and people*, third edition, London, 1997, pp.51–2.

103 SLA A7/12a/11 investment file 1958.

104 Ibid.

105 SLA A7/12a/13 investment file 1960, memorandum on property transactions p.7.

106 SLA A7/12a/13 investment file 1960 memorandum on property investments p.4.

107 SLA memorandum on Hammerson Property Investment Company, 1990.

108 SLA A7/12a/12 and A7/12a/13 investment files 1959 and 1960.

109 SLA A7/12a/14 investment file 1961 memorandum on further finance for the Hammerson Group, pp.4–11 and memorandum on Hammerson Group, op. cit.

110 SLA A7/12a/13 and 14 investment files 1960 and 1961 memoranda on property investments; Peter Michael Scott, *Financial Institutions and the British Property Investment Market 1850–1980*, University of Oxford D.Phil thesis, 1992, pp.234–5.

111 Blakey, op. cit., pp.62–3.

112 SLA A7/12a/15 investment file 1962 memorandum on long term equity policy in relation to sterling new money.

113 SLA A7/12a/17 investment file 1964.

114 W.J. Reader & D. Kynaston, *Phillips & Drew – Professionals in the City*, London, 1998, p.98.

115 SLA A7/12a/15 investment file 1962 memorandum on long term equity policy in relation to sterling new money pp.14–20.

116 SLA A7/12a/19 and A7/12a/20 investment files 1966 and 1967.

117 SLA A7/12a/16 investment file 1963.

118 SLA A7/12a/17 investment file 1964, memorandum regarding City Wall Properties Limited.

119 SLA A1/3/26 encl. 149 City Wall Properties Limited, memorandum by Investment Manager, 26 August 1969 and A1/3/10 private minute book no.10, pp.362 and 363, and 378.

120 SLA memorandum on property investment by P.J. Henwood for Turnberry investment conference 1972.

121 SLA A7/12a/13 investment file 1960.

122 Richard Saville, *Bank of Scotland: A History 1695–1995*, 1996, pp.673–4. In this account Standard Life is reported to have owned part of Capital Finance at the time of the Bank's first involvement, which was not the case.

123 SLA A7/12a/18 investment file 1965 memorandum regarding Capital Finance Company Ltd.

124 SLA A7/12a/19 investment file 1966 memorandum regarding Capital Finance Company Ltd.

125 SLA A7/12a/20 investment file 1967.

126 SLA A1/3/25 encl. 112 memorandum on Capital Finance Co. Ltd.

127 SLA annual report 1967 p.12.

128 SLA A1/3/10 private minute book no.10 p.347.

129 Ibid. p.352 and A1/3/26 encl. 152 memorandum on Capital Finance, 7 October 1969.

130 Glover, op. cit., pp.127–8.

131 SLA A7/12a/21 investment file 1968, memorandum on long-term equity policy.

132 SLA board papers 1970–74, encl. no.4/73.

133 Butt and Treble, op. cit., chapter 8, pp.23–6.

134 *The Economist*, insurance supplements, 1950–74.

135 SLA annual report 1970 p.14.

136 SLA annual report 1969 p.19.

137 D. Kynaston, *Cazenove & Co. – A History*, London, 1991 p.250.

138 SLA A7/12a/20 investment file 1968, memorandum on long-term equity policy p.18.

139 SLA annual report 1961 p.4.
140 Glover, op. cit., pp.101–5.
141 *Standard Review* 1964 pp.66–7.
142 *Standard Quarterly*, 1953 no.92, p.2.
143 Ibid., 1970 pp.53–5.
144 Ibid., 1969 pp.56–8; Glover, op. cit., p.121.
145 *Standard Review*, 1951, opposite p.542.

Feature: 'The coming of the computer' (p.268)
1 SLA board papers encl. no.33/82.
2 Ibid., 1959, p.18, and information supplied by G.C. Philip.
3 SLA oral history project interview with Alison Hewat, 1998.
4 SLA A1/5/10 GPC 1962, second meeting, p.25.
5 J. Butt and J.H. Treble, *History of Standard Life 1825–1975* (unpublished), ch.8, p.62.
6 *Standard Review*, 1967, pp.98–102.
7 SLA GPC A/5/12 1970 first meeting, p.69.

CHAPTER 7: MAKING PROGRESS: 1970–88
1 SLA A1/5/17 Property and General Purposes Committee Meetings (PGPCM) 1975 p.8.
2 SLA A1/5/13 PGPCM 1st meeting 1971, p.93.
3 F.T. Blackaby (ed.), *British Economic Policy 1960–74*, London, 1978, pp.52–72.
4 Jorg Finsinger, Elizabeth Hammond, and Julian Tapp, *Insurance Competition or Regulation?*, London, 1985, p.25.
5 *The Economist*, 31 July 1971, p.69.
6 *Linked Life Assurance – Report of the Committee on Property Bonds and Equity-Linked Assurance*, London, cmnd. 5281, 1973.
7 SLA annual report 1973 p.11.
8 G.P. Glover, *Standard Life Assurance Company – A Story* (unpublished), 1996, p.137.
9 SLA A/1/3/27 encl. no.P5/72 and information provided by Iain Lumsden.
10 SLA A1/3/27 encl. P17/73.
11 SLA A1/5/13 PGPCM 1971, p.4.
12 SLA Ibid. encl. P12/71.
13 SLA A1/5/13 PGPCM 1971, p.37

and A1/5/14 1971, p.53-4.
14 SLA F.S. Jamieson, Investment Procedure Paper no.1, 1972, p.12.
15 L. Dennet, *A Sense of Security: 150 Years of Prudential*, London, 1998, p.315.
16 SLA F.S. Jamieson, Investment Procedure Paper no.1, September 1972 and memorandum on investment procedure, 17 October 1972.
17 SLA S.C. Keppie, Long-term investment policy Paper no.3, September 1972 and The 'Home Fund' ordinary share portfolio paper no.4, September 1972.
18 SLA P.J. Henwood Property investment paper no.5, September 1972.
19 SLA property investment report, 1973.
20 SLA A1/3/27 board papers encl. no.P14/71.
21 SLA report of Standard Life directors and executive meeting at Turnberry Hotel, 7 October 1972, p.6.
22 SLA A1/5/14 PGPCM 1972, p.4.
23 SLA A1/5/16 PGPCM 1974, p.12.
24 SLA A1/5/13 PGPCM 1971, p.91 and A1/5/14, 1972, p.118.
25 SLA A1/5/15 PGPCM 1973, p.138, and A1/5/16, 1974 pensions report, p.3.
26 SLA A1/5/16 PGPCM 1974, pensions report, p.10.
27 SLA A1/5/15 Ibid, 1963, p.138.
28 SLA A1/5/17 PGPCM minutes 1975 p.12.
29 SLA A3/2/8 home branch reports, 1978, p.104.
30 SLA home branches reports, 1985.
31 Neil Buchanan, *Know Your Pension Rights*, London, 1977, p.8.
32 SLA A1/5/15 PGPCM 1973, pp.139–40, and A1/5/16 1974, pensions report pp.8–9.
33 *Better Pensions Fully Protected Against Inflation*, London cmnd. 5713, 1974 and SLA A1/5/16 PGPCM 1974, pensions report pp.7–8.
34 SLA A1/5/16 Ibid., pp.8–9.
35 Ibid., p.7 and information provided by G.P. Glover and G.D. Gwilt.
36 SLA A1/5/17 PGPCM 1975, pp.103–4, and Leslie Hannah, *Inventing Retirement: The Develop-

ment of Occupational Pensions in Britain*, Cambridge, 1986, pp.61–2.
37 SLA board papers, a summary of the life assurance case against nationalisation, 12 October 1976, and letter to policy-holders 1 March 1977.
38 SLA A1/3/27 board papers encl. no.P10/73.
39 SLA A1/3/27 board papers encl. no.P9/72.
40 A.J.C. Britton, *Macroeconomic Policy in Britain 1974–87*, Cambridge, 1991, pp.23–4.
41 George G. Blakey, *The Post-War History of the London Stock Market: Fifty Years of Business, Politics and People*, London, 1997, p.175.
42 SLA board papers encl. no.4/74, property investment report, 1973, pp.10–13, and property investment report, 1974, p.16.
43 SLA A1/5/16 PGPCM 1974, p.7, and Margaret Reid, *The Secondary Banking Crisis, 1973–75: Its Causes and Course*, London, 1982, p.135.
44 Finsinger et al., op. cit., pp.153-4.
45 Finsinger et al., op. cit., pp.26–8 and 153–5, and information supplied by G.C. Philip.
46 SLA board papers 12 April 1976.
47 Finsinger et al., op. cit., p.155.
48 SLA A1/5/16 PGPCM 1974, pp.6–9.
49 SLA board papers encl. no.2/75, and Reid, op. cit., p.126.
50 SLA board papers encl. no.P21/74.
51 SLA board papers letter Gordon Richardson to T. Risk, 27 December 1974.
52 Dennett op. cit., p.338 and information supplied by G.C. Philip.
53 A.D. Shedden 'The Strength of the Company', *Standard Review*, 1974, p.22.
54 SLA board papers encl. no.4/75 and annual report 1974.
55 SLA A1/5/16 PGPCM 1974, pensions report.
56 SLA board papers encl. no.10/75.
57 SLA A1/5/17 PGPCM 1975, pp.13–4.
58 SLA A1/5/17 PGPCM 1975 and A3/2/6-8 home branches reports and Canadian branches reports 1977–79.
59 SLA A3/2/8 home branches reports

and Canadian branches reports 1978, p.10.

60 SLA A3/2/6 home branches reports and Canadian branches reports 1977, p.11.

61 SLA board papers encl. no.14/78.

62 Information supplied by Tom King.

63 SLA home branch reports 1981.

64 Information supplied by A.D. Sheddon.

65 SLA A3/2/8 home branches reports and Canadian branches reports 1978, pp.102–4.

66 Ibid., pp.100–5.

67 SLA A3/2/9 home branches reports and Canadian branches reports 1979, p.37.

68 SLA board papers memorandum on investment targets, 29 November, 1979.

69 SLA board papers encl. no.11/80.

70 Information supplied by G.D. Gwilt and annual report, 1981.

71 SLA board papers memoranda on Cutler Street and agricultural property, 25 October 1977.

72 Penelope Hunting, *Cutler's Gardens*, London, 1984.

73 SLA Property investment reports, 1978–83.

74 SLA A1/3/26 board papers encl. no.185.

75 SLA Canadian file ii.

76 SLA A1/5/13 PGPCM 1971, Canadian report.

77 SLA A1/5/15 PGPCM 1973, Canadian report.

78 Ibid.

79 Ibid.

80 SLA annual report 1975, p.11.

81 SLA board papers letter Tom Risk to Lucien Rolland 10 October 1975.

82 SLA board papers report on Visit to Canada 25 November 1975.

83 SLA board papers Risk to Rolland, op. cit.

84 SLA Canadian file 11 Barry to Donald, 15 April 1977, and endorsement.

85 SLA A1/3/29 board papers encl. no.P11/77 and Canadian file Donald to Burns 15 September 1976.

86 SLA Canadian file 11 (summary information given to the board, 26 April 1977).

87 Ibid.

88 Ibid. report of visit to Canada, 16 May 1977.

89 Ibid. review of the Quebec problem, 30 June 1977.

90 Ibid. memorandum on Canada, 2 May 1977.

91 SLA A3/2/5 Canadian annual report, 1976.

92 SLA A3/2/6 Canadian annual report, 1977.

93 SLA A3/2/6 home branches report and Canadian branches report 1977.

94 SLA Canadian file 11(i) memorandum, 22 August 1977.

95 Ibid. memorandum Canada, 22 March 1978.

96 Ibid.

97 SLA Reminiscences of the ManuLife bid by John Burns, 1981.

98 SLA A1/3/29 board papers, encl. no.P1/78.

99 SLA Canadian file 11(i) notes on basis for assessing surplus in Canada, March 1978.

100 SLA A1/3/29 board papers encl. no.P9/78.

101 SLA Canadian file 11(i), Lucien Rolland to A.M. Hodge, 21 April 1978.

102 SLA A1/3/29 board papers encl. no.P12/78 letter Lucien Rolland to A.M. Hodge 21 April 1978, and encl. no.P14/78.

103 SLA Reminiscences of the ManuLife bid by John Burns, 1981.

104 SLA A1//329 board papers encl. no.P12/78, memorandum business in Canada, 25 April 1978.

105 SLA Canadian file 11(i) memorandum on Canada by Waterlow, 9 May 1978.

106 SLA A1/3/29 board papers encl. no.P15/78 and encl. no.P16/78.

107 SLA Canadian file 11(i) memorandum on Canada by Waterlow, 9 May 1978, p.4.

108 Ibid. Donald to Rolland, 10 May 1978.

109 Ibid. Donald to Humphreys, 17 May 1978.

110 Ibid. extract of minute, 17 May 1978.

111 Ibid. and Canadian file 11(d) papers, May–July 1978.

112 Ibid, press release, 25 July 1978.

113 SLA board papers for meeting 26 July 1978.

114 SLA board papers letter Lucien Rolland to A.M. Hodge, 24 August 1978.

115 SLA Canadian file 11(d) notes of telephone conversation between Donald and Jackson, 24 August 1978

116 Ibid. Donald to Bell, 5 October 1978

117 SLA A1/3/29 board papers encl. no.P19/1978.

118 SLA Reminiscences of the ManuLife bid by John Burns, 1981.

119 SLA Canadian file 11(d) Donald to Eckler, 13 October 1978.

120 Ibid. memorandum of 8 November 1978.

121 Ibid. press release, 20 November 1978.

122 SLA A1/3/29 board papers encl. no.P20/1978.

123 Ibid. encl. no.P22/78.

124 Ibid. encl. no.P23/78.

125 SLA annual reports 1978 and 1983.

126 SLA board papers Canadian reports 23 January 1979.

127 SLA board papers report on visit to Montreal, 2 May 1979.

128 SLA board papers for meeting of 17 July and 18 December 1979.

129 'Mr. D.W.A. Donald', *Standard Review*, 1979 and information supplied by Sir William Kerr Fraser.

130 Hannah, op cit., p.62.

131 Britton, op. cit., pp.44–66.

132 Ibid., p.320.

133 SLA A1/3/6 encl. no.P30/80.

134 Insurance Ombudsman annual report and case review, London, 1995, p.ii.

135 Review of Investor Protection, cmnd. 9125, 1984.

136 SLA marketing newsletter, Richard Lambert 'Anatomy of the Gower Report', *Financial Times*, 1982.

137 Richard Roberts, *Schroders Merchants & Bankers*, London, 1992, p.448.

138 SLA marketing newsletter 1982–83, Rosemary Burr 'When the consumer is the casualty', *Financial Times*.

139 Roger Hardman 'Why pact on life policy was killed', *Sunday Standard*,

SLA marketing news, 1982–83 and SLA home branch reports, 1982.

140 SLA annual report 1982, p.2 and information supplied by G.P. Glover.

141 SLA marketing news 1983–84, 'Borrie accuses insurers of giving customers poor deal', *The Times*.

142 SLA annual report 1982, p.2.

143 G.D. Gwilt 'The Company's Future', *Standard Review*, 1981, pp.6–10.

144 SLA home branches reports 1983 and annual report 1983, p.3.

145 SLA annual report 1984, p.2.

146 SLA annual report 1987, p.7, and SLA home branch reports 1987.

147 SLA annual report 1984, p.7.

148 SLA home branch reports 1984 and 1985.

149 SLA home branches reports 1983.

150 Occupational Pensions Board, *Report on Greater Security for the Rights and Expectations of Members of Occupational Pension Schemes*, London, 1982.

151 Nigel Vinson and Philip Chappell, *Personal and Portable Pensions for All*, London, 1983.

152 SLA annual report 1984, pp.3–4.

153 See for example T. Miller, 'Case for Money Purchase' in *FT, Pensions in 1984: A Time for Change*, London, 1984.

154 SLA marketing newsletter, 20 August 1984.

155 DHSS, *Personal Pensions: A Consultative Document*, London, 1984.

156 DHSS, *Reform of Social Security*, London, 1985.

157 *Reform of Social Security Programme for Action*, London, 1985.

158 SLA annual report 1985, p.4.

159 Binder Hamlyn, *A Pocket Guide to Personal Pensions*, London, 1987.

160 SLA annual report 1986, p.5.

161 Britton, op. cit., pp.74–80.

162 SLA board papers encl. no.28/82.

163 See for example SLA board papers encl. no.14/85.

164 SLA A1/3/30 encl. no.P7/82.

165 SLA board papers investment reports 1976–85.

166 SLA board papers encl. no.25/84 and encl. no.12/85 p.4.

167 W.J. Reader, and D. Kynaston, *Professionals in the City: A History of*

Philips & Drew, London, 1998, p.186.

168 See for example Andrew Lycett, *From Diamond Sculls to Golden Handcuffs*, London, 1998, pp.143–5.

169 SLA A1/3/30 encl. nos.P7/84 and P11/84 and P16/84 and information supplied by Sir Robert Smith.

170 SLA board papers encl. no.42/87.

171 SLA board papers encl. no.12/86 and encl. no.19/87.

172 SLA Investment Committee minutes, 1985–87.

173 SLA Property investment reports 1982–86.

174 SLA board papers encl. no.27/86.

175 SLA Property investment reports 1981–86.

176 Richard Saville, *Bank of Scotland: A History 1695–1995*, Edinburgh, 1996, pp.778–9. Saville states that the negotiations began in November; but both Sir Thomas Risk and Sir Robert Smith confirm September.

177 SLA marketing news, 1983–84, Barry Riley, 'Sassenach Swipe at Standard Life', *Financial Times*.

178 Tom King, 'Proven Commitment to the Agency System', *Brokers' Monthly and Insurance Adviser*, March 1986, p.145.

179 G.P. Glover, 'Why independents must fight back together', *Money Marketing News*, 29 November 1986.

180 SLA annual report 1987 pp.10-11.

181 SLA annual report 1985, pp.4–5.

182 Information supplied by G.P. Glover and Tom King.

183 SLA marketing news 1985–86 'Will your insurer go bust?', *The Times*.

184 SLA board papers encl. no.26/86.

185 SLA annual report 1983, p.4 and information supplied by Sir Robert Smith.

186 SLA annual report, 1985, p.9.

187 SLA home branch report 1985, p.22.

188 SLA home branch report, 1985.

189 SLA marketing news 1 April 1986, 'Eight from Standard', *Unit Trust Management*.

190 SLA annual report 1986, pp.4–5.

191 SLA marketing news 1 April 1986.

192 SLA home branch report 1987, p.12.

193 Information supplied by A.S. Fernie.

194 SLA board papers encl. no.7/81.

195 SLA board papers encl. no.9/82.

196 SLA board papers encl. no.5/84.

197 SLA annual report 1983, p.12.

198 SLA board papers encl. no.5/84.

199 SLA board papers encl. no.8/85.

200 SLA annual report 1987, p.14.

201 SLA board papers encl. no.7/86.

202 SLA board papers encl. no.40/88.

203 SLA board papers encl. no.30/84.

204 SLA annual reports 1983–86.

205 Ibid., 1984, p.9.

206 Information supplied by John Brindle.

207 Information supplied by John Brindle.

208 SLA home branch report 1981.

209 SLA home branch report 1984.

210 SLA annual report, 1986.

211 SLA annual report, 1987, pp.4–5.

212 Helen Pridham 'A Standard Triumph', *Money Observer*, 2 February 1987.

CHAPTER 8: AIMING FOR EXCELLENCE: 1988–2000

1 SLA annual report, 1987.

2 See for example SLA minutes of executive group, 19 April 1988.

3 SLA annual report, 1988.

4 SLA board papers encl. no.51/98.

5 SLA Group corporate objective.

6 SLA The business model, 1989.

7 See for example S. Roux-Levrat, *The Strategic Management of a Life Insurance Company*, Edinburgh University Management School, 1994.

8 SLA board papers encl. no.17/91 and the financial strategy version 1, 1994.

9 SLA board papers encl. n. 51/98, p.7, and encl. no.44/90 p.8.

10 SLA board papers encl. no.17/91.

11 SLA board annual report research & planning 1991, pp.4–6.

12 SLA board papers encl. no.57/88.

13 SLA board annual report research & planning 1991, pp.12–14.

14 SLA letter: A.S. Bell to all members of UK staff, 27 May 1992.

15 SLA board papers encl. no.27/92.

16 SLA board papers encl. no.50/92.

17 Standard Life annual report, 1992.

18 Ibid., 1993.

19 SLA board papers encl. no.27/93 and minutes of meeting held at Dalmahoy, 18 and 19 April, and Turnberry, 1 June 1995.
20 SLA board papers encl. no.12/96 and balanced scorecard, 1994/5.
21 SLA annual report, 1995.
22 SLA board papers encl. no.76/97.
23 SLA board papers encl. no.57/88.
24 SLA board papers encl. no.23/89
25 Ibid.
26 SLA Papers for private meetings of the board, 28 February and 20 April 1989 and 18 December 1990.
27 SLA minutes of the meeting of the directors' investment group, 19 December 1989.
28 SLA annual report of the investment division, 16 May 1990.
29 See for example *European Fund Industry Directory*, 1989.
30 SLA minutes of the meeting of the directors' investment group, 1990–91.
31 SLA board papers encl. nos.17/91 and 5/92.
32 SLA board papers encl. no.6/92.
33 SLA board papers encl. nos.4/93 and 5/93.
34 SLA board papers encl. no.45/93.
35 SLA annual reports, property investment department, 1988–94.
36 SLA House view, January 1995.
37 SLA minutes of directors' investment group, 27 June 1995.
38 SLA minutes of the directors' investment group 28 February 1995.
39 SLA minutes of the directors' investment group 24 October 1995.
40 William M. Mercer, *European Pension Fund Managers Guide*, London, 1996.
41 SLA Bank of Scotland private file, 1996.
42 SLA board papers encl. no.72/97.
43 SLA board papers encl. no.28/98.
44 *The Scotsman*, 8 September 1999, p.27.
45 SLA Standard Life Investments launch literature, 1999.
46 SLA Standard Life Investments private equity fund brochure, 1999.
47 See for example Geraldine Kaye 'Current Regulation' in Bernard Benjamin et al, *Pension – the Problems of Today and Tomorrow*, London, 1987.
48 SLA board papers encl. no.39/88.
49 SLA board papers encl. no.56/88.
50 SLA Letter: A.S. Bell to IFAs, 11 January 1989.
51 SLA Letter: J.D. Birrell to A.S. Bell, 1 February 1989.
52 SLA board papers encl. no.15/90.
53 SLA board papers encl. nos.38/90 and 40/90.
54 SLA board papers encl. no.33/90.
55 SLA board papers encl. no.3/90.
56 Ibid.
57 SLA board papers encl. nos.25/89 and 26/89.
58 SLA board papers encl. no.3/90.
59 This issue was discussed at every executive meeting during 1989 and 1990.
60 Standard Life annual report, 1988.
61 SLA board papers encl. no.25/89.
62 SLA board papers encl. no.47/89.
63 SLA marketing news, John Willman, 'Wanted: a user-friendly system of City regulation, *Financial Times*, 1991.
64 Standard Life annual report, 1991, pp.14-15.
65 Standard Life annual report, 1992, p.14.
66 SLA board papers encl. no.27/92
67 SLA board papers encl. no.25/93.
68 SLA board papers encl. no.12/96.
69 SLA board papers encl. no.4/94.
70 Ibid.
71 SLA board papers encl. no.44/93.
72 SLA board papers encl. nos.11/94 and 12/94.
73 SLA board papers encl. no.43/93.
74 SLA UK senior executive – minutes of meeting 2 February 1995.
75 SLA UK senior executive minutes of meeting 3 March 1995.
76 SLA board papers encl. no.12/96.
77 SLA board papers encl. no.12/96.
78 SLA board papers encl. no.24/93.
79 Standard Life annual reports 1993 and 1994.
80 SLA board papers encl. no.40/93.
81 SLA company operational plan, 1993–94, United Kingdom.
82 SLA board papers encl. no.25/93.
83 SLA UK senior executive minutes of meetings of 16 January and 13 February 1995.
84 SLA board papers encl. no.1/94.
85 SLA board papers encl. no.51/94.
86 SLA board papers encl. no.57/93.
87 SLA report on compliance, 27 June 1995.
88 see for example *Euro-Forum – the Life Insurance Industry*, London, 1995.
89 SLA board papers encl. no.12/96.
90 SLA board papers encl. no.4/95.
91 Harriet Dawes and Jane Samsworth, *Guide to Pensions Act 1995*, London, 1995.
92 Frank Field and Matthew Owen, *Private Pensions for All – Squaring the Circle*, London, 1993.
93 See for example E. Philip Davies *Pension Funds: Retirement-Income Security and Capital Markets – An International Perspective*, Oxford, 1995, pp.268–70.
94 Christopher Daykin, F*unding the Future? Problems of Pension Reform*, London, 1998, pp.30–8.
95 A new contract for welfare: Partnership in Pensions, cmd. 4179, 1998.
96 SLA UK senior executive minutes of meetings 18 and 19 April 1995.
97 See for example SLA UK senior executive minutes of meetings of 3 June of 4 November 1996 and board papers encl. no.79/96.
98 SLA board papers encl. no.79/96.
99 SLA board papers encl. no.100/97.
100 SLA board papers encl. no.99/97.
101 SLA board papers encl. no.33/98.
102 SLA Prime Health annual reports 1994–98.
103 SLA UK senior executive minutes of meetings 18 March and 8 April, 1997.
104 SLA board papers encl. no.46/97.
105 SLA board papers encl. no.01/98
106 SLA board papers encl. no.9/98.
107 SLA board papers encl. no.25/99.
108 SLA board papers encl. no.40/88.
109 SLA board papers encl. no.7/98.
110 Ibid.
111 SLA board papers encl. no.9/90 and Canadian annual review, 1989.
112 SLA board papers encl. no.8/92.
113 SLA board papers encl. no.35/91.
114 SLA board papers encl. no.48/92.
115 SLA board papers encl. no.31/93.
116 SLA board papers encl. no.32/93.
117 Canadian annual review, 1993.

118 SLA board papers encl. no.44/93.
119 Canadian annual review 1993.
120 SLA board papers encl. no.13/96.
121 SLA board papers encl. no.10/96.
122 Canadian annual review 1996.
123 Canadian annual review 1998, SLA Canadian balanced scorecards 1997–98, and SLA board papers encl. no.105/98.
124 SLA board papers encl. nos.102/97 and 5/98 and Canadian annual review, 1997.
125 SLA board papers, Canadain Investment annual report, 1989/90.
126 SLA board papers encl. no.102/98.
127 SLA board papers encl. no.3/90.

128 SLA board papers encl. no.2/91.
129 Standard Life annual report 1993.
130 SLA board papers encl. no.3/90.
131 Standard Life annual report 1993.
132 SLA board papers encl. no.50/92.
133 SLA board papers encl. nos.33/98 and 40/99.
134 SLA board papers encl. no.51/89.
135 SLA board papers encl. no.22/90.
136 SLA board papers encl. nos.44/90 and 40/91.
137 SLA board papers encl. no.10/93.
138 SLA board papers memorandum on acquisition prospects in Spain, 25 April and encl. nos.54/97 and 33/98.

139 SLA board papers memorandum on Germany, 23 May 1995.
140 SLA board papers encl. no.33/98.
141 SLA board papers encl. no.40/99.
142 SLA board papers memorandum on India, 27 June 1995.
143 SLA board papers memorandum on joint venture in India, 22 August 1995.
144 SLA board papers encl. no.40/99.
145 SLA board papers memorandum on China, 23 May 1995.
146 Standard Life annual report, 1996.
147 SLA board papers encl. nos.33/98 and 40/99.
148 SLA board papers encl. no.89/99.

PICTURE CREDITS

An enormous amount of work has gone into finding the images used in this history. Details of how to obtain these are available upon application to the archivist at Standard Life. Unless otherwise stated, the illustrations are the property of The Standard Life Assurance Company. The majority of the inhouse photography has been undertaken by Chris Close Photography and Stewart & Baxter of Edinburgh, and thanks go to both them and to Barry and Steven McCleery of Capscan for all their hard work.

The following Standard Life Group staff have all been extremely helpful in the search for suitable images: Standard Life: Mary Thomson, Lorna Fleming, Tricia McKinlay, Susan Boyd, Fiona McMorran, Catherine Graham, Heather Scott, Helen Shoemark, Alex Zhang and Gregor Cunningham. Standard Life Investments: Catherine Knowles, Jackie Lennie and Garry Latimer. Special thanks must go to the marketing design department, in particular Jacquie Dryden, Sandra Glen, Louise King, Guillermo Navarro-Oltra and Gary Porter, for recreating a number of images.

Frontispiece © Chris Close Photography.

p.8   © Stewart & Baxter. GD354/1/1 loaned by National Archives of Scotland and with permission of Royal & SunAlliance Insurance Group plc.
p.10   © Jeremy Cockayne, York.

CHAPTER 1

p.16   by courtesy of Edinburgh City Libraries.
p.18   Thomson publication © the Bodleian Library, University of Oxford (ref: 49.532 front cover).
p.18   from Sir William Fraser, *Memorials of the Montgomeries*, vol.1, 1859.
p.19   by courtesy of Perth Museum & Art Gallery, Perth and Kinross Council.
p.21   GD 354/1/1 p.379 Reproduced by courtesy of the Keeper of the Records of Scotland and with the permission of Royal & SunAlliance Insurance Group plc.
p.22   The Scottish National Portrait Gallery for the image of Henry, Lord Cockburn, by Sir John Watson Gordon.
p.23   by courtesy of Edinburgh City Libraries.
p.24   with thanks to Althea Parsons. Image reproduced by Benedict Parsons.
p.27   The Scottish National Portrait Gallery for the image of the seventh Earl of Mar and his family by David Allan. © The Earl of Mar.
p.28   by courtesy of Edinburgh City Libraries.
p.35   © His Grace the Duke of Buccleuch.
p.36   © Lloyds TSB Bank Scotland plc, with thanks to George Fraser.
p.40 and p.42 Reproduced with permission from the George Washington Wilson Collection, Aberdeen University Library (Ref A123/GWW 184).
p.44   with thanks to Patricia McCarthy, archivist, Cork Archives Institute, Christ Church, South Main Street, Cork.
p.46   by courtesy of Robert Steuart Fothringham.
p.47   with thanks to the Earl of Elgin.
p.49   with thanks to Rusty McLean, archivist, Rugby School © Rugby School.
p.50   with thanks to Lynn MacNab, the Print Room, the Guildhall Library, London, and Geremy Butler Photography, London. © News International.
p.51   by kind permission of the Marquess of Ailesbury, Savernake Estate © Marquess of Ailesbury.
p.52   by kind permission of the Hon. Mrs M. Williams, Udny Castle.
p.53   by courtesy of Edinburgh City Libraries.

CHAPTER 2

p.56   From the *Illustrated London News* (1855) by courtesy of the Mitchell Library, Glasgow, Cultural and Leisure Services, Glasgow City Council, and with thanks to Moira Thorburn, photographer.
p.58   Professor Sir Robert Christisson: by kind permission of the Royal College of Physicians of Edinburgh.
p.58   Professor Anthony Todd Thomson: by kind permission of the Royal College of Surgeons of England.
p.60   with thanks to Colum O'Riordan, the Irish Architectural Archive.
p.66   Calcutta reproduced by permission of the British Library Oriental and India Collections (ref: Neg No B12471 (pol)/Photo 147/A (44) 7).
p.68   the drawing of the Hope Street Offices; from the *Baillie Magazine* (1891) by courtesy of the Mitchell Library, Glasgow, Cultural and Leisure Services, Glasgow City Council.
p.69   From *The Illustrated London News* (1848), by courtesy of the Mitchell Library, Glasgow, Cultural and Leisure Services, Glasgow City Council, and with thanks to Moira Thorburn, photographer.
p.72   Henry Houldsworth – from *The Beginnings of the Houldsworths of Coltness* by William Houldsworth McLeod, Glasgow, 1937; kindly

lent by Nigel J.H. Houldsworth, St Boswells, Roxburgh.

p.72 Thomas George, twelfth Earl of Strathmore – with thanks to the Earl of Strathmore and Kinghorn. Photo: The Pilgrim Press Ltd (ref: GL.83).

p.73 Lundin House ©:Royal Commission on the Ancient and Historical Monuments of Scotland (Ref: FID/225/1).

p.74 Leven Links and Largo Law: by courtesy of the Valentine Collection, Special Collections, University of St Andrews Library; with thanks to Cilla Jackson (ref: JV-620).

p.74 Lundin Gold Medal: loaned by kind permission of the Leven Golfing Society. Photograph © Chris Close.

p.74 Golf trophies: Standard Life: © Chris Close.

p.75 Davidson Cup for football: Standard Life. Photograph © Chris Close.

p.76 Gordon Urquhart, © Glasgow Conservation Trust West.

p.77 by courtesy of London Borough of Ealing Library Service, with thanks to Maureen Gooding.

p.78 by courtesy of Hartlepool Museum Service.

p.79 Peebles Union Poorhouse ©:Royal Commission on the Ancient and Historical Monuments of Scotland (Ref: B 629 84 and B 629 85).

p.79 The London Hospital for Women – from London Metropolitan Archives (ref: H1/RW/21/1) Reproduced by permission of the Special Trustees of St Thomas' Hospital and Guy's Hospital and with thanks to London Metropolitan Archives.

p.80 by courtesy of the Shaftesbury Society, London.

p.81 by courtesy of The Board of Trustees of the National Museums and Galleries on Merseyside (The Merseyside Maritime Museum).

p.83 from the *Illustrated London News* (1855) and by courtesy of the Mitchell Library, Glasgow, Cultural and Leisure Services,
Glasgow City Council.

p.85 Albert Insurance Co. publication – © The Bodleian Library, University of Oxford (John Johnson Collection).

p.89 © The Library of Congress, courtesy of the Museum of the Confederacy, Richmond, Virginia, with thanks to Terri Hudgins, photographic dept, the Museum of the Confederacy, and John Adhlas, curator.

p.92 AA NEG 1865 Sydney West Cove © Commonwealth of Australia 1999, with thanks to Shirley Mahoney.

p.98 Punch cartoon (1882) with thanks to Dr George Dyke, CDM Dept, Rothamsted Experimental Station.

p.99 by courtesy of Gordonstoun School, with thanks to Richard Oliver.

p.101 Watercolour by the Rev. Thomas Kilby, by courtesy of Wakefield Art Gallery, Education, Libraries and Museums Department.

CHAPTER 3

p108 Kenmare House – the National Photographic Archive, the National Library of Ireland.

p.108 Earl of Kenmare – the Library, Muckross House, Gardens and Traditional Farms, the National Park.

p.110 by courtesy of *Bord Failte* – Irish Tourist Board.

p.111 © Royal Commission on the Ancient and Historical Monuments of Scotland (ref: SU/811).

p.112 © The John Rylands University Library, University of Manchester (ref: Hindustani Ms.1 Laur – Chanda) detail of elephants from *Bibliotheca Lindesiana*.

p.113 Standard Life: Barnhill Poorhouse image redrawn after an original glass negative from Glasgow City Archives, the Mitchell Library, Glasgow.

p.114 by courtesy of Hocken Library, Uare Toaka o Hakena, University of Otago, Dunedin: (ref: c/n E3403/43).

p.115 Main image St James Street, Montreal © National Archives of Canada/ C–8840.

p.115 Image of St James Street/Victoria Square Montreal and Archbishop Fabre of Montreal – © McCord Museum.

p.117 © Robert Fleming & Co.

p.118 Barrow shipyard – by courtesy of the Cumbria Record Office, Barrow-in-Furness.

p.118 Burmeister and Wain – by courtesy of Copenhagen City Museum.

p.119 © National Archives of Canada/PA-13228.

p.124 by courtesy of the Community and Leisure Services Department, City Library, Newcastle Upon Tyne.

p.126 typewriter advertisement – redrawn after a Trade Directory in the Glasgow Room, the Mitchell Library, Glasgow City Council, Cultural and Leisure Services.

p.126 George Stewart – with thanks to Liz Blair.

p.126 Atlantic liner – reproduced by kind permission of Keeper of the Records of Scotland from Glasgow University Archives and Business Record Centre.

p.127 from the *Illustrated London News* (1891) by permission of the National Library of Scotland.

p.129 © Trustees of the National Museums of Scotand.

p.132 advertisement – from *The Times of India* (July 1880) by permission of the British Library.

p.136 *Hungary: An Illustrated Fortnightly Society* newspaper, 1909, p.194, by permission of the British Library.

p.140 © The Bodleian Library, University of Oxford (24787e.4 front cover).

CHAPTER 4

p.146 by permission of Jocelyne Cunningham.

p.152 by permission of Sir Stephen Furness.

p.158 © (IB 2-285) Copenhagen Archive Collection/Image Bank, with thanks to Roddy McRae.

p.160 © Carl Engler, National Archives of Canada/PA-1875516/.

p.166 South African campaign from the *Illustrated London News* (1915) by permisssion of the Mitchell Library, Glasgow, Cultural and Leisure Services, Glasgow City Council.

p.168 © ICI Technology and Brunner Mond (UK) Ltd, with thanks to Sharon Loak.

p.169 by permission of the Clerk of the Records acting on behalf of the Beaverbrook Foundation. Photographs in the custody of the House of Lords Record Office.

p.171 © University of Berkeley, California.

p.172 by courtesy Kilmainham Gaol and Museum.

p.174 © BBC and with thanks to Bobbie Mitchell, BBC visual archives.

p.176 Scottish Army officers – *The Scots Pictorial* (1914), by permission of the Mitchell Library, Glasgow City Council, Cultural and Leisure Services.

p.180 sketch of Carnegie by permission of the Andrew Carnegie Birthplace Museum, Dunfermline.

p.180 Carnegie Medal with thanks to Jocelyne Cunningham.

p.180 citation and entry in roll of honour by permission of The Carnegie Hero Trust Fund, Dunfermline.

CHAPTER 5

p.189 © (IB F11EVGN) Uruguay Archive Collection/Image Bank.

p.195 © (IB 2411) Wall St Crash Archive Collection/Image Bank.

p.197 from *Goodwill in Industry being the Semi-jubilee Souvenir of Burton* by Sir John Forster Fraser (1925).

p.198 © National Museums & Galleries of Northern Ireland/Ulster Folk & Transport Museum.

p.201 from *Camera in the Works*, London, 1970, and by permission Cambridge University Library and Vickers plc.

p.202 by permission of the Imperial War Museum, London (ref: Q.23665).

p.208 Metrovickers image – from Dummelow, J., *Metropolitan Vickers 1899–1949*, Manchester, 1949 © the Bodleian Library, University of Oxford.

p.208 Taylor Woodrow policy – with thanks to Taylor Woodrow plc.

p.208 logos reproduced by permision of J. Sainsbury plc; Fortnum & Mason plc; H.P. Bulmer Ltd; Scottish & Newcastle plc; Charles Letts (Scotland) Ltd and Ryvita.

p.211 by kind permission of John Norman.

p.217 Blitz image – from Standard Life Archives (ref: PH/00273) image © News International.

p.219 *1245 Sherbrooke Street* © John C. Little, Canada.

CHAPTER 6

p.229 © The Post Office. Reproduced by kind permission. All rights reserved.

p.235 brochure – with thanks to J.A. Burgess of Save and Prosper Group.

p.242 Rover Group image – by permission of British Motor Industry Heritage Trust Archive/The Rover Group.

p.262 © Scottish Daily Record and Sunday Mail Ltd. From the *Daily Record*, 1962, and with thanks to Moira Thorburn, photographer, and Martin O'Neill (for scanning) in the Science and Technical Department of the Mitchell Library, Glasgow, Cultural and Leisure Services, Glasgow City Council.

p.271 © John James (personal collection).

CHAPTER 7

p.277 © Stephen Scrase Photo Coverage, London.

p.279 © Seagrams Ltd, with thanks to Yvonne Thackeray and Iain Russell.

p.280–81 © Stewart & Baxter.

p.288 © Dennis Gilbert Architectural Photography.

p.289 © J. Wharton.

p.291 © Stephan Poulin.

p.292 with thanks to John Burns.

p.307 © Dennis Gilbert Architectural Photography.

CHAPTER 8

p.321 © Stewart & Baxter.

p.322 © Stewart & Baxter.

p.327 © Nick Wood.

p.328 © Scotsman Publications Ltd.

p.329 Standard Life House – © the Michael Laird Partnership.

p.333 © Katz pictures.

p.335 by courtesy of IFA Promotion, and with thanks to Peter Glover.

p.337 © Peter Cook.

p.347 © Stewart & Baxter.

p.351 © Graeme W. Baxter.

p.353 © Bernard Bohn and by kind permission of K-mart.

p.356 Simpson's foyer: © Stewart & Baxter.

p.356 © Lindsey Robertson at Strawberry.

p.357 Live175 thermometer © David Boni.

p.358 © Yves Beaulieu of Yves Beaulieu Photographe Inc.

p.361 © Betty Latimer.

p.367 historical: © (P188021) Shanghai Image Bank.

p.368 With thanks to Ronnie Knight.

p.369 © Stewart & Baxter.

Every effort has been made to obtain permission for the reproduction of the illustrations and photographs in this book; apologies are offered to anyone whom it has not been possible to contact.

BIBLIOGRAPHY

Allen, Joseph, *An inquiry concerning all the life insurance offices . . . having agencies in the United Kingdom.* [On cover *Where shall I get the most for my money?*] 10th ed., London 1883, and 13th ed., London 1888.

Anderson, James L., *The Story of the Commercial Bank of Scotland Limited during its hundred years from 1810 to 1910*, Edinburgh, 1910.

Anderson, John, *A History of Edinburgh from the earliest period*, Edinburgh and London, 1856.

Andras, H.W., *Historical Review of Life Assurance in Great Britain and Ireland*, London, 1912.

Armitage, Seth, *The Future of Mutual Life Offices*, Edinburgh, 1996.

Arnold, Percy, *Bankers of London*, London, 1938.

Banbury, Philip, *Shipbuilders of the Thames and Medway*, Newton Abbot, 1971.

Beaumont, G.D., *The Law of Fire and Life Insurance*, London, 1846.

Beckett, J.V., *The Aristocracy in England 1660–1914*, Oxford, 1986.

Bellott, H.H.L., and Williams, R. James, *The Law relating to Unconscionable Bargains with Money Lenders*, London, 1897.

Benjamin, Bernard, et al., *The Problems of Today and Tomorrow*, London, 1987.

Besant, Arthur Digby, *Our Centenary being the history of the first hundred years of Clerical, Medical & General Life Assurance Society*, London, 1914.

Better Pensions Fully Protected Against Inflation, London cmnd. 5713, 1974.

Beveridge, Sir William, et al., *War & Insurance*, London, 1927.

Binder Hamlyn, *A Pocket Guide to Personal Pensions*, London, 1987.

Blackaby, F.T. (ed.), *British Economic Policy 1960–74*, Cambridge, 1978.

Blake, David, and Orszag, Michael, *The Impact of Pension Funds on Capital Markets*, London, 1998.

Blakey, George G., *The Post-War History of the London Stock Market – fifty years of business, politics and people*, London, 1997.

Bourne, William, *Expenses Ratios of Life Offices*, Liverpool, 1886.

Bourne's Handy Insurance Manual, Liverpool, 1888–1939.

Britton, A.J.C., *Macroeconomic Policy in Britain 1974–87*, Cambridge, 1991.

Burke, Kathy, *Morgan Grenfell 1838–1938*, London, 1989.

Buxton, Tony, Chapman, Paul, and Temple, Paul, *Britain's Economic Performance* (2nd ed.), London, 1998.

Cairncross, Alec, *The British Economy since 1945*, Oxford, 1992.

Cameron, A., *Bank of Scotland 1695–1995: A Very Singular Institution*, Edinburgh, 1995.

Campbell, R.H., *Owners and Occupiers – Changes in Rural Society in South-West Scotland before 1914*, Aberdeen, 1991.

Capie, Forrest, and Webber, Alan, *A Monetary History of the United Kingdom, 1870–1982*, London, 1985.

Chadwick, Edwin, *Report on the Sanitary Condition of the Labouring Population of Great Britain 1842* (edited by Flinn, M.W.), Edinburgh, 1965.

Checkland, Olive, Nishimura, Shizuya, and Tamaki, Norio, *Pacific Banking 1859–1959 – East Meets West*, London 1994.

Checkland, S.G., *Scottish Banking – A History, 1695–1973*, Glasgow and London, 1975.

Clapham, Sir John, *The Bank of England: A History – Volume 2 1797–1914*, Cambridge, 1944.

Clayton, G., and Godden, A.H., *Insurance Company Investment, Principles and Policy*, London, 1965.

Clow, Rob, *Ayrshire & Arran – An Illustrated Architectural Guide*, Edinburgh, 1992.

Cockburn, Henry, *Memorials of His Time, 1779–1830*, Edinburgh, 1856.

Cockerell, H.A.L., and Green, Edwin, *The British Insurance Business – A Guide to its History & Records* (2nd ed.), Sheffield, 1994.

Cottrell, P.L., *Industrial Finance 1830–1914 – The Finance and Organisation of English Manufacturing Industry*, London, 1979.

Cox, Charles, *Facts & fallacies of life insurance*, London, 1904.

——, *How and where to insure*, London, 1903.

Culmer, F.G., *How Shall I Insure?*, London, 1934.

Cumper, G.E. (ed.), *The Economy of the West Indies*, Kingston, Jamaica, 1960.

Daunton, M.J., *A Property-Owning Democracy – Housing in Britain*, London, 1987.

Davidoff, Leonore, and Hall, Catherine, *Family Fortunes – Men and Women of the English Middle Class 1780–1850*, London, 1987.

Davidson, Andrew Rutherford, *The History of the Faculty of Actuaries in Scotland 1856–1956*, Edinburgh, 1956.

Davis, E. Philip, *Pension Funds – retirement-income security and capital markets, an international perspective*, Oxford, 1995.

Dawes, Harriet, and Samsworth, Jane, *Guide to Pensions Act 1995*, London, 1995.

Daykin, Christopher, *Funding the Future? Problems of Pension Reform*, London, 1998.

Denholm, James M., *One Hundred Years of Scottish Life: A History of the Scottish Life Assurance Company 1881–1981*, Edinburgh, 1981.

Dennet, Laurie, *A Sense of Security: 150 Years of Prudential*, Cambridge, 1998.

Dent, George Middlewood, *A dialogue, showing how to select a life office so as to secure the maximum of security*, Manchester, 1888.

Devine, T.M., *The Great Highland Famine – Hunger, Emigration and the Scottish Highlands in the Nineteenth Century*, Edinburgh, 1988.

DHSS, *Personal Pensions: A Consultative Document*, London, 1984.

DHSS, *Reform of Social Security*, London, 1985.

Dickson, P.G.M., *The Sun Insurance Office 1710–1960*, London, 1960.

Dilnot, Andrew, et al., *Pensions: The Problems of Today and Tomorrow*, London, 1987.

Dodds, J.C., *The Investment Behaviour of British Life Insurance Companies*, London, 1979.

Donelly, James S. jnr., *The Land and the People of Nineteenth-Century Cork*, London and Boston, 1975.

Dougan, D., *The History of North-east Shipbuilding*, London, 1968

Dougharty, H., *Pension, Endowment and Life Assurance Schemes*, London, 1927.

Dow, J.C.R., *The Management of the British Economy 1945–60*, Cambridge, 1964.

Drummond, P.R., *Perthshire in bygone days – one hundred biographical essays*, London, 1879.

Dummelow, J., *Metropolitan Vickers 1899–1949*, Manchester, 1949.

Dunlop, A. Ian (ed.), *The Scottish Ministers' Widows' Fund, 1743–1993*, Edinburgh, 1992.

Dupree, Marguerite W., 'Other than Healing: Medical Practitioners and the Business of Life Assurance during the Nineteenth Century', *Social History of Medicine*, pp.79–103, 1997.

Edwards, H.H., and Murrell, R., *Pension Schemes in Theory and Practice*, London, 1927.

Europe-Forum, *The Life Insurance Industry*, London, 1995.

Fergusson, William, *Scotland – 1689 to the Present – the Edinburgh History of Scotland Volume 4*, Edinburgh, 1987.

Field, Frank, and Owen, Matthew, *Private Pensions for All – Squaring the Circle*, London, 1993.

Field, Frank, *Stakeholder Welfare*, London, 1996.

Finsinger, Jörg, and Pauly, Mark V., *The Economics of Insurance Regulation – A Cross-National Study*, London, 1986.

Finsinger, Jörg, Hammond, Elizabeth, and Tapp, Julian, *Insurance Competition or Regulation?*, London, 1985.

Foster, Roy, *Modern Ireland 1600–1972*, London, 1988.

Franklin, Peter J., and Woodhead, Caroline, *The United Kingdom Life Assurance Industry*, London, 1980.

Fraser, Derek, *The Evolution of the British Welfare State* (2nd ed.), London, 1984.

Freestone, John, *Where to Insure*, London, 1890.

FT, *Pensions in 1984 – A Time for Change*, London, 1984.

Gibson, James, *The indicator for industrial & ordinary life assurance agents*, Burnley, 1893.

Gifford, John, *The Buildings of Scotland – Highlands and Islands*, London, 1992.

Glendinning, M., MacInnes, R., and MacKechnie, A., *A History of Scottish Architecture from the Renaissance to the Present Day*, Edinburgh, 1997.

Good, Roy, *Pension Law Reform – the Report of the Pension Law Review Committee*, London, cmnd. 2342–1, 1993.

Gosden, P.H.J.H., *SELF-HELP – Voluntary Associations in the 19th Century*, London, 1973.

Gower, L.C.B., *Review of Investor Protection*, London, cmnd. 9125, 1984.

Grant, A.T.K., *A Study of the Capital Market in Post-War Britain*, London, 1937.

Gray, M., 'Scottish Emigration: The Social Impact of Agrarian Change in the Rural Lowlands, 1775–1875' in Fleming, D., and Bailyn, B. (eds.), *Perspectives in American History VII*, Cambridge, Mass., 1973.

Green, Edwin, and Moss, Michael, *A Business of National Importance – the Royal Mail Shipping Group, 1902–37*, London, 1982.

Habakkuk, John, *Marriage, Debt, and the Estates System – English Landownership 1650–1950*, Oxford, 1994.

Hannah, Leslie, *Inventing Retirement – the Development of Occupational Pensions in Britain*, Cambridge, 1986.

Hare, F.A.C., *Bonuses: An aid to the selection of a life office*, London, 1883.

Henderson, E. Piercy, *Insurance Questions Plainly Treated for Plain People*, London, 1906.

——, *Latest Supplement to Insurance Questions Plainly Treated for Plain People*, London, 1910.

Henry, Jardine, *The hand-book for life assurers* (2nd ed.), Edinburgh, 1887.

Hicks, Ursula K., *The Finance of British Government 1920–36*, Oxford, 1938.

Hodgins, Frank E., *Life insurance contracts in Canada*, Toronto, 1902.

Holms, A.R., and Green, Edwin, *Midland: 150 Years of Banking Business*, London, 1986.

Hoppen, K. Theodore, *The Mid-Victorian Generation 1846–86*, Oxford, 1998.

Hoskins, Gordon A., *Pension Schemes and Retirement Benefits*, London, 1960.

Howson, Susan, *British Monetary Policy 1945–51*, Oxford, 1993.

——, *Domestic Monetary Management in Britain 1919–38*, Cambridge, 1975.

Huebner, S.S., *The Economics of Life Insurance*, London, 1927.

Hume, John R., *The Industrial Archaeology of Scotland, Volume 1. The Lowlands and Borders*, London, 1976.

Hunting, Penelope, *Cutlers Gardens*, London, 1984.

Hutchison, I.G.C., *A Political History of Scotland 1832–1924 – Parties, Elections and Issues*, Edinburgh, 1986.

Innis, Mary Quayle, *An Economic History of Canada*, Toronto, 1943.

Insurance Policyholders' Mutual Protection League Ltd, *Profit or Plunder? In Respect to Life Insurance Etc.*, London, 1888.

James, Leslie, *A Chronology of the Construction of Britain's Railways 1778–1855*, London, 1983.

Johnson, Christopher, *The Economy under Mrs Thatcher 1979–90*, London, 1991.

Johnson, Paul, *Saving and Spending – The Working-Class Economy in Britain 1870–1939*, Oxford, 1985.

Kay, John, *The Future of Pension Schemes*, Liverpool, 1987.

Kennedy, Liam, and Ollerenshaw, Philip, *An Economic History of Ulster 1820–1939*, Manchester, 1985.

Kirkaldy, A.W. (ed.), *British Finance during and after the war, 1914–21*, London, 1921.

Kynaston, David, *Cazenove & Co. – A History*, London, 1991.

——, *The City of London, Volume I – A World of its Own 1815–90*, London, 1994.

——, *The City of London, Volume II – Golden Years 1890–1914*, London, 1995.

Laing, Gerald, *A Retrospective*, Edinburgh, 1993.

Lawson, W.R., *The Scottish Investors' Manual*, Edinburgh, 1884.

——, *British War Finance 1914–15*, London, 1915.

Leigh-Bennett, E.P., *On This Evidence: A Study in 1936 of the Legal & General Assurance since its formation*, London, 1936.

Liveing, E., *A Century of Insurance: The Commercial Union Assurance Group, 1860–1960*, London, 1961.

Lowe, Rodney, *The Welfare State in Britain since 1945*, Basingstoke, 1999.

Lycett, Andrew, *From Diamond Sculls to Golden Handcuffs*, London, 1998.

M. (A.A.), *Life insurance up to date*, Edinburgh, 1890.

McInroy, Charles Colqhoun, *Scottish Equitable Landmarks – Our First 150 Years 1831–1981*, Edinburgh, 1981.

Maclean, Joseph B., *Life Insurance*, 1924.

Macmillan, Hugh, and Christophers, Mike, *Strategic Issues in the Life Assurance Industry*, London, 1997.

McNaught, Kenneth, *A Penguin History of Canada*, London, 1988.

Macnicol, John, *The Politics of Retirement in Britain 1878–1948*, Cambridge, 1998.

Mantle, Jonathan, *Norwich Union – The First 200 Years*, London, 1997.

Maxwell, Sir Herbert Eustace, 7th Bart., *Annals of the Scottish Widows' Fund Life Assurance Society, 1815–1914*, Edinburgh, 1914.

Michie, R.C., *Money, Mania and Markets – Investment, Company Formation and the Stock Exchange in Nineteenth-Century Scotland*, Edinburgh, 1981.

Miles, David, and Ibran, Andreas, *The Reform of Pension Systems: Winners and Losers Across Generations*, London, 1988.

Mingay, G.E., *The Agrarian History of England and Wales, Volume VI 1750–1850*, Cambridge, 1989.

Morgan, E.V., *Studies in British Financial Policy 1914–25*, London, 1952.

Morris, R.D., *Life Assurance from the National and Personal Standpoint*, London, 1909.

Moss, Michael, and Russell, Iain, *An Invaluable Treasure – A History of the TSB*, London, 1994.

Munn, C.W., *The Scottish Provincial Banking Companies 1747–1864*, Edinburgh, 1981.

Newlands, John, *Put Not Your Trust in Money – a History of the Investment Trust Industry from 1868 to the Present*, London, 1997.

Norman, G.A.S., *The Overseas History of The Standard Life Assurance Company*, Volumes 1 & 2, Edinburgh, 1950.

——, *The History of the London City Offices and the Early English Branches of Standard Life*, Edinburgh, 1962.

Nursaw, W.G., *Principles of Pension Fund Investment*, London, 1966.

O'Shea, James, et al., *Special Report – Demutualisation*, London, 1996.

Occupational Pensions Board, *Report on Greater Security for the Rights and Expectations of Members of Occupational Pension Schemes*, London, 1982.

Occupational Pensions Board 1973–97 Final Report, London, 1997.

Ogborn, M.E., *Equitable Assurances – The Story of Life Assurance in the Experience of the Equitable Life Assurance Society, 1762–1962*, London, 1962.

Partnership in Pensions: A New Contract in Welfare, cmd. 4179, 1998.

P., Q., *How to buy life insurance*, London, 1905.

Pollard, Sidney, and Robertson, Paul, *The British Shipbuilding Industry, 1870–1914*, Cambridge, Mass., 1979.

Pressnell, L.S., and Orbell, John, *A Guide to the Historical Records of British Banking*, London, 1985.

Pugh, Peter, *Number One Charlotte Square*, Edinburgh, 1987.

Rae, George, *The Country Banker – his clients, cares, and work from an experience of forty years*, reprinted privately, London, 1976.

Raleigh, S., *Scottish Widows' Fund Assurance (Mutual) Society, and the Proprietery Companies Claiming to Give Greater Benefits*, Edinburgh, 1864.

——, *Scottish Widows' Fund (Life Assurance) Society, 'Mutual and Proprietary Life Assuance Compared'*, preliminary note, Edinburgh, 1863.

——, *Scottish Widows' Fund Life Assurance Society, Benefits to Policy-holders and Comparative Results in the Standard Life Assurance Company, The Life Association of Scotland, The North British and Mercantile and The Caledonian Insurance Company*, Edinburgh, 1863.

——, *Scottish Widows' Fund Society, Explanatory Memorandum Regarding the Financial Position, Estimation of Liabilities and Assets, and the Free Surplus*, Edinburgh, 1864.

Rankine, John, *A Treatise on the Rights and Burdens incident to The Ownership of Lands and other heritages in Scotland* (4th ed.), Edinburgh, 1909.

Raynes, Harold E., *A History of British Insurance*, London, 1984.

Reader, W.K., and Kynaston, David, *Professionals in the City – A History of Philips & Drew*, London, 1998.

Recknell, G.H., 'Life Assurance versus Investments', *Post Magazine and Insurance Monitor*, 7 November 1925.

——, *King Street, Cheapside*, London, 1936.

Reed, M.C., *A History of James Capel & Co.*, London, 1975.

Reid, Margaret, *The Secondary Banking Crisis, 1973–75: Its Causes and Course*, London, 1982.

Roberts, R., *Schroders: Merchants & Bankers*, London, 1992.

Robertson, Bernard, and Samuels, H., *Pension and Superannuation funds*, London, 1928.

Rose, Thomas George, *Cost price life assurance*, originally published as: *Costless life assurance*, London, 1897.

Rothermund, Dietmar, *An Economic History of India from Pre-Colonial Times to 1991* (2nd ed.), London, 1993.

Saville, Richard, *Bank of Scotland – A History 1695–1995*, Edinburgh, 1996.

Sayers, R.S., *Financial Policy 1939–45*, London, 1956.

——, *The Bank of England 1891–1944*, Cambridge, 1976.

Schooling, Sir William, *Life assurance explained*, London, 1897.

——, *Alliance Assurance 1824–1924*, London, 1924.

——, *The Standard Life Assurance Company 1825–1925*, London, 1925.

Scott, J.D., *Vickers: A History*, London, 1962.

Scott, Sir Hilary, *Linked Life Assurance – Report of the Committee on Property Bonds and Equity-Linked Assurance*, London, cmnd. 5281, 1973.

Scott, Peter, *An Outline of the Property Investment History of the Standard Life Assurance Company:1825–1980*, unpublished thesis, Oxford, 1991.

Scottish Land – The Report of the Scottish Land Enquiry Committee, London, 1914.

Seyd, Isabel, *Eagle Star – A Guide to its History and Archives*, Cheltenham, 1997.

Simmonds, R.C., *The Life Insurance Textbook*, London, 1929.

——, *The Institute of Actuaries 1848–1948*, Cambridge, 1948.

Sinclair, Keith, *A History of New Zealand*, London, 1985.

Sked, Alan, and Cook, Chris, *Post-War Britain* (2nd ed.), London, 1984.

Skidelsky, Robert, *John Maynard Keynes – The Economist as Saviour, 1920–37*, London, 1992.

Smith, Josiah W., *The Law of Real and Personal Property*, London, 1855.

Spensley, C., *A thousand tips about Life Assurance Offices*, Sheffield, 1893.

Stenton, Michael, *Who's Who of British Members of Parliament, Volume 1 1832–85*, Hassocks, 1976.

Steuart, M.D., *The Scottish Provident Institution*, Edinburgh, 1937.

Stevenson, John, *British Society 1914–45*, London, 1984.

Strang, C.A., *Borders and Berwick – An Illustrated Guide to the Scottish Borders and Tweed Valley*, London, 1994.

Stone & Cox, *Ordinary Branch Life Assurance Tables*, 1940–88.

Street, Eric (ed. by Glen, Richard), *The History of the National Mutual Insurance Society*, London, 1980.

Supple, Barry, *The Royal Exchange Assurance – A History of British Insurance 1720–1970*, Cambridge, 1970.

Swain, A.H., *The War and Life Insurance, with-profits policy-holders' precarious position*, Leicester, 1915.

Teasdale, W.A., *How to distinguish the safest and most profitable life offices*, Manchester, 1898.

The Northern and Allied Companies, 1836–1936, Staff Magazine – centenary number, vol.XVI, no.4, 1936.

Thomson, William Thomas, *Notes on the pecuniary interests of heirs of entail, with calculations regarding such interests in reference to Acts of Parliament affecting entails and tables showing the values of liferent interests*, Edinburgh, 1849.

——, *Further suggestions with reference to the amendment of the Joint Stock Companies Registration Act as regards life assurance institutions*, Edinburgh, 1852.

——, *Lenders and Borrowers on Landed Securities*, Edinburgh, 1855.

——, *Answers to observations by the Scottish Widows' Fund on the comparative merits of Life Assurance Companies and Mutual Assurance Societies*, Edinburgh, 1863.

——, *The Standard Life Assurance Company and The Scottish Widows' Fund*, addition to 'Further Answer', 1863.

——, *The rate of interest on landed securities in Scotland*, Edinburgh, 1868.

——, *An address to the Actuarial Society of Edinburgh*, Edinburgh, 1874.

Tindall, George Brown, and Shi, David E., *America – A Narrative History* (4th ed.), New York and London, 1996.

Trebilcock, Clive, *Phoenix Assurance and the Development of British Insurance, Volume I 1782–1870*, Cambridge, 1985.

——, *Phoenix Assurance and the development of British Insurance, Volume II 1870–1984*, Cambridge, 1999.

Tregoning, David, and Cockerell, Hugh, *Friends for Life – Friends' Provident Life Office 1832–1982*, London, 1982.

Turton, Alison, *Managing Business Archives*, London, 1991.

Van Selm, R., *History of the South African Mutual Life Assurance Society 1845–1945*, Johannesburg, 1945.

Vinson, Nigel, and Chappell, Philip, *Personal and Portable Pensions for All*, London, 1983.

Walker, F.A., *The South Clyde Estuary – An Illustrated Architectural Guide to Inverclyde and Renfrew*, Edinburgh, 1986.

Wallace, William, *The Law of Bankruptcy in Scotland* (2nd ed.), Edinburgh, 1914.

Watkins, M.H., and Grant, H.M., *Canadian Economic History – Classic and Contemporary Approaches*, Ottawa, 1993.

Watson, R. Cook, *Life Assurance Premiums Charged by Various Companies*, Newcastle upon Tyne, 1900–15.

Westall, Oliver M. (ed.), *The Historian and the Business of Insurance*, Manchester, 1984.

——, *The Provincial Insurance Company 1903–38, Family, Markets and Competitive Growth*, Manchester, 1992.

Wilkie, Patricia, *The Making of the Actuarial Profession in Scotland 1815–70*, unpublished MA thesis in Sociology and Social History, Edinburgh, 1972.

Wilson, Sir Harold, *Committee to Review the Functioning of the Financial institutions*, London cmnd. 7937, 1980.

Withers, Hartley (ed. Nicholas, Conan), *Pioneers of British Life Assurance*, London, 1951.

Woodruff, Archibald M., *Farm Mortgage Loans of Life Insurance Companies*, London, 1937.

Worswick, G.D.N., and Ady, P.H., *The British Economy*, Oxford, 1952.

INDEX

NOTE: page references in italics denote illustrations

Kemp, George Lucas, in Calcutta, 102, 130–4, *130*

Kenmare, Valentine Augustus, 4th Earl of (1825–1905), 108–10, 173, 197

Kenmare, Valentine Charles, 5th Earl of, *108*, 110, 197

Kenmare house *see* Killarney house

Kennedy, A.E., Governor-General of Vancouver Island, 80

Keppie, Simon, 289

Kerr, William Hackney, accountant, Edinburgh, 30–1

Keynes, John Maynard, 175, 194

Kia-Ora Ltd, 207

Kidderminster shopping centre, 306

Killarney House, 108, *108*, 173

Killyheagh Spinning Co., Belfast, 99

Kilmaron Castle, Fife, 41

Kimber, Edward Scipio, 166

King, Albert Edward, 75, 183–4, 194–6, 215–16 , *215*, 371

King, F.E., 238

King, Leonard, 224, 251

King, Tom R., 276, 308, 310, 319, *320*, 321, 323–4, *347*, 350

Kingsmeadows, Peebles, 271, *271*

Kingswood, Surrey, 216

Kinloch of Kilnie, John, 34

Kinnaird, George William Fox, 9th Lord, (1807–78), 70, 80

Kinnear, David, journalist, Edinburgh, 63–4

Kinnear, James, lawyer, 57, 64

Kirkintilloch, 101

Kitcat & Aitken, stockbrokers, 194

Kitson, W. E., 165

K-Mart, Canada, 353

Knight, Robbie, 366

Kraft Cheese, 207

Kylsant, ist Lord, 198fn

Lahore, 103

Laing & Cruickshank, 194

Lamont, Lt-Col A.M., 253

Laing, Gerald O., *280–1*, 328, *337*

Laird, Michael, Partnership 328

Lancashire & Yorkshire Railway, 98

Lancashire Insurance Co., 82

Lang, Thomas, 75, 103, 130–4, *130*, *132*, 138

Langdale, Lady, widow of the Master of the Rolls, 100

LAPR, 301–2

Latzko & Popper, Budapest, 136

LAUTRO *see* Life Assurance and Unit Trust Regulatory Organisation

Law Fire Insurance Society Ltd, 82

Law Society of Scotland, 230

Law Union & Rock Co., 172.

Lawes, Sir John Bennet, 1st Bt, (1814–1900), 98, *98*

Lawrence, General Sir Herbert (1861–1943), 202, *202*

Lazards, merchant bankers, 331

Leeds, 22, 79, 82, 138, 197, 237, *237*

Leeds Permanent Building Society, 278

Legal & Commercial Fire Assurance Co., 95

Legal & Commercial Life Assurance Co., 93–4

Legal & General Assurance Society Ltd, 156, 181, 202, 206, 221–2, 226, 242, 257, 265, 272, 278, 281–2, 287–8, 298, 317, 332

Lemoine, Benjamin H., cashier, Québec, 65

Lenegan, Major J.D., Trinidad, 214

Lerwick, 32

Lessels, Norman, 319, 331

Leth, C.A. & K., Copenhagen, 158

Letts Diaries, 208

Leven Links golf course, *74*

Lévesque, René, 291–2

Levitt Group, 338

Lewis, Dr D.J., surgeon in the Confederate Army, 88

Lidstone, George, 163, 184

Life Association of Scotland, 124–5, 128, 283

Life Assurance Companies Act 1870, 105

Life Assurance Corporation of India, 365

Life Assurance Premium Relief *see* LAPR

Life Assurance and Unit Trust Regulatory Organisation (LAUTRO), 309, 335–6, 338, 342

Life Insurance Company of Scotland, 15–31

Life Offices Association, 174, 179, 200, 202fn, 205, 221, 239, 244, 253, 283, 285, 300, 303fn

Lifeguard, 283

LIFFE *see* London International Financial Futures Exchange

Limerick, 44, 69

Limerick, county 110

Littledale, Harold, of Liverpool, 39

Littlewoods, 207

Liu, Ming Kang, *368*

Live175 charity activities, 356, *356*

Liverpool, 45, 78, 81, *81*, 124, 127

Liverpool, The, 127

Liverpool and London and Globe Insurance Co. Ltd, 181

Livs-og Genforsikringsselskabet, 159

Lloyd George, David (1863–1945), 155, 169, *169*, 175, 179

Lloyd D. Jackson Square, Hamilton, Ontario, 266, 315

Lloyds Bank, 203

Loch Lomond Golf Tournament 350, *351*

Lochgilphead poorhouse, 79

Loganlea, Edinburgh, 79

London, 39, 45
    Abchurch Yard, 221
    Blitz damage, 216–17, *217*
    board of Standard Life, 45, 61, 86, 89, 97, 98, 109, 124, 141, 144, 147, 170
    branch of Standard Life, 86, 132, 169, 187, 199, 203, 240, 242
    Cannon Street office, 93, 187, *217*
    Castrol House, 258
    Cutler's Gardens development, 288–9
    inspectors, *239*
    King William Street office, 187
    Lombard Street office, 49, *50*, 68
    Queen Victoria Street office, 187, 216, *217*
    staff, cartoon of reservists, *217*
    West End branch, 93, 100, 102, 139, 165, 169, 170, *170*, 186–7, *186*, 276

London & Globe, 127

London & Lancashire Insurance Co., 128–9, 133, 148

London & Provincial Joint Stock Life Assurance Co., 94

London Asiatic and American Co., 130

London, Brighton & South Coast Railway, 97

London County & Westminster Bank, 167

London Hospital for Women, 79, *79*, 174

London Indemnity & General, 283

London International Financial Futures Exchange (LIFFE), 305

London Life, 345

London School of Economics, 221, 241

London Stock Exchange, 175, 196, 282, 289, 305, 321, 327

Londonderry, 69

Londonderry, Frederick William Robert, 4th Marquess of (1805–72), 70

Lord, Cyril, 263, 265

mortgages, 193, 197, 199
Muckross Abbey Estate, 110, *110*
Mugford, Stanley, 165
Mulholland, W.D. 'Bill', president of the Bank of Montreal, 295fn, 298
Mulroney, Brian, leader of the Canadian Conservatives, 314
Munich crisis 1938, 220, 258
Municipal Mutual Insurance Group (MMI), 345, 363
Munro, Lt-Col John, 21
Munroe, Mrs Sophia Urquhart (widow of Captain Charles Munroe), 25
Murray, J.V., in Jamaica, 214
Murray, James, surgeon in Leith, 25
Musicians' Union, 281
Musselburgh, 75
Myreside, Midlothian, 21

Nanchang, 133
Napance, Canada, 90
Napier, Lord, 197
Narodny Bank, Moscow, 263
National Association of Pension Funds, 302fn
National Bank of Scotland, 51
national debt, 36
National Health Service, 349
National Housing Act, Canada, 245
National Indian Life Assurance Co., 162
National insurance, 123, 221, 241–2
National Life Assurance Society, 283
National Mutual Life Assurance Society, 194–5,
National Provincial Bank, 203
National Savings, 207, 220
Nationwide Building Society, 278
Naudie, Roy, 319, 352
Navigation Acts, repeal of, 55
New Brunswick, 63
New Deal, 196
New Poor Law 1834, 78
New York, 47, 57, 67, 89, 128
New York Life, 128
New Zealand, 59, 67, 81, 93, 103, 114, *114*, 116
    Matakanui sheep station, *114*
    Maoris, land purchase from, 116
    Maori Wars 1863, 88
New Zealand and Australian Land Co., 114
New Zealand Scotch Trust, 99
Newcastle-Upon-Tyne, *124*, 217
Newfoundland, 63–4, 128
Niagara Falls Park & River Railway Co., 119

Nichol, W., Birmingham, 124
Noble, Ernest, 148, 159
Noble Lowndes, 240, 242
Norman, George A.S., 211, 237, 276
Norske Forenede Forsikrings Selskab, 159
North America, 37,48, 57, 107, 126, 128, 135, 148, 170–1, 177, 194, 207, 323, 362
North American General Insurance Company, 247
North American Life, 253
North British & Mercantile Insurance Co. Ltd, 122, 127, 133, 140, 202–6, 210–11, 214–15, 226
North British Insurance Co., *see also* North British & Mercantile, 17, 20, 27, 41
North Central Wagon Co., 257
North Leith poorhouse, 79
North West Provinces of India, 93, 133
North West Securities Ltd, 263–4
Northern Bank, Belfast, 144
Northumberland & Durham District Bank, 77
Norway, 135, 158
Norwich Union Fire Insurance Society, 21
Norwich Union Life Assurance Society, 20, 21, 25, 32, 156, 160, 165, 257, 272, 283, 289, 325, 336, 345
Nova Scotia, 64, 127

Oceanic Steam Navigation Co., 198
Oceanic Steam Navigation Realisation Co., 198
Occupational Pensions Board (OPB), 280
Occupational Pensions Regulatory Authority (OPRA), 345
Occupational Schemes Joint Working Group, 302
OEICs (open-ended investment companies), 334
Office of Fair Trading, 206, 309
O'Hagan, John, 90–2, 93, 101, 139
O'Hanlon, Bertie, 315, *315*. 317, 361
Oliver, George, *130*, 133, 136, 139, 144, 147
O'Malley, Brian, 281
Ontario, 90, 127, 359
    Canadian National Railway building, 266
    Hamilton, 89, 266, 314
        Lloyd D. Jackson Square, 266, 314
    Kingston, 90

Yonge Street office block, 266
open-ended investment companies *see* OEICs
Ordonios, Battel, 165
Oregon, 48, 171, *171*
O'Reilly, James, 69
Oriental & General Marine Insurance Co., 131
Orkney, Thomas John, 5th Earl of (1803–77), 73
Ottawa, 90, 224, 266
    Confederation Square, 355
Oxenden, Sir Henry Chudleigh, 54
Oxford Institute of Statistics survey 1953, 229

Palladium Life & Fire Assurance Co., 17, 45
Palmer, Charles, shipbuilder, Tyneside, 113
Paradell, Ramon, 188, 213, 218, 224, 251
Parekh, Deepak, *366*
Parizeau, Jacques, 296
Parkinson, Cecil, Secretary of State for Trade, 306
Parker, Alexander Davidson, 63–4, *63*, 89
Parker Gerrard Ogilvie & Co., 64
Parker, John, of the Register Office, Edinburgh, 63
Paton & Baldwins Ltd, 207
Paton, George, Caithness, 29
Patton, George, advocate, 57
Pattullo, Sir Bruce, 308, 331
PDFM *see* Philips & Drew Fund Management
Peabody, Houghteling & Co., 171
Pearl Assurance Co., 226
Pearce, Harry H., 276
Peat, T. Dick, 171, 194, 199
Peddie & Brown, architects, 142
Peddie, William, secretary, 22, 29
Peebles Parochial Board poorhouse, 79, *79*
Pegasus computer, 268
Pelican Life Assurance Co., 18, 21
Pembroke, Canada, 127
Penang, 133
Penny & McGeorge, stockbrokers, Glasgow, 119
pension schemes, 139, 167, 199, 200, 202–3, 213, 216, 218, 222–3, 238, 230–1, 240–1, *243*, 281, 287, 312, 285, 302–3, 311, *341*, *348*, 358, 361
pensions, stakeholder, 346–7